Books by
GILBERT FRANKAU

WORLD WITHOUT END

A Novel

by
GILBERT FRANKAU

HUTCHINSON & CO. (Publishers), LTD.

LONDON :: NEW YORK :: MELBOURNE

TO
SUSAN

WORLD   WITHOUT   END

Conceived in the United States of America.   Summer 1939.
Concluded in England.   Summer 1942.

PRINTED IN
GREAT BRITAIN,
AT THE ANCHOR
PRESS, TIPTREE,
::   ESSEX   ::

BOOK ONE

"IT'S CRAZY OF JIM TO GO WITH A SHINNER GIRL", THOUGHT MILES RADCLIFFE.
"But then we're all a bit crazy in our detachment. That's part of the fun."

A watery moon was just setting over this utter desolation of bog and
moorland which was Ireland. So Jim had been with Molly Maguire for
more than an hour. And it must be a good twenty minutes since this
menacing silence one had come to know so well—this curfew silence during
which one's imagination always strained to hear the taut breathing of men
acrouch behind walls or in ditches—had been broken by the swish of bicycle
tyres along the narrow bog-road at the end of the lane.

"If they'd come this way——" thought Miles Radcliffe.

The Bergmann automatic rifle—his most cherished possession—still lay
across his knees. Fingering the smooth wood of the stock, the metal
magazine which projected from the short barrel, Miles remembered how he
had come by this weapon and the ashen-faced boy in the fieldgray uniform
crying, "Kamerad", as it dropped from his shaking hands.

"Scared stiff", he remembered. "Thought the old tank was going to
roll him flat."

Queer—how some chaps got the wind up. Queer—how others fell in
love. Perhaps they couldn't help it. Perhaps he himself would fall in love
one day. Jim said it was quite different from just wanting to have a woman.
Not that he'd ever really wanted that either. Not since that night in
Amiens . . .

Memory flashed him fragments of another picture—a cobbled street—a
dark doorway—a blousy woman in a dressing gown.

"*Pas toute suite, cheri*", said the woman. "*Plus tard. Dans une petite
demi-heure, peut-être. Faut attendre ton tour, tu sais.*" Waiting one's turn.
Queueing up for it . . .

Hallo! More bikes.

Memories vanished. Quietly as a cat, every muscle under perfect
control, Miles slid from the driving seat of the Ford; took cover between it
and the hedge; rested his Bergmann on the radiator, and sighted for ground
line at the mouth of the lane.

The old, cold, utterly pleasurable excitement of battle was on him. Fine
nostrils flaring, he took one deep breath; and waited, motionless as the leaves
he could just feel at his neck. If only the Shinners came this way. They'd
never see him here. He'd let 'em come on. Let 'em come to within twenty
paces. Then, just a squeeze at the trigger—just one burst . . .

But never a figure showed against the starlight at the mouth of the lane;
and presently Miles heard the swish of the tyres going away from him along
the road.

"Only more of 'em on the run", he thought. "On their keeping, as they
call it. No luck."

After waiting another minute he climbed back to the driving seat, and
rested his rifle against the dashboard. Just as well, perhaps, that he hadn't

5

needed to fire. The Bergmann—its ammunition irreplaceable—was only for very special occasions.

"Less than a hundred rounds left", he reminded himself; and his hands played with the butts of the two forty-five Colt pistols he wore, one in the shoulder holster given to him by an American soldier, one low at his right hip. Plenty of ammunition for them anyway. But there wouldn't be much more chance of using it. The I.R.A. had had about enough. They'd cave in any day now. Dominic said so. And what Dominic Mahoney didn't know about Shinners wasn't worth knowing. How he hated them.

"Funny", thought Miles. "I don't. Some of 'em are swine, of course. Simply thugs. But some of 'em are jolly gallant. It's all very well for Dominic to say they don't fight fair. But how else can they fight? They haven't got any tanks, or any artillery, or any aeroplanes, or a navy. And after all, this is their country."

But Ireland—or Eire as the Shinners called it—was Dominic's country too. The ghost of a breeze whispered in the silence. Shutting off thought—the more one thought about Ireland, the more muddled one became—Miles looked at his watch.

Nearly two hours now since Jim Bowlby had sneaked through the coppice at the other end of the lane to the cabin where Molly Maguire lived with her deaf and dumb mother. If he didn't come back pretty soon, one would have to give him the bird call.

Miles waited another five minutes. Another ten. Best go after Jim now. He'd had plenty of time for his lovemaking. Land himself in a nice mess one of these nights. "And me too", thought Miles.

Still making no more noise than a cat on the prowl, he stooped for the automatic rifle; cuddled it into the crook of his right arm; dismounted, turned, and tiptoed the few yards along the hedge to the other end of the lane. From here a path led into the coppice.

Through the trees he could just make out the thatched roof of the Maguires' cabin. Putting the fingers of his left hand to his mouth, he gave his bird call—the hoot of an owl. Almost simultaneously Jim hooted in reply. Within less than a minute his tall figure, capped with the big tam-o'-shanter Scottish bonnet, appeared along the path.

"You've been a nice time", grumbled Miles.

"Just kissing her goodbye when you signalled", laughed Jim. "The darling. My God, I do feel played out. I shan't half be glad to get back to barracks."

They made their way to the car. Jim climbed aboard, and switched on the electric sidelights with which Miles had replaced the original oil lamps. Miles handed him the rifle; started the engine with one swing of the handle, took the wheel, opened the throttle, and pushed at the pedals.

"Home, John", laughed Jim. "And don't spare the horses."

His voice was a little thick. His breath smelt vaguely of poteen. As their tyres churned last year's leaves, he put a cigarette between his lips, and tapped the pocket of his flapped Flying Corps jacket for matches. The spurt of the match revealed long-lashed dark brown eyes, a golden moustache, and a nose that would have delighted an ancient Greek sculptor. What a handsome fellow Jim was. And what guts he had.

"There were some Shinners about a while ago", said Miles.

"Muck 'em", grunted Jim Bowlby. "Muck 'em all to hell."

6

He lit up, and blew out the match. Their Ford bumped up the lane, bucked on to the road. The bog stretched empty under the starlight, rising to rocky moorland ahead of them and on either side.

"How many?" asked Jim.

"Two parties. About twenty in each I should say."

"Which way were they going?"

"Into the hills. Confound this Tin Lizzie."

The engine had stopped. Miles jumped out; and cranked again.

"If I weren't so bloody tired", said Jim, "we might go after the bastards."

"And run into a nice ambush."

"Ambush my foot. I'd like to get a Shinner tonight."

"We're going back to barracks", said Miles firmly.

But at that moment both saw a flicker of orange light in the sky beyond the brow of the first hill.

The light disappeared. Now, gazing up the road, they could only see stars, blurred by an occasional slather of mist. Then the light flickered again, and Miles leaped back to the wheel.

"It might be Major Adair's place, Jim."

"I shouldn't wonder. The old duck's been asking for it ever since the Troubles started."

"We'd better go along and see, I suppose."

"You bet we had, kid."

Miles pushed first gear in; swung the wheel over, and advanced the ignition. As he changed up, Jim Bowlby rested the Bergmann against the back of the driving seat; took a swig from his flask; pulled a revolver out of one of his pockets, and broke it to make sure it was loaded in all six chambers.

"Why do you always do that?" asked Miles.

"Habit, kid", grunted Jim, reclosing the service Webley with a click.

"I wish he'd chuck calling me kid", thought Miles. "I'm not so young as all that."

Halfway up the hill, he switched out their sidelights. The narrow road grew even narrower. Rocks closed in on them. Just the place for an ambush—a couple of trees, or a trench across the road. But the rocks opened again, and soon they were on the brow of the first hill.

Jim held up a hand. Miles braked. Jim peered over the low windscreen into the next valley. They could hear a stream burbling; and the breeze, stronger here, soughing through dry bracken. Jim stood up, looking this way and that.

"Seems quiet enough", he began.

Then, suddenly, they heard the shots.

There were only a few shots; but, while they still echoed, light flickered again. A red light this time—midway up the next hill—on the edge of that dark patch of woodland.

"It's Castle Kilranan all right; that'll be the lodge", said Jim; and sat down again as the Ford jumped to the gear.

II

Once more that old, cold, utterly pleasurable excitement—only experienced in battle—took hold of Miles Radcliffe. He drove fast; but his thoughts

7

drove faster. It was half a mile of crooked going from the major's lodge to his big rambling house. If the Shinners had left the gates open they might just catch 'em on the hop.

He put the plan to Jim.

"Good enough", said Jim. "But don't stop if they aren't open or we shall be for it."

He had a revolver in each hand now, and was dangling the one in his left by the trigger guard. Another habit of Jim's. As usual before action, too, a steady stream of blasphemy flowed from his lips.

"I wonder why he does that", thought Miles, who never swore.

The road dropped steeply, curved sharply, forcing him to use the hand-brake. Reaching the valley, they could no longer see the fire. But, as they climbed again, wisps of smoke came down wind; and within a few seconds they saw the glare of the flames.

Jim stopped swearing to ask, "Is this the best you can get out of her?"

"She'll pick up in a minute. It's pretty steep here."

"We'd be better in a Crossley."

"We'd be better in barracks", grinned Miles. "Geoffrey'd kick up hell if he knew what we were doing."

"Muck Geoffrey", grunted Jim.

Miles gave the Ford all she'd take. She picked up slowly, shaking and rattling.

"Four spools and an old tomato can", he quoted. "Can you see if the gates are open?"

"It looks like it, kid."

"Then here goes."

The road levelled out as Miles spoke. He gave the Ford full throttle. The engine spat, backfired, thuttered, but gathered speed. He gave her full ignition.

Four, three, two hundred yards to go. Grand, if they did catch the Shinners on the hop. Gosh, how the lodge was blazing. Were the gates open? Yes, by jove. A nice bump that. Nearly had her off the road and Jim overboard. Another bump—and Jim cursing one's lights out.

"Fun", thought Miles.

A hundred yards to go. Fifty. The Shinners might have posted sentries. If they had, Jim would take care of 'em.

Out of the tail of his left eye Miles saw the muzzles of Jim's revolvers lifting. A rifle cracked. He heard a bullet ping past his head, another bullet. But Jim held his fire.

The Ford jumped again. Miles swung the wheel hard over; caught a glimpse of open gates, of blazing thatch, of a figure in a trench coat with a Mauser at its shoulder.

Jim let fly with both Webleys. The figure fell. They hurtled through blood-red smoke, past crackling timber, into sudden gloom under shadowy trees.

"Got the blighthawk", Jim was shouting. "Slow up while I reload, kid."

Past the first bend in the drive, Miles slowed, asking, "What's the next move? They're bound to have heard the shooting".

"I wonder." Jim had already reloaded. "Even if they have, they can't know we're only two. They'll be firing the house any minute now. I'm for pushing on."

8

"All right. If you say so. What do you think's happened to the major?"

"God knows. He always swore he'd shoot if they started any of their tricks on him. There's his wife too. Can you see all right?"

"Pretty well."

Miles accelerated. This drive had not been touched since the Troubles began. There were potholes here, puddles there, stones everywhere. And anywhere they might hit a trench or a tree trunk. He thought of switching on the sidelights, thought better of it. They splashed, skidding, through another puddle; hit their off front wheel against a log; ricocheted against another log; made the clearing where the drive forked.

"Right here", ordered Jim. "And pull up when I tell you."

What a map of a mind Jim must have. They'd only been inside this place once. The day they were hunting Mick Shanahan's gang.

"Stop", ordered Jim; and, jumping out, "Back her. Left lock. All you've got." He kicked at the front wheels to help them round. Miles pushed the reversing pedal. Shrubs scraped at his right elbow.

"That'll do", ordered Jim. "Switch off."

Miles picked up his precious Bergmann and dismounted. Jim signalled for silence; signalled for him to follow along a path between ragged rhododendrons. Soon Jim dropped to ground and wriggled forward on his knees and elbows. Miles wriggled at his heels.

"Haven't done this in years", he caught himself thinking; and, just for the split of a second, memory flashed him yet another picture—Railway Wood—and men, himself among them, crawling out through a gap between the wire into No Man's Land.

Then Jim stopped; and, crawling up to him, lifting his bonneted head, Miles saw that they were less than a hundred yards from Castle Kilranan.

The big rambling house lay a little below them. Between them and it sloped rough turf. Half right was a clump of trees.

Lights shone from the ground floor of the house. A torch flashed and went out at one of its upper windows. Miles could just perceive a cluster of figures round the porch.

"They can't have heard us", whispered Jim. "Let's get a bit closer."

He crawled away down the slope. Crawling alongside him, Miles thought, "I could wipe that lot out with three bursts".

They reached a furrow in the turf; and lifted their heads again. More figures were emerging from the house. Miles clicked off the safety catch of the Bergmann and cuddled the stock to his shoulder.

"How about it, Jim?"

"No. Wait."

At that moment the girl screamed.

The scream—quite obviously a girl's—came from the little clump of trees now about fifty yards to their right. Simultaneously a tongue of fire leaped from the upper window where they had seen the torch flashing.

In the second that followed, Miles—glancing towards the trees—saw the stacked cycles, the two bodies, and a figure that could be the girl's wrestling with other figures.

Then Jim barked, "Cover my flank. Don't let that lot get to their bikes"; jumped to his feet, bellowed, "Come along, lads. Charge 'em"; and ran straight for the clump.

9

"Good bluff", thought Miles.

Flames leaped from another window as he sighted low for the bunch of men round the porch. Both elbows planted, left hand gripping barrel to keep it down, he squeezed trigger, held it back. One, two, three figures toppled to his first burst. The rest scattered. He ceased fire ; heard revolver shots from his right ; heard a high bullet sing over.

The men he had scattered were taking cover. Mindful of Jim's order, he watched the ground between the house and the trees. Had Jim's bluff succeeded ? Had he got to the girl ? Who was the girl anyway ? Some servant perhaps. Why had she screamed ? Whose were those two bodies ?

Riflefire from the men round the house stopped speculation. They hadn't spotted him yet. They were shooting wildly.

One last revolver shot from his right. To his front, five men up and running for the clump. He squeezed the trigger again. Two men fell sprawling. Three dropped to ground. He rammed another magazine into the Bergmann. More riflefire. A dozen bullets plopping into the turf. That last burst must have given away his position. More flames from the house. Too much light. Inside another minute they'd be able to see him. That'd be about the end of it. He'd give 'em a run for their money, though. And maybe Jim would be able to get the girl away.

"This is where I get scuppered", he caught himself thinking. But the thought held no fear, only an excitement which transcended any he had ever known. And instantly he was firing again, single shots now, at the flashes of the rifles.

The cowards. Why didn't they rush him ? By jove, they were rushing him. Seven of 'em. What was that ? A klaxon ? Nonsense. He was crazy. One last burst. And if that didn't stop 'em, it'd be pistol work.

He realised that he must have fired his burst ; that he had let the rifle go ; that he was on his feet, one hand at shoulder holster, the other at hip holster— and that someone was shouting, "Jasus. The Tans".

Miles Radcliffe emptied both Colts as the klaxons blared again and the white sword of acetylene headlights stabbed down at the red daggers of the flames.

III

"I've a damn good mind to put you both under arrest", drawled Sergeant Geoffrey Thirkell of the Auxiliaries, his green eyes sulky, his heavy, clean-shaved, full moon of a face the colour of lard in the glare of the burning house.

"What for, Geoffrey ? Killing Shinners ?" mocked Jim.

"You'd have been killed yourselves, both of you, if O'Reilly hadn't got through to barracks before they cut the telephone wires."

"Who's O'Reilly ?"

"After he'd given Tony the S O S he told him he was Major Adair's batman. He didn't have time to say any more, I imagine."

"One of them shot him in the back. It was the same man who killed my uncle."

The girl spoke ; and Miles looked at her, thinking, "She's only a flapper. She's still got her hair in a pigtail".

"Would you recognise the man if you saw him again ?" asked Geoffre Thirkell.

10

"I don't think so. He had a mask over his face."

"You don't happen to remember if he wore a ring?"

"A ring?"

"A gold ring with a diamond in it?"

"Why, yes. I'm sure he did."

"Mick Shanahan", said Geoffrey; and called, "Ronnie—come here a minute, will you, old boy?"

Meanwhile Miles Radcliffe was still looking at the girl—and the girl at Miles.

Despite all the terrors she had experienced in this last hour, Rosaleen Adair's impression was the sharper. "The kid", as she remembered the tall man beside her calling him while they lay among the trees, had the clearest eyes—darkish gray, one imagined—long-lashed under eyebrows so narrow that they might have been plucked. His pale complexion was almost girlish. So were his lips, very red and curved almost in a Cupid's bow under the narrow line of a moustache, jetblack as the hair—a little curly, perhaps? —one could see under his bonnet. But there had been nothing girlish about the way he fought.

"Don't worry. The kid'll stop 'em. He's a perfect little tiger in a scrap", she further remembered the tall man saying. But "the kid" wasn't really little—just the right height, not too tall and not too short.

This "Ronnie" who had just run up really was too short—a wizened little monkey of a man, dwarfed by his tin hat, by the long dirk and the huge holster he wore at his hip. He had eyes like a snake's; but a nice smile.

"So this young woman recognised Mick", he was saying. "Somehow I opined it was his lot, Geoffrey. He's no among the wounded. But I'll just take another look at the deaders."

Miles saw the girl shudder. She must have had a pretty thin time. Not a bad-looking girl. A bit on the gawky side. Good teeth. By jove, her mouth was bleeding and her blouse torn. Approaching her, he asked:

"I say, are you hurt?"

"No. At least I don't think so."

"One of the brutes hit her in the mouth." Jim spoke. "But he won't hit anyone again." And, laughing, "You two haven't been introduced yet. Miss Adair, this is Miles Radcliffe, commonly called the kid".

"I don't know how to thank either of you", said Rosaleen Adair.

"What a nice voice", thought Miles.

She held out a hand. Her thin fingers were red, rough and as dirty as her face. He grasped them awkwardly. Again they looked at each other. He had an idea that her big eyes were hazel and her hair a golden brown.

"Oh, that's all right", he said, still awkward.

Jim cut in, "I'll go and see if I can get you a coat. There may be one in the tender".

He loped off. From behind the burning house echoed a fusillade.

"Is that . . . an execution?" asked Rosaleen.

"*We* don't shoot prisoners, Miss Adair."

Miles's voice, usually gentle, rose several semitones. A sudden glint in his eyes—elephant-gray, they were—made her realise that she had annoyed him.

"I'm—I'm sorry", she stammered.

11

"Oh, that's all right", repeated Miles.

She dabbed at her mouth with a soiled handkerchief. His own was clean. He offered it to her.

"Thanks", she said. "Thanks awfully."

Geoffrey had followed Jim. They were alone now. The house blazed and blazed—lighting up the woods behind it—the rhododendrons through which one had followed Jim—the slope of turf down which one had crawled—the stacked bicycles—this clump of trees.

"It's lucky the wind isn't this way", went on Miles.

The girl did not answer.

More shots echoed. They heard timber and slates crashing; saw smoke and sparks billow high beyond the branches under which they stood.

"It's all so terrible", said Rosaleen Adair. "And I don't know what I'm going to do now that they're both dead."

The two bodies Miles had seen—apparently those of her aunt and uncle—were already on the Crossley. He remembered watching them being taken away. A sudden sympathy—the first ever experienced for a girl—touched him. Not knowing what to say, he put a hand on Rosaleen's shoulder.

"Did Mick shoot your aunt too?" he asked—and thought, "What a fool I am. I ought to be kicked for asking her that."

He could feel her shoulder, bare and bony under his fingers (he'd forgotten her blouse was torn), shaking as she answered:

"No. She had a bad heart. She just fell down. Please—I don't want to talk about it".

"I couldn't find you a coat"—it was Jim speaking—"but here's a blanket. Geoffrey wants us to push off in the Ford and send out another tender. You'd better come with us if you feel up to it."

He draped the blanket round her. She smiled wanly.

"I'd like to get away", she said.

"Then come on."

Jim gave her an arm. They left the clump. He helped her up the slope. Following them, rifle at the carry, Miles thought, "If Mick escaped she won't be safe anywhere in Ireland"; and turned his head to see the other gable of Castle Kilranan topple in sparks and smoke.

They came out of clear flamelight into the flickering shadows of the rhododendrons. Jim helped the girl mount the Ford. Once more Miles handed him the Bergmann and swung the crank.

"It was lucky you had this with you", said Jim as Miles took the wheel. "The silly devils must have thought it was a Lewis. I was damn lucky, too."

Rosaleen Adair, seated between them, said nothing. Miles could feel her thigh, her elbow, pressing against him.

"I wonder if Fluke and Enid could do anything for her", he caught himself thinking as he let in the gear.

The last of the flamelight showed him his way back to the clearing. Once in the main drive, he switched on the side lamps. The lodge was just a mass of glowing ashes near which lay the dark shape of the first man Jim had shot.

"Oughtn't we to take his rifle?" asked Miles.

"No. The others'll find him all right. Geoffrey said we were to get a move on."

"Right you are."

They turned through the gates on to the bog-road. Miles opened the throttle, advanced the ignition lever. The Ford bounded swaying down the hill.

Up the next slope she needed coaxing. But once past the lane that led to Molly Maguire's cabin they made a good forty.

"Must we go quite so fast?" asked Rosaleen, holding the blanket tightly round her.

"Sorry", said Jim. "But I'm afraid we must."

He explained why. Without bicycles, the Shinners would find it difficult to get away. If they possibly could, they must catch Mick Shanahan.

"A firing party's too good for that young murderer", added Jim. "What he needs is a nice rope round his neck. And, once we catch him, your evidence'll do that."

"Oh, don't", said Rosaleen Adair.

Her words were so low that only Miles heard them. Her knee pressed his convulsively. He thought, "Jim's a brute to talk like that. She's all in. And no wonder".

He put a hand on her knee. It steadied. Another quarter of an hour at this pace would take them to barracks. Once there, he'd give her a good stiff whiskey and send her to bed.

They switchbacked on; made the crossroads.

"We're nearly home now", he told her. Jim said, "Slow down before we come to Monk's Wood, kid". The wood loomed ahead. Miles throttled back.

Jim leaned over Rosaleen, and put a hand to the rubber bulb of the horn. Fifty yards from the pines he began to toot—three longs and a short, three longs and a short. The answering torch flashed three shorts and a long. Miles braked. Jim called to a shadowy figure at the foot of a tree:

"Is that you, Bert?"

The figure stepped into the road; called back, "Yes. Is that you, Jim? Anything doing?"

"Lots. Geoffrey wants another tender out."

"No difficulty about that, old thing. We're all standing to. Where's the party?"

"Castle Kilranan. They've done the old major in."

"Thought they would one day." The torch beam swept the car. "Who's that you've got with you?"

"The major's niece."

"Rightyho. Carry on, old thing."

"Carry on, kid", echoed Jim; and a minute later they were through the wood.

It was lighter now. Peering between the folds of the blanket, Rosaleen could just perceive, beyond a pillared gateway, through which a carbine barrel poked, whitewashed walls, closed shutters, a tile roof and various outbuildings. A voice shouted, "You there. Who are you? Halt". They braked again. The man who had fetched her the blanket called, "Don't shoot, Martin, you bloody fool. Can't you see who we are? Open the gate and be quick about it".

The voice barked, "All right, Jim. Keep your wool on, even if you have

13

got a V.C.". A key turned in a lock. The gate swung back. They drove through—the bulb horn tooting and tooting. A door in one of the whitewashed walls opened, letting out a stream of lamplight, and half a dozen men in nondescript uniforms who crowded round the car.

"Where's Dominic?" asked Jim.

Someone answered, "Still counting his chips. The blighter held a straight flush".

" 'Twas a royal straight flush too." Another man, who wore a dark green police jacket, khaki breeches and fieldboots, had appeared in the doorway. "And phwat might you be making all this shindy for, Jim? Has Molly Maguire been after pulling your hair out, or is that her you've got with you?"

Everyone laughed; but Jim's first words silenced them.

More men had come running from the house. Rosaleen Adair heard Dominic Mahoney's booming orders, "Billy and George, get the tender out. Tom—Oi'll need you and your Lewis. No, Harry. Oi'll take eight—and not one more. That's Geoffrey's orders".

The men scattered. Four or five dashed into the house; dashed out again, cramming bonnets on heads, cramming weapons into pockets or legholsters. Two had darted to one of the outbuildings. Rosaleen saw double doors flung wide; heard a crank swung, the sudden roar of a big engine. Within the doors, a match spurted. Instantly acetylenes flared, almost blinding her.

Then the open tender, with the steelshod planks lashed to its running boards, was driven out, and the men clambered over the tailboard, seated themselves back to back on the form down the centre. Dominic Mahoney jumped up beside the driver. His Irish voice bawled, "All aboard for Castle Kilranan. Let her go, Billy".

He waved a revolver at them as the Crossley was driven off, its headlights showing up the sandbagged trenches and the barbed wire between the gates and the house.

The door of this house—Rosaleen Adair saw, as Miles led her inside it—was loopholed and had an inside lining of metal plates.

IV

"These shutters are lined with steel too", said Miles. "So you're quite safe here. Drink this up, and you'll feel ever so much better."

"I don't feel as bad as all that. And I really don't like whiskey."

"Never mind if you like it or not. It'll do you good, really it will."

Miles and Rosaleen were alone again in a little room, lit by an oil lamp, its only furniture the chair on which she was seated, the table on which the lamp stood, a canvas washstand and a bed. The bed had been turned back. On it lay a pair of silk pyjamas.

"This is Geoffrey's room", said Miles. "But I'm sure he won't mind your having it. Geoffrey's an awfully good chap. He's our sergeant."

He gave her the glass he was carrying. She sniffed at it, took one sip, made a wry face, and put it down on the table.

"Go on", he coaxed, and repeated, "It will do you good. Really it will."

14

"Aren't you having any?"

"I've had one already. I'm not much of a drinker."

She took a second sip, and a third.

"I'd better be going now", said Miles.

"Oh, please don't go. Sit and talk to me a little."

"But aren't you sleepy?"

She shook her head. Their eyes met. Again sympathy touched him. Vaguely he realised that she was afraid of being alone.

He moved to Geoffrey's bed; perched himself on it. For the first time, she noticed his clothes—black boots and belt, dark green trousers, a vari-coloured muffler, an old khaki jacket with the three stars of a captain on the shoulders and several medal ribbons at the left breast. He had taken off his bonnet; she saw that the thick black hair really was a little curly, and a queer patch of white at his right temple.

"How old are you?" she asked.

"Nearly twenty-two. At least, I was twenty-one in January."

"I'm fifteen. And today's my birthday."

"I say, I am sorry."

Again he thought, "What a fool I am. That's not a bit what I meant to say". But she seemed to have taken his meaning, for she smiled at him.

"Perhaps you'd like something to eat", he went on—quickly, to cover his mistake. "I can cook you some eggs if you like."

"I'd much rather talk. Tell me, how long have you been a Black and Tan."

"We're not Black and Tans. We're Auxiliary Cadets. There are only fifteen hundred of us—all ex-officers."

He explained the difference, adding, "I was one of the first to volunteer. It's been jolly good fun so far".

"Fun?"

"Well, you see"—he spoke shyly—"I like fighting. I say, do finish your whiskey."

She emptied the glass. He made to rise.

"Please don't go", she repeated. "Tell me some more about yourself. Have you done a lot of fighting?"

"Oh, a fair amount. Not as much as Jim, of course. I didn't get out to France till the end of sixteen."

She seemed to be counting with her fingers.

"But you were only a schoolboy then", she went on.

He admitted that he had run away from school and "joined up as a Tommy".

"I was in the infantry when I went out", he continued. "Then I was lucky enough to get my commission and a transfer to the Tank Corps."

She looked at his left sleeve. "Aren't those wound stripes?" she asked.

"Yes. I got cut over twice. Once in the leg, and once"—he pointed to the white patch of hair over his right temple—"just there. Lucky I had my battle bowler on, wasn't it?"

Falling silent, he took a battered cigarette case from a top pocket, opened and offered it.

"I don't smoke", said Rosaleen.

"Perhaps you'd rather I didn't."

15

"Oh, I don't mind a bit."

He lit up. She noticed what nice hands he had, and that he must have washed them. She hadn't yet washed hers. Or her face either. "I ought to have", she thought. He said suddenly:

"Now tell me about yourself. Have you always lived in Ireland?"

"Oh, no. I only came to live with uncle after mummy died. There was nowhere else for me to go, you see."

"Then your father's dead too."

"Yes. Daddy was killed in the Great War."

She in her turn fell silent, thinking of her own future.

"I shan't have a penny", she thought. "And I'm not old enough to be a governess, though I do speak French quite well. Oh dear, I wish I hadn't taken that whiskey. It's making me feel so funny."

Aloud she said, "Would it matter if we had the window open?"

He rose, opened the window, and unbolted the steel-lined shutters.

It was almost dawn. Over the hills, stars began to pale. The wind had died down. Soon cocks would be crowing. He pitched his cigarette on to the gravel, and felt the girl's hand clutch his arm.

"I'm—I'm afraid I'm going to faint", she was saying. "But I'll try not to."

Her fingers tightened their grip. Half turning his head, he saw that her face had gone quite gray. He freed his arm; circled her shoulders, and supported her back to the chair.

"Put your head down", he ordered, and there was a new note of command in his voice. "Right down. Between your knees."

Her eyes closed as she obeyed him. Thought went. After a while she grew hazily conscious that he had lifted her, that he was carrying her. When her eyes opened again she saw the round shadow of the lampshade on the whitewashed ceiling, and felt his fingers at the laces of her gym shoes.

"You'll be quite all right now", he was saying.

The sleep of complete reaction overwhelmed Rosaleen while she was still wondering how she came to be in bed.

V

"This is a funny kind of thing to have happened to me", thought Miles Radcliffe.

He had turned out the lamp and drawn the chair to the bedside. Dawn—growing lighter and lighter beyond the unshuttered window—showed him the back of the girl's head, the top coils of the golden brown pigtail, the curve of her left cheek, and one ear which struck him as rather pretty. How quietly she slept. Not a bit like Jim. When Jim was asleep you could hear every breath he drew through his nostrils. Or Ronnie, who always lay with his mouth open. Or Martin, who snored.

He had thrown a blanket over her. But one of her stockinged feet was still uncovered. He leaned forward, and twitched the blanket a little lower, thinking again, "It's lucky I knew how to deal with faints".

Who had taught him that trick of making people who looked like fainting put their heads between their knees? That doctor man on the Rhine? No. Enid. Enid had been a V.A.D. before she married Fluke.

His thoughts came back to the present. Somehow or other one felt responsible for this girl. She'd be got out of Ireland all right. Dublin Castle would see to that. They'd probably send her to England in a destroyer. But what would happen to her once she got there?

"I think I'll telegraph Fluke", decided Miles. "Only I'll have to be careful what I say. Oh lord, I am hungry. I wonder if I could leave her."

He thought of bolting the shutter; thought better of it (the Shinners never attacked in daylight); rose; tiptoed from the room, closing the door gently behind him, and made his way to the kitchen. There he found Martin, just relieved from sentry duty on the gate.

Martin Halliburton was boiling water and making toast. He said, "Hallo, kid. Not been to bed yet?"

"No. I've been looking after the major's niece."

"The devil you have. I should have thought that was more Jim's line of country. He's our poodlefaking specialist. Did you kiss her good night and tuck her little tootsies up properly?"

"Is that what you do to your yellow girl in Hong Kong?"

Martin's imaginary "yellow girl" (you placed her in Hong Kong, Pekin, Tokyo, or any other spot out East for which you had a fancy) was a standing joke in the detachment. A further legend had it that he prayed to the little jade Buddha he wore, instead of an identity disc, on a thin gold chain round his neck.

He acknowledged the legpull with his customary, "She's only yellow in spots and she doesn't show them to strangers for less than a dollar"; and ladled two eggs into a saucepan.

Miles fetched four more eggs and a dozen rashers of bacon from the larder, another saucepan and a frying pan.

"I'm jolly hungry this morning", he said, joining Martin at the stove.

"When aren't you? You eat enough for six. By the time you're my age, you'll have chronic dyspepsia."

They chaffed on—Miles obviously enjoying it, the set lines of Martin Halliburton's sinister countenance hardly relaxing. Miles remembered Jim's first judgment of him, "Once the bloody little colonel, always the bloody little colonel". But in a tight place Martin was every bit as good as Jim; and his black eyes, though they looked so fierce under those enormous eyebrows, could display the keenest understanding. They displayed it now, as he said:

"You're worried. What about? That girl?"

"Well, I am rather."

"Why? She's not your responsibility."

"I know she isn't. But, look here, I wish you'd give me your advice."

"I never give advice on an empty stomach."

Martin Halliburton lifted his eggs from the saucepan and dropped them into the eggcups. He took his toast to the table and buttered it. Miles, who rather prided himself on his cooking, poached his own eggs and arranged them neatly on the fried bacon.

He talked while he ate, and Martin listened carefully till he had done.

"It doesn't sound a bad scheme", he admitted. "How old is this brother of yours?"

"Oh, Fluke's almost as old as you are. He's my half brother really."

17

"And is his christian name really Fluke?"

"No. That's his nickname."

Miles talked away, while Martin Halliburton thought, "Nice lad. Pity he's such a pal of Bowlby's. Bowlby'll go to the bad. Drinks too much. Womanises too much. Maskee. It's none of my business. Don't suppose I'll see any of 'em again once this show's over".

He lit a pipe and went to his toilet. Miles finished his eggs and bacon, and was just draining his third cup of tea when he heard an engine. Jumping up, running out, he saw a tall foxy-haired man with red tabs and the crossed swords of a brigadier general on his khaki jacket dismounting from a Vauxhall. Beyond the gates were three armoured cars.

Miles, recognising the local Military Governor, commonly known as "The Ferret", stiffened to attention and said, "Good morning, sir".

The Ferret grunted, "Morning. The Divisional Commissioner phoned me you chaps had a bit of a scrap at Castle Kilranan last night. Anybody back yet?"

"The tenders are still out, sir. But I can tell you most of what happened."

"So you were in it, eh? Well, fire ahead."

Miles told as much as he thought advisable. The Ferret's lean face twitched.

"Johnny Adair of Kilranan was my father's best friend", he said between set teeth. "I often stayed there when I was a lad. Mick Shanahan's going to hang for this. I'll find him if I have to beat every hill from here to Connemara. Any witnesses?"

"One, sir. A girl."

"Where is she?"

"Here."

"Right. Phone your District Inspector at once. Use the new code."

"Very good, sir."

"What's your name, by the way?"

"Radcliffe, sir."

"And your sergeant's name?"

"Thirkell, sir."

"Right."

The Ferret jumped back into his Vauxhall, which was driven away at full speed—one of the armoured cars ahead and two following it—into the eye of the rising sun. Miles ran back to the house.

In the slip of a room Geoffrey used for an office he found Tony Shaw, who grumbled "How much longer am I supposed to stay on this blasted phone? Everybody out having fun—and I've been here since midnight".

"I don't mind taking over for an hour if that's any good to you. As a matter of fact I've got a message for the D.I. The Ferret's just been here."

"Ferreting?"

"Yes."

Shaw lit a cigarette and went out. Miles got out the code book; sat down at the table; twirled the telephone handle, and asked for the district inspector's number. A known voice answered, "He's just been hauled out of bed by the commissioner and gone off breathing fire and slaughter. It appears that the Ferret's on the warpath".

18

"I've got a code message from him."

"All right. I'll take it down."

Miles dictated slowly. When he had finished, the voice at the other end said, "I'll decode this right away and give it to Charlie the moment he comes back". He replaced the receiver; rang off; drew a piece of paper towards him; took out his fountain pen and wrote after much thought: "*P.L. Radcliffe. The Firs. Plinley Green. Herts. England. Am sending a friend of mine to stay with you* stop *she's rather young and has nowhere else to go* stop *give her my room or if occupied will pay for one outside Miles*".

On further thought he cut out the "P.L.", which seemed rather extravagant, hoping that his half brother would understand the need for secrecy with every telegraph and telephone line liable to be tapped.

The telephone rang as he screwed the cap on his pen. The known voice spoke again, excitedly, for a long minute.

"I don't believe it", said Miles.

"But I tell you the letter's in the *Examiner*. It's just come in. Lloyd George wrote the bloody thing himself. To de Valera, if you please. The old goat calls him 'the chosen leader of the great majority of Southern Ireland'.

"And my brother was murdered in Grafton Street yesterday afternoon", added the voice at the other end of the wire.

VI

Rosaleen Adair woke to hear two men talking outside a narrow window through which sunshine streamed.

"I tell you we've been doublecrossed", one of the men was saying. "And I'll tell you something else, kid. I'm going to send my decorations back. The King's welcome to them, and, as for the blasted Country, it's not worth fighting for."

The other man said, "Don't talk rot, Jim. And don't talk so loud. She's still asleep."

Boots trod gravel. The voices were silent. Memory flooded back into her brain.

Starting up, she looked at her wristwatch. Three in the afternoon. But it must be even later. She had forgotten to wind her watch. The second hand wasn't moving. She swung her feet to the floor, saw her gym shoes and groped for them. Habit made her think, "What am I going to wear today?" Then she remembered that she had nothing to wear except these clothes in which she had bolted from her little room at the Castle when the rifle butts crashed on the front door.

There was a jug of water by the canvas washstand, over which hung a man's shaving mirror. She found soap and a nailbrush; began to wash and tidy herself.

Before she could finish, a green-eyed moon of a face capped with a huge bonnet peered in through the window; and a voice she recollected from overnight said:

"Hallo. So you're awake, are you? What about a nice cup of tea?"

"Yes. I should like that", answered Rosaleen, feeling rather self-conscious.

19

The moonfaced one bawled, "Miles. The Adair girl's awake. Get her some tea, will you?" and left the window. She dried her hands on a towel that might have been cleaner; searched the hem of her short skirt for a safety pin that ought to be there; found it, and pinned up the rent in her blouse.

Presently she heard feet on floorboards and the rattle of china against a tray.

Miles knocked. She called, "Come in".

"How are you feeling?" he asked, depositing the tray on the bed. "I've brought you some bread and butter and a boiled egg. You can have some cold beef if you like."

"Oh, that'll be quite enough, thanks."

He appeared to hesitate.

"I say——" he began; then quickly, "The—the convenience is quite close. It's the first door on your right."

He went out; and, just for a moment, her sense of humour returned. It must be awfully awkward for all these men to have a girl billeted on them.

"Shall I have to stay another night?" she wondered; and was still wondering about that when, some twenty minutes later, Miles knocked again.

"Geoffrey thinks", he began, "that you'd better put these on. The slacks'll go under your skirt and the coat'll cover that. Your gym shoes won't show once we're in the car. This is Ronnie's cap. I hope it'll fit you."

He laid a pair of khaki trousers, a greatcoat, and a bonnet with the crowned harp badge on the bed; picked up the teatray and made to leave.

"But why have I got to dress myself up?" asked Rosaleen.

He explained that she was being driven into the town, and that the Shinners mustn't know about it because, "they've got spies everywhere—you see".

"The district inspector's sent a car for you", he added. "They'd like to start as soon as ever you're ready."

"Aren't you coming?"

"Well, Geoffrey's sending a tender in. So I thought I might—that's to say if you've no objection."

"It would be nice if you would."

He went out again. The trousers—curiosity discovered that they were marked "M. Radcliffe. 30.9.1920"—fitted perfectly round her waist; but she had to turn the ends up because they were so long. The tam-o-shanter bonnet fitted even better. "It rather suits me", she decided, examining herself in the glass.

But the greatcoat, which happened to be Martin Halliburton's, fell nearly to her feet.

Once more humour came uppermost, almost obliterating the repressed thoughts, "Uncle and aunt are both dead. You don't even know what's happened to their bodies. You're all alone in the world. And you haven't got a shilling".

Then Miles knocked once more; and led her through the house to the front door, close by which stood a big motorcar, two men in dark green ackets and peaked caps on the front seat and one behind.

All the men were armed. She saw that Miles, too, was wearing a pistol; and a tender just beyond the gates.

"Mind if I come along?" Miles asked of the man in the rear seat. "There's something I want to talk to Charlie about."

"The more the merrier", answered the man, who wore the khaki trousers of "The Tans".

He opened the door. They climbed in, seated themselves. The driver klaxoned. The tender beyond the gates began to move. So did they. Within two minutes she was clutching her bonnet.

She had not been in a motorcar half a dozen times—and never in one like this. Speed blinded her, took all thought from her. She could feel the dust caking on her eyebrows.

They slowed at last. She saw the tender just ahead and that they were in the outskirts of the town.

Soon she was wondering why uncle had never allowed her into the town. It seemed so peaceful. All the shops were open—except one or two whose windows had been boarded up. Carts were clip-clopping along; and "jaunting cars", as her ignorance still called them. Cyclists darted here and there. On the pavement, women with shopping bags stood at gossip. She heard a newsboy shouting, saw the bill he carried, "All about LL G's letter to Dev".

Only the armed Black and Tans, walking two by two, and the realisation that her own escort had drawn their pistols, spoke to her of war.

The tender stopped. They drew up behind it, their tyres scraping the kerb. She saw two more Black and Tans, in their green jackets and khaki trousers, standing either side of a door, which opened.

She was out and across the pavement and through the doorway almost before she understood the orders she had been given.

The door closed. Miles said, "Jolly good work. I don't see how she could have been spotted". The man who had come in with them said, "You never know with Shinners. I expect the D.I.'s in his office. You can take her in to him if you like".

"Right. I will."

Miles took her by the arm. They came along a passage to a door marked, "Royal Irish Constabulary. District Inspector". Miles turned the handle, and a square-headed pugnacious-looking young man in a dark green uniform rose from a table at which he had been writing.

"Hallo, Charlie", said Miles. "This is Miss Adair. We thought it better to dress her up a bit."

"Good idea."

The young inspector offered her his hand, and a wooden chair, saying, "I'm afraid you must have had a pretty rotten time. But you'll be all right with us".

He smiled, showing good teeth. A short silence followed. Then Miles spoke.

"I'll have to be off in a minute or two, Charlie. Geoffrey wants the tender back. But there's something I want to tell you first. It's about Miss Adair. Of course she'll be sent to England."

"I presume so."

"How soon, do you think?"

"My dear chap, how should I know? You'd better ask the military. Evacuations are their pidgin, not ours."

Rosaleen saw Miles's eyelashes—he had the longest eyelashes—flutter.

"You needn't be so jolly official, Charlie", he countered. "The point is that Miss Adair doesn't know anybody in England. So this afternoon I got Geoffrey to let me send a telegram to my half brother, asking him to look after her when she arrives. I ought to have an answer by tomorrow, or the day after at the very latest."

"I see."

The district inspector picked up a fountain pen and tapped it against his teeth. Miles turned to Rosaleen.

"My half brother lives quite near London", he went on. "He's married. I'm sure he and Enid—that's his wife—will make you quite comfortable."

Gratitude made her blush. The knowledge that she was blushing made her stammer.

"It's—it's awfully good of you, Captain Radcliffe."

Another silence followed. Then Miles said:

"Well, I'll have to be off now".

He held out his hand; took hers, and appeared in his turn to be blushing.

"About money", he blurted out. "You'd better let me lend you some."

"Oh, but I couldn't do that."

"Why not?"

They were still holding hands. Watching them, the district inspector thought, "What kids they are, both of them".

"Why not?" repeated Miles. "You can pay me back any time."

He dropped her hand and dived into one of his trouser pockets, from which he drew a neatly folded note.

"It's only a fiver", he continued. "You won't have to pay for your ticket or anything. The moment I hear from my brother, I'll let Charlie know his address and all that."

"You'd better give me the address right away", cut in the district inspector.

"Yes, perhaps I had."

They exchanged glances. Miles gave the address. The inspector wrote it down. It struck Rosaleen that both of them looked a little worried—and that she was being treated like a child.

"But I suppose that's all I really am", she caught herself thinking—and wanted to blush again as she took the note.

VII

"I wonder if I ought to have given her more", worried Miles, as he climbed over the tailboard of the waiting tender and sat down on the form. "I wonder if it'll be all right about Fluke. Supposing he doesn't telegraph."

But before they were halfway back to barracks he gave up worrying—because after all he had done his best, and, as Martin said, the girl wasn't his responsibility.

"Don't know why I butted in", he thought. "It isn't even as if I liked girls."

Meanwhile the other men in the tender were talking, as everybody had been talking ever since they first got wind of it, about Lloyd George's letter to Dev.

22

"No terms with the murder gang", quoted Tony Shaw. "That's what they said only the day before yesterday. I'll be sugared if I can understand it."

"Nor I", put in Jack Ellington, who was at the wheel.

"You would—if you knew as much about the Castle as I do", Mark Merrivale, a newcomer to the detachment, informed them. "There's a blighter in that outfit who'd sell the whole damned Empire for forty pieces of silver. For two pins I'd ask for a spot of leave, and put a bullet into him."

"Name?" asked Tony.

"No names, no packdrill. But everybody in Dublin knows that he and Michael Collins are as thick as a couple of thieves. You mark my words, this is their doing."

"Off with your safety catches", snapped Jack over his shoulder. "There's a cart across the road."

But the cart backed through a gate almost before he pushed the brake pedal; and once again, as they swept past it, the June sun, which had hidden itself behind a little cloud, shone on the white road, on green woods and brown moorland and the far blue-gray of the hills.

Miles rested his elbows on his knees.

"Lovely country", he caught himself thinking; and the voices of his companions seemed to recede, while, in their stead, he heard the voice of a poet singing:

> "Down thy valleys, Ireland, Ireland,
> Down thy valleys, green and sad,
> Still thy spirit wanders wailing,
> Wanders wailing, wanders mad".

And, "I expect that's about right", he thought drowsily. "There is something mad about Ireland". Then his head fell slowly forward on to his hands; his eyes closed, and he heard no more voices, only a vague scrunching, which he still knew to be the noise of their tyres, till Jack Ellington shook him by the shoulder, bawling, "All change for Sligo."

"Sorry", said Miles, wide awake on the instant. "Have I been asleep?"

"You've been giving a jolly good imitation of it. I'm just going to put this tender away. So hop out. And if you take my advice, you'll go and lie down for a bit."

"I believe I will. I haven't been to bed since the night before last."

But in the dormitory they shared with Martin and Ronald Wallace and Dominic and three others, Miles found Jim, cursing to himself while he cleaned his Webleys.

"Drunk?" said Jim in answer to his question. "Not yet, kid. Not by a long chalk. But if I don't get drunk tonight, my name's not Bowlby."

"Nor mine Mahoney", boomed Dominic, entering by the other door. "Let's get Miles sewed up too. Not that I ought to be after drinking with Englishmen. 'Tis a lot of treacherous bastards, ye are, all of you."

"Stow that, Dominic."

"Oi'll say what I damn plaze."

Jim rose, gun in hand, and they faced each other. Miles saw Dominic's blue eyes suffuse with rage. His shock of red hair seemed to bristle. His big body stiffened. His hands clenched.

23

Jim's face had gone white; but his pose, as always, was the easy, carefree pose of the beau sabreur. He tossed his gun on to his bed.

Then he smiled, and his hands, too, clenched; and Miles stepped quickly between them.

"Easy on", he said. "Both of you."

"Out of me way, whippersnapper", bellowed Dominic. "Or it's the pair of ye Oi'll be eating."

Miles Radcliffe's nostrils flared. His elephant-gray eyes glinted.

"Try it", he said.

"Hallo. A fracas."

Martin Halliburton spoke, sarcastically, from the doorway. The three turned to him. He approached them. Behind him, Miles saw Ronnie Wallace and Geoffrey Thirkell.

"What's up?" asked Geoffrey.

"Only a slight difference of opinion about my parentage", answered Jim.

" 'Twas not you in particular I called a bastard", muttered Dominic; and suddenly his hands unclenched; suddenly laughter shook him through and through.

"Jasus", laughed Dominic Mahoney. "Jasus, but it's funny. There's me wanting to batter the face off Jim, and Jim itching to belt the lights out of me. And all for why. Becase one sloimy little Welshman's sold the pair of us, and all Oireland with us, to the corner bhoys. That's God's gospel truth, and ye know ut as well as I do, Jim. So what would we be foighting for? There'll be foighting enough in Oireland from this day on. But it won't be us, nor the Black and Tans, nor the military that'll do the foighting. 'Twill be Oirish against Oirish. Mick Collins's boys against de Valera's boys. But the shame of ut, the black shame of ut, will be England's."

And, "By Christ", said Jim Bowlby, "you're damn right about that, Dominic". But Geoffrey Thirkell, green eyes blazing, intervened while they were still shaking hands:

"You chaps are as bad as Shinners. Worse in my opinion. I've a damn good mind to put you both under arrest for talking treason".

"A verra sound idea, Geoffrey." The diminutive Ronald Wallace—eyes emotionless as a snake's, his wizened face betraying none of the passions which had been boiling in him all day—spoke pawkily. "But you'd better put the whole detachment under arrest while you're about it."

"You agree with them?" Thirkell puffed out his fat cheeks.

"Of course I agree with them. And so does everybody else."

"I don't", said Martin Halliburton. "I think Lloyd George is quite right to try and settle things."

"Settle things", Dominic broke out. "If you think this'll settle things, you're a loon. Oi know Oireland. And you don't. Oi love Oireland. That's why I've been foighting for her—foighting to give her a bit of peace. But this won't mane peace. This'll mane civil war. And it'll mane more than that. It'll mane that in the end—after the country's run with more blood than we and the Tans spilled betwane us—both soides'll jine up against England, and de Valera'll get his republic. And phwat'll happen to loyalists like meself before he gets his republic? Oi know if you don't, Martin. Oi know if you don't, Geoffrey. We'll be hunted for our loives, and the loives of our womenfolk, we'll be beaten up, we'll be boycotted, we'll be stripped of everything we possess. And all for why? Just becase we were loyal." His voice rose hysterically. "Just becase we were loyal. And ye expect me to go on being loyal. Ye tell me I'm talking treason when I tell ye the truth. You know it's the truth as well as Oi do, Geoffrey. And so do you, Martin. So why can't ye face it, like Jim here, like Ronnie here?"

"Because it isn't the whole truth", said Geoffrey Thirkell; and Martin added, "Precisely. I don't pretend to know as much about Ireland as you do, Dominic. But there's one thing I do know. And that's this. That there've been as many faults on our side as on theirs. If we'd have given them Home Rule——"

"Home rule, Rome rule", quoted Ronnie, who was a fanatical presbyterian. "I'm a' for discipline, Geoffrey. But a fact's a fact. If there's any treason, it's in Westminster. And it's treason to the whole Empire. We were sent here to keep order—and ye canna deny we've kept order. But we canna go on keeping it. Not now——"

"I can", drawled Geoffrey. "And I'm bloody well going to. So get that into your heads everybody. And get something else into your heads too. This detachment's still on active service. I won't have anyone in it talking mutiny.

"Mutiny", he repeated—and Miles Radcliffe realised, not for the first time, that this fat man, nearing forty, wih the pale hair receding from his forehead and the cold green eyes which so rarely showed anger, was at least as reckless, and far more dangerous, than Jim, or Dominic, or even Ronnie, who had been known to kill with his bare hands.

Maybe Jim and Dominic and Ronnie realised that too. For none of them spoke; and after a while Martin eased the situation with a semi-sarcastic:

"I fancy there's still time for a little drink before we haul down the Union Jack and hang out the green white and orange. We might even mix Scotch and Irish, just to show there's no ill feeling. Come along, you wild mutineers".

He made for the door. After a little hesitation the three followed him.

"What about you, Miles?" asked Geoffrey Thirkell.

"I don't think I will, thanks. I really am most awfully sleepy."

"And no wonder." To Miles's surprise Geoffrey laid a fat hand on his shoulder. "You put up a damn good show last night. But I'm afraid that kind of fun's pretty well over. For us anyway. Those three lunatics are quite right about that. The only trouble with them is that they talk so much. You don't. And I don't imagine you care so much either—about Ireland, I mean. You're like I am—out for what you can get. Or aren't you?"

His eyes probed. He removed his hand.

"Do you mean the pay?" asked Miles, feeling that the question was rather stupid.

Geoffrey laughed.

"In my case", he said. "But not in yours. You must have a bit of money of your own, otherwise you couldn't have offered to pay for that girl's board and lodging. Still, money's always useful. And when this job's over, I might be able to show you how to make quite a packet. It'd mean a lot of fun too. We must have a yarn one of these days."

He went out, closing the door behind him. Miles took off his boots.

Geoffrey had been right. He didn't care much about Ireland. Ireland was just another adventure. Like the war. By jove, he had enjoyed the war. If it hadn't been for the war—and Ireland—he might be swotting at a desk in Fluke's office.

"But I don't care about girls either", he thought. "So why did I send Fluke that telegram? And why am I in such a stew that he won't answer it in time?"

The "stew" kept him awake nearly ten minutes—a long time for Miles.

26

BOOK TWO

I

ROSALEEN ADAIR FITTED THE COVER ON HER TYPEWRITER AND LIT A CIGARETTE. She had only just taken to smoking, and could never quite make up her mind. whether she really enjoyed it, or whether she only smoked because "one felt so out of things if one didn't".

"One does so hate being different", she thought. Yet of course one was "different", because one "simply hated being kissed". Other girls seemed to like it. Why?

Such moods of introversion were rare; and this one, brought on by an incident already two nights old, soon passed. Casually she re-read her typescript of the notes Fluke had dictated before leaving the office: "You'll never get reception right, Until you take to Radcliffite . . . The green crystal in the special cup . . . The secret's in the cup . . . Radcliffe Cats' Whiskers are the cat's whiskers . . . The Radcliffe high tension battery plug means less plugging . . . A Radcliffe coil, Means far less toil".

How Fluke loved rhyming his ads.

She finished her cigarette and looked at the clock. Five past five. She could go. But perhaps, if she waited a little longer, this rain would stop. Such soft rain. It reminded one of Ireland. What a long time ago that seemed.

"More than four years", Rosaleen remembered. "And it's three since I saw Miles. I hope he'll write this Christmas. He only sent me a card last time. I wonder what he was doing in Paraguay. It seems such a funny place to go. But then Miles is funny. He's not a bit like Fluke."

Memory flashed her the picture of her first meeting with Fluke—after that "trip up the river" in the despatch boat—and that other trip in the destroyer when she had nearly disgraced herself by being seasick—and that long railway journey to London.

"I'm Philip Luke Radcliffe", she remembered him saying. "You know, Miles's half brother. My wife ought to have met you. But we're having a spot of servant trouble and she can't leave the two kids. I hope you like kids. Because—well, to be quite frank with you—I rather thought you might help Enid to look after them. Just for a start anyway."

Fluke's son Simeon had only been two and his daughter Phyllis still in her cradle when he brought her to The Firs. Arthur had been born last year, just before Fluke and Enid moved to Rosemary Lodge, just after she started work in this office.

Fancy, she'd been working in this office for nearly two years.

Thought returned to Miles. How excited she'd been when Fluke told her, "He's been demobbed. He'll be down tomorrow". How different he'd looked, coming up the steps in that blue suit, that soft green hat. And what an argument he and Fluke had had about Ireland that first evening.

Fluke was always a bit noisy when he got into an argument; but Miles had never even raised his voice.

"All right, old chap", Rosaleen could almost hear him saying, "have

27

things your own way. If you'd been in the show, you mightn't feel quite so sure. As far as I'm concerned, it's over."

And after that they had fallen to arguing about Miles's future—Fluke resolute that he "must get down to brass tacks and earn a decent living"; Miles equally resolute, "If you mean that I've got to sit on my tail in some rotten office for the rest of my life—well, I'm not cut out for that and I'm not going to do it".

But when Fluke asked, "Then what are you going to do? You can't just mooch about on four pounds a week, and that's pretty well all you can expect six thousand quid to bring you in, even though they have taken a bit off the income tax", Miles had only laughed, "I shan't be mooching about, as you call it, for more than another month".

And in less than a month, during which they scarcely saw anything of him, he had just disappeared, only reminding them of his existence with an occasional postcard, an even more occasional letter.

What could Miles have been doing with himself all these years—he never so much as mentioned his own doings—in places like Havana and the Bahamas, in Tampico and New Orleans, and more especially Paraguay?

"He's a regular puzzle", thought Rosaleen; and looked up towards the door, which had just opened, showing her the lanky, shaggy-haired, sports-coated, gray-trousered figure of the man to whom Fluke always referred as "My chief engineer".

Derek Grayson, the one and only engineer of "Radcliffe Radios Limited", blinked at her through hornrimmed spectacles, and said, "Where's our lord and master? Gone home. Oh, blast. I've just had a real brainwave. There's only one thing wrong with our new valve holder, and that's . . ."

He overwhelmed her with technicalities; cadged a cigarette, and vanished. Rosaleen walked to the window, which had no blind, and looked out on to the courtyard of the little factory, its asphalt just beginning to dry.

Through the lighted panes opposite she saw workgirls still at their benches, and Alf, the foreman, bending over one of the tables on which they wound the coils. From the one window of the grandiloquently styled "Scientific and Experimental Department" the "latest triumph of Radcliffe research—a loudspeaker set you can make in your spare time" seemed in two minds whether it were giving a lesson in morse or playing "Don't go down the mine, daddy".

The morse lessons led at a crackling canter while she fixed the blue hat firmly on to her bob of golden brown hair; but "Don't go down the mine, daddy" challenged it to a fighting finish as she belted the mackintosh round her waist.

"Fluke's right", she decided. "We'll never sell that set unless we give them an Amplion with it. Derek's loudspeaker doesn't work."

"Moggles", the night watchman, had just come on duty. He gave her, "Good night, miss", as she let herself out by the glass doors on her way to the shed where she kept her bicycle.

Mounting, she thought, "We shall have the new sign up after Christmas". But, once outside the gates, the traffic along the newly opened bypass drove all other thoughts from her mind.

Tonight there seemed to be more cars than ever. Their oncoming headlamps kept on blinding one. Their overtaking horns kept on deafening one. And as for one's splashed stockings—well, one would just have to wash them out as soon as one got home.

She pedalled along, becoming crosser and crosser, for three flat miles. Then the tarmac rose, and she had to change into low gear. By the time she reached the red sign of the new garage at the top of the little hill she was feeling quite exhausted.

After another mile the headlamps of an overtaking car showed her the fingerpost, "Plinley Green Station"; and soon she was between the bare hedges of the old country road, down which she remembered wheeling Simmy and Philly in their double perambulator.

Presently, to her right, she could see the many lights of Albanford; and, ahead, the first streetlamps of her own suburb—always to be referred to, she reminded herself, as a "rural district".

How Miles had laughed when Fluke remonstrated with him for using the derogatory word "suburb"!

II

Rosaleen Adair was still thinking about Miles Radcliffe, and this struck her as rather surprising because she had not thought about him for "ages and ages", when she reached "Fairholm", the little house where she boarded with Stephanie Archer, the younger of Enid's two sisters.

Stephanie was already home. She came to the front door while Rosaleen stabled her cycle—a young woman of twenty-seven, already cut out for a spinster, dark hair Eton cropped, tall figure rather mannish, not even a fleck of powder on her severe features.

But there was nothing severe about Stephanie's lips as they smiled, "You must have had a beast of a ride, dear"; and the hand which drew Rosaleen into the little hall could hardly have been more tender or better kept.

"You'd better have a bath", went on Stephanie. "I've ordered the taxi for a quarter past seven. Are you going to put on your new frock? I should, if I were you. You look so nice in it."

Rosaleen took off her shoes—Stephanie being so fussy about the new staircarpet—before she went up to her room and drew the chintz curtains. How lucky she was to have this nice room, this plain wallpaper, this white furniture. What good taste Stephanie had. Much better than Enid's.

She took off her frock, put on a dressing gown, washed her stockings, and—leaving them to soak in the lavatory basin—went to the bathroom. This new gas geyser was a perfect joy. It functioned automatically the moment one turned the hot tap.

Back in her bedroom, she spent a little longer time than usual at her dressing table, on which, in a folding frame of tooled leather, stood the photographs of her father, looking very much the soldier (though, of course, he'd only been a temporary one) in his khaki, and her mother, rather old-fashioned with her long hair and her heavy jewelry.

"I can remember the day she sold that necklace", thought Rosaleen. "They were always selling or pawning things. The poor darlings."

But they'd been the silliest darlings. And sometimes one couldn't help resenting it. Because after all one oughtn't to be a typist, living in a suburb.

"Snob", she chided herself. "You're no better than anyone else just because your father happened to be an honourable. And his family were quite right not to have anything more to do with him. He was simply hopeless about money, and—and he did drink."

Still—"the family" might have done something for oneself. They might have taken some trouble to find out what had happened to one after Uncle John was killed and Aunt Hetty died. For all they seemed to care, one might still be in Ireland.

"Not that *I* really care", concluded Rosaleen's thoughts. "I don't want charity. I'd far rather earn my own living."

She gave her nose, which always struck her as a little too small, a last dab of powder; rose, and slipped into her new evening frock, which barely came to her knees. Stephanie called up from the hall, "It's nearly ten past. Are you ready?" She called back, "Just coming", and put on her cloth coat.

"The child gets prettier every day", thought Stephanie, when Rosaleen came down the staircase; and, chiding herself as usual for sentimentality, "Not that she's really pretty. She's nothing like as good-looking as Enid was at her age."

All the same, one couldn't deny that men ("boys" she corrected herself contemptuously) were attracted by Rosaleen, or that one of these fine days "some idiot" would propose to her.

"And when she does get married", concluded Stephanie's thoughts, "it'll be pretty bleak for me."

The crunch of tyres on gravel sent them to the door. It was raining again. They jumped into the taxi quickly, Stephanie calling to the driver in her rather harsh voice, "Rosemary Lodge. You know, Mr. Philip Radcliffe's house".

"On the Avenue, isn't it?"

"No. Clareville Grove. Past the golf course, up the hill, and the first on your right."

The driver said, "Oh, that Mr. Radcliffe. I thought you meant the other one"; and set off.

Five minutes took them past the gates of the club house, its windows brilliantly lit, into a narrow road under high trees. The road forked and climbed towards street lamps. They turned away from the lamps at a sign which read, "Clareville Grove. No through traffic". Another hundred yards brought them between brick pillars to a white doorway.

The door opened to show a parlourmaid in yellow linen, whom Stephanie, having told their driver to be back at ten o'clock, greeted with, "Good evening, Betty. I hope we're not the last".

"Oh no, miss. There's only Mr. Paul here so far."

"Good."

They took off their wraps, and laid them on a narrow mahogany table which Rosaleen remembered from The Firs. By this, against the light oak panelling, stood a walnut grandfather clock, also remembered.

An oak door at the far end of the hall stood ajar. Stephanie pushed her way through; Rosaleen followed.

"Help yourselves to drinks", said Enid from her armchair. "And you can both thank your stars you're not in the family way."

Paul, standing by the fireplace, pursed his thin lips.

The eldest of the Archers, managing director of the family provision

30

business, churchwarden of St. Mary's, Albanford, and prominent member of the Albanford branch of the League of Nations Union, might have been ten years older than his actual thirty-three. His fair hair was already receding from his lined forehead. Spectacles with very thick lenses magnified the blue eyes whose poor sight had kept him out of the Great War. As always, he looked his worst in the dinner jacket on which Enid had insisted.

"You needn't be so shocked", Enid chaffed him. "This is nineteen twenty-five, I'll have you know."

She patted a curl slightly more golden than nature intended with a plump hand on which rings glittered. Her eyes, larger and of a deeper blue than his, twinkled with fun. Tonight she wore three rows of pearls, too large to masquerade as real, round her white throat.

"Let me pour you out a cocktail, Rosaleen", said Paul, stepping to a side table.

"Hallo. Not late, am I?" boomed Fluke.

His dinner clothes—Rosaleen realised as she looked towards the doorway —really fitted. And although you couldn't call him handsome—his nose was a little too bulbous, and his ears a little too prominent, and his eyes, a paler blue even than Paul's, goggled a little too much under those sandy brows—he looked very much of a man, nearly six feet tall, broad-shouldered, with a ruddy complexion, and a moustache, which was still clipped soldier-fashion, of the same sandy colour as his hair and eyebrows. He had a nice smile too. Everybody liked Fluke. The men and girls in the factory would do anything for him.

Simultaneously with his entrance, they heard voices from the hall.

"Mother and father", said Enid, rising.

Mildred Archer, like her son Paul, had aged prematurely. A little old lady at fifty-three, who had not been much to look at even on her wedding day, she wore the clothes of another generation; and was apt, under the stress of excitement, to drop a betraying h.

"And 'ow are you, my dear?" she asked, as her eldest daughter kissed her on both cheeks.

"Oh, I'm grand, mother."

Meanwhile Walter Archer surveyed the scene with satisfaction. Enid had done well for herself. This new house really was the last word in comfort. And one couldn't want for a better son-in-law than Philip—though he did play games on a Sunday instead of going to church.

He gave Fluke a gnarled hand; refused a drink; and stood playing alternately with his gray whiskers and the heavy gold watchchain he wore across his black silk evening waistcoat.

"How's business?" he asked.

"Top hole", answered Fluke; and again they heard voices in the hall, followed a moment later by the entrance of Timothy Archer and his wife Lucy.

The dark-haired Timothy, who sported a soft shirt with his double breasted dinner jacket, kissed his two sisters with considerable affection; and held Rosaleen's hand for a little longer than the occasion warranted. "A damn pretty girl", thought Timothy. "Wouldn't mind taking her out dancing. Lucy's a rotten dancer." Not that he'd ever be unfaithful to Lucy. Still—a chap did like his bit of fun.

His dark eyes, losing their twinkle for a moment, surveyed his young, fat, fair-haired wife. What had come over Lucy? One could hardly drag her out of the house these days. And what was the use of making two or three thousand a year at his age just to stay at home?

"Lucy's so damn placid", continued his thoughts.

III

Betty announced dinner. They went in unceremoniously.

"I ought to have got a man for you, Rosaleen", said Enid. "We're really two men short. You and Stephanie had better sit together."

But Fluke, as usual, arranged the oblong table to his own liking; and Rosaleen found herself next to him, with Paul on her other side.

Fanny, the young housemaid, helped Betty to serve soup, fried sole, and a brace of pheasants which Fluke carved himself. They drank claret.

"We ought to start a wine department", said Paul.

"As long as I'm alive", said his father, "Archers will not sell intoxicating liquor."

"But you don't mind drinking it yourself", retorted Fluke.

"I know when I've had enough, Philip"—the chairman of Archers Limited never indulged in nicknames—"the modern generation, more's the pity, doesn't. It's the same with smoking"—he looked at Stephanie—"and dancing. Amusement and self-indulgence are all that young people think of nowadays."

"You can't say that about me", cut in Enid.

Her father eyed her through his goldrimmed spectacles, pronouncing: "I don't call thirty-two young".

Betty brought in the sweets.

"Christmas pudding", announced Enid. "It's the first one we've tried. Tell me what you think of it, everybody. Fluke darling, can you light the brandy?"

Fluke functioned with his usual efficiency.

Lucy launched into the latest achievements of "my Peter and my Pamela". Mrs. Archer said, "It's such a pity Constance and her husband aren't here. Then we'd be a complete family party. I had a letter from her yesterday. She says they're having the most dreadful weather in Manchester".

"When don't they?" laughed Fluke.

"And she tells me", went on his mother-in-law, "that George has just bought her one of your new wireless machines. George is always so extravagant. I wrote and told her I'm sure you'd have let them have it at wholesale price."

"Does it work?" asked Fluke.

"Oh, yes. Constance says she wouldn't be without it for anything. The children simply love somebody called—now let me see, what was he called?"

"Uncle Arthur?"

"Yes. I believe that was it. Oh, and I was to tell you that George believes you're on to a really good thing. He thinks everybody will have a wireless machine sooner or later."

Enid cut in, rising:

"Now don't be long, you men. You know I don't mind cigars in the drawing room".

Alone, the four men fell to discussing the recently signed treaty of Locarno.

"It really does mean peace, and about time", opined Fluke. "And now that the Irish boundary question's settled too, we really ought to be all right."

"The League", said Paul, "has done jolly well over this business between Greece and Bulgaria."

"I've been thinking, father", interrupted Timothy, who never lost the chance of a commission, "that you might do worse than buy yourself some Austrian loan. They bring you in a jolly good rate of interest."

"Five per cent's good enough for me, Timothy."

"Then how about you, Fluke ?"

"My dear chap, every penny I've got's tied up in my business—and I haven't finished settling up for this house yet."

Betty brought in coffee. Fluke, who always envied Timothy his Military Cross, said, "I shan't be able to turn up at your British Legion do on Saturday. Enid's taken seats for *Rose Marie* that evening".

Timothy, always a little jealous that Fluke had finished his career in the Sappers as a major, whereas he wasn't even entitled to call himself captain, turned to Paul.

"To be quite frank with you", said Paul, "I don't approve of the Legion. It smacks too much of militarism."

Fluke asked her father-in-law, "How do you find these cigars ?"

"Excellent, my boy. How much do you pay for 'em ?"

Fluke took a pound a hundred off the price ; was duly congratulated on his business ability ; and fell to thinking what a fortunate man he was—only just thirty-five, with a good business, as jolly a wife as a chap could wish for, three kids, and another on the stocks. He got on so well with his wife's family too. Pity about his own. There was only "that lunatic Miles". But what could one expect with a mother like Miles's ?

"I wonder what's happened to her", he mused. "I wonder whether she really was as lovely as I used to imagine. I was only eleven when she ran away. Rotten of her. Especially with the pater being a clergyman. Poor old pater."

Remembering his last talk with his father, who had abandoned his country parish to join up as an army chaplain in nineteen-fourteen and been killed by a stray bullet at Neuve Chapelle, Fluke indulged in a little sentimentality.

Come to think of it, one owed a lot to the pater. One's education, for instance. Torrington College mightn't be Eton, but it was one of the best little public schools going. Hadn't he put his own Simmy, his own Arty, down for it the moment they were born ? And the pater had been quite right on insisting one must go to Cambridge. He'd send Simmy and Arty there too. If he could afford it.

"But of course I'll be able to afford it", decided Fluke. "Nothing's going to stop me making money. I know a good thing when I see one. Not that I haven't been lucky."

For of course it had been a stroke of luck—getting a job with Marconi the moment one left the Varsity.

Paul, Timothy and his father-in-law were now discussing other invest-

B—WWE

ments. Fluke continued to think about his own luck. He might have been making the mistake of his life when he chucked his job with the Marconi Company to join up. Instead, he'd fallen in with Grayson—a bit of a genius in his way, but with no more commercial sense than a rabbit. Why, the fellow hadn't even realised—the day he took one down to Writtle to see those first experiments of Peter Eckersley's—that there might be big money in broadcasting, if only one could supply all the components for amateurs to make their own listening-in sets.

"I saw that right away", he prided himself. "But I wonder how long the component business will last. Not much more than another five years, I reckon. The standard ready-made set's the thing to push. Make one's name before there's too much competition. It isn't too easy for us firms outside the ring even nowadays."

A statement by Timothy, "I'll tell you another thing there may be money in, Paul, gramophones", interrupted thought. Pulling out his father's gold watch, Fluke saw that it was nearly ten minutes past nine; and asked the customary question. Shortly afterwards they joined the ladies in the drawing room; and Timothy, squashing himself between Stephanie and Rosaleen on the smaller of the two sofas, asked:

"Well, how's the bun shop?"

"My bun shop, as you call it", answered Stephanie, "is doing quite well, thank you. How many dud shares have you sold today?"

Brother and sister continued to spar. Rosaleen, never quite sure whether she liked Timothy, kept silent. Presently the telephone rang from Fluke's study, and Enid said to her, "See who it is, will you, dear? Betty and Fanny won't have finished washing up".

IV

The study was at the other end of the hall. It took Rosaleen a few seconds to find the light switch. Before she could lift the receiver from its hook, the bell ceased ringing. After she had jerked the hook up and down for several more seconds, the local operator condescended to say, "It was a trunk call. They've gone off now. But they may come on again. Please replace your receiver". She did so, and sat down at Fluke's desk, on which in an identical silver frame stood a duplicate of the photograph he kept at the office—Enid, with Arty on her lap, supported by Simmy in dark velveteen, and Philly in light cotton.

"I'd like to have a lot of children and a house of my own one day", she thought; and, inconsequently, "But I don't think I'd care to be married to a man like Timothy."

By the photograph frame stood a silver box, inscribed, "To Major P. L. Radcliffe R.E. from his old comrades on the occasion of his marriage". She opened the box, took out a cigarette, and lit up.

Just as she was thinking, "I expect it was a wrong number", the phone rang again.

"Plinley Green two-o-two", said the voice in the receiver. "Don't go away, please. I want you."

The next voice said, "Hallo, there. Can I speak to Mr. Philip Radcliffe, please?"

Surprise kept Rosaleen silent till the question had been repeated. She was conscious of the queerest little choke in her throat as she answered :

"Yes. This is Mr. Radcliffe's house. You're Miles, aren't you ?"

"Sure I'm Miles." He seemed to have developed a suspicion of an American accent. "Who am I talking to—Enid ?"

"No." She was feeling perfectly normal again. "I'm Rosaleen."

"Why, of course you are. I ought to have known. Then you're still living with them ?"

"Oh, no. I'm only here to dinner. Where are you telephoning from, Miles ?"

"Southampton. We only got in this afternoon."

Curiosity made her ask, "Who's we ?"

"I only meant the boat." He chuckled. "What did you think I meant ? Did you imagine I'd brought a wife with me ?"

She hadn't imagined that ; but somehow the knowledge that he was still without a wife pleased her.

"I'm spending the night here", he went on, "and coming up to London tomorrow. What I really wanted to know was whether Fluke could put me up for Christmas ?"

"I'm sure he'd love to. Hang on, and I'll go and ask him."

"No. Don't bother. I'll ring him up at the factory as soon as I get to town. Do you happen to know the number ?"

"It's Albanford double five. I work there now."

"What—making gadgets ?"

"No. I'm Fluke's secretary."

"Are you, by jingo. Oh, confound it. The girl says our time's up. No. I don't want another three minutes. Cheerio, Rosaleen."

The wire went dead. She picked up her cigarette from the ashtray, and returned to the drawing room with her news, which seemed to please Fluke inordinately.

"I wonder what the young devil's been up to all this time", he said ; and Enid, "I wish the spare room weren't so tiny."

As they drove back to Fairholm, Stephanie remarked, "I don't think I really care for Miles".

"But you hardly know him."

"I believe I'm afraid of him", thought Stephanie. But that thought she kept to herself.

v

Jim Bowlby said, "Well, I'll be blowed if it isn't the kid. How are you, old boy ?"

Miles Radcliffe said, "I'm fine. What are you doing with yourself these days ?"

"Oh, I'm in business", answered Jim, stroking his golden moustache. "Just wait a tick till I write out this cheque."

He bent over the bank counter ; and Miles, who had developed an eye for such details, noticed that the sleeve of his waisted blue overcoat was a little shiny. He tore the cheque out of the book, and passed it through the grille to the cashier, who said, "I hope you won't mind if I keep you waiting just a moment, Captain Bowlby".

Jim lit the cigarette he had been holding. He carried himself as well as ever; but his dark brown eyes looked faintly bloodshot, and his bowler hat, though as carefully brushed as his overcoat, also showed signs of wear.

The cashier returned, and passed him three pounds through the grille. Miles handed in his own cheque; was asked, "How will you take this, please?"; answered, "I'd like nine five-pound notes if you've got 'em, and can I have a pound's worth of silver?"; trousered his change and filled his notecase.

"You seem pretty flush", commented Jim.

The experience of these last years warned Miles that this man—once so admired—might have deteriorated; and he hesitated a moment before asking him to lunch.

Jim pretended to hesitate before answering:

"Well, I'm pretty busy. But, after all, one doesn't meet old pals every day; and I must say I'd like a yarn".

They left the bank together.

"Where shall we go? I don't know very much about London", said Miles; and Jim Bowlby hesitated again, thinking, "I can't take him any-where posh in that rig. And where the devil did he get that hat from?"

For Miles's hat might have been a cowboy's; and his suit, which had padded shoulders, was of a flamboyant green that contrasted horribly with a pair of yellow boots. Although it was freezing, he wore no overcoat and no gloves. Tucked under his arm was a long stick with a peculiar handle.

"How about a drink first?" hedged Jim.

"Yes. That's a good idea."

They cut through St. James's Square and up into Jermyn Street, where they entered a bar. As they seated themselves on their stools, Jim noticed that the white patch of hair at Miles's right temple had grown distinctly larger, and that his features had lost their girlishness.

"Nothing of the kid about him now", he decided, ordering a double whiskey. Miles took beer.

"If you're not too busy after lunch", said Miles, "you might show me where to get some decent reach-me-downs. I look pretty awful, don't I?"

His elephant-gray eyes twinkled. His smile, at least, had not changed.

"Well, you're hardly dressed for London, old boy."

"And I'm certainly not dressed for Plinley Green."

He explained that he'd only arrived in town that morning, and that, "Plinley Green's where my halfbrother lives".

"Wasn't that where you sent that girl—you know, the one we rescued from the Shinners?"

"Yes. She's still there too. I was talking to her on the phone last night, and again this morning."

"Really."

Miles insisted on buying two more drinks. They fell to talking of Ireland. Soon the years dropped away from them; and Jim was saying:

"Do you ever see any of the old crowd? I ran into Ronnie Wallace about a year ago. He was home on leave from Somaliland. Dominic went to America. Martin Halliburton sent me a card last Christmas. He's out East. I often wonder what happened to Geoffrey Thirkell".

"Geoffrey's living in Trinidad", said Miles—and stopped.

More than a year ago, he and Geoffrey had parted company. But there was always the chance that they might join up again. And anyway the less information one volunteered the better.

He changed the conversation, asking, "What kind of business are you in?"

"Well, as a matter of fact", said Jim, reddening, "it's silk stockings."

"Silk stockings!"

"Yes. I'm a kind of a traveller really." And he in his turn changed the conversation, saying:

"By the way, I'm married. You must meet my missus one of these days".

"I'd like to. And now what about some food? I've rather a lot to do this afternoon."

"Well, we could lunch here. They've got quite a decent place upstairs I believe."

Miles said, "That suits me okay. *Vamos, amigo*", and Jim, had he spoken the language, might have deduced from his accent that the Spanish was not that of Castille.

Jim Bowlby, however, was too preoccupied with personal thoughts to notice much more. "What about some oysters to start with?" he asked, once they were at table; and followed up his oysters with a steak and Stilton cheese.

Afterwards Miles called for cigars.

"It's rather good to be home", he said, drawing his first puff. "I've been away more than three years." And, smiling, "Tell me some more about the silk stocking racket, Jim. Is there any money in it?"

Jim reddened again, and stroked his golden moustache with a nicotine-stained finger.

"Not much", he admitted. "If you want to know, I peddle 'em from door to door. In the suburbs mostly. Nice job for a V.C., isn't it?"

"I say, that's too bad."

The sudden sympathy—and the two double whiskeys he had drunk—disarmed Jim.

"It's my own fault, old boy", he confessed. "I've had plenty of chances."

Miles hesitated a moment. On principle he disliked lending money. But this—dash it all—was Jim, the man he had once admired more than any other.

"Broke?" he asked.

"My dear chap, I'm always broke."

"Can I help?"

"You can lend me a tenner if you like", began Jim; then, suddenly, "But don't fool yourself I'll ever pay you back."

Miles hesitated another moment or so. "I'm a nice idiot", he thought, pulling out his cheque book and calling to the waiter, "Get me a pen and ink, will you?"

The cheque he wrote was for twenty pounds. Staring at it, Jim said, "You may as well know the truth. I made up my mind to try and touch you for something the moment we met".

"So what?" laughed Miles.

37

He asked for the bill and paid it. They walked downstairs and out into the street.

"I know just the place for you to get your duds", said Jim; and something of his old selfconfidence seemed to come back to him as he swung along, bowler hat on the back of his head, umbrella at the carry, his dark brown eyes quizzing every girl they met.

"What do you actually want?" he asked, steering Miles into the big man's store on Regent Street.

"A complete rig-out. The ants got into my trunks while I was up country."

"The what?"

"Ants. They did in pretty well everything. Boots included."

He vouchsafed no further information; and during the next two hours, spent with one assistant who accompanied them from department to department, Jim was again aware of the changes in the man who had once been called "the kid". Except in action, there had always been something diffident about Miles. There was no diffidence about him now.

"That'll be the lot", he said, having finally selected two suitcases. "You know where to send 'em. And I want everything there by the day after tomorrow. Tell me how much I owe you altogether."

The bill came to some seventy pounds. He paid half in cash, gave his cheque for the balance, and insisted—despite Jim's, "Hang it all, let me pay for this lot"—on standing him tea.

Before parting, they exchanged addresses, Miles giving Fluke's, which Jim wrote down in a little notebook, and Jim handing out a card, "Captain J. Bowlby. The Unladderable Hose Company", on which he had written in ink, "16 Muirhead Mansions, S.W. 11." and his telephone number.

"Poor old fellow", thought Miles, alone in his modest hotel that evening. The sentiment, nevertheless, did not prevent him from realising he might have made "rather an ass of himself".

Such "borrowers"—the experience of these last years had taught him— always came back for more.

VI

Except for the guncase and the ancient bedding-roll of green Willesden canvas which formed part of his luggage, nothing appeared to distinguish the Miles Radcliffe whom a taxi decanted at Euston three days after his meeting with Jim Bowlby from any of the other young men who caught the five-five to Plinley Green.

In his blue suit, black shoes and gray felt hat he might have been a bank clerk, an insurance agent, or any other city employee taking his usual way home. It was distinctly unusual, however, for third-class passengers to give one a shilling; and the porter who pocketed that tip couldn't help speculating about its donor while he watched "the steamer" (as Plinley Green calls it) roll away from the platform.

Meanwhile Miles, also, was speculating—about these seven fellow passengers, all of them with their umbrellas, their evening papers, their pipes or their cigarettes.

"They do this every evening", he thought. "Don't know how they stick it. Blowed if I could." And from that he fell to remembering a line of poetry, "Romance brought up the nine-fifteen".

"But I don't want romance", he thought next. "Romance is all poppy-cock anyway."

What did he want, then? Just what he'd got. Freedom. And by jingo he'd keep his freedom. No Plinley Greenery for him!

The phrase sounded rather good. His mind repeated it. What did Plinley Greenery imply? Doing the same thing every day? No. More than that. Life without risk, without adventure. Why did fellows choose that life? Just to make a little money? Or because they really liked it? If so, well and good.

"None of my business really", he decided; and glanced through his own evening paper, one article in which—headed, "Woman, the driving force of modern civilisation"—seemed singularly futile.

For if this railway carriage represented modern civilisation, the sooner one escaped back to the Alto Parana or anywhere else in the wilds of South America the better. While as for women—once they got hold of a chap he was sunk.

"Tie a chap down", thought Miles. "Insist on having children. Unless they're tarts, of course. And all they want is money."

Still—one couldn't do without an occasional woman. Not once one had started. One got . . . kind of hungry. Thank goodness one didn't get that kind of hunger too often. Like Geoffrey. Geoffrey—when one came to know more about him—had been even worse than Jim.

The train stopped. Two men got out of the compartment; four entered. Squeezing himself in his corner, Miles continued to think about Geoffrey Thirkell—a stout fellow, if ever there was one; clever as paint, too; never slipped up over his staff work.

And it had taken some staff work—to buy the stuff, to get it shipped and unshipped, to deliver it just at the right place, just at the right time.

"Fun we used to have", thought Miles; and memory unreeled the picture of a boat without lights, nosing its way through oily waters; and of himself, in the bow of that boat, clicking off the safety catch of his Bergmann to Geoffrey's whisper, "Hijackers. Stand by to give 'em the works". They'd never had one of their cargos hijacked; and as for the revenue cutters, had Geoffrey known how to deal with those blokes or hadn't he? He'd known when to chuck the game too.

"Getting too damn well organised", Miles remembered him saying. "No room for small outfits like ours. There's a mug just out from home who wants to buy the boats and what he calls the goodwill. I've asked him three thousand quid. If it comes off, you can take that South American trip you're always talking about."

And here was the end of the trip—Plinley Green.

Boards and lamps flashed the words. A porter was shouting them. Miles opened the door. Several others followed him on to the platform and hurried away.

"Living by the clock all the time", he thought. "Wouldn't suit me."

The porter removed his luggage from the van and put it on a trolley. Queerly, he remembered arrivals at other stations—Indian women smoking cigars, men in gaucho hats and pyjama jackets, barefooted boys fighting to carry his saddlebags.

He sauntered down known stairs and along an underground passage. The trolley rattled ahead of him. He came into open air; saw the church spire outlined against the first stars of a frosty night.

Memory reached back to his last arrival at this station. It had been daylight then. Summer. If one climbed those wooden steps and took the asphalt path between those railings—curious, that one should recollect the smell of the stinging nettles—one would come out quite close to The Firs.

In that moment his mind conceived the clearest picture of his last homecoming to The Firs, and of Rosaleen, stooping over the perambulator, looking up at the sound of his footsteps to say, "Miles! What a lovely surprise. We didn't expect you down till much later".

But the trivial business of telling the porter, "I'll have the guncase inside, please", drove the picture away.

He tipped the porter with another shilling, and told the taximan, "I want you to take me to Rosemary Lodge, Clareville Grove".

A hundred yards brought them under railway arches to a main road, off which they turned to their left. Here were street lamps, little villas with lit windows and trimmed garden hedges. Imaginatively Miles saw himself condemned to spend the rest of his life behind such hedges.

"Never", he swore; and visualised a different picture—the face which had been haunting him intermittently for the best part of a year.

Dusky red hair framed the perfect oval of that face, the broad forehead, the cheeks creamy white as a jungle flower, the lips redder than any jungle fruit, the eyes set slightly aslant and blacker than the waters of Lake Ypacarai on some thunderous night.

"Who can she have been?" he asked himself. "Can I have only dreamed her?"

But, of course, one hadn't dreamed her. One knew—to a day, to an hour, almost to a minute—exactly when one had seen that face which was lovelier than any dream.

Seeking distraction, he leaned forward and asked the taxidriver, "How much farther is it?"

The man answered, "We're just about there, sir"; and a few moments later the white door opened to show Fluke, just a shade bulkier than one's recollection of him, standing under a huge bunch of mistletoe.

"Thought it must be you", boomed Fluke. "So you caught the five-five all right. Betty—where are you, Betty?"

A door in the oak panels behind him opened. A tall woman in a cap and apron said, "Here I am, Mr. Radcliffe"; and made to help the taximan bring in the luggage.

"You'd better let me do that", suggested Miles; but another servant appeared; and between them they carried away all his belongings.

"Take your cloak and bonnet off, and we'll have a snifter in my den", went on Fluke.

He led the way to a fair-sized room with a red and blue Axminster carpet, brown velvet curtains, two saddlebag chairs covered in green leather, and a desk which Miles remembered since childhood. Above the desk hung two paintings—one of their father in clergyman's black, one of Fluke's mother in a tight-waisted frock of the nineties.

"Cigarette?" asked Fluke, proffering a silver box. "Cocktail or whiskey?"

"Whiskey. Only don't make it too strong."

They sat down, facing each other, on the saddlebags.

"You're looking very fit", began Fluke. "What have you been doing with yourself all this time?"

"Oh, lots of things. This last year I've been running about South America."

"That sounds pretty expensive."

"It wasn't really."

"How did you come home?"

"In the glory hole", laughed Miles.

"What the hell's that? Steerage?"

"No. I shipped as a stoker. It was rather fun."

"Then you're broke?"

"Far from it."

Again Miles laughed; and Fluke eyed him, saying to himself, "He always was a bit crazy". Aloud he said, "Well, there's no accounting for tastes. It wouldn't be my idea of a picnic. Give me home comforts. And, talking of them, Enid's going to have another baby".

"That'll make four, won't it?"

"Yes. Just the right number. As I was telling her only yesterday, it's time we closed the book. No sense in overdoing it. Kids cost the earth nowadays. And what with one thing and another I've got about all I can carry."

Fluke began to talk about himself, about "this new house, I'll show you round in a minute", and "the car", and "the factory, you'll have to see that, too".

Listening to him, glancing at the two paintings, Miles thought, "He's got the same voice as father, though he doesn't look a bit like him".

For Fluke, in more ways than one, took after his mother, the sandy-haired daughter of a Yorkshire worsted-spinner. It was really her money—Miles remembered—that they had inherited on their father's death.

And after that, with his halfbrother still talking, Miles remembered the little he had been told about his own mother, who must be comparatively young if she were still alive.

"She must be a little like I am", continued his thoughts. "I expect that's why she ran away from the vicarage."

VII

Fluke divested himself of the slightly flamboyant dressing gown which Enid had given him for his thirty-fifth birthday; hung it on one of the hooks in their bedroom door; and inserted his body between the sheets.

"And what do you make of the prodigal?" he asked.

"I think he's devastatingly attractive", answered Enid from the other pillow.

"That's all you women ever think of—sex."

41

Fluke chuckled, and fondled her.

"That's all you men ever think of", she retorted—hoping that he would "leave her alone".

He continued to fondle her. She did not protest. Wives shouldn't. And she was so terribly fond of Fluke. She couldn't have asked for a better husband.

"But apart from his looks", he went on. "Don't you think he's a bit queer ?"

"Why ?"

"Oh, I don't know. That's the way he strikes me."

"It takes all sorts to make a world", said Enid, who was rather given to platitudes. "Can I put out the light, darling ?"

"Are you as sleepy as all that ?"

"I am rather tired. It's started to kick. I believe it's going to be another girl. Philly went on just the same way. I hope it is a girl, don't you, darling ?"

"Well, they're certainly a bit cheaper. Put out the light if you want to, old thing. I don't want to be a nuisance."

"You're never a nuisance", prevaricated Enid.

She turned over to click off the light, and Fluke kissed the back of her neck, thinking, "Best wife a man ever had. I'll play a couple of rounds tomorrow".

Meanwhile, alone in the spare bedroom which adjoined the day nursery, Miles lit the very last of the black cigarettes he had bought in Pernambuco ; and drew back the blue taffeta curtains. How pale these stars were, and how few !

Directly below him lay a garden. He could see the hard tennis court of which Fluke had spoken with such pride, and beyond it the shadowy golf-course. Here and there, to right and to left of him, other windows radiated light.

It was still very early, not yet half past ten. He finished unpacking his new clothes ; putting them away very quickly but very carefully. Tomorrow he'd have to get a few more things out of his valise, which had been left in the corridor because this room was so small. He'd have to take a squint at his guns too. There'd been no time to look them over since he landed. Why not do that now ?

His guncase lay under the bed. He pulled it out ; laid it on the eider-down, and unlocked it. What a fuss that chap at the Customs had made till one showed him one's firearm certificate. Lucky he hadn't spotted that it wanted renewing. One would have to see about that.

Busy with cleaning rod and oil bottle—one must be careful not to make a mess—he fell to wondering why he had returned to England. But by half past eleven, with the guncase under the bed again, he began to feel drowsy ; and, once in bed, he slept till a maid appeared with a teatray to tell him, "Mr. Radcliffe won't be going to the factory today, so breakfast isn't till a quarter to nine".

Habitually Miles shaved, bathed and dressed himself in twenty minutes. Dawdling, he managed to stretch the process to half an hour. Passing the day nursery on his way downstairs, he encountered Fluke's two elder children

"I'm Simmy", said the little boy, "and this", indicating his sister, "is Philly. You're Uncle Miles, aren't you?"

"Yes. That's right."

The little boy offered a hand. It was obvious that the little girl expected a kiss. Flaxen-haired, they resembled their mother more than their father. Neither seemed at all shy. Thank the lord they weren't his.

"Jolly kids, though", thought Miles, leaving them; and told Fluke so, when he appeared in plus fours at the breakfast table. Fluke beamed and picked up his newspaper.

"Enid's taking it easy this morning", he said. "I'm going to play golf. Would you like a round?"

"I'm afraid I haven't any clubs."

"Oh, that's all right. You can use Enid's."

"And I haven't played for years."

"That doesn't matter a damn. I'll give you a stroke a hole. One beauty of golf is——" And Fluke continued to elaborate on the beauties of golf till they left the house and made their way through the garden on to the course.

A wintry sun shone through thin clouds as they drove off. Miles took the first hole with a perfect five. Halfway round, Fluke grumbled, "I thought you said you hadn't played for years?"

Miles thought a moment before laughing, "It's quite true. I haven't had a club in my hand since the last time I stayed with you". And it was then that Fluke remembered their father showing him a report from Miles's housemaster at Torrington, "A born games player. If only he were a bit keener!"

"If you'd take a few lessons", he said at the fifteenth, "you'd get down to a six handicap in no time. Why, you might even be a scratch man before you'd finished."

"And what good would that do me?" thought Miles.

They lunched at the clubhouse, where Fluke seemed to know everybody. He was obviously popular, and for a very good reason. All these people interested him. He knew what their businesses were, if their wives were in good health or bad, how many children they had, what make of car they owned or contemplated buying, and, of course, their golf handicaps.

But that he went a little out of his way to be popular was equally apparent. "Not quite as interested in 'em as he pretends to be", decided Miles; and tackled him with this as they walked back to Rosemary Lodge after eighteen more holes.

"That's pretty cute of you", laughed Fluke. "But, damn it all, I'm a businessman. And nowadays a businessman has got to be a good mixer. Besides, I may be wanting a spot more capital one of these fine days. And most of those chaps have got money. By the way, I suppose you wouldn't like to put a thousand or two into Radcliffe Radios? We ought to pay tenpercent this year".

"Not on your life", decided Miles instantly. But the experiences of these last years made him say, "Well, I might think it over"; and, just as he said that, Enid hailed them from the garden gate, "Hallo. You're just in time for tea".

A girl stood by Enid. As they approached, Miles recognised her for Rosaleen.

"But how you've changed", he said when they shook hands.

Memory grew active in him as they walked side by side past the tennis court towards the red brick house. Three years ago, when he came back from Ireland, this girl had still seemed little more than a child. She'd been shy then—and how poorly dressed.

Today there seemed no shyness in her. And her tweed clothes looked as good as Enid's. He imagined that she must have grown a good inch taller; and that her golden brown hair had turned a shade darker. The pigtail, of course, had disappeared long ago.

Her complexion—it seemed to him—was clearer, and even her eyes—nice hazel eyes, she had—somehow different. Her white well-kept hand contrasted strangely with the red, rough, dirty paw he could remember grasping to Jim's, "One of the brutes hit her in the mouth".

"You've changed too", she said. "Tell me—what were you doing in Paraguay?"

"Oh, just looking it over. I might settle down there one of these days."

"But what would you do with yourself?"

"I might grow yerba."

"Whatever's that?"

"It's called maté tea over here. Maté's really the gourd one drinks it out of. It's jolly good stuff, too."

Another girl—tall and slightly mannish, her dark hair Eton-cropped—came towards them from the house.

"You remember Stephanie", said Rosaleen.

"Why, of course."

Stephanie said, "Hallo. I heard you'd turned up"; but did not offer to shake hands.

"I'll have to be off", she went on. "We're always so busy the day before Christmas, and the girls aren't to be trusted. What time will you be home, Rosaleen?"

"Oh, about the usual."

"Well, don't be late. You know Paul's having supper with us."

She went for her bicycle.

"Who's Paul?" asked Miles.

"Her elder brother. Didn't you meet him when you were here last time?"

"I don't think so. If I did, he didn't make any impression."

"He doesn't", smiled Rosaleen as they followed Fluke and Enid into the house.

Simmy and Philly joined them after tea, during which Miles ate four crumpets and two hefty slices of cake despite Enid's, "You'll only spoil your dinner". The two children obviously adored Rosaleen. She made rather a pretty picture—thought Miles—with the little girl on her lap and the boy at her feet.

44

But there his interest in her ended; and they did not meet again until Boxing Night—celebrated, as usual, by a fancy-dress dance at the Albanford Assembly Rooms.

Miles dug into his valise for that occasion, and appeared in the riding trousers which your South American calls *bombachas*, the cummerbund which is known as a *faja*, a red shirt and an enormous belt of black leather studded with brass. Soft boots, silver spurs and a gaucho hat almost completed the cowboy illusion, which only lacked the lasso, the flat-thonged whip and the gun.

"I feel a perfect ass in 'em", he confided to Rosaleen, whom Stephanie had dressed up as a shepherdess. "But Fluke insisted I had to put on some costume or other, even if it was only a mask and domino. And it took me the best part of the afternoon to mend these pants."

He showed her the mends, explaining, "I like to be able to do everything for myself, otherwise one feels so helpless.

"Like Fluke", he went on.

"But Fluke isn't a bit helpless."

"Isn't he? Where'd he be without someone to cook his meals, and darn his socks, and press his trousers, and look after his motorcar for him."

"He pays other people to do that sort of thing."

"And works like a galley slave to make the money."

"But he likes work. Don't you?"

Miles thought that over.

"Not office work", he said finally; and asked for the supper dance, which she had half promised to Paul.

For a girl, she struck him as fairly companionable, though he would far rather have been talking to a man; and said as much to Fluke, disguised as Sir Francis Drake at two guineas for the evening's hire, on their way back to Rosemary Lodge with Enid, who had not been able to dance.

"Our Miles is a funny chap", grunted Fluke, with just one glass of champagne too many inside him. "Isn't he, old thing? Fancy not caring for girls at his age. Why, when I was twenty-five—now let me see—when was that?—nineteen fifteen—I came home on leave in Christmas fifteen . . ."

"Oh, we all know what a devil you were with the girls when you were a soldier", interrupted Enid; and adding, with a happy smile, "They say reformed rakes make the best husbands", she let her blond head droop to his shoulder.

Fluke put an arm round her. They fondled each other.

"Goofy", thought Miles.

IX

New Year's day came in to the twelve strokes of Big Ben on a Radcliffe Radio. The party at Rosemary Lodge, which included all the Archers except Constance and her husband, linked hands and sang "For auld lang syne". Hot punch and a considerable amount of kissing followed. Miles wondered whether he was expected to kiss Rosaleen, but confined the attention to Enid.

"You're the fish out of water", mocked Stephanie, to whom he had taken one of his very rare dislikes.

"I know what you're thinking", she went on. "You're thinking we're all very suburban. Well, why shouldn't we be if we enjoy it ?"

"I wasn't aware that I'd lodged any objection", he smiled at her, stroking his narrow jetblack moustache. "And anyway I'm leaving at the end of the week."

"Well, that's a comfort anyway."

"Why ?"

Their eyes clashed. Stephanie looked away.

"I oughtn't to have said that", she admitted. "I'm sorry. I didn't realise you were going away. I thought you were going to join Fluke in business. Aren't you ?"

"No."

She stalked off to the other side of the room, where Rosaleen stood by the fireplace. Her brother Timothy came over to say, "I've just remembered something. You and I met during the war. I'll tell you when it was too". He elaborated his memory, jogging Miles's back to a night in Arras.

"Seems a long time ago", said Timothy. "What have you been doing with yourself since then ?"

"Oh, just drifting about."

"I'm on the Stock Exchange. Do you ever do anything that way ?"

"I haven't so far."

"Well, if you ever feel like a flutter in something really good, give me a tinkle."

He handed over a card. The party began to break up. When the last of his guests had gone, Fluke said, "I don't feel a bit sleepy. How about just one more tiddler in my den, Miles ?" And there he grew a little sententious, and just a little too much the elder brother for Miles's taste, beginning, "Of course it's your own affair entirely", and ending, "But I think you're making a big mistake not to join me in the business".

"I thought you only wanted me to put some money into it", parried Miles.

Fluke hedged. Of course the business did want more money. What business didn't ? Quite apart from that, though—after all, Radcliffe Radios could always raise a bit more capital—Miles couldn't just go on amusing himself all his life. He'd have to settle down sooner or later.

"Why ?"

The question seemed to puzzle Fluke. His blue eyes goggled. He smoothed his sandy hair with a freckled hand before answering :

"Well, one of these days you'll want to get married, and you can't do that on your income".

The idea struck Miles as ludicrous. He said so.

"But supposing you fell in love ?" persisted Fluke.

Miles burked the last question with a jesting, "If ever that happens I'll come to you for a job" ; and they separated amicably.

Alone in his bedroom, however, he fell to resenting Fluke. Fluke wanted to boss him. And he wasn't going to be bossed by anybody. Thank goodness he was his own master. No marriage, no Plinley Greenery, for him.

He slept on that thought—and woke to it. After breakfast, with Fluke already away to the factory, he walked into Albanford, and bought himself some Havana cigarettes. Next door to the tobacconist's, a mullioned window displayed the sign, "Morning Coffee". He walked in, and seated himself at an oak table, to which—a moment later—came Stephanie, bareheaded in a flowered overall. She said good morning; and volunteered in answer to his question, "Yes. This is my shop".

Another girl brought his coffee. Stephanie retired behind the cake counter. Various customers came in. She served them. He called across, "Can I smoke here?" She called back, "Sorry. But I don't allow smoking till two o'clock".

In the street again, he fell to wondering why they should dislike each other. And from that, somehow or other, he fell to thinking of Rosaleen. In a very little while, however, his thoughts drifted to his own affairs.

One still had about five hundred pounds of the money one had made rum-running with Geoffrey. Still, neither five hundred pounds nor four quid a week went very far in England. And—wasn't one getting just a wee bit bored?

"Getting a bit soft, too", he decided. "Time I hit the trail again." And, hiking back to Rosemary Lodge, his imagination played with an advertisement, "Ex-officer, good shot, rider, fluent French, German and Spanish, wants temporary employment abroad. Danger and distance no object".

Feeling restless, and rather lonely, he took another walk after lunch; and arrived home in a frosty dusk to hear the telephone ringing.

"It's a gentleman for you", said Betty; and a moment later he was listening to Jim's, "Hallo, Miles. Is that you? Who do you think I'm with? Dominic Mahoney. He wants to talk to you."

"Right. Put him on."

Dominic's brogue was still fairly rich, but he had acquired a transatlantic accent; and his first question took Miles by surprise.

"When did you and Geoffrey quit?" he asked. "About a year ago, eh? Well, he always was the wise guy. Oi've been in the same racket meself. Better than a guinea a day for being plugged by Shinners. See here, Oi'm throwing a party tomorrow noight. Can you come along, and bring a lovely with you?"

"I don't know so much about the lovely."

"You wouldn't." Dominic's laugh had not changed. "But don't come alone, because Jim can't spare his missis and Oi'm not lending mine to anybody either."

He gave the name of a West End hotel—said, "We're meeting at half eight. Wear a tuxedo. If you haven't got a girl friend of your own bring some other fellow's", and hung up.

"Why don't you take Rosaleen?" suggested Enid, when Miles told her of the invitation. "You'll have to bring her back, so you'd better stay another night. I expect Fluke'll lend you the car if you ask him nicely."

Fluke agreed; but Rosaleen, to whom Miles telephoned after supper, seemed in two minds. He gathered—during pauses in their talk—that she was consulting Stephanie.

Her hand on the transmitter prevented him from hearing Stephanie's final, "All right. Go if you're so keen. Only—don't get any silly romantic ideas into your head. Because that young man doesn't care for anybody in the world except himself".

47

X

Stephanie's judgment repeated itself, not too pleasurably, to the young mind of Rosaleen Adair, as Miles drove her rapidly towards London. It was so obvious that this car interested him far more than she did. He talked about it all the time; and the way he cut in and out of the traffic, though it did not frighten, annoyed her.

"Why the hurry?" she asked.

"Because Dominic wants us there by half past seven. You remember Dominic, of course?"

"No. I can't say I do."

"But you must. He was the chap who took out the second tender."

She had always tried to avoid such memories; but her first sight of Jim Bowlby and Dominic Mahoney in the hall of the hotel brought them back with a rush.

Both wore dinner jackets, and carnations at their buttonholes. With them were two young women in short-skirted evening dresses. The little one with mousy hair, pale gray eyes and a rather sad smile, was Mrs. Bowlby; the tall blond, slightly overscented and flashing with false jewelry, was Mrs. Mahoney. Mrs. Mahoney seemed almost too happy to be real.

"Glad to know you, Miss Adair", she said; and her red-headed husband, whose chest seemed too big for his stiff shirt, "Who'd believe ut. The last toime Oi saw her she was wearing trousers. And very noice she looked in 'em too."

Something of the old shyness overwhelmed Rosaleen as she refused a cocktail. But Mrs. Bowlby said, "There's nothing to apologise for. I don't drink either"; and offered her a cigarette.

"Jim's often spoken about you", she went on. "But I never expected to meet you. I don't go about very much, you see. We simply can't afford it. He has to work terribly hard, poor lamb."

"Is he in business?"

"Yes. And business is so bad nowadays."

She looked at her husband, still as handsome as Rosaleen's memory of him with that heavy golden moustache and those long-lashed dark brown eyes. Transparently, he was her whole life. "She's what Stephanie calls a doormat", decided Rosaleen; and turned her attention to Mrs. Mahoney. There was nothing of the doormat about her, though she addressed her husband as "honeybun" and stroked his arm, with a hand so wonderfully manicured that it made Rosaleen a little jealous, whenever she expressed a wish.

Meanwhile Miles's attention, also, was concentrated on Edla Mahoney, who might or might not be legally married to Dominic, but whose type he had recognised at once.

"New York girl", he decided. "Probably been on the stage. Tough as blazes. Out for what she can get, and doesn't care how she gets it."

"We'd better be toddling now", said Jim. "How many can you take in your bus, Miles?"

"All of you, if you don't mind squashing up a bit."

"Foine", said Dominic, and told the waiter who had brought their drinks, "Gimme the check and Oi'll soign it."

The waiter brought him a cheque form and he roared with laughter. Miles translated, "Major Mahoney only wants to sign the bill".

They pushed their way through the revolving door of the hotel. The three women took the back squab of Fluke's car, and Jim a folding seat. Dominic sat next to Miles.

"Edla was just crazy to see London", he began. "She wants me to quit the booze game. And Oi'm not sure Oi won't. There's a little oidea Oi've got up me sleeve."

Jim interrupted with a question.

"Sure Oi'm in that racket", Dominic flung over his shoulder. "In the transport end. We run the stuff across from Canada. Miles and Geoffrey used to run it in down south—till the bigshots put the kybosh on outside competitors."

"You never told me that, Miles", said Jim.

"Why should I?" thought Miles.

Rosaleen, who could not help overhearing the conversation, began to feel a little uncomfortable. Had Miles really been a gangster—the sort of man one saw on the films? If so, he ought to be ashamed of himself. But, mingled with that thought came a sneaking admiration. How brave he must be—and how unlike the silly boys who tried to kiss one after dances.

"Here we are", said Jim.

XI

Jim told Miles where to park, and handed the three ladies out of the car. A porter in uniform saluted him, saying, "It's nice to see you with us again, captain". They passed under bright lights into a narrow vestibule. This place—decided Rosaleen—must be a club, for he had to sign a book before another porter ushered them into a circular room beyond which, through glass doors, she saw a dance floor set with tables.

"Jim's an honorary member", explained Mary Bowlby.

"And so I ought to be, considering how much I used to spend here in the old days."

"Well, don't you forget it's my party tonight, old horse", said Dominic.

"I'm not likely to do that."

The three women went to the cloakroom to take off their wraps. Edla's mink coat and Fifth Avenue evening frock made the other two feel rather shabby. They returned to find the three men waiting for them. A maître d'hôtel escorted them across the dance floor to an alcove table, and handed them menus. Glancing at hers, Rosaleen was shocked by the prices.

"I guess we'll start with caviar", said Edla. "Tell the captain to bring us some wine rightaway, honeybun."

"We call them head waiters over here, Mrs. Mahoney", said Miles; and she smiled at him, "Okay. I'll remember. What do you call wine?"

"Champagne, usually."

"Well, you can call me Edla."

"Okay, Edla."

"They seem very much at ease with each other. I wonder why", thought Rosaleen. "I don't feel a bit at my ease. I wish I hadn't come."

The food, however, was the most delicious she had ever tasted—and the

49

people who came crowding in soon began to interest her. This was the sort of place, these were the kind of men and women, one read about in the gossip column of one's newspaper. One could even recognise some of the women from their photographs.

She asked Mary Bowlby to confirm one recognition, and Mary Bowlby said, "Yes. That's Fiona Dering, and the man with her is Harold Lamberton".

The man nodded to Jim. So did one or two others. But the nods—it seemed to Rosaleen—were perfunctory. She wondered why.

Towards the end of dinner the small orchestra, which had been playing soft music, left the dais; and a jazz band took its place. Miles asked Edla for a dance and they left the table. Dominic took Mary Bowlby. Jim said, "Well, that only leaves you and me, Miss Adair. So how about it?"

"Mayn't I finish my ice first?"

"Do. And I'll have a cigarette.

"I say, you have altered", he went on.

"Have I?"

"I should just think so. That wasn't half an adventure we had."

He poured himself another glass of champagne.

"Miles is a grand fellow", he told her a little later. "And so's Dominic. They're luckier than I am. Nothing I do nowadays seems to come off. I don't mind for myself so much. But it's rotten for Mary."

He broke off to quiz a passing girl. Something made Rosaleen say, "I don't believe in luck".

"You would if you had mine", he laughed. "And how about that little business of yours with the Shinners? Supposing Miles and I hadn't happened to come along?"

She thought that over before admitting, "Well, of course, that was lucky".

At the same moment Edla Mahoney, still dancing with Miles, said, "Say, you're out of step".

"Sorry", muttered Miles, still staring over her blond head at that vision in the doorway—at the woman whose face had been haunting him, intermittently, for the best part of a year.

As they approached, the face was averted. He could see only dusky red curls of cropped hair, the curve of a prominent cheek, the thick creamy skin of neck and shoulder, and the lines of that exquisite body under the white and silver frock.

"Can't be the same woman", he tried to tell himself. But there had been no doubting his one sight of those eyes, of that mouth.

XII

The music stopped. Miles led Edla back to their table. A waiter brought coffee. Dominic offered him a cigar. But he had no desire to smoke. He was only conscious of one desire—to see his vision again. And here she came. Straight towards him.

There was a man with her—a tall foreign-looking man, heavily moustached, slightly brown of skin, in a perfectly fitting tail coat and a white waistcoat with elaborate buttons which matched the studs in his shirtfront. A maître d'hôtel escorted the pair to the next table.

"*Te gusta, Halcyon?*" asked the man, pronouncing it "Althion".

"*Si, Severo.*"

They seated themselves, and continued to talk Spanish. At close range the woman seemed more beautiful than ever. She had the loveliest hands and arms. The white and silver frock was cut low at the bosom. That first time she had worn riding costume.

"Halcyon", thought Miles. "Happiness. What a marvellous name for her."

The waiter, consulted about their food, addressed the man as "Señor Aramayo", and the woman as "Señora". It seemed fairly obvious that they were a married couple.

The band struck up a new tune.

"Let's dance, shall we ?" said Miles to Rosaleen. For the proximity of this Halcyon was disturbing—and his immediate instinct to escape.

Once on the floor, he tried to laugh at himself. What could have happened to him ? Was he in love ? Nonsense. He'd never even spoken to the woman.

"Enjoying yourself, Rosaleen ?" he asked.

"Yes. At least I think so. Though I feel rather like Cinderella. It seems funny that some people do this sort of thing every night of their lives. Are you enjoying it ?"

"Up to a point. By the way, what's this tune called ?"

"Don't you remember ? We danced to it on Boxing Night."

She half whispered, half sung, three lines of "I want to be happy".

Secretly he caught himself comparing her with that other. "She's really rather plain", he thought. "And of course she's only a kid. Barely nineteen. I wonder how old Halcyon is. No older than I am."

But such thoughts seemed idiotic; and he suppressed them before the end of their dance.

Bringing Rosaleen back to the table, he happened—though any clumsiness was rare with him—to brush against the Aramayos', and said automatically, "*Dispensa usted, señor*".

The man answered, "*No hay de que, señor*"; but he did not smile, and the woman appeared completely oblivious to the interchange of courtesies. When she next spoke, however, it was in a much lower tone than before.

The first shock of this strange meeting seemed to pass. Miles asked Mary Bowlby to dance. But he still found conversation a little difficult; and her, "Jim told me how good you were to him—it made such a difference to our Christmas", made it no easier.

"Oh, that's all right", he said, a trifle gruffly. "Jim and I are the oldest pals, you know. How long have you and he been married ?"

"Nearly three years now."

She fell silent for several turns of the room.

"Last year he tried to get a job with a flying company", she resumed abruptly. "But I'm glad he didn't."

"Why ?"

"Because the air frightens me."

Edla and Dominic swung alongside, swung by them. Mary fell silent again. She was a poor dancer—and poor company. He wondered why Jim, of all people, should have fallen in love with her. Poor old Jim. He ought to get out of England. "And so ought I", decided Miles.

51

The tune went on and on. The floor grew fuller and fuller. How hot they kept this place. What an idiotic life these people led. Plinley Greenery was boring enough. But this . . . this just stifled a chap.

At last the music stopped. Seated again, he lit a cigarette. Jim was chaffing, "Well, your old pal Dev isn't President of the Irish Republic yet, Dominic".

Dominic said, "But he will be before he's done, and Oireland's giving her contracts to Germany, and you British are evacuating the Rhoineland. It's glad Oi am to be taking out me papers".

"You mean, you're becoming an American?"

"And phwy not? If there's ever another war, do you think Oi'd foight for the British Empire?"

Jim flushed, but held his tongue. Nowadays one couldn't afford quarrels. Least of all with chaps who had money. Then the band struck up a tango; and, glancing sideways, Miles saw Halcyon put down the gold-tipped cigarette she was smoking. A moment later she and Aramayo had begun to dance.

Watching her, he felt a little pulse hammering at his forehead, and was scarcely conscious of Rosaleen's, "Don't those two do it beautifully?"

"I guess they're in the business", said Edla. But somehow Miles knew that wasn't true.

The couple returned to their table before the end of the tango. Severo Aramayo, still speaking Spanish, asked, "What thinkest thou, little one? Shall we go?"

"*Si. Vamonos*", answered Halcyon; and she added two words in the Guaraní language which Miles happened to understand.

The pulse at his forehead was still throbbing as he watched her go. His imagination followed her. For the very first time he was conscious of an excitement which transcended even the excitement of battle—not cold, but so hot that he could feel his palms sweating.

Dominic had ordered another bottle of champagne. The wine waiter was just filling his glass. He drank the lot at one gulp. For the very first time he wanted to get drunk. But the wine seemed to have no more effect than water. His imagination remained with Halcyon. Imaginatively, he saw her lips, red as jungle fruit, parted for a kiss, her black eyes blazing passion, her hands outstretched. The white and silver frock lay at her feet. He was lifting her, carrying her, beating down her resistances—only, was she resisting?—conquering her—only, did she need conquering?

"But this won't do", he managed to tell himself. "This won't do at all."

He drank another glass of champagne. Gradually the imaginative pictures faded. At half past twelve he suggested to Rosaleen, "Don't you think it's about time we made a move?"

Edla, however, protested; and, after he had taken her to dance again, Dominic asked, with an assumption of casualness, "Say, Jim, can you still floy a plane—because if so Oi might have a job for you?"

Jim's eyes kindled; but Mary cut in at once, "He's not going to fly again if I can help it, Major Mahoney"; and Rosaleen was surprised at the vehemence in her voice.

"Well, you know best, Mrs. Bowlby." Dominic shrugged his bulging shoulders. "And maybe Jim'd be too old for the job anyway."

"Old! Damn it, I'm only thirty-two. Where is this job?"

"Somewhere in South America", said Dominic; and turning to Miles, "That was Spanish you were speaking to that guy at the next table, wasn't it? Well, Oi'll be needing someone who can talk that lingo. That's to say if Oi take up the proposition Oi'm thinking about."

"What a kind of a proposition is it?" asked Miles.

"It's nutty." Edla spoke. "I've told him so till I'm tired. The Irish are all nuts anyway."

Dominic's blue eyes hardened. Blood suffused his cheeks.

"You keep out of this, angel face", he snapped.

For answer she rose, gathered up her bag, and made for the cloakroom. Mary Bowlby went after her. Rosaleen, not knowing what else to do, followed them.

"You'd better call for our check, Jim", said Dominic; and, turning to Miles again, "We're off to Paris in a couple of days. Maybe she'll change, her moind. Or maybe Oi'll have to change it for her. Anyway, Oi'd like to have a talk with you. How about tomorrow?"

"That suits me all right. Where and when?"

"Make it three at my hotel. She usually sleeps after lunch. Oi'll be in the hall waiting for you."

"Don't you want to see me too?" asked Jim.

Dominic brooded.

"Oi guess not", he said finally. "Nothing'll change Mrs. Bowlby's mind for her. Besides, it isn't a married man's job anyway."

"But you're married."

"Sez you", laughed Dominic Mahoney. "Edla and Oi picked up on the boat coming over."

He paid the bill, and they went for their hats and coats.

XIII

Dominic and his Edla, Jim and his Mary, departed in taxis. A few flakes of snow were falling as Miles helped Rosaleen into Fluke's car.

"You won't drive too fast in this snow, will you?" she said; and for the first time he was aware of conflict between their wills.

"Just as you like", he answered casually. "But we're pretty late, you know."

"We'll be later still if we have an accident."

"Accident!" scoffed Miles.

She was aware of some change in him. Just for a moment, remembering the many glasses of champagne he had consumed, she wondered if he were a little drunk.

"Do you remember the way?" she asked.

"I shall, once we get into Park Lane."

It was just after he inquired his way of the policeman on point duty at Hyde Park Corner that Miles also began to wonder whether, by any chance, he were a little drunk. For the question he had really wanted to ask appeared to be, "Can you tell me anything about a woman called Halcyon Aramayo?" And the palm of his right hand, as he wound up the window, was sweating again. His brain, however, seemed quite clear.

Snow continued to fall, and Fluke's single-bladed electric screenwiper was out of order. He gave it a twist with his fingers.

"Won't it work?" asked Rosaleen. The silly fool, couldn't she see that for herself?

An arc light showed him her face in the driving mirror. Once again he compared it with Halcyon's. Once again his imagination ran away with him. Once again he caught himself saying to himself, "But this won't do at all".

Conversation seemed the only escape. He asked Rosaleen what she thought of Mary Bowlby.

"She's nice, I think."

"And Edla?"

"I didn't like her much."

"Why not?"

"Well, she's common."

"Isn't that rather a snobbish thing to say?"

"Yes. I suppose it is. But one can't help one's likes and dislikes."

"True", thought Miles; but disputed the point, because it seemed the best way of reassuring himself of a determination not to be carried away by his feelings about a woman whom he had only seen once previously and might never see again.

"Talking of likes and dislikes", he said a little later, "what's the matter with your pal Stephanie? She always looks at me as though I were something out of a bottle."

Rosaleen hedged. He mustn't take any notice of Stephanie. That was only her way. She didn't like men.

Something made him ask, "Do you?"

She answered, a trifle primly, "I don't dislike them as much as Stephanie does".

"She is silly", thought Miles. "But then so are most girls. I wonder what she'd do if I tried to kiss her." But the thought seemed an idle one; because he didn't want to kiss her. He wanted . . . Dash it all, what was the use of thinking about that?

He cleared the screen again. His instinct for distance told him that they had done about five miles; his sense of direction indicated a left turn at the top of this rise, just past that row of shops.

The car skidded as he pressed the accelerator. He corrected the skid automatically. They topped the rise and swung left past a garage on to the bypass, white except for the occasional track of wheels.

Snow still fell.

"I can't see a thing my side", said Rosaleen. "Shall I work that wiper for you?"

"No. I can manage all right."

"Oughtn't you to put on the headlights?"

He laughed, "Who's driving this machine? You or I?"

She felt snubbed, and faintly resentful. Stephanie was quite right. Miles cared for nobody in the world except himself. Not that it mattered. He'd soon be going away. And as far as she was concerned he could stay away. She'd been silly to think about him so much, to have been so excited when he asked her out dancing.

Thought stopped. She began to feel sleepy, and told him so. He said, "Then why don't you drowse off for a bit? It's okay by me".

More resentful than ever—he *didn't* care for anybody except himself—and why must he use that dreadful Americanism?—she closed her eyes; but remained fully conscious, thinking, "Why was I so excited when he asked me out? Did I really imagine he'd try to kiss me on the way home? How I should hate it if he did".

Presently the car stopped.

"What's the matter?" She pretended to wake up.

"Nothing. I only wanted to make sure this was the right turning."

He wound down the window and clicked on the spotlight. The fingerpost read, "Plinley Green Station". A few minutes afterwards they neared the gate of Fairholm, which was open.

"Don't drive in", said Rosaleen, "we'll only wake Stephanie."

"But you can't walk through all this snow."

"Of course I can."

"Nonsense."

"Please stop here, Miles."

"I'll do nothing of the sort."

His obstinacy infuriated her—mainly because she knew he was right; that if she did "walk through all this snow" she would ruin her evening frock. But why he should be so infuriated, Miles did not know at all. He only knew that he'd never been in such a state in his life.

Slowing, changing down, steering in through that narrow gate, he said to himself, "This girl does need a lesson". Braking at the porch, he said to Rosaleen, "You really are a little fool", and when, too angry to answer, she would have opened the door, he gripped her by the elbow, and heard his own voice—only could it be his own voice?—threatening, "No, you don't. Not till you've admitted what a fool you are. Supposing we have woken your precious Stephanie, she can go to sleep again, can't she?"

"Miles!" There was no fear in her voice, only temper. "Let me go. You must be drunk to talk like that."

One part of his mind urged him to say, "Sorry. I'm not drunk, but I am feeling a bit funny"; and through that part of his mind moved memories—of a blazing house, of a girl with a cut mouth to whom he offered a handkerchief. But another part of his mind seemed to be saying, "Beat down her resistances; conquer her—she needs conquering"; and through that part of his mind moved very different memories—of eyes black as the water of Lake Ypacarai on some thunderous night and lips redder than any jungle fruit.

His left hand was still gripping Rosaleen's elbow. Hardly knowing what he did, he drew her closer, put his right arm round her shoulders.

"Miles!" she repeated, her lips half open. Confound the girl. Didn't she know what was wanted of her? Well, she'd soon find out.

His lips met hers, silenced them. He was aware that she had struggled, that she had ceased to struggle, that the hunger was on him, that he was telling himself, "You can't do this. She's decent. She's only a kid".

But the pulse was hammering at his forehead, and he kissed her again before he let her go.

She stared at him for a moment. Then she began to fumble in her bag. Her hand trembled as she drew out her latchkey. He took it from her, dismounted, helped her out, and opened the front door. Light blazed up, showing him Stephanie at the top of the staircase. He heard himself say— this time in his usual voice and quite calmly, "Hallo! We're a bit late. Sorry if we woke you. Good night, Rosaleen".

She did not answer. He handed her back the latchkey, turned, closed the door quietly, and went out into the snow.

BOOK THREE

I

"ANY FOOL OUGHT TO BE ABLE TO FLY", THOUGHT MILES RADCLIFFE, EASING back the joystick of the open Moth, and pushing gently on the rudder bar with his right foot.

It had been cloudy when he took off. But now the April sun was breaking through, lighting up the whole chequered map below.

He checked his height—three thousand—by the altimeter; centred the joystick; gave one more touch of right rudder, and let the plane fly itself. Peering overside through his goggles, he again made sure of his direction. These railway lines would bring him over Albanford in about seven more minutes. That train with the cottonwool smoke-puff wouldn't arrive there for at least another quarter of an hour.

"Toy train", he thought. "Toy country. Little fields and kindergarten towns and dolls' houses. Thank goodness I'm getting out, even if it is only on a wild-goose chase."

Automatically he looked at his windspeed indicator. The needle stood steady at a hundred. According to his revolution counter that meant a twenty-mile head wind. He rechecked his mental calculation of the flying time to Albanford, and found it correct.

In the air—he had discovered during his first flight solo—his memory worked far more rapidly than on the ground. He let it work; and it showed him Dominic, in the lounge of his hotel, that day after the party.

"Maybe Edla's roight and Oi am nuts", Dominic was saying. "But if Oi choose to spend ten thousand bucks of moy own money looking for treasure it's moy own business. Only—we've gotta find someone who can floy a plane, because it's the only way I can see of getting there. Say, as we can't take Jim, why shouldn't you learn to floy?"

"And I have", thought Miles.

An air pocket recalled him sharply to the present. The Moth bumped and lost height. He eased back the joystick. When he next looked overside, he saw that he was a little off his course. Steering over the railway lines again, he saw the cruciform bulk of Albanford Abbey, flat against dwarfed trees.

"A wild-goose chase", thought repeated. "But Dominic didn't ask me to put up any money. And if we do find anything I'll get my cut."

Almost at once the map below showed him the streets of Albanford town. He grew conscious of the wildest impulse. If he pushed this joystick forward, the plane would dive. He imagined it diving; imagined those buildings coming up at him, those streets opening out, those tiny figures of people scurrying for cover as they heard his engine roar close over their roofs. What a scare one could put into 'em. Serve 'em right if one did. They shouldn't be so smug, so safe, so comfortable.

The wild impulse passed. One wasn't allowed even to fly over towns. He gave the Moth left rudder. She banked. Albanford spun slowly like a card on a pin.

Now memory flung him a picture of Rosaleen. He'd been a bit crazy, that night he kissed her. Maybe he ought to have apologised. Maybe he would have, if she'd given him an opening. But she never had. Standoffish little fool with her, "How are you, Miles? I'm all right, thank you, Miles. No—I don't think I care to play golf, Miles".

What an idiot he'd made of himself that night. Dash it all, he didn't even like the girl. She stood for everything from which he most wanted to escape—Plinley Greenery, the little houses behind trim hedges, the eight-thirty up and the five-five down, the men with the umbrellas and the newspapers, "Safety First" and all that sort of thing, "Keep your schoolgirl complexion", "Where are my bath cubes, Betty?" "Enjoy life listening-in on a Radcliffe Radio". Faugh!

A little surprised at the violence of his own antipathies, he saw the flat expanse of Plinley Green golfcourse directly below. That doll's house was Fluke's. That tiny figure in the garden must be Enid's. She'd been up a whole week now. What an ass Fluke had made of himself over the confinement. As though it were his first child instead of his fourth.

Plinley Green slid astern. Ahead, smoky beyond the chessboard of fields and villas, lay London. Miles glanced at the clock. He'd been in the air more than fifty minutes. One was only supposed to be up an hour. He'd better begin to look for the aerodrome. It ought to be about fifteen degrees right. Yes. There lay the road intersection, the electric railway, the hangars. Which way was the wind. North west. Dead astern. He eased the stick forward; dropped five hundred, another five hundred; banked; turned; saw the windsock pointing straight at the Moth's nose; throttled down, throttled up again; skimmed trees, and felt his wheels touch ground in a perfect three-point landing.

II

"Fun", thought Miles as he slid his legs over the Moth's fuselage.

He took off his helmet and goggles; told the mechanic, "That engine's much smoother since you changed her plugs, Bert", and walked slowly towards the little club house. There he gossiped for half an hour with Betterton, his instructor—a retired squadron leader of the Royal Air Force, who knew Jim.

"I haven't set eyes on him for a couple of months", said Miles in answer to Betterton's inquiry.

"I saw him about a week ago. He's got some new job or other. Says it's going to make his fortune."

The news was pleasant, though Miles doubted that fortune. Jim's wasn't the moneymaking type. To make money one had to be like Fluke, according to whom the political situation was "pretty serious. These labour people are out for trouble. I shouldn't wonder if they didn't call a general strike".

That too—Miles decided—might be rather fun. But, back at the obscure London club he had joined because it was cheaper to live there than at a hotel, he found a cable from Dominic: "*Everything fixed hope ship all equipment Barranquilla end May suggest we meet there cable date your arrival care Western Union New Orleans Edla sends love*".

58

So Dominic and Edla were still together; and maybe she'd come part of the way with them. Pity if she did. You didn't want women about on that kind of job. You didn't want women about anyway. Didn't you, though?

And that night—after a long and not too satisfactory afternoon spent at various shipping offices—Miles Radcliffe scrutinised, for the first time in many weeks, a photograph he had cut out of an illustrated paper and folded away in his notecase.

The caption under that photograph read, "The wife of a distinguished Bolivian now visiting England, Señora Halcyon Aramayo, only daughter of the late Don Juansilvano O'Donnel y Cardozo and Donna Serafina Cardozo de O'Donnel of Asuncion, Paraguay".

Halcyon's picture really didn't do her justice. In the flesh she was infinitely more beautiful. But one mustn't think of her in the flesh. Because that always brought on the hunger.

"I'd better tear this up", he decided; and did so, rather quickly, dropping the little shreds of paper into the fireplace.

Nevertheless he dreamed of her. A strange dream in which they rode together past blue-black waters into a dense green jungle which he seemed to recognise; till a voice called, "All aboard for Barranquilla", and a steamer hooted, and Halcyon galloped away.

III

Stephanie Archer said, "No newspaper. Did you ever hear of such a thing? And the trains aren't running. But I don't care. I shall go to business just the same".

"So shall I", declared Rosaleen. "Though Alf said our workpeople might have to come out this morning. He's simply furious about it. And so are most of them."

"If I had my way, I'd shoot these trade union leaders. What does Fluke think about it?"

"Fluke's got the funniest idea." Rosaleen folded her serviette and rose from the breakfast table. "He said last night at dinner that if the newspapers didn't come out it'd be the making of the radio business."

"Then he isn't frightened there's going to be bolshevism?"

"Not a bit. Though Miles telephoned just before I left to say there was quite a bit of rioting in the East End. Apparently he'd been down there to have a look at it."

"That's just the sort of idiotic thing he would do. Serve him right if he gets his head broken."

"Why do you hate Miles so much, Stephanie?"

"Well, don't you?"

The retort made Rosaleen blush. She had been a fool to tell Stephanie—that night while she was going to bed—about Miles's behaviour in the car. He'd only been a little bit drunk. Lots of boys got drunk when they went dancing. But, thank goodness, she hadn't told Stephanie everything. "I didn't really mind", she remembered. "After the first one, I . . . I rather liked his kissing me."

Then the telephone rang; and, having run to answer it, she heard Paul.

"I hope you're not going to the factory", he began.

"Of course I'm going. Why shouldn't I ?"

"It may be rather dangerous."

"What on earth makes you think that ?"

"I'm at the office. I got here early. We've just had a call from London. The strikers have held up some of our food vans. The government's called out the military. This means civil war in my opinion."

He talked on—obviously in a panic. Stephanie came to the phone. Rosaleen heard her say, "You don't seem to be keeping your head very well. What does father think ?"

Leaving them to it, she went upstairs, put on her outdoor shoes and a hat. Taking a last glance in the mirror, she remembered Ireland. But England wasn't like Ireland. If people tried to riot, the police would soon deal with them. Couldn't Paul see that ? What was the matter with the man ? At his age he ought to have more sense.

She said goodbye to Stephanie and mounted her bicycle. As she pedalled away from Fairholm, everything seemed normal—except that one missed the noise of the trains, and that there were so many cars about. Every car, crammed to capacity, seemed to be making for the bypass. Halfway down the old country road a block of traffic forced her to dismount.

"A nice business, I don't think", the driver of the car by which she had halted was grumbling to the woman beside him. "At this rate we shan't be in London before ten o'clock."

The woman said, "It's no good getting into a temper about it". The man blew his horn.

This was followed by an epidemic of hornblowing which lasted a good two minutes. Then the block began to move again; and Rosaleen, alternately mounting and dismounting, was carried forward—only to be stopped at the fingerpost by a special constable, whom she recognised, to her surprise, for Timothy Archer.

"Hallo", said Timothy; and told her that he had been up since "four g.m."

"We were warned we might be wanted a week ago", he went on. "Ramshackle Mac hasn't caught the Government on the hop this trip." He turned to the motorist who had started the hornblowing epidemic, and said, "No, sir. You can not go on. You must stay put for the present".

The motorist swore. Timothy smiled. Three motorcyclists in khaki hared by along the bypass. A convoy of lorries, also driven by soldiers, followed; then an armoured car reminiscent of Ireland, and more motorcyclists, rifles on their backs.

With the road clear Timothy signalled her forward; but at the garage on the top of the hill she was held up again; and it was nearly half past nine before she dismounted at the gates of the factory, thankful to be away from the fumes of the exhausts.

The gates were open. By them, obviously on guard, stood Moggles, the night watchman. He gave her the news. More than half the girls had turned up. She stabled her cycle; passed through the glass doors, and heard Fluke booming into the phone, "Never mind about that. All I want is a window show". In the passage that led past Fluke's room to her own she encountered Derek Grayson, who said, "Come and help pack".

"Pack what?"

"Every set we've got. Fluke's sending 'em out on sale or return. I think——"

"Never mind what you think, Derek", interrupted Fluke, appearing at his own door.

His telephone rang again. He ran to it. "Is that you, Thompson?" Rosaleen heard him say. "Good. Hop in your car and come straight here. I don't care a hoot in hell if you've got twenty appointments."

Syd Thompson was their traveller for the home counties. Rosaleen found Alec Jones, their London man, hanging up his hat and coat in her own room.

"I don't know what's got into Mr. Radcliffe", he said without preamble. "He routed me out of bed before it was light and told me to hire a taxi for the day. Nice job I had to find one."

She could see the taxi in the courtyard. Fluke entered. He had a piece of notepaper in one hand and a child's paintbox in the other.

"You cut along to the packing room, Jones", he ordered. "Load up the taxi as quick as you can. Rosaleen'll be getting on with the showcards."

Jones ran off. Fluke handed her the piece of notepaper, across which he had printed, "Break the strike with a Radcliffe Radio!" and laid the paintbox on her desk, saying:

"You know those cards we had done for the exhibition. Get fifty or sixty and paint this slogan right across 'em. There's plenty of blank space. Black and red would be best. Never mind how roughly it's done as long as it's legible. Jones'll need the first twenty. We've got to get him off by eleven. Thompson'll need about thirty, and I'll take what's over".

His phone rang again. He left her. She ran to the stockroom, found the cards, and brought them back. The paintbox—she recognised—had been her Christmas present to Arty. Setting to work, she thought, rather queerly, "Fluke's clever. He never misses a chance. What a pity Miles isn't more like him".

IV

Rosaleen's first effort at painting seemed a bit of a mess. But the next card she finished looked "quite decent"; and she had done ten more by the time Fluke reentered.

"Not bad", he said. "Not bad at all. But be a dear and hurry."

As he spoke, Jones came in to say, "We can't get more than twenty-five sets into the taxi".

"Oh, yes, you can, if you sit outside with the driver."

"But that isn't allowed; and besides, there's no seat."

"I don't give a tinker's curse what's allowed. Sit on the driver's lap. Here, I'll talk to him."

They went out together. Continuing to paint, she heard great argument from the courtyard. But Alec Jones and forty sets with showmatter were away for London by ten minutes past eleven, and Thompson drove up five minutes later. She heard Fluke booming at him, "This is the chance of a lifetime". He was away, with fifty sets, by one thirty. She and Grayson, Fluke and Alf, the foreman, lunched off sandwiches fetched from the local public house by the office boy.

"How many more can we rake up?" asked Fluke.

"Twenty-five", answered Alf. "But we've only got batteries for eighteen."

"Oh well, some of the shops'll have batteries. Get 'em all into my bus, and you go on with your painting, Rosaleen."

"Where are you going with your lot?" asked Grayson.

"Albanford."

They got Fluke off by half past two. Immediately afterwards a boy on a bicycle brought the first telegram, "*Send urgent fifty Radcliffite crystals, fifty coils, fifty valve holders, hundred high tension battery plugs Studd Manchester*". The next order came by telephone. More followed. Fluke returned at five o'clock with the news, "The customers are just grabbing 'em off the counters".

Shown the orders, he grinned, "What did I tell you? We'll have to get the girls to work overtime. They'll do it all right if I talk to 'em".

Next morning Alf reported that only ten girls had not clocked in. Fluke called a meeting for the lunch hour. It was the first time Rosaleen had heard him make a speech; and again, as he boomed, "I don't know how you all feel about it, but what I feel is that if people want to work, nobody's got the right to stop them", she could not help comparing him with Miles.

"Miles is such a fool", she thought that night. "Why doesn't he come into the business? Why doesn't he settle down and get married?" But the significance of that thought escaped her; and for the next week she was too busy by day and too tired of a night to think about anything except her own particular job.

Only with the collapse of the General Strike did she remember one of the last things Miles had said to her: "I shall be leaving England pretty soon. Of course I'll come down to say goodbye to everybody". And the very casualness of that "everybody"—at least he might have said "you"—hardened her against sentiment. What if he had kissed her? What if she had liked being kissed by him? You didn't allow yourself to become sentimental about young men who got drunk.

v

At the back of Rosaleen's mind, nevertheless, lurked a doubt as to whether Miles had been drunk; and this doubt seemed very active on that sunny Saturday afternoon late in May when, seated near the tennis court with Enid and the new baby, she watched him stroll out of the house and towards them. Could he have driven so well—through all that snow, too—if he'd taken even one glass too much?

Hatless, Miles wore a blue shirt with a soft collar and a plain tie, gray trousers and a homespun sports jacket. She noticed the smallness of his waist, the set of his powerful shoulders, and that his narrow jetblack moustache had been newly clipped. His hair was still a little curly. The white patch at his right temple still attracted one's attention. His elephant-gray eyes twinkled with sheer fun as, kissing Enid, he said, "And how's the last shot in Fluke's locker?"

"Her name's Gladdy", smiled Enid. "And there's no need to be coarse."

He shook hands with Rosaleen and seated himself on the grass.

"It's nice of you to put me up for the night", he went on. "I've brought some gear I'd like you to keep for me till I come back. Will it be all right?"

"Yes. Betty'll keep an eye on it. I hope you packed everything with mothballs."

"You bet."

He began to talk about the strike. It hadn't been bad fun. He'd volunteered to drive a lorry and been billeted in Regent's Park. One night some silly asses tried to stop him. Quite a good scrap while it lasted.

Willynilly, Rosaleen interrupted:

"That was the part you liked best, I suppose?"

Glancing up at her, he answered, "I certainly got a kick out of it. Any objection?"

As their eyes met, she was conscious of antagonism. "You mind your own business", he seemed to be saying. She thought stupidly, "I wish he weren't so good-looking"; and then, "I wonder why he's learned to fly. I wonder where he's going to this time".

Fluke, wearing white flannels and an old Torringtonian blazer, appeared from the house. Two other men followed him. He called, "Hallo, Miles. Can you make up a four? That damn fellow Timothy has let us down at the last moment". Miles rose, saying, "I don't mind. I've got a pair of sneakers in my bag, only you'll have to produce a racket".

He went off. Sneakers—it transpired when he came back—were gym shoes; and his forehand drive—from the moment the men began to knock up—almost untakable.

"Fluke says", confided Enid at the end of the first set, "that Miles could be first class at any game he cared to take up. Isn't it funny that games don't amuse him? Oh, dear, it's time for Gladdy's bottle."

She carried the baby away. Fluke boomed, "Radcliffes v. The Rest this time. Toss you for service". He spun his racket, and took the service. Once again Rosaleen was forced to compare the halfbrothers. On the court all the advantages seemed to be with Miles. Lithe, graceful, sure as a cat on his feet, he made the sandy-haired Fluke appear fat and clumsy.

Every time Fluke missed a ball his face changed—his customary bonhomie giving way to irritation. Occasionally he swore. Miles never swore; and his expression—that faint smile—never altered. When they broke off—by which time Fluke dripped perspiration—Rosaleen saw that he was still as cool as when he began playing. Curiously, this annoyed her; so did his conversation over the tea which Betty carried on to the lawn.

Enid had come back by then, bringing Arty with her. Simmy and Philly—she explained—had gone to a party. Arty clambered to Rosaleen's knee. Listening to the four men argue about the strike, she came to the conclusion that Miles had only volunteered for what he called the fun of the thing. Memory suggested that he had only been an Auxiliary in Ireland for the same reason; and again flung up Stephanie's judgment, "That young man doesn't care for anybody in the world except himself".

At about half past five it began to rain. By six o'clock it was pelting. "You'd better stay for supper, Rosaleen dear", said Enid. "You'll only get sopped to the skin if you cycle home in this."

VI

Instinct urged Rosaleen to go; but Enid, who could be stubborn, insisted. Rosaleen helped her and the nurse put Simmy and Philly, back from their party, to bed. Tidying herself afterwards, she felt altogether jealous of Enid, who had everything a woman could want—enough money, a nice home, children, and a husband who adored her. But Rosaleen's main envy—she knew—was the children. One day, she must have children of her own.

The two guests, primed with generous drinks, drove away in a two-seater. Over supper Fluke asked Miles, "Where are you off to this time?" To Rosaleen's surprise, Miles answered at length.

A pal of his was organising a treasure hunt in Colombia ("No. Not British Columbia. The one in South America.") The chances of their finding any treasure were "pretty slim". Still—they might dig up something. And anyway it ought to be good sport.

"Going to cost you a bit getting out there", said Fluke.

"Not more than thirty quid. I don't travel in liners, you know."

Miles's eyes glinted, his nostrils flared a little, as he talked on. Rosaleen had visions of him—standing at the bow of a ship over which spray broke, sleeping by a camp fire, climbing into an aeroplane. And a sudden depression—never previously experienced—opened like a pit in her mind.

"I'm being silly", she thought. "I've been silly all day—ever since Fluke told me he'd be here this afternoon and that I'd better come over and say goodbye to him." Her sense of humour recalled a caption in a film, "You should worry. Let him go fly his aeroplane". But films were silly too. Why did one waste one's time going to them? Miles's whole life was a waste of time. Oh, bother Miles!

After supper he fetched the big atlas from Fluke's study, turned to the map of South America, and pointed to "Bogota, that's the capital of Colombia". Soon his finger moved south across the Rio Negro and the upper reaches of the Amazon and down through Bolivia to Paraguay.

Then he began to talk about his last journey; and more visions came to Rosaleen—showing her a vast river, turgid under those banks he called *barrancas*, down which floated great islands of weeds, called *camelotes*. On the other side of the river stretched dense jungle, hundreds upon hundreds of unmapped miles, through which one hacked one's way with a weapon called a *machete*. Fierce fish ("*pirañas*, they're absolute cannibals") swarmed in the river waters, and alligators lurked there. Jaguars haunted the jungle, and peccary hogs infinitely more dangerous than jaguars, and snakes, giant anacondas, rattlers, and a particularly poisonous one known as *ñandurié*.

"You'll give me the creeps if you don't shut up", protested Enid. "I had an awful nightmare about the reptile house the last time I took Simmy and Philly up to the Zoo."

Miles laughed and closed the atlas.

64

"There's no accounting for tastes", platitudinised Enid. "But fancy wanting to go anywhere where there are tarantulas and mosquitos. Give me Plinley Green."

She rose and walked to the drawing room window, across which the curtains had not yet been drawn.

"It's setting in wet", she went on. "Rosaleen can't possibly go in this."

Fluke said, "Tell you what. Miles can drive her back to Fairholm and she can fetch her cycle tomorrow".

"I'll be all right——" began Rosaleen; and stopped.

Miles was looking at her again. "Afraid?" his eyes seemed to be saying. "Don't worry. I shan't try to kiss you." As though she were afraid of that!

Some vague fear, nevertheless, tried to impose itself on her as she continued, with just a touch of artificiality, "Well, perhaps that would be best. It's awfully good of you, Fluke"; and, putting on her hat, she felt an unaccustomed tremble in her fingers. "You are being a goose", she chided herself. "It isn't as if you were the least bit in love with him."

By the time she had said goodbye to Fluke and Enid the car was already chugging outside the porch. Miles held the door open for her. Switching on headlamps and screenwiper, he remarked, "It wouldn't have done you much good to cycle home in this, would it?"

"No."

He drove carefully through the gates, along the hundred yards of private road and down the hill. There he began abruptly, "Look here, there's something I've wanted to say to you for some time. Only somehow there's never been an opportunity".

He paused, apparently in need of prompting.

Rosaleen prompted, "Yes, Miles". But he still hesitated, and there was a touch of the old shyness in his voice when he continued, "I'm afraid I behaved rather badly that night I took you out dancing".

Rosaleen, in her turn, hesitated.

"Oh, that's all right", she said finally. "I expect you'd had one over the eight, as Fluke calls it."

"Probably. Dominic had been setting 'em up a bit. Though as a rule I'm pretty abstemious."

He broke off. His obvious intention to dismiss the subject roused a resentment which found vent in a quiet, "I'm glad of that. I always think it's so silly of men to get drunk, especially when they're driving".

"Well, you must admit I'm quite sober tonight", answered Miles.

They were passing the club house by then. The glare of the brilliantly lit windows showed her the same faint smile she had observed on the tennis court. Resentment faded. Again she grew aware of depression. Why need he go? Why couldn't they be friends? One had so few real friends. Only Stephanie. Spontaneously she asked, "Will you be away long?"

"Oh, quite a while, I expect."

"But won't you miss England?"

"Miss it? Good lord!" And he went on—he too, she realised, speaking spontaneously, "I don't know what I'd do with myself if I had to live in England. I should be bored stiff. Can you see me catching the eight-thirty up every morning and the five-five down every night?"

"But most people have to."

"Poor devils."

He broke off again.   They were almost in sight of Fairholm.

"You needn't be so scornful", protested Rosaleen.

He slowed the car, saying, "You're wrong there.   I'm not scornful.   I'm only sorry for them".

"Why?"   Resentment was on her again.   "Because you want them all to be like you?"

"My dear girl, I don't expect anybody to be like me.   All I ask is that they shouldn't expect me to be like them."

Rosaleen's resentment vanished.   But her depression remained.   "So now *you* know what to expect", depression seemed to be suggesting; and her fingers wanted to tremble once more when—a few minutes later—the time came for them to part.

"No.   I won't come in", he smiled, "it wouldn't be popular with Stephanie"; and she, too, managed a smile as she said, "Then I'm afraid this'll have to be goodbye, Miles.   I shan't be able to fetch my bike till after church, and you'll be off by then."

"Yes.   I must be in town before one because I've asked Jim to lunch with me.   Shall I give him your love?"

"You can if you like.   And Miles, take care of yourself.   Don't have any flying accidents."

"Not more than I can help.   Besides, one's usually enough at that game."

Fear, no longer vague, struck her speechless.   He released her fingers and climbed back into the car.

His hand waved.   She managed to wave back.   The red rear light vanished.   The purr of the engine dwindled down the road.

It had stopped raining.

Maybe that was a good omen.

What of?

VII

All that June of nineteen hundred and twenty-six Rosaleen was conscious of occasional depressions and occasional fears.   These came on—she discovered—every time memory threw up some picture of Miles.   Accordingly she began to repress all thought of him; and by July—or so it seemed—she was her normal happy self.

In August she and Stephanie took their holiday together.   The coal-miners were still on strike, but nobody in the little hotel at Worthing seemed to care.

During that fortnight Stephanie, too, was at her happiest.   A middle-aged widower who always wore a rose at the lapel of his blue flannel jacket, spoke with a Lancashire accent, and proclaimed himself in the textile business, paid her much attention.   Chaffed about this, she retorted, "I'd as soon marry a codfish, but it does amuse me when he grovels".

Rosaleen's temporary admirer was more youthful, and the reverse of a groveller.   She bathed with him every day; danced with him most nights, and let him kiss her occasionally.   But his apparent ardours left her cold.

There was only one thing—Rosaleen decided at twenty—that she wanted

66

of any man. And that one thing summed itself up in the word "Home". That her home would contain children seemed axiomatic. Otherwise, why marry? All this talk, all these books and films about the "sex motive", were "just rot". She told her admirer so on their last evening together. He retorted, a trifle bitterly, "The trouble with you is that you're undersexed".

Secretly this judgment worried her; but not much and not for long.

VIII

That summer Fluke only joined Enid and the children in the house he had taken in Westgate for the weekends. Business—he told Rosaleen on her return—was "going great guns". Before the strike only a million people had taken out B.B.C. licences. By Christmas the figure would be three million. He'd decided to "stick another wing on the old factory" and to give her a rise of ten shillings a week.

October found him cursing "the sanguinary bank" because they wouldn't let him have "a couple of lousy thousand more overdraft". In November Timothy said across the supper table at Rosemary Lodge, "The thing for you to do, old lad, is to float Radcliffe Radios as a public company—and the chap you ought to get in with is Cuthbert Brendon".

Three days later Rosaleen took down a telephone message from Timothy, "Tell Fluke I've fixed up a lunch. Monday at the Savoy Grill. One o'clock sharp. Brendon's bringing his publicity man along".

Paul dropped in to supper at Fairholm that evening. After he had gone, Rosaleen said, "We seem to be seeing rather a lot of Paul these days"; and Stephanie, "I shouldn't wonder if he weren't in love with you". But the idea of the myopic Paul being in love with anybody seemed so ridiculous that Rosaleen only laughed.

She always looked her best—Stephanie used to think—when one could make her laugh. In repose her mouth was a little too set, and her hazel eyes a little too serious.

Next morning, when they came down to breakfast, they found a picture postcard with the first news they had received from Miles since his departure.

The picture—of a Spaniard, bare-headed but in full armour, with a lace ruffle round his neck and a blue cloak hanging from his right shoulder—bore the legend, "El famoso conquistador Gonzalo Jiménez de Quesada, Fundador de Bogotá". Underneath Miles had written, "All the best. We've been held up here for a month or so but now we're off".

Cycling through thin fog over frosty roads to the factory, Rosaleen experienced another mild attack of depression; but, from the moment Fluke arrived, this passed. For, these days, Fluke simply exuded optimism; and once he had lunched with Cuthbert Brendon, there was, to quote Enid, "no holding him".

Before Christmas, with the coalminers back at work, the accountants were in. With nineteen hundred and twenty-seven barely a week old, Rosaleen was typing, "My dear Brendon, I've just been looking through that draft prospectus", and to Fluke's solicitors, "Here are the two contracts I spoke to you about yesterday—my own and Grayson's. What I want to know is: Are they absolutely ironclad?"

All this while orders poured in, and they continued to engage more staff,

67

and Fluke spent at least two days a week in London. He had taken to wearing a red carnation, and rarely appeared without one cigar in his mouth and several others in the left top pocket of his waistcoat. "Radcliffe Radios Limited, Chairman, Mr. Cuthbert Brendon, Vice-Chairman and Managing Director, Mr. P. L. Radcliffe, Technical Adviser, Mr. Derek Grayson" was floated on a sea of press publicity (with two and a half per cent underwriting commission to the firm of stockbrokers in which Timothy Archer was now a junior partner) by the middle of March.

IX

The morning of the flotation brought another card from Miles, very dirty and the postmark indecipherable except for the first five letters Sogam— Underneath the picture, of some Indians, he had written, "Having a grand time. No Plinley Greenery about this bunch!"

"He's probably got a squaw of his own by now", sniffed Stephanie.

"What a filthy idea", snapped Rosaleen; and, because she so rarely snapped at one, Stephanie wondered—for the first time in nearly a year— whether by any chance she could be in love with Miles; but decided, thankfully, that she was not.

"I shall know if she ever falls in love", Stephanie reassured herself; and from that her thoughts took a strange turn, brought on by a recently banned book. Why couldn't she herself fall in love? Were her feelings for Rosaleen . . . a little abnormal? The mere idea made her shudder. "I'm the most normal woman alive", she determined; and all that spring she devoted herself more and more to the business of her teashop, which flourished, and to local politics, in which she had always taken a certain amount of interest.

It was through a local politician, who kept a small hotel at Plinley Common, that Stephanie first heard about "The Beehive".

"If that place were properly run", he told her, "there'd be a little fortune in it. You could buy the lease and goodwill for a song. But you'd have to spend a bit—say fifteen hundred to two thousand—on improvements."

The following Sunday, mere curiosity sent her cycling to the Beehive. She saw its attractions at once; but doubted whether even the full two thousand pounds could convert this house, garden and paddock which an ex-officer had bought with his gratuity and the idea of becoming a chicken farmer (an idea eventually abandoned for the hardly less precarious trade of restaurant keeper) into a profitable business. For one thing the approach, nearly half a mile of rough track from the bypass, was too difficult, and for another it had no electric light.

"Charlie always meant to have the electricity put in", she was told by the ex-officer's widow. "And he tried to get the road tarmacked. But the Albanford Company asked three hundred pounds to run a main—and you know what rural district councils are like about having roads made up. He always said, too, that the pond would make the loveliest swimming pool."

Pedalling back to Fairholm, Stephanie decided, "Even if I could get the money out of father, it would be too much of a job for me". About a week afterwards, however, Bob Hartley, of Hartley's Limited, the principal caterers of Albanford, encountered with Paul at a meeting of the League of Nations Union, said, "That teashop of yours is a bit of a nuisance to us, Miss

68

Archer. You're too close, you know. Not that we really mind competition. Still, we'd rather buy you out—that's to say if you'd be a willing seller".

"It looks to me as though he's dead keen", opined Paul, when he drove her back to Fairholm.

Stephanie told him a little about the Beehive.

"Too much of a risk", said Paul.

Next day, towards closing time, Bob Hartley strolled into the teashop, and, having opened, "What do you think of this fellow Lindbergh flying the Atlantic?" suggested a cocktail at the Peacock, over which he again broached the topic of "us buying you out".

The day after—by a most curious coincidence, it seemed to Stephanie—Jeremiah Treason, of Treason and Purchase, the Plinley Green house agents, rang her up to ask, "Have you ever thought of selling Fairholm, Miss Archer? Because if, by any chance, you did want to get rid of it, I believe I've got a buyer".

And the last evening of May found Stephanie closeted with her father in the little dreary sitting room of the Victorian villa where he and her mother had lived ever since their marriage.

"You've always been a good daughter", said Walter Archer after a full hour's discussion, all through which he had stroked his gray whiskers with one veined hand while the other twisted at the gold albert chain festooned across his broadcloth waistcoat. "But two thousand five hundred pounds takes a lot of making. And you'll want credit for your provisions as well, you say. So I think I'd better have a talk with Paul. You understand, of course, that if I do lend you the money and you don't pay it back, it'll have to come off your inheritance?"

"Of course, father", said Stephanie. "But I warn you frankly that Paul will be against it."

X

Paul's opposition, nevertheless, stubborn at the outset, underwent a most peculiar change on the June Saturday afternoon of Rosaleen's twenty-first birthday.

He brought her a present that afternoon—a wristwatch set with little diamonds, which had cost him "the special price to you, Mr. Archer" of twenty-five pounds at Glaisyer's, the best jeweller in Albanford.

As Rosaleen buckled the present on her wrist, thinking, "What on earth made him give me this, it looks awfully expensive?" Stephanie burst out:

"Oh, Paul. What do you think has happened? This morning Rosaleen got a letter from a firm of solicitors. Some great-aunt of hers has died and left each of her great-nephews and nieces seven hundred and fifty pounds. Isn't it too marvellous? We've been talking about what she's to do with the money ever since lunch. And do you know what we've nearly decided? That if only you and father agree to my buying the Beehive, she's to come in as a partner".

"Is that what you really want to do, Rosaleen?" asked Paul, eyeing her through his thick glasses.

"Rather. It'd be so grand to be working for oneself. And Stephanie says she simply must have someone she can trust to keep the accounts and look after things generally."

69

To the surprise of the potential partners Paul said, "I quite agree. But there's one thing I don't agree about. Rosaleen oughtn't to put her whole legacy into the business. Five hundred's quite enough for her and fifteen hundred's quite enough for father. I'll make up the rest myself".

"You darling", said Stephanie—and kissed him for the first time since New Year.

XI

Kempton and Kempton, the solicitors who had written to Rosaleen about her legacy, asked for a birth certificate and suggested a personal interview.

"I should go if I were you", said Stephanie; and Rosaleen, having demanded a day off from Fluke, took the early "steamer" to town.

Kenneth Kempton, a typical lawyer, with whom she spent nearly three quarters of an hour, had known both her father and her mother.

"You're not much like either of them", he said, eyeing her through his pincenez. "But anyone can see you're an Adair." And he went on, "Would you care for us to invest this money for you? I don't think I'm giving away any family secrets; but there'll be a bit more coming to you when Lady Caroline's three sisters pass on. They're spinsters, too, you see".

The legacy had increased Rosaleen's selfconfidence. She answered, speaking with more decision than Kenneth Kempton anticipated: "It's very kind of you, but I'm going to put the money—most of it anyway—into a business"; and left the office thinking, "The family ought to have done something for me years ago. Now I've learned to look after myself".

She made her way to Oxford Street, and passed the afternoon buying clothes. To spend the best part of fifty pounds in one go was a thrill.

"But I mustn't ever allow myself to grow really extravagant", she told herself as the electric train—which, unlike "the steamer", stopped at every single one of the eighteen stations between Oxford Circus and Plinley Green—jerked her homeward. And, when she brushed her hair that evening, memories of her childhood were very active in her mind.

Her parents' fecklessness about money had ruined most of her childhood. Her own children, when the time came for her to marry, must have financial security, won, if it were possible, by her own efforts.

She did not confide this thought to Stephanie. The elder woman, nevertheless, was subconsciously aware of a change, or maybe only of a development, in her friend's character. Nor did this change quite escape Fluke, who returning to his Enid on the Friday, confided, "Rosaleen's given me notice. I offered her another five bob a week if she'd stay on, but she wouldn't hear of it. She says she wants to be independent".

"Well, I suppose you can do without her", said Enid.

"Do without her? Of course I can. Shorthand typists are two a penny. That isn't the point."

"What is the point then?"

Fluke hesitated, and began to prowl up and down the drawing room—a habit which always fidgeted her.

"Perhaps you're in love with the girl", she suggested. "Men are always supposed to fall for their secretaries."

"Don't be such an ass." To her surprise he spoke crossly. "You know perfectly well I'm not that sort of man."

"Then why are you so annoyed at her leaving?"

"I dunno. I expect it's because I've always looked on her as one of the family." And that, decided Fluke, was the truth.

Subsequently told more about their plans by Stephanie, he shook his sandy head. They'd probably make a mess of things. It was all very well for women to run dress shops or teashops. But this was quite a different proposition. For one thing, if the place were to succeed, it must be advertised. Advertisement cost a lot of money.

"We thought you might help us there", put in the tactful Stephanie. "You're so clever at it."

"Well, of course I might be able to think up something."

Thus flattered, Fluke eventually made up his mind to put "a hundred quid, just to show there's no ill feeling" into the private company they had decided to call "Beehives Limited". Another hundred was wrung from Timothy, who introduced a hatchet-faced man of his own age as, "Dick Simmons. He and I soldiered together. Dick's an architect. Of course you'll need an architect". And that August, with the builders already working, Stephanie and Rosaleen were far too busy and far too excited to dream of a holiday.

Paul only went off for a week; and spent most of those seven days on the Lakes moping. Naturally timid with women, he kept on recalling various experiments all culminating in shameful disaster, and the fact that he was fourteen years older than Rosaleen. On his return his mother happened to say, "You do look thin, Paul dear. Perhaps you ought to consult a doctor about your digestion".

He made an appointment with Doctor Maxleigh, reputed to have the best practice in Albanford; but could not screw up sufficient courage to broach the obsessing topic. The doctor prescribed a tonic, a laxative, and more exercise. Paul took up, detested and gave up golf.

Meanwhile Rosaleen and Stephanie had moved from Fairholm; and the *Albanford Herald* was carrying an advertisement, suggested by Fluke, "The New Beehive. A honey of a place for lunch, tea or supper. Intimate dances every Saturday. Music by Radcliffe Radio. Open—the twenty-fifth of September".

That opening day, the three girls Stephanie had brought with her from the teashop served twelve lunches, twenty-one teas, and eight suppers in the pseudo-Tudor refreshment room of Dick Simmons's designing. Mrs. Cranbourne, the ex-officer's widow, whom they had engaged for two pounds a week and all found, did the cooking; Stephanie, very authoritarian in tweeds, acted maître d'hôtel; and Rosaleen made out the bills.

"If only my poor Charlie had been alive to see it", sentimentalised Eliza Cranbourne after closing time. "We must have taken fifteen pounds if we've taken a penny."

Alone with Rosaleen in the big bedroom they had decided to share "until we've got these beastly decorators out of the place", Stephanie said, "What a fool that woman is. Does she imagine the takings are all profit?" And until December the New Beehive showed a small weekly loss.

"Never mind, dear", Stephanie used to say every time Rosaleen made out the accounts. "We're bound to do fairly well over Christmas."

But just before Christmas they were snowed up; and on Boxing Day their only customers were Paul, who had to leave his car on the bypass, and a couple of young men who arrived across country on skis.

XII

Paul caught the influenza as a result of his little adventure.

"I can bear that", grinned Stephanie, when her mother telephoned the news. "What I can't bear is that while this infernal weather lasts they won't make a start on our road."

It was not until the middle of March, indeed, that the rural district council—and how Stephanie had coaxed those bucolic obstructionists into action still remains Stephanie's secret—began operations by erecting a barricade and chalking, "No thoroughfare" on a large board.

Frantic phone messages changed the notice on this board to "Work in progress" and removed half the barricade. Not even free teas to the foreman and his gang, however, could induce them to hurry; and the few motorists who heralded Easter had to squeeze their cars between a traction engine, immobilised till after the bank holiday, and what Timothy called "a regular tank trap" of tar barrels.

"Another six months at this rate", gloomed Stephanie, "and we shall have to put up the shutters."

But during Whitsun she cheered up a little; and by midsummer of nineteen hundred and twenty-eight they were covering their expenses. In July they made their first profit—nearly seventy pounds.

Credit for this was due largely to Paul, who persuaded the Albanford branch of the League of Nations Union to hold its "first al fresco rally—principal speakers, Mr. Godfrey Spoonface, M.P., and the Reverend Lionel Papworthy" at the New Beehive; and a little to Timothy's suggestion that members of the British Legion, if wearing their badges, should be given a special rebate of a penny in the shilling. Once the new road was open, moreover, Fluke "followed his money", to use his own language, by making the Beehive, less than five miles from the factory, his lunch headquarters.

Fluke's new car, driven by a chauffeur, usually contained one guest, frequently three or four, and always some bottles.

"Damn it all, Stephanie", he used to boom, "why the deuce don't you get a licence to sell liquor? Packets of money in this place if you could only wangle it."

"And what would father have to say?"

"He might blow up, but he'd blow down again when you started paying off his debentures."

"Well, I'll think it over."

"Think it over my foot. This is a go-getters' world. You go get that licence and shove in a cocktail bar."

He almost chucked Rosaleen under the chin in his exuberance; called to his guests, "Come along, you chaps—no rest for the wicked", and departed. Paul, who motored over that evening, admitted—after considerable argument—that he might be right.

That summer, Paul took no holiday—and seemed to be taking unusual care with his appearance. The fair hair receding from his furrowed brows was always carefully brushed and redolent of barber's wash. He had changed

72

his old-fashioned spectacles for a more modern shape—"real tortoiseshell", he informed them. At weekends he sported white flannel trousers on his thin legs, a blue blazer with brass buttons across his narrow chest, and a pseudo-Panama hat on his egg-shaped head.

In October business slacked off; and Stephanie went away for a week, staying with a schoolfriend at Cambridge. On her return, Rosaleen said, "Old Paul's invited me to go to the pictures with him tomorrow evening". The adeptness of the still-silent screen hero in the becaptioned scenes with his heroine, however, made Paul so overconscious of his own imaginary short-comings that his clammy hands could not even attempt to hold Rosaleen's in the friendly darkness of the cinema, and he always needed both of them when he drove his car.

They parted at the side door of the Beehive; and Rosaleen, alone in her own room afterwards, could not help feeling a little sorry for the man—his final, "You will come out with me again, won't you?" having been as obvious as his behaviour during the past week.

"Why doesn't he pluck up his courage and propose?" she thought. "Then I could put him out of his misery."

But Christmas came round again—a busy Christmas this time—with Paul, as she phrased it to herself, "still hovering"; and New Year's Eve brought a surprising letter from Miles.

XIII

Miles's letter ran to twelve pages of his tiny neat handwriting. Rosaleen answered with four, and addressed her envelope to a bank in Buenos Aires. She gave the Argentine stamps on Miles's envelope to Fluke's Simmy, now ten years old and very keen on his collection. The letter itself she locked away in a battered jewelcase which had belonged to her mother. It was too interesting—she decided—to destroy.

Even more interesting—she sometimes thought—was the speculation, "What made him write to me?" And every now and again during the weeks that followed she would see pictures of Miles in one or other of the scenes he described—the finding of the golden idols ("only they turned out to be brass")—the crashing of the plane—his parting from Dominic and Edla—his lonely trek from Colombia into Ecuador—that cargo boat on which he had worked his passage from Guayaquil to Mollendo—the train climbing up from Arica to La Paz, and down from La Paz to Sucre and Potosi. But somehow or other all such pictures—especially that last one, in which she would visualise him actually sitting down to begin, *"It's raining like the devil and doesn't look as if it would stop for hours. This place is called Victoria Colony. It's in the Argentine province of Misiones. I may settle down here. A chap's made me an offer to go into a kind of partnership with him"*—proved more disturbing than pleasurable.

Accordingly she began to repress them; and on that last Sunday morning in April when Stephanie called to her, "Come along, slug, breakfast's on the table," there were no more images of Miles Radcliffe in her conscious mind.

That Sunday the five waitresses they now employed could hardly cope with the rush of customers—many of whom insisted on being served in the garden; and on the following day, with the sun still shining, Dick Simmons brought them the first plans for "The Honeycomb Cocktail Snuggery", as Fluke insisted they should call it.

"A little bird told me you'll be getting your licence at the next sessions", said Dick; and after they had approved his rough sketches, he continued, "Do you know what I'd do with this place if it belonged to me? I'd build on half a dozen double bedrooms, each with its own bathroom and a little sun parlour. People are beginning to look for that sort of thing."

"What sort of people?" asked Stephanie with a malicious grin.

"Oh, married people, of course", answered Dick.

Next day they passed the idea on to Fluke, who asked, "But where's the money to come from?" And Paul took the same line, till Rosaleen twitted him, "The trouble with you is that you're too cautious". At which he flushed.

"Well, there'd be no harm in your asking Simmons for an estimate", he hedged before he drove back to Albanford; and on the following afternoon he telephoned from his office, "I say, there's a talking picture on at the Playhouse. You've never seen one, and neither have I. Do come with me tomorrow evening."

His voice sounded exceptionally nervous. She could not help being rather flattered. But all through the picture she herself felt just a little nervous, though this seemed "perfectly futile", because after all it wasn't the first time that a man had held her hand.

It was past eleven when they emerged under the arc lamps of Albanford High Street, and walked to the car park.

"Let's go round by the Abbey", said Paul. "It always looks wonderful by moonlight."

His car had one of the new sunshine roofs.

"Shall I open it?" he asked. "Or would you find that too cold?"

"No. I think it would be rather nice."

He fumbled with the catch. The roof stuck. She had to help him pull it back. Their hands met again. His skin seemed as though it were burning. The engine needed several pushes at the starter button, and he let in first gear clumsily. Poor old Paul!

No longer nervous, she gave her attention to what he was saying: "This is rather a nice road. I've always wanted to live in this road. But of course", giggling, "a chap can't very well live by himself".

"Why not?" she asked, pretending to be disingenuous.

That silenced him. They turned out of Elderberry Avenue and up the hill towards the Abbey. Near a little house on the green which faces the cloisters he slowed, and put his hand to the brake lever, but took it away again immediately.

"Fluke and Enid were married in the Abbey", he said while they circled the green. "Did you know?"

"Of course. There's a photograph of them, taken on those steps. It used to be in the parlour at The Firs."

"Fluke's done jolly well for himself since those days."

"Yes. Hasn't he?"

"I haven't done too badly either. And when father retires I shall have control of the business."

"Is he going to?"

"Well, not yet, of course. He's only just over sixty."

"And Paul can't be more than thirty-six", thought Rosaleen. "Funny. He seems like a hundred."

He steered away from the green down Monks Road. Here were larger residences, standing well back from the pavement.

"That one belongs to me", said Paul, indicating a double-fronted house of red brick. "It's let for two hundred a year."

Greatly daring, he took a hand from the wheel and laid it on her knee. The contact left her entirely frigid. All the same, when one did marry, it would be nice to feel that one's husband had some good solid investments. "He's a steady old stick", she caught herself thinking. "And he wouldn't be much trouble."

Then, curiously, her mind flashed her a picture of her mother. They were together in a frowsy boarding house. (They had lived in so many frowsy boarding houses.) Her mother was reading a telegram. "Is that from father?" Rosaleen remembered herself asking, and the answer, "No, darling. But it's—it's about him." And after that came the tears, and the weak arms round her, and the broken cry, "I've only you now. Oh dear, oh dear, what shall I do without my Harold?"

"Isn't it a lovely night", said Paul.

She wrenched her thoughts back to the present. They had just recrossed the High Street and were making for the bypass. His hand had removed itself from her knee. Maybe he wasn't going to propose after all. That would be a pity. Why? Surely she had no intention of accepting him? One shouldn't marry unless one were in love. But again—why? All sorts of fools married for love. Look at mother. A nice mess she'd made of her life. No security!

"And I", she thought, "must have security. For my children."

"Have you ever seen such a moon?" asked Paul.

The question irritated her. She wanted to answer, "Yes. Often", but changed it to, "And the stars are so bright".

Paul edged carefully on to the bypass. Once again his hand rested on her knee. Suddenly she felt sorry for him. He'd be happier if he were more like that scallywag Timothy. The cheek of Timothy, asking one to go dancing in London with him. And how cross he'd been when one refused. "All right, if you don't want to have a good time", Rosaleen remembered him saying, "there are plenty of others who do."

The hand on her knee tightened. Paul drove slower and slower. A lorry hooted and passed them. A pair of undimmed headlamps flashed in their faces. "That's a nice caddish way to drive", he muttered. "There ought to be a law about it."

She said, a trifle tartly, "You didn't dim either".

"Didn't I? I always do."

"Well, you forgot to that time."

More headlights grew visible. The hand left her knee for the dimmer. A mile ahead—she knew—they would come on the sign, "First left for the New Beehive".

"I don't believe I'm going to like talking pictures as much as silent ones" said Paul.

The remark seemed too inappropriate to answer Why didn't the man get it over? Hadn't he any guts?

She could see the sign now. At this hour of night it oughtn't to be still illuminated. That time switch must be out of order again. And electricity cost money. Children, too, cost money. Heaps of it. She'd never be really happy without children. Two at least. Four would be nicer. Two boys and two girls. Like Fluke and Enid.

The lights in the sign went out. They passed it; and Paul turned down the sideroad, asking, "Do you mind if I pull up for a moment?"

Without waiting for her answer, he braked in the shadow cast by the hedge, switched off his engine, removed his hat and threw it behind him.

"Rosaleen——" he began, turning to her and fumbling for her hands.

Placid, she let him have both her hands.

"Rosaleen", he repeated, panting a little, "there's something I must tell you. I'm in love with you. I've been in love with you ever so long. I want you to marry me. Will you?"

Emotion struck him speechless. Instinctively his hands tried to pull her close. Instinctively she resisted him.

"I do love you so much", he managed. "Couldn't you love me just a little?"

His thin lips remained half open. He seemed to find it difficult to breathe. His eyes, magnified by the thick lenses of his spectacles, were like a hungry dog's.

She could feel his emotion communicating itself to her; feel her instinct to resist his hands waning. "You poor thing", she wanted to say, "if you're so crazy for me, why don't you kiss me? Other men have. Miles did."

Miles!

Paul managed more words. He loved her so much. He'd be so good to her. She should never want for anything. Wouldn't she let him kiss her? Just once.

"No", she heard herself say. "No."

"Please. Please, Rosaleen, my . . . my darling."

His hands were feverish on hers. His half open lips were very close. They had touched her cheek. She felt her skin goosefleshing.

"No", she repeated. "Don't. There's a dear. It's no good. It really isn't."

"Even though I love you so much?"

"However much you love me."

"Oh."

There was pain in that little gasping cry. His head went back; but his fingers still clung feverishly to hers. Her own fingers were cool and untrembling. Her heart beat normally. No man could have moved her less.

"I'm sorry", she heard herself say. "I really am sorry, Paul. You're awfully decent, but I could never marry you."

His teeth closed with a funny little click. He dropped her hands; fumbled for the ignition key, the starter button. She was aware that the engine fired, that they were moving, that they had left the shadow cast by the hedge. Soon they reached the side door of the Beehive.

She opened the door and sprang out. He followed her. For a moment they faced each other in the moonlight. It seemed to her that he was almost in tears. Poor Paul. Poor dear old Paul. Had she hurt him so much?

"I really am sorry", she repeated. "But it's no use pretending about that sort of thing. Don't be angry with me."

"Of course I won't be." He forced a smile. "You can't help the way you feel any more than I can."

"But you must try to, Paul."

"I will. I want us to go on being friends."

"So do I."

"Honestly?"

"Yes. Honestly."

"You really mean that, Rosaleen?"

"Why, of course I do."

He forced another smile. She gave him her right hand. He held it for a moment, released it and climbed back into his car.

She watched him turn in the parking place; heard his tyres on the gravel. Queerly, as she unlocked the side door, she seemed to hear other tyres—on snow—on the soft snow at the gates of Fairholm. And, as she tiptoed upstairs to her own room, she could not quite suppress the thought, "I wonder where Miles is tonight".

XIV

Night, however, had not yet fallen on that inland lagoon by which men come, upstream from Corrientes or downstream from Concepcion, to the city of pastel shades which is Asuncion. And Miles Radcliffe, who loved that city more than most, could feel the tropic sunshine of late afternoon hot through the awnings on the upper deck of the Mihanovitch steamer, as he emerged from his cabin and leaned over the rail to survey the wharf.

Another car had just been driven on to the wharf. "Posh car for Paraguay", he thought, still sleepy from his siesta. "Don't see many of them about."

Then the car halted—a chauffeur sprang to one of its rear doors—and out of that door stepped a woman—and Miles Radcliffe felt the last veil of sleepiness snatched, as some rough hand might snatch a girl's mantilla, from his eyes.

His eyes stared. His heart seemed to have stopped beating.

Could that woman, all in black, even to the parasol she had just opened, be the young woman of whom he had dreamed for years? Could she be alone? Could she be coming aboard this very boat?

Yes, she was alone—she was coming aboard this very boat—and she was, she was Halcyon.

His heart beat again, his elephant-gray eyes glinted, and his nostrils flared a little, as those long hands in the black lace gloves furled the parasol and those little feet in the Parisian shoes trod the gangplank.

"*É como me gusta tu cuerpo!*" The words of a song heard the previous evening sang madly through his mind . ..

77

BOOK FOUR

I

"Querido de mi alma", MURMURED HALCYON. "IT IS STILL SO EARLY. PUT your arms round me and let us sleep for another hour."

Miles snuggled closer. His left arm circled her. Through the spider-web *ñanduti* lace of the nightgown her heart still beat fitfully under his hand.

Gradually the heartbeats subsided. Another murmur of love words—and she was asleep. How quietly she slept. One could hardly hear her breathing. The miracle—the sheer miracle—of possessing this Halcyon. Only—did he possess her? Was not he the one possessed?

He closed his eyes for a while; opened them to see dawn light filtering in under the brocade curtains. This traffic he could just hear, far and far below these windows, was the traffic of New York.

A day and a night now, since they had arrived in New York—nearly three months since he had won her? Only—had he won her? Was not the victory hers?

"Maybe", he thought; and conjured up the memory of her alone at the ship's rail, of his trepidation, of his approach, of the first words he had ever spoken to her, "The *señora* looks lonely. Perhaps she will permit me to introduce myself? Captain Radcliffe".

"Capitan inglés?"

"Si, señora."

"But you speak such good Spanish. And—and I have seen you before."

"Yes. Once in San Bernardino, and once in London."

"I do not remember the time in San Bernardino, but I remember the time in London. I was with my husband."

"Your husband is not on board, *señora*?"

"He is dead. Otherwise I should not be travelling alone, *señor capitan*."

"And how far are you travelling, *señora*?"

"Eventually to the *Estados Unidos*. But I am in no hurry. I may stop in Buenos Aires. I might even stop over in Rosario."

He, too, had stopped over in Rosario; and there they had first danced together—a polka Paraguayano, by moonlight, on that wide terrace under the arc lamps. Later, with dancing done, and the lamps out, and the breeze which heralded the Argentine dawn just rustling the palm fronds, he had attempted his first embrace.

"You are very inexperienced, *señor capitan*", he remembered her saying, "A man of experience does not ask a woman to let him kiss her. When the moment comes, he knows it without asking.

"But maybe", she had added, "I shall like you all the more because you are so lacking in experience. Tell me something. That girl I saw you with in London. Were you in love with her?"

"No."

"Have you ever loved?"

"Not till now."

"Not till now." Lying here beside her, he could see her actual smile as she repeated his words, could actually feel her hand on his sleeve, as she continued, smiling, "*Palabra inglés*—on your word as an Englishman?"

"*Si, señora. Palabra inglés.*"

Halcyon stirred in her sleep. He caressed her, and she lay quiet again. More memories crowded on his drowsy mind. He relived the hunger—sharper and more poignant than any hunger previously experienced—of two more days, of two more nights, all through which she seemed to mock his inexperience, treating him like a lovesick boy.

"But I am not a boy", he remembered himself saying; and her semi-scornful, semi-provocative, "Then why are you so afraid of me?"

"I am not afraid of you."

"The brave soldier. Yet his hand shakes. Why does your hand shake, *amigo mio*?"

"It is steadier than yours."

"No. Both my hands are quite steady. Look!"

But, although she held out both her hands, he had not looked at them, only into her eyes; seeing, suddenly, something of tenderness in her eyes; and, suddenly, behind that tenderness, the dark blaze of desire. Yet even so he had not dared to loose his own desire, until she whispered, "When the moment comes, he knows it without asking", and his mouth met hers in the long, fierce, breathless frenzy of their primal kiss.

Once more Halcyon stirred. Once more he passed his hands over her body, asking himself, as he was always asking himself, "Is she mine or am I hers?"

The noise of the traffic along Fifth Avenue grew more insistent. Now, so much light filtered in under the brocade curtains that he could see the whole room. Such a luxurious room. Everything to do with Halcyon stood for luxury, for the soft ways of living he had hitherto despised.

Love, too, he had despised. Because both love and the soft ways of living caged a man. Was he, Miles Radcliffe, caged at last? Could this woman force him to marry her? Last night, for the first time, she had talked of marriage. Lightly. Mockingly. But then, at first, she had talked so lightly, so mockingly, of love, saying:

"Love never lasts. Sooner or later one of us will tire of the other".

And another time—in Trinidad, where they had stayed with Geoffrey Thirkell—she said, "We are too alike, you and I. We are both very greedy. In love, one should be a little greedy and the other a little grudging".

Strange idea. But then she was altogether a strange woman, with many different bloods in her veins.

The blood of those early *Conquistadores* who had adventured up the Plate in their heavy armour, taking their Spanish ladies with them; the blood of a Portuguese admiral who trafficked with the Brazils; the blood of a wild Irishman who soldiered for Lopez in the days when that mad dictator would have made himself emperor from the Amazon to Tierra del Fuego; the Indian blood of a Guaraní woman—all these had gone to the making of this Halcyon, whom Europe and North America had provided with an education, and to provide for whose luxuries Paraguayans hauled the quebracho trees in the steaming lowlands of the Gran Chaco and Bolivians hewed the tin in the mines of the high Andes beyond Villa Montes.

That much—and a little of her dead father, from whom she had inherited the quebracho forests, of her dead husband from whom she had inherited a share in the tin mine—Miles knew. And today, for the first time, the knowledge of her wealth fretted him, because both the money he had saved from his own small income and the few hundreds he had made in Misiones would soon be exhausted.

"I could never be happy living on her money", he thought.

Yet could he ever be happy without her? Could any other woman satisfy this new hunger, so unlike the old, which had always been transient and always impersonal, a mere appetite that left no memory behind?

Halcyon's dark eyes opened. Her flame-coloured head lifted from his shoulder. Then her lithe body turned to him, and her soft arms enlaced him; and once again their breaths were as one breath . . .

II

"You are being unkind", said Halcyon, some mornings later. "And what is worse, you are being unintelligent. If this were my home, you would not mind accepting my hospitality."

"But this isn't your home. It's a hotel."

"A hotel which I have made my home ever since I first came to New York. A man can be too proud, *caro mio*. Let us consider this matter reasonably. Let us imagine, for example, that you are the millionaire, and that I am a poor girl with whom you have fallen in love. In that case——"

"But that isn't the case !"

"You mean—you are no longer in love with me?"

"You know I do not mean that."

"Then come and kiss me."

"No."

"You are angry enough to refuse me a kiss, just because I have settled one little check ?"

"It is not so little."

Miles fell silent, upper teeth biting lower lip. Halcyon shrugged her fine shoulders, and lit one of her rare cigarettes.

The receipted card for their first week's hotel bill, brought up by the waiter with their breakfast, still lay on the tablecloth. Glancing at it, she continued, "*Mas ó menos*, it only comes to five hundred dollars. And you paid the bootlegger. You paid for our dinner at the Colony last night—and at Jack and Charlie's afterwards".

"It is I who should pay for everything."

"*Que tontería* ! What nonsense. If we were Indians and I were your woman, you would be quite content that I should work for both of us. So why should I not pay for both of us ?"

"Because I'm not a gigolo !"

Still in a dressing gown she had given him, Miles rose, walked to the window, flung it open, and drew the air deep into his lungs. For the second time in his life, he knew himself on the verge of losing his temper. "If we were Indians", he caught himself thinking, "I could beat her." But the mere thought of beating her seemed so idiotic that he could not help smiling. And almost immediately Halcyon was at his side.

She laid a hand on his shoulder. At her touch, anger vanished. He put an arm round her; kissed her, lightly, on the temple. Silence held them while they looked down on New York.

Directly below them, so far down that the foreshortened figures on its sidewalks looked like walking dolls and its vehicles like clockwork toys from some nursery cupboard, lay the straight canyon of Fifth Avenue. A little to their right, and equally far below, Central Park might have been a mere garden. Level with them rose the stone forest of other recessed pinnacles, with here a copper dome and there a gilded belfry, all clearcut and shining against the October sky.

At this height the drone of the traffic was scarcely audible, though every now and again they could hear bells jangling or horns tooting or the shrill of a whistle, and always the clack-clack-clack of the riveters which told of new pinnacles abuilding.

"*Lindo*", said Halcyon; and Miles thought, "We ought to have a word like *lindo* in English. You can use it to admire anything, from a girl's face to a view."

"*Muy lindo*", she continued. "I am always happy in Manhattan. Though I would not live here always. Tell me, am I forgiven?"

"Yes. But I can't pretend I like being paid for."

"Be a little patient. And I will teach you how to make plenty of money."

The telephone in the sitting room rang. Unhurried, Halcyon went to answer it. Before she could reach the instrument, her bedroom telephone was rung impatiently, as is the habit of New York.

Miles closed the window. She curled herself on the sofa and put the microphone to her ear.

"Yes", he heard her say in her curiously accented, almost overcorrect English. "This is the Señora Aramayo. You will put the gentleman through, please." But the conversation which followed was in Guaraní; and, despite the lessons she had given him, he could understand only an occasional word.

"What was all that about?" he asked when she recradled the telephone.

"Those accursed Bolivians." Her eyes blazed. Her lips quivered. "With the sixty million dollars loaned them by America they have given another order for arms. To an English company this time. The war draws closer. It draws closer every day."

She rose and began to pace up and down the luxurious carpet. Never before had he seen her in this mood.

Then the telephone rang again; and, controlling herself, she spoke Spanish for several minutes. "Very well", she ended. "I will consent to discuss the matter. But I warn you, it will be quite useless to talk to me of *acciones*. If you buy, it must be for cash."

That time, when she replaced the instrument, she smiled to herself. But her mood—Miles realised—had not changed.

"I go to dress", she said. "At eleven o'clock someone is coming to see me. It would be better if you went out."

The waiter knocked, entered, and wheeled away the breakfast table.

This new mood of Halcyon's puzzled Miles. Bolivia had been rubbing Paraguay up the wrong way and pinching bits of her territory for some years. But only six months ago their dispute about the Chaco had gone to

81

arbitration. And the Chaco wasn't worth fighting for. Anyone who'd ever been there knew that.

He picked up the paper, and glanced idly at the headlines: "Markets hit all time high. Record car loadings. 'U.S.A. leading world back to prosperity' says head of Boston department store. Radio sales show 100% increase".

Smaller headlines read: "London Exchange Sensation. Statement by prominent financier".

The name of the financier struck a chord in Miles's memory. "Cuthbert Brendon?" he thought. "Didn't Fluke have something to do with that fellow?"

And, thinking of Fluke, his thoughts turned, just for an instant, to Rosaleen. Didn't he owe her a latter?

But the telephone—curse the machine, what a nuisance it was making of itself this morning—shrilled again while he was making up his mind to send Rosaleen a postcard; and, answering it, he heard a man's voice, which also struck a chord in his memory, say:

"Is that Miles Radcliffe? I bet you don't know who this is. I saw you at Jack and Charlie's last night. I didn't like to come over and talk to you. You and your lady didn't look as though you would appreciate your tête-à-tête being interrupted. But I managed to find out where you were staying—they seem to know most things about their customers at that particular place—so I thought I'd just ring you up on the off chance that you and your lady might be able to lunch with me and my yellow girl".

"You and your yellow girl?" repeated Miles. "Then of course I know who you are—Martin Halliburton. What on earth are you doing in New York?"

"Honeymooning, for one thing."

"I say, congratulations, old chap. When were you married?"

"About three months ago in Hong Kong."

Martin Halliburton went on, "I need hardly say my Mary's no more yellow than you are"; and suggested, "How about our hotel for lunch? It's not quite as posh as yours and rather a long way down town. But they don't do one at all badly".

"I'll just ask", answered Miles; and, putting down the telephone, tapped on Halcyon's door.

She was just slipping into her dress. He waited until her head emerged from the chiffon.

"*Un amigo?*" she said, mock-jealous. "Or perhaps *una amiga*? Anyway, you had better go by yourself."

"But why?"

"Because I shall probably be busy all day. Now, please run away and let me finish my dressing."

There was a new note of imperiousness in her voice. "What's got into the girl?" he thought. For according to European standards she was only a girl. Hadn't they celebrated her twenty-seventh birthday last night?

Martin Halliburton, told that one would be alone, sounded a trifle relieved.

"He always was a bit of an old stick about women", decided Miles. "And he knows I'd have told him if we were married."

82

It was nearly eleven by the time Miles took that curious stick which had once attracted Jim Bowlby's attention and sauntered out into the long corridor towards the elevator. In the lobby he heard a man inquiring for "Señora Aramayo, please. I have an appointment with her"; and, appraising him with a quick glance, saw that he was tall, youngish, faintly olive of complexion, somehow familiar, and inordinately well dressed.

For the very first time in his whole life he experienced a twinge of that suspicion which is the forerunner of jealousy. "Crazy of me", he thought. But then nearly all his feelings during these last months had been rather crazy. That was the real trouble about falling in love.

He put on his soft hat, lit a cigarette and strolled out into Fifty-seventh Street. A long walk would do him good. He had been living too high; needed more hard exercise. Dash it all, even his feet were going soft on him. Sooner or later this craziness would have to stop.

The thought quickened his stride. As he swung across Madison and into Park Avenue his mind ranged away from Halcyon, and from this city whose only values seemed to be money values. "Not my life", he caught himself thinking. Yet what would his life be without Halcyon? Next year he'd be thirty. Quite an age!

Nearing Grand Central Station, with the traffic lights against him, he stopped for another cigarette. An empty cab drew to the kerb. The driver looked at him, looked at him again and ejaculated, "Say, have I got the heeby-jeebies or are you another guy's double?"

"Not unless you're Jake Folinshaw's double", laughed Miles. Jake, keen-eyed still, but grown a little flabbier with good living than one's last recollection of him, leaned out of the window and wrung Miles warmly by the hand.

"Jump in and let's go some place where we can talk", he said; and, with the lights changing, "First thing I recognised was that sword cane of yours. Have you still got that Heinie tommy gun? Me—I haven't toted a gun in years. I quit when you did. This is my own machine, so don't you worry about no fare. I've got me a wife, too. We live over to Brooklyn. You must come see us some night. Only don't you tell Sadie I was ever in the booze racket, 'cause that's one of the things about me she's not wise to."

Ten minutes, with Jake talking through the partition all the time, brought them down the slope past the station, out of Park and into Fourth Avenue. Off Twenty-fifth Street, they turned left and stopped at a parking place.

"Seen the boss lately?" asked Jake, taking Miles by the arm and steering him towards a narrow doorway.

"Yes. I saw him about six weeks ago. He's living in Trinidad."

"Swell guy to work for. Here we are."

They passed along a narrow passage. Jake pressed a buzzer in what appeared to be a wooden partition. A peephole shutter clicked, an eye inspected them, and half the partition slid back, disclosing another doorway, through which they came, over a sanded floor, to the bar of the speakeasy.

"They don't skin you here like they do some places", said Jake.

He addressed the barman by name, shook hands with him, ordered a couple of beers—and proved even more inquisitive than in those days, seven years ago now, when Geoffrey used to say, "Folinshaw'll ferret that out for us. He's a perfect wizard at getting information". His eyes opened their widest when he heard where Miles was staying.

"I guess that sets you back good and plenty", he remarked. "My Sadie, she don't hold with throwing money around ; and she don't hold with me playing the markets either. So I keep that under my hat, same as I do me having been in the booze racket."

Then he began to talk, as most New Yorkers down to the coloured men who blacked one's shoes seemed to be talking, about stocks and shares.

Presently Miles ordered two more beers. "I'll have to be on my way pretty soon", he said, glancing at his old wristwatch.

"You got a lunch date ?"

"Yes."

"Where ?"

Told the name of Martin's hotel, Jake said, "I'll drive you there. 'Twon't take more than a few minutes. Meeting you's made me feel kinda . . . kinda homesick. I get that way now and again. Owning one's own machine, and having a wife like Sadie, and playing the markets, and going to ball games or the movies,—you'd say that's a swell life for any guy. And mostly it is. Only—sometimes it's a bit . . . a bit tame, see".

"Yes, I see."

And, "His Sadie or my Halcyon", thought Miles. "It boils down to the same thing. Once a man's got a woman permanently tagged on to him, he's stuck."

Before they left, Jake took a piece of paper and a stub of pencil from one of his capacious pockets ; slowly wrote down his address and phone number ; handed over the paper, and said, "Gimme me a ring any time. If I'm not home, just leave a message with Sadie".

"I'll do that", promised Miles.

IV

A few minutes—Jake drove his taxi as he had once driven Geoffrey's speedboats—brought him and Miles to the intersection of Broadway and Fourth Avenue, and through Union Square to Halliburton's hotel.

"Like hell you'll pay anything", laughed Jake. "Don't forget to ring me" ; and he waved as he cruised off.

Entering the hotel, Miles found himself in a modest lobby. Almost immediately Martin materialised through a glass door, saying, "This is great. Come along and meet Mary. Or would you rather wash first ?"

Miles elected to wash. The meeting with Jake had made him, also, feel "kinda homesick". This meeting set up a different reaction. It was making him feel most absurdly young.

Martin really did look like a colonel nowadays—and a retired colonel at that. The hair and moustache one remembered almost as dark as one's own were nearer white than gray. There seemed to be no colour in that saturnine face. The black eyes under those enormous eyebrows had lost most of their fierceness. Only the figure, slim and upright as ever, remained the same.

"You haven't changed much", said Martin, as though reading his thoughts. "Let's see, what age are you ? Just about thirty, isn't it ? My Mary's twenty-eight."

They returned upstairs, to a room papered with a flower pattern and furnished in dark mahogany. Lace curtains covered the three windows. An old-fashioned coal fire burned in the open grate. Martin's wife rose from a sofa in the far corner and came across the faded carpet to shake hands.

Her eyes were the same hazel as Rosaleen's. She was the same height and had much the same way of speaking, an almost identical smile. But there the resemblance ended—Martin's Mary being definitely plain.

As they went to a lunch of chicken okra, pot roast, the inevitable salad and the equally inevitable ice cream, in a long room which held only half a dozen other guests, Miles could not help comparing her with Halcyon. He wondered how Martin could be so much in love—as he must be from the way he looked at her and patted her arm whenever the occasion offered— while they told him of their wedding, of their journey from Hong Kong ("I said to Martin, 'I simply must see Japan, and Honolulu'"), of their three days in San Francisco ("Luckily we're both used to fogs. One gets plenty on the Peak") and their trip to Yosemite.

The meal over, she said, "I'm sure you two are just dying for a chat, so I think I'll go out and do some shopping. Can I have some money, please, dear ?"

"Take what you want", smiled Martin, handing over his notecase.

Mary counted herself out twenty dollars ; handed back the notecase, and left them. "That's the way it ought to be", thought Miles.

He and Martin adjourned to a smoking room, where another coal fire was burning, and seated themselves in leather armchairs.

"A chap we met in Yosemite recommended us to this place", said Martin, filling himself a pipe. "They only charge us four dollars a day each with our food ; and, of course, we've got our own bathroom. You pay rather more, I expect."

"Slightly."

Miles laughed ; but the laugh—it seemed to Halliburton—was rather selfconscious. Further, it seemed to him that the kid, though he looked fit enough, had been going the pace.

"Pity", thought Halliburton. "None of my business, though" ; and— deciding that his warning to Mary, "I shouldn't say anything about that woman he was with if he doesn't", had been apt—asked the general question :

"And what have you been doing with yourself all these years ?"

"Oh, just messing about."

"In the States ?"

"No. Mostly in South America."

"What part ?"

"All over the shop. Paraguay. The Argentine. Ecuador. Colombia. You remember Dominic Mahoney, of course ?"

"That mad Irishman", said Halliburton. "Rather."

"He and I were together in Colombia. We went treasure hunting."

"Did you find anything ?"

"Three brass idols and about three million mosquitos." And Miles, anxious to turn the conversation, went on, "I was staying with Geoffrey not long ago. Do you ever run into any of the old crowd ?"

"No. But I had a letter from your pal, Jim Bowlby, just before I got married."

"Really. What did he have to say for himself?"

"Among other things, he wanted to know if I could find him a job. It was rather cheek, I thought."

"You never cared for Jim, did you?"

"No. I always felt he'd come to a foggy finish."

Martin Halliburton fell silent for a while, puffing at his pipe. "Tell me some more about Geoffrey", he continued. "Is he as fat as ever?"

"Fatter." And again Miles turned the conversation, asking, "Have you been in the East ever since you left Ireland?"

"Yes. This is my first trip home; and, if I hadn't got such a cushy job, I wouldn't go back."

"What is your job?"

"I'm with Carradine's. We're general merchants, and we do a bit of banking. We run a few ships too."

"Sounds all right."

"That shows how much you know about what's going on in the Far East", growled Halliburton; and, suddenly animated, he burst out:

"When I went to China as a lad, one was jolly proud to be an Englishman. Nowadays one's damn well ashamed of it. Talk about losing face. Since nineteen-eighteen we've lost so much face that all the Chinese can see of us are our back collar studs. And the Japs can't even see that. Do you realise what happened in Hankow in twenty-seven?"

"I seem to have read something about our giving up our concession."

"Giving it up." All the old fierceness blazed from Halliburton's eyes. "We were bloody well pansied out of it. And by our own fool Foreign Office. Our chaps weren't even allowed to put up a fight. They just had to stand to attention and be spat at. A lot of good that did our prestige! And ever since then things have gone from bad to worse. Even now, we could put 'em right by backing Chiang Kai-shek."

"Who's he?"

"Who's Chiang Kai-shek?" Halliburton laughed bitterly. "He only happens to be the President of the Republic, and the one man in all China who can save it from the Japs. I know the Japs; and what they're after is sticking out a foot. They think they've got a divine mission to boss the whole of the Far East. That's why they've been behind the Chinese revolution ever since it started. Now that Chiang Kai-shek's trying to unify the country, they'll do their very damnedest to stop him. And, by God, they'll succeed or come precious near it—if they don't pinch Manchuria within the next couple of years I'm a Hottentot—unless England and America pull their socks up. But will they? Of course they won't. It makes me sick, I tell you. You come out and see for yourself if you don't believe me."

But with that Martin Halliburton again fell silent, realising how little Miles Radcliffe, like nearly everyone to whom he had opened his heart since leaving China, cared.

v

Somehow or other Miles's hour alone with Martin had proved rather depressing. "I suppose I ought to be more patriotic", he thought; and from that he fell to remembering his last day at Torrington, his sudden decision, "I'm fed up with being at school. I think I'll run away and enlist".

86

Why had he enlisted? Not entirely for the fun of the thing. And it wasn't entirely for fun that he'd joined the Auxiliaries. He'd felt differently about patriotism then.

The mood passed. Again, he began to think about money. How much had he still got in the bank?

Acting on impulse, he decided to find out; and set off, walking his fastest, down Broadway. Soon there were no more street numbers, only names—Walker, Leonard, Worth, Chambers. Presently he was passing City Hall.

He had never been so far downtown before—all his business with the American bank to which, acting on Dominic's advice, he had transferred his investments when the dollar reached parity, being transacted by correspondence.

The lack of sunlight, the height of the buildings, the crowds along the sidewalks, seemed to stifle him. Queerly, he remembered himself in an English railway carriage, edged between two men with umbrellas reading their newspapers; and the words "Plinley Greenery" formulated themselves to his mind.

"Cities to sweat in, suburbs to go home to", he caught himself thinking. "I'd rather be a farmer." Yet what life could be duller than a farmer's? Who wanted to stay in one place all the time anyway?

A show of baggage in a store window attracted him. He stopped to stare; stopped again before a shipping office whose window displayed posters of the East; made to enter the shipping office; changed his mind, and swung on again till he came to a church.

There he stopped once more, to ask a middle-aged man passer-by, "Excuse me, sir, can you tell me which is Wall Street?"

His man grinned, "Sure I can, son"; and jerked his thumb across the street. The lights changed, and a crowd swarmed over as he spoke.

The narrow granite cleft of Wall Street seemed even more stifling—and even more dwarfing—than Broadway. Yet somehow it impressed one's imagination. Here men thought in, dealt in, millions. Here, for the first time in one's life, one felt positively a pauper. It was almost a surprise that one should encounter so much politeness, when, jerked to the eighteenth floor of this marble-panelled skyscraper, one was conducted through an open office where many clerks were working to a mahogany desk from which a fattish man in hornrimmed glasses rose, saying, "Captain Radcliffe, my name's John Parker, and I'm sure glad to meet you".

"Glad to meet you, Mr. Parker", said Miles. "I just came in to see how my account stands."

Mr. Parker, having offered him a chair, pressed a key and called an order into the house telephone. Three minutes later an extremely attractive young woman, carrying a letter file and two large yellow sheets, emerged from behind a mahogany screen. She gazed at Miles with considerable interest, thinking, "Gee, he's handsome", before she disappeared.

"Including day to day interest and this month's dividends", said Mr. Parker, "your balance last night was fifteen hundred and sixty-two dollars and thirty-seven cents."

He passed the yellow sheets across the desk; and, having looked through the file, continued, "You're what I call a really cautious investor, captain".

"Does that mean you think I'm too cautious?"

Mr. Parker seemed to hesitate. "Well, it's better than being the other way", he said finally ; and, after a little more conversation, Miles took his leave.

It was raining when he emerged into Wall Street. He made for a cafeteria, and ordered himself some coffee. "That chap thought me a bit of a mug", he decided. "But I'm dashed if I see the sense of risking my little bit of capital. If I lost that, I should be a real pauper." Then, just for a moment, his thoughts turned to Fluke.

Curious, the difference between himself and his half brother. Fluke had never minded risking money. But one just couldn't imagine him risking his precious skin.

Miles paid for his coffee, finished his cigarette, and made a dive for the subway, already crowding though the rush hour had not begun. Here again he was reminded of the men with the umbrellas and the newspapers.

"New York or London", he thought. "Paris or Buenos Aires. Life's pretty much the same in all of 'em. And it seems to suit most people. But, by jove, it doesn't suit me."

Uptown, rain had ceased. Once more in open air, he breathed freely, lingering by the windows of two more baggage stores before he entered the hotel. With his key the clerk handed him an envelope postmarked, "Trinidad". The letter was from Geoffrey Thirkell. He read it before entering the elevator. The last paragraph ran : "*Regards to madam. It wouldn't surprise me if you and she were married by the time this reaches you. I'm meditating a little trip to Italy. You remember my telling you what a lot of money there was in . . . macaroni*".

Miles remembered that conversation perfectly ; and his eyes glinted, his nostrils flared a little, as he unlocked the door of his bedroom.

From the sitting room came the sound of voices. He put his hat and swordstick away in the closet ; hesitated a moment, and walked in.

There were three men with Halcyon, at her ease on the sofa between the two windows across which curtains had not yet been drawn.

She greeted him in English. Her three visitors rose. One of them, whom Miles recognised for the tall youngish man with the faintly olive complexion he had seen in the lobby that morning, she presented as, "My brother-in-law, Francisco Aramayo". The other two—Mr. Dutton and Mr. Thorogood—were obviously Americans.

Miles said, "I hope I'm not butting in".

Halcyon smiled, "Oh, no. We're pretty well through. That's so, isn't it, Mr. Dutton ?"

Dutton, well past middle age, with a mane of silvery hair, dryshaved a heavy pink jowl with a fat white hand before answering, "If Mr. Aramayo is agreeable, I am". Halcyon turned to her brother-in-law, saying in Spanish, "Don't be a mule, Francisco. You can argue from now till Christmas, but you won't get me to abate a *centavo*".

"A million dollars", grumbled Francisco Aramayo. "A million *duros americanos*. Between one member of a family and another, too."

But a few moments later he was kissing her hand, while Dutton snapped, "The legal end of the deal is up to you, Mr. Thorogood. Take care of it rightaway, please".

The young lawyer, who might have posed for a collar advertisement, snapped back, "I'll have the contract ready by five o'clock tomorrow after-

88

noon, Mr. Dutton. Presumably it'll have to be stamped at the Bolivian consulate".

"And don't forget", interposed Halcyon, "that my dear brother-in-law has to pay all the expenses."

"It is very sad", smiled Aramayo, "that one who is so beautiful should be so grasping"; and he kissed her hand again before the three took their leave.

VI

As the door of the sitting room closed, Halcyon sprang from the sofa.

"Victory", she cried. "Victory over that *maldicho boliviano*, my brother-in-law, whom I detest even more than he detests me. Kiss me, my dear one. Kiss me your hardest."

At the touch of her lips, all those yearnings for escape which had fretted Miles throughout the day vanished. One arm round her pliant waist, he drew her towards the window. His mood—both their moods—matched the magic of the twilight, which was just falling over New York. Night came, floodlights silvered domes and belfries and the recessed pinnacles of the skyscrapers, while she told him of her day's doings. Presently she talked, for the first time frankly, of her dead husband, whose share in the tin mine she had just sold.

"Severo was not like Francisco", she said. "He did not belong to the militarist party. He believed in peace between our two countries. That made us sympathetic. Then we fell in love. Yet when he died, I could not weep for him. I used to wonder why that should be. But now I know. It is because my way of love is more a man's way than a woman's. And, sooner or later, a man's love burns out. There are only two loves that never burn out—the love of the parent for the child and the love of a patriot for his country."

And, during the days which followed, she talked much of her own country, and of that war—history, these sixty years—when Paraguay fought on against the massed armies of the Brazilian Empire, and Ecuador and the Argentine Republic, until, in all her borders, there were no males left except her dotards and boys too young to sire a child.

Miles, increasingly restless, was apt to be a little bored by such talk. But on the day her money was paid over to her she asked, "Tell me, how does one buy rifles, and how many can one buy for a million dollars?" and all sense of boredom left him.

"I'll soon find that out," he answered, his nostrils flaring a little.

For here, it seemed, might be a gun-running adventure after his own heart; and that very afternoon he wrote a careful letter to Geoffrey Thirkell, which began: "*Thanks for yours about the macaroni. I believe I've found a customer for you*".

It was just as he sealed his letter—thinking, "But there won't be any money in it for me, and I can't stand much more than another month living at this rate",—that he heard the telephone bell ring, and Halcyon asking in Guaraní, of which she had been teaching him a little more every day:

"Are you sure? Are you quite sure?"

Then, twice, she used the word *Angabey*, which means "Danger"; and he ran into the sitting room.

She had already recradled the instrument; but her hand still grasped the vulcanite; and he saw that she was frowning.

"*Que hay?*" he asked. "What's the matter?"

"*Nada*. Nothing. Leave me alone. I must think. I must think very carefully."

Miles lit a cigarette and sat down at the far end of the room.

Suddenly the frown cleared from Halcyon's face; and she came towards him; bent over him; put her hands on his shoulders.

He was conscious of decision in her, and of a new imperiousness, and of a force against which every instinct told him that he must battle.

"Do you remember my telling you", she asked, "that if only you would be a little patient I would teach you how to make plenty of money?"

"Yes. I remember."

"Well, the moment is here. It only needs a little courage. Listen."

But, as he listened to her, Miles's courage failed him for the first time; and, when she had done, he said slowly:

"You're asking me to risk every penny I've got in the world. I could'nt do it. I couldn't do it even for you, Halcyon".

"Risk half then."

"No."

"Coward."

"You can call me a coward if you like. But I won't do it."

"Well—put up five thousand dollars?"

"No."

"Even if I loan you the money?"

"No."

He threw her hands from his shoulders, and sprang up. Their eyes clashed, blue-black against elephant-gray. For the very first time in all his life, temper mastered Miles Radcliffe.

"I don't take loans from women", he shouted. "You're welcome to any cash I've got. But I won't gamble a penny more. Not one single penny."

"And how much cash have you got?" asked Halcyon, smiling.

"*Mas ó menos*, a thousand dollars."

"*Pobrecito*. My poor little man." She was still smiling. "And that is all you will risk for me?"

"If you insist. But I warn you. Once that's lost——"

"It will not be lost. It will be doubled, trebled, quadrupled."

Still furious, Miles thought, "She's crazy. But I'm crazier. My grief, why did I ever fall in love with her? I could go all round the world for a thousand dollars".

But Halcyon was once more at the phone.

"That is perfectly correct", she said in her meticulous English. "I wish to sell, not to buy. Tell me how much cover you will require. Two hundred and fifty thousand dollars? Very good. You shall have them tomorrow morning. If you want more, you have only to ask me."

Miles's temper was under control again. How infernally certain she seemed.

Maybe he ought to warn Jake.

BOOK FIVE

I

IT HAD ALL HAPPENED MONTHS AGO. THEY WERE IN ITALY NOW. TOMORROW Geoffrey Thirkell should be back from La Spezia. But how often—thought Miles Radcliffe—one relived those last days of October in New York.

Mad days they seemed—as one lay, drowsy after luncheon, in this high room through whose windows poured the spring sunshine of Liguria —days, and nights, which had shaken one's nerve as it had never been shaken by battle, though all one stood to lose was a paltry thousand dollars.

A coward, Halcyon had called one. And how rightly. Why—even Jake Folinshaw had lost more than that, and written off his loss without batting an eyelid.

"Guess I ought to have listened to you", Miles remembered Jake laughing from his driving seat as they sped downtown. "Those bozos on Wall Street sure have given me the works. Scalped, that's what I am. I can take it, though, as long as my Sadie don't get wise."

But the average New Yorker—the men and women to whose talk one had listened, whose faces one had seen in the hotels, in the stores, in the speak-easies or on the sidewalks—hadn't been like Jake.

Scraps of conversation came back to him.

"Market's going to break." "The ticker's an hour behind already." "My broker's just been on the phone. He wants more cover." "D'you know what Steel is? D'you know what Montgomery Ward is? I tell you what this is going to be—it's going to be a panic."

Panic. With all the newspaper headlines screaming, "Break in the Stock Market". And all the radios blaring, "Slump on the Stock Market". And everywhere one went, those chalk-white cheeks, those shaking hands, those trembling lips, those eyes that stared as though, as though . . .

"As though they were facing a firing squad", thought Miles.

He took a cigarette from the pack on the side table by his rockingchair.

"Scared stiff", he thought next. "So was I. But Halcyon never turned a hair, even before the crash, when they asked her to put up another quarter of a million dollars." And her, too, he could remember laughing, as she recradled the telephone and fingered the orchids at her shoulder, "*Que hay? Nada.* Nothing. The shares we have sold short closed a little higher, so the brokers are nervous. That is all. Do not worry about it, *querido.* Let us go dancing. *Mañana ó pasado mañana* we shall be able to buy back the shares very cheaply—and you will make four or five thousand dollars".

Five thousand dollars. A thousand pounds. He'd made quite that. And, dash it all, he could have made twenty-five thousand without risking a penny. Why hadn't he accepted Halcyon's offer of a loan? Because he was too proud; or because, if they'd lost, he'd have felt obliged to pay her back?

"A bit of both", he decided. "Besides, I wasn't only scared of losing my thousand. I was scared because if I'd lost my dollars it would have meant losing her too."

Yet his scare had gone deeper than that. Even after the market broke, even after they'd bought back their shares and banked their money, he'd still felt jittery—he, who'd never known what it meant to have the wind up before.

"Guess it must have been in the atmosphere", he brooded. Then, once again, he remembered himself speeding downtown in Jake's cab.

"Lost one of my best customers last night", Jake was saying. "It's all in the paper. As nice a guy as ever I drove. Cleaning his gun, it says. But I reckon he must have shot himself for his insurance money. And not the only one either. To hell with Wall Street."

And after Jake pocketed his three dollars, grinning, "Thanks a lot. Sorry I can't give you no more free rides, gasolene costs dough", Miles had stood for a while, deep in peculiar meditation, just outside the doorway of that huge building which housed his bank.

"Suicide", he remembered himself meditating. "Can't see myself doing that even if I did lose all my money. Life's too much worth living."

It was in that moment he had heard the screams.

The incoherent screams tore through the traffic noises and the clip-clop of shoes on the sidewalk, like the screams of a mechanical saw through the quiet of a forest. Jerking his head round, he saw that they emanated from a woman close beside him; and that the woman was pointing, with rigid fingers, on one of which a diamond glittered, to a window more than two hundred feet above them on the other side of the street.

The tiny figure of a man had climbed through that window; stood poised there—just as though it were a diver's. And in that split second the screams had become incoherent words, "Harry! Don't! For Christ's sake. You promised. You promised me".

And now, in his recollection, his hands were on the woman; and he was pulling at her; and the figure slipped, plummeted, arms out, head down, straight at them, growing larger, larger . . .

He heard other people screaming, and a rush of air, and a thudding crash, and what might have been the detonation of a shell bursting in soft ground, as he dragged the woman into the shelter of a doorway; as blood and brains spattered them and she went limp in his arms.

The picture which Miles Radcliffe's mind had been making faded out in a rush of faces milling all about him, to the sound of indrawn breaths, to the click of a press photographer's shutter and the glare of his flash bulb, to the bellowing Irish voice of a traffic cop, and the shrilling gong of an ambulance.

He took another drag at his cigarette; blew the smoke through his nostrils. In the next room Halcyon was just astir. He heard her yawn, heard the creak of the bedsprings, the tip-tap of her mules on the parquet, water running.

She had been running water on her hands when he came back from Wall Street.

"These *gringos* are all alike", he remembered her saying. "They drive themselves to death for money. But they only want money for their women."

It was that saying—of course—which had really given him the jitters. It still seemed infernally true.

As long as he hadn't got a woman tagged on to him, no man in good health—and certainly no man with a bit of capital—need ever worry his head

92

about money. But once he fell in love—especially if he married and had children—either the woman demanded money of him, or his own pride demanded that she must be as well dressed, must have as good a home, as good a time, as fine an automobile, as the other fellow's. And even if his wife had money of her own, no man worth his salt would take any from her.

So wasn't one better off without a wife?

Obviously.

But on that, Halcyon called "Meelés. Meelés. I am awake. Did you remember to order the *coche*?"

And as he called back, "*Como no, cara*", thought vanished from his conscious mind.

II

"*Che bellina*", mused the hall porter, as Miles handed Halcyon into the waiting carriage ; and, being a Neapolitan, his musing did not stop there.

The horses trotted off between brown cliffs, which had been blasted to make a roadway, and a turquoise sea. Miles lit another cigarette. Watching him sideways from under the lace brim of a hat she had bought herself in Milan, Halcyon wondered, "Is he a little tired of me? Shall I let him go?"

The roadway twisted, opened—showing her the sea scarcely afoam where it met the rocks, pine trees, and the red roof of a villa above a wall of masonry yellow with mimosa bloom.

Automatically she said, "Look. *Que lindo*" ; and laid a hand on her lover's knee. The coachman turned, and, pointing with his whip, told them, "That villa belongs to an English *signora*. The gardens are very beautiful". Miles asked him, "How does the Englishwoman call herself?" And they chatted for a moment or so.

Still speaking automatically, Halcyon said, "How clever you are at languages. You have learned to talk Italian in less than a month".

Her flattery seemed to please. There was really no reason to let him go. His passion for her had not yet burned itself out. Maybe it never would.

"But mine?" she asked herself. "Sometimes he is still *crudo*. And always he is a little stubborn. I can never make him believe the Bolivians will attack us. He is like all *gringos*. He has no imagination."

Aloud she said, "I am not happy about Don Geoffrey. I believe he is going to fail us".

"Geoffrey doesn't usually fail."

"If there are no rifles for sale, how can he buy any?"

She relapsed into silence. The horses jogged on—downhill at a slow trot—till they reached a fishing village, where a barefooted boy in ragged shorts pointed and called, "*Rubia!*"

"They seem to like your hair in this part of the world", laughed Miles.

Beyond the village they circled a little bay.

"Much fish here", volunteered the coachman, turning again. "My father is a fisherman. He is *molto vecchio*, over ninety. He can remember Garibaldi. He says Garibaldi was a greater man than Mussolini."

"Do you agree with him?" asked Miles.

The coachman's face might have been a Chinaman's, as he answered,

93

"Once upon a time I was very interested in politics. But nowadays it is better that poor people like myself do not meddle with them. See—*soldati*".

He pulled to the side of the road. A company of foot swung into view.

"*Bersaglieri*", he went on. "I have a son in the *Bersaglieri*. He is a corporal."

The plumed files came abreast of the carriage.

The officer at the head of the company turned his head to appraise Halcyon. Most of the men did the same. The officer who brought up the rear smiled at her. She smiled back and he saluted.

"A real soldier", she said with a touch of contempt in her voice, "would not have done that."

The coachman drove on. Soon they were in a little town of shops and boarding houses and seaside hotels. Here, too, all the males stared at Halcyon; and another ragged boy called, "*Americana!*"

She took a lira from her bag and flung it at him. He caught it and flung her back a kiss. A man in a black shirt with a pistol at his belt signalled the coachman to stop; cuffed the ragamuffin on the head; took the lira; approached the carriage, and handed her back the coin, saying, "The *signora* will pardon me, but in Fascist Italy it is strictly forbidden to beg".

"He was not begging", retorted Halcyon in Italian.

"If he did not beg, he accosted you. In Fascist Italy it is forbidden to accost a lady. The *signore* and the *signora* will please favour me with their passports."

"Passports? Why?"

"Because I demand them."

Halcyon's temper was quick. Miles had seen her lose it before—with a customs official in Trinidad, with a carabineer at Genoa.

"Our passports are at the hotel", he interposed.

"The name of the hotel, please. And your own names."

Given the required information, the blackshirt wrote it down, touched his silver-tasselled cap, and said, "*Grazie*, *signore capitano*. You may proceed".

As they trotted away from the little town, the coachman turned to remark, "You were fortunate. He was of the militia, that one. He might easily have detained you". Halcyon whispered in Guaraní, "If he had, it would only have been for one purpose. Did you observe his eyes? They made me feel naked. What is the matter with the men in this country? They all seem to be starving. I am beginning to feel quite sorry for them".

Miles said, "As long as you are not too sorry for them"; and smiled at her. Smiling back, she thought, "That was not at all *crudo*. He is very handsome. I do not think I shall let him go".

Presently they came to that place where many lovers have dreamed—a square of cobbles in the centre of which plays a fountain, bounded on one side by a tiny harbour and on another by a church which was three centuries old before the young Michelangelo hewed his first block of Carrara marble. Above them towered a gray cliff with a castle at the summit.

"*Il castello*", said their coachman, "belongs to an Englishman who is *molto ricco*." And he drew rein at an inn whose proprietress gave him a few *soldi* for every foreigner he brought to the tables under her vine.

The woman came bustling out as they alighted. Miles ordered coffee and "*biscochos*".

"*Biscotti* in Italian", corrected Halcyon. "This place is *muy lindo*. We might stay for supper."

While they were drinking their coffee and eating their biscuits, two fishing boats, one with a red sail and one with a yellow, glided towards the harbour. Afterwards they went arm in arm across the cobbles to inspect the catch; and Miles practised his Italian again, finding the dialect spoken by the fishermen a little difficult.

The sun was still well above horizon when, leaving the harbour, they strolled towards the steps of the church.

"In the old days", said Halcyon, "there would have been beggars. Italy was more picturesque then. And people laughed more."

She mounted the steps and pushed her way through the leather screen. Hat in hand, Miles followed.

The church was very small, and—to his idea—rather tawdry. Halcyon genuflected, made the sign of the cross, and moved towards a little shrine where candles burned. There, she knelt.

III

Whenever they entered a church or a cathedral—and they had entered quite a number since their arrival at Genoa—Halcyon prayed. This always made Miles feel rather uncomfortable. Because after all he and she, religiously speaking, were "living in sin".

"Don't see how she can", he thought. "Unless Romans feel differently about it."

And suddenly, since the word "Romans" for "Roman Catholics" had been his father's, his mind conceived a picture of his father, warming his clerical coat tails at the fire as he said, "There are one or two things I want to talk to you about before you go to Torrington, my boy. You're rather young to have to know them, but if I don't tell you, the other boys will".

And after that talk (queer, how faraway it seemed) his father had spoken about his mother, saying: "You've always thought she died when you were born. Well, she didn't—at least not physically. She only died spiritually. Your mother was one of those women I've been warning you to avoid, Miles. She sinned against me, and against you. God knows I've tried to forgive her often enough . . ."

"But he never succeeded", thought Miles.

Halcyon rose; smiled at him, and called his attention to the picture which hangs over the altar.

An acolyte, who had been cleaning the candlestick of a nearby shrine, piped up, "The *signora* is quite right. The picture is by Fra Lippo Lippi. It is our great treasure".

As they recrossed the square, she pointed to some words roughly tarred round the base of the fountain, "Up with Fascism. Let the priests keep to their churches", saying:

"One day the good God will make them pay for such blasphemy. The old Italy was better than this. It was the natural Italy—the Italy of our *vetturino* and of those fishermen and of that boy who is singing a love song to his guitar".

The boy stood at the door of the inn. He ceased playing and took off his cap as they approached. Halcyon gave him five lira.

"Your friend the militiaman will be after you", Miles chaffed her.

"He can go pleasure himself", smiled Halcyon; and to the boy, "Do you know a song which goes like this?"

She hummed a tune. The boy shook his head. She stamped her foot at him, crying, "Give me your instrument"; and began to strum on it, began to sing that song which begins:

> "*La luna nuova su su quel mare*
> *Stende la faccia d'argento fino*".

Her contralto rang true in the twilight. A little crowd began to gather. Presently, as her voice rose on the lines, "The white prow might be an altar rising, O'er the little waves where the love stars glitter", Miles was aware of two men coming to a halt near them.

Then the song ceased; one of the men touched him on the shoulder, saying with a strong Scottish accent, "It's a lang way from Castle Kilranan to Castello Gandolfo. What might you be doing in this part of the world?" and he found himself looking down at the wizened face, into the snakelike eyes, of Ronald Wallace, who seemed smaller than ever in contrast to his companion—a perfect tower of a man, his complexion the colour of mahogany, with a bristling black beard.

"This is my friend Ras Imajum", went on Ronnie.

The Abyssinian, who wore European clothes, said in English, "Any friend of Major Wallace is my own"; and offered a muscular hand.

When Halcyon had given his guitar back to the boy, Miles presented them.

"A wee drink", said Ronnie. "For auld lang syne."

He shrugged a knapsack from his shoulders, signalled to the proprietress, and ordered a bottle of Chianti. The Ras said to Halcyon, "You sing very beautifully. I had great pleasure in listening to you. You are not an English-woman, I feel".

"No. I am a Paraguayan."

"Forgive my ignorance. But all I know about Paraguay is that it is somewhere in South America."

"Forgive mine. Is 'Ras' a christian name?"

"No. It is a title."

They seemed to take to each other at once. When the wine had been poured, the Ras toasted, "*Viva Paraguay*" and Halcyon toasted back, "*Viva Ethiopia*". Miles asked Ronnie, "Are you two on a walking tour?" Ronnie answered, "No. We're staying here. We just happen to have been for a walk".

Since their time in Ireland, he had shaved off his moustache. His skin, nowadays, looked rather like the stitched leather of a Mexican saddle. Miles sensed that he would rather not be asked what he and his strange companion were doing in Italy. Halcyon intervened, "I think we will sup here"; and went off to wash. Ras Imajum said, "That is a very intelligent lady. Are all Paraguayan ladies so beautiful?"

"Hardly", answered Miles.

They refilled their glasses.

"When I left the Auxiliaries", volunteered Ronnie, "I went back to Somaliland. But there was no enough money in my job. And no enough excitement either. So I thocht I'd become a hunter and trader; and I began my trading with Abyssinia. Now I have a farm near Harrar. You should come out one of these days. I could show you some grand sport—lion-spearing."

"Good lord, you don't mean to say you spear them?"

"Aye, but we do. On foot."

"He saved my life from one", interrupted the Ras. "That was why I gave him the farm."

Ronnie talked on; until, listening to him, Miles experienced a touch of jealousy. These last months his own life had been tame almost to boredom. So far Geoffrey hadn't succeeded in buying a single rifle. And even if he did, one wouldn't have the sport of running them. According to present plans, they'd just be a gift from Halcyon to her government.

She returned while Ronnie was telling another lion story. A waitress laid a tablecloth. The electric light had been turned on—here under the vines, there by the fountain and the church and along the harbour. A nice place. For tourists. But not for him. He needed to be somewhere freer, wilder. He needed more risk, more excitement. This war Halcyon was always talking about might be just his cup of tea. But of course it wouldn't happen. She'd just got a bee in her bonnet.

What could a woman know about war?

IV

Throughout supper Halcyon's conversation had been inconsequent; Ronnie's dour; and the Ras's informative—but only up to a point. The Abyssinian was in Italy "on my Emperor's business". Ronnie appeared to be acting as his adviser.

Asked if they were making a long stay at Castello Gandolfo, Ronnie answered, "I dinna fancy so. We're due back in Rome shortly". Invited over to meet Geoffrey, he said, "Aye. I'd like that weel, if it can be managed", and went on, "What is he doing here?"

"Oh, he's got some sort of deal on", hedged Miles.

Ras Imajum, who appeared to be enjoying one of those virulent weeds known as *toscani*, sucked the straw mouthpiece reflectively, and pronounced, "It is not easy to do deals with the Italians". Ronnie said, "They're better than the French anyway". And talk veered to international politics. Bored, Miles called for his bill.

This meeting with Ronald Wallace, like his meeting with Martin Halliburton, hadn't really been enjoyable. Comrades in Ireland, they now seemed little more than acquaintances. All the same, it might be rather fun to accept that invitation, renewed at parting, "Dinna forget there's a warm welcome for ye at the farm if ever ye drift oot oor way".

But how could one—with Halcyon on one's hands?

The moon rose as their *vetturino* cracked his whip and they were trotted away over the cobbles. Halcyon, who had drunk a little more wine than usual, edged closer. Miles laid an arm along the top of the seat and she rested against it. Presently she took off her hat and dropped her head on to his shoulder, sighing, "I wish it were not such a long way back. I want to be made love to now. Let us stop the carriage and go for a walk. Or perhaps we could find a boat. I should like you to make love to me in an open boat".

"*Tonta!*"

"Yes. Perhaps that is rather silly. Do you still love me, Meelés?"

"You know I do."

"But tonight you would prefer to spear a lion."

Her intuition fretted him. He kept silence. They came to the seaside town, and she sat upright, singing to herself, "*L'onde, le stelle, sfavillan d'amor*".

Once they were beyond the town, her head dropped to his shoulder again, and one of her long hands caressed his cheek. Silver moonlight showed him the swell of her bosom under the thin frock, the curve of a hip. She had crossed her left leg over her right. Her free hand fastened on him.

The headlamps of a passing car flashed in their faces. A momentary revulsion, the first he had ever experienced with her, set him thinking, "We must look a couple of fools". But the touch of her hands, the perfume of her, the whole abandonment of her attitude, were excitements that his body could hardly control.

"*Querida*", he heard himself whisper, "*querida de mi corazon*"; and his heartbeats seemed to choke him as his mouth bent for hers.

At the kiss, a shudder ran clean through her. Released from it, she lay speechless—her lips half open, the pupils of her eyes grown enormous.

"*Esta noche*", she said at last. "*Todas las noches. Dios mio*, if only I could die in your arms."

Shame, and a touch of chivalry, overwhelmed him. He must never give her up.

Yet even so he could not help knowing that he had wanted to give her up —not once, but several times during these last months.

"I'm not myself any more", he caught himself thinking. "And I want to be myself again. Standing on my own feet. Free to come as I like and go as I like. Answerable to nobody for my actions."

More headlamps flashed by. Halcyon sat upright again. She was laughing now, "Meelés, how silly we are. It might be our first night. Do you remember our first night? In Buenos Aires. Do you remember what you said to me—about your dreams?"

"Yes. I remember." He felt the blood flush to his cheeks.

"It was so sweet of you. I like to think that you used to dream of me— before I gave myself to you."

They were through the fishing village, just passing the place where they had encountered the Bersaglieri. His mind showed him a picture of the cocks' plumes on their heads, of the rifles at their shoulders, of their dusty boots. And suddenly he remembered himself on guard, his automatic rifle across his knees, while Jim Bowlby made love to Molly Maguire.

How young he'd been then, and how ignorant—to think it queer because chaps got the wind up, because chaps fell in love.

The coachman, who had not turned his head since they left Castello Gandolfo, pulled his horses to a walk. They climbed away from the sea. Twisting walls of rock closed on them; opened out again as their wheels rolled them past the wall on which mimosa bloomed, into sight of their hotel.

Halcyon smoothed her hair and put on her hat. Miles handed her out; and asked how much they owed.

"I leave it to the *signore*", answered the coachman. "We have been out for seven hours. According to the *tarifa* that should be forty-two lire."

"*Da le ciento*", whispered Halcyon.

Miles passed up the hundred lira bill. The man jabbered gratitude.

"See that your horses have a good meal", Halcyon told him. "They are too thin. If you are not careful, they will have the *mal de caderas*."

"What is that, *signora*?"

"A disease."

"It is not a disease horses have in Italy."

"No? Here, I think, you have only one disease. The black fever."

The coachman glanced at the door, which was still closed. Then, having glanced up and down the road, he grinned, "*La signora ha ragione*. But red fever or black, it is all the same for us poor people"; and drove off.

The white-haired night porter let Miles and Halcyon into a long hall whose tiled floor echoed to their footsteps, handed her some letters, took them up in the lift, wished them "*Buona notte*", and stood watching them till they entered her room.

"I have always had too much imagination", thought that night porter. "Nor, alas, does it diminish with age. How I envy that young man. How I envy all young men." And, having been rather addicted to poetry in his own youth, he remembered those lines about Isaotta of the soft hands which run:

> "To the flower of her youth
> But one thing is meet.
> All else is vain
> Save love all-sweet".

But all the sweetness of love deserted Halcyon while she was reading the first of her letters; and even love itself seemed vain to her as she blazed:

"*Locos*. They are all mad. Why am I not a man? If I were a man I would sail for home tomorrow and take my rifles with me and put these politicians against a wall".

V

Halcyon—her other letters lying forgotten on the bed—raved away for a good ten minutes. Why be a patriot? What was the use of loving one's country? What was the good of offering half one's private fortune to men who were so frightened of provoking the enemy that they would not even accept a gift of arms?

"The cowards", she cried. "They spurn my offer. They will not let me ship one single case of rifles to Asuncion. Read what they say for yourself."

She tossed the typewritten sheets across the bed.

"What are you going to do?" asked Miles.

"What can I do? Without a permit, nothing."

"Couldn't we run the stuff?"

"How? You know Paraguay. There are only two ways in—up the river or by the railway from the Argentine."

She stopped, biting her lips.

"And only this afternoon", she resumed, "I prayed to the Virgin that she would help me in my quest. I should have prayed differently. I should have asked her to let our *politicos* see reason. For now, even if Don Geoffrey succeeds, it will be useless."

And a little later, after she had glanced through her other letters, one of which was from her mother, she said, "I will sleep alone tonight. I am no longer in the mood for love".

VI

Miles shrugged his shoulders and went to his own room. For nearly an hour the tip-tap of Halcyon's mules on the parquet kept him awake. Next morning, when he went in to her, he found her already half dressed.

"I shall go home", she said. "One effects nothing by correspondence. Maybe, if I could see the President, I could persuade him. Only, first, I must be sure that the arms are purchasable. You will come with me, of course."

"Why 'of course'?" thought Miles.

As usual, he ate breakfast alone on the wide terrace which overlooked the sea. Drinking his second cup of coffee, he remembered one of the figures which had haunted his overnight dreams. The figure had worn khaki, but with a chaplain's collar and badges. Presumably it must have been his father's—though he could not recall any face.

Curious, that he should have recollected his father while he watched Halcyon at her prayers. More curious, that—this morning—he could think of her so angrily. How dared she say, "Of course"? He was her lover, not her lackey. No wonder Geoffrey had nicknamed her "*la conquistadora*". Geoffrey wouldn't stand any woman telling him, "I will sleep alone tonight".

"So why should I?" thought Miles.

Seeking distraction, he asked the waiter to bring him the Continental *Daily Mail* and skimmed the headlines. Things at home seemed pretty grim. No protection for industry. Nearly a million and three quarter unemployed. And they'd raised the income tax to four and six in the pound. Lucky one's own money was in America. Safely invested, too. No more gambles for him.

Skimming on, he came to another of those articles about women which seemed such a feature of all home newspapers. This one was captioned, "What Great Statesmen have owed to their Wives". Balderdash, most of it. And who wanted to be a great statesman anyway?

"Not I", he decided; and thought snapped back to Halcyon, who would be expecting him upstairs. Confound the girl, she expected altogether too much of him. He wouldn't go.

She appeared while he was still brooding. They could walk into the town.

She had a little shopping to do. Didn't he need some more shaving soap? And he really ought to buy himself a new hat.

"What's the matter with this one?"

"The colour is fading."

"Very well. If you say so." After all, why argue with her? She always won.

The road to the town led along the sea and over a bridge. They stopped to look at the statue of Christopher Columbus, and again by the war memorial.

"One day", said Halcyon, "this Mussolini will make them another war. *Viva il duce!* Pah. All dictators are alike. They end by wanting to be Napoleons. If once the military junta gets the upper hand in Bolivia——"

"There she goes again", thought Miles.

Walking on, they came to a hairdresser's. While he bought his soap, Halcyon demanded "French perfumes". It took her nearly twenty minutes to make up her mind, "Your prices are too high. I shall wait till I am in Paris". In the window of another store she saw some blond tortoiseshell, and spent twenty more minutes bargaining for a dressing-table set, which she eventually bought. Followed the best part of an hour at a draper's. It was close on midday by then—and Miles's patience nearly exhausted.

"But we haven't yet found you a hat, *caro*."

"My new *sombrero* can wait."

He hailed a carriage, and they were driven back to the hotel. On the terrace they found Geoffrey Thirkell, moonfaced and bulky in silk clothes, a gin and lime at his elbow. He rose heavily, beaming, "Hullo, *conquistadora*", and kissed Halcyon's hand.

"What news?" she asked.

"I'll tell you after lunch."

"Yes. Perhaps that would be better."

She went to wash.

"Drink?" asked Geoffrey; and his eyes—green and deceptively lazy under pale brows and lashes—inspected Miles with all their old shrewdness, as he continued, "Slight rift in the love lute, old boy?"

"Good lord, no. What makes you think that?"

"Dunno. Just an idea of mine. I picked up with quite a nice little piece in La Spezia. Nearly brought her along with me."

"Why didn't you?"

"Because I don't believe in mixing up business and pleasure. By the way, it looks as though we'll have to try some other country for our macaroni."

"You didn't bring it off then?"

"No."

VII

The reappearance of Halcyon prevented Miles from saying more. Lunch over, the three of them adjourned to her room, and Geoffrey told his story. His bloke at La Spezia didn't want to play. As far as he could make out, nobody in Italy wanted to play. They needed all the arms they could manufacture for themselves. And they couldn't import any more from England, because the English had sold them everything they'd got to dispose of.

"And a nice profit the Eyeties must have made passing them on", said Geoffrey. "My bloke let out they were buying our surplus machine guns at ten pounds apiece when they were worth forty, free on board, Genoa. I vote we try Germany next."

"But I thought"—Miles spoke—"that the Boches weren't allowed to make armaments?"

"Lots of things done that aren't allowed", winked Geoffrey. "Shall we take a little trip to Berlin, *conquistadora*?"

"No. It is not worth while. Not for the moment anyway."

She, too, told her story; and dismissed them, saying that she wanted to take a siesta. They returned to the terrace.

"So that's that", said Geoffrey. "Pity. I stood to make a nice bit of bunce out of her order. Still, I've got quite a few other customers. What are you going to do with yourself?"

"She wants me to go back to Paraguay with her."

"Cost you a bit—the way she travels. How's the bank balance?"

"Oh, I've still got a few dollars left. That's not the trouble."

Miles fell silent, fingering his narrow moustache. Geoffrey Thirkell—who knew perfectly well what the trouble must be, and had been anticipating it ever since the three of them left America together—did not question him further. Instead—Miles having already told him of yesterday's meeting—he began to talk of Ronnie Wallace, suggesting, "Let's find out if that inn's on the telephone, and ring him up. I would like to see the old chap again". And, "Talk of the devil", ejaculated Geoffrey a moment later, "here he is".

Ronnie Wallace had motored over alone. Ras Imajum—he explained —would be writing letters the whole afternoon. Geoffrey offered him a drink. He said, "Whiskey wouldna be unacceptable", and perched himself—rather like a vulture, it seemed to Miles—on the marble balustrade of the terrace. In full daylight you saw how the sun had bleached his hair and the mark of the topee on his wrinkled forehead.

"Where's your leddy?" he asked Miles.

"Having her siesta."

"She's a very lovely leddy", said Ronnie; and, biting off the end of a cigar he took from his pocket, lit up.

He and Geoffrey began to gossip over their pegs. For a little, Miles, who had refused a drink, listened in silence. Gradually, however, he found himself being drawn into the conversation. This was the sort of talk he had always enjoyed. Men's talk. Of sport. Of faraway places. Of strange people. Of skirmishes never chronicled in any newspaper.

"Your Abyssinians seem a tough crowd", he said after one of Ronnie's tales.

"I wouldna say that. They're all richt as long as they're treated richt. Give 'em a raw bullock to eat once a week and they'll do anything for ye."

"What language do they speak?"

"Oh, Amharic'll get ye most places, though the Gallas have got their own lingo. Ye ken that the Queen of Sheba was an Abyssinian?"

Talk turned on women.

"I dinna hold wi' white men taking natives to live with them", pronounced Ronnie. "For mysel', I've got a French girl from Jhibuti."

"Geoffrey prefers blonds", laughed Miles; and Geoffrey laughed back at him, "I've had a redhead or two in my time, but they're liable to be too much for a man of my age. Our kid's come on a bit since the old days in Ireland, eh, Ronnie?"

"Aye. But he had the roots o' the matter in him even then. D'you remember the major's wee niece. I wouldna be surprised to lairn he seduced her that night in barracks—and her wi' her hair doon too."

They chaffed on. For a minute or so Miles's thoughts switched to Rosaleen. He remembered the one time he had kissed her—and why. How long ago that was. More than four years. He hadn't known much about women then. Or about himself either. He'd only kissed her because . . . because he'd been so excited after seeing Halcyon.

"*La signora*", interrupted the hallporter at his elbow, "has just telephoned to say would the *signore* please go up to her."

"*Va bene.*"

Somehow the message, though, made one feel rather a fool.

VIII

Miles found Halcyon still on her bed. She demanded a kiss, and that he should sit beside her. When he said, "But, look here, Ronnie turned up while you were having your siesta", she retorted imperiously, "He is not alone. Don Geoffrey is with him. I heard you all talking. That was what woke me. *Oiga*, I have made up my mind. I wish to return home at once. I want you to arrange everything. I would rather be on an English ship. Of course we must have the best cabins. And I should like to know when we arrive as soon as possible. Because I have been reading mamma's letter again, and I am afraid she is not so well as she pretends, so I wish to send her a cable that we are coming. You will like mamma. And I am sure she will like you. But of course she will want us to be married. Perhaps we ought to marry before we start, Meelés. What thinkest thou? It would certainly be more *convenable*".

She smiled at him, and demanded more kisses. "Is she serious?" he asked himself; and the question chilled him, seemed to take all the ardour from their embrace.

After he had left her, Halcyon lay pensive. Why hadn't she been born a man? Life was so much easier for men. Nobody minded if a man kept a mistress. She would rather keep Miles as her lover than marry him. But mamma had always been *muy religiosa*. She couldn't very well take him home. And Asuncion was such a little city. If she visited him at the hotel, there would be gossip.

The Guaraní word "*Cué*" formulated itself in her mind; and, because that word signifies anything which is over and done with, she frowned, biting her lips, telling herself, over and over again, "No. No. I have been so happy with him. And he will never be so happy with another woman".

Yet would he ever be happy with a wife?

103

IX

"You've been a hell of a time", said Geoffrey Thirkell when Miles returned to the terrace. "And you don't look too pleased with yourself. How about a cup of tea? We've just ordered some."

"Thanks. The porter's been doing some telephoning for me. But we can't find out anything here. Now he's trying to get Cook's in Genoa."

"So the *conquistadora's* determined to be off, eh?"

"Yes."

Miles smoothed the white patch of hair at his right temple—a habit, Geoffrey knew, which betokened perplexity.

"Ye'll gang with her?" asked Ronnie Wallace.

"I expect so." But would he?—Miles asked himself. Not if she insisted on marriage. She was too rich for one thing. And for another, the mere idea of getting married gave him the jitters. He'd rather stand up to machine-gun fire any day. All the same . . .

"All the same", he decided, sipping the apology for tea a waiter brought them, "I can't really contemplate parting from her. I'm still too much in love with her. Even though she does boss me about so." But that evening —Ronnie having insisted that Geoffrey motor back with him to meet Ras Imajum—Halcyon proved strangely submissive, saying, as they sat over their coffee, "Forgive me for sending you away last night, *querido*. My country means so much to me".

And that night she rekindled all the fire in him, so that the moon was setting before he left her drowsy on her tumbled pillows, and went to his own room.

x

Next morning, just as he finished breakfast, a page summoned Miles to the telephone; and, after a few sentences, he found that he was talking Italian to an Englishman, who said, "I think I'd take a Royal Mail boat from Southampton if I were you, Captain Radcliffe. There's one sailing a week from tomorrow. I'll telegraph and find out what accommodation we can secure. She may be rather full up. Would one big stateroom suit you?"

Answering, "No. I'm afraid it wouldn't", Miles saw Geoffrey come down the staircase. He finished his conversation. They strolled on to the terrace, and sat down for a smoke.

"I think I'll start for Berlin this evening", began Geoffrey. "Pity you can't come with me. They say it's gayer than Paris these days." And he added, with studied inconsequence, "I shall miss you two a lot. The *conquistadora's* a grand woman. And she seems to have oodles of money".

Off his guard for a moment, Miles said, "A jolly sight too much".

Geoffrey Thirkell did not press the point too hard. Ras Imajum, also—he went on—seemed to have oodles of money. Ronnie was on a good wicket. Trust a Scot to look after number one.

He lounged off to consult the hallporter about trains. Presently Halcyon called down from the verandah outside her bedroom, "Have Cook's telephoned yet?"

Miles called back, "Yes. They're telegraphing to England about our cabins".

"When shall we know?"

"Either this evening or tomorrow morning."

"Thank you, *caro*."

At her laziest, she spent most of that morning on a long chair in the sunshine. Geoffrey packed. Miles read an Italian novel for an hour; went to write a few letters; but compromised with picture postcards—one of which he addressed to Fluke and another to Rosaleen.

"If we sail from Southampton", he thought, "I might just get a chance of picking up that gear I left with Enid." And, so thinking, he experienced—for the first time since he had left England—a faint twinge of homesickness. But this passed before the three of them sat down to lunch.

Geoffrey's train left at two o'clock. His farewell to Halcyon was strictly businesslike. It was a pity their little deal should have fallen through. But his office in Trinidad always knew where to find him. If she ever needed his services, she had only to cable. Meanwhile he'd be at the Adlon for at least a week. To Miles he said, "If you've nothing better to do, old boy, come and see me off".

A taxi took them through the town in ten minutes. Geoffrey registered his trunk, and entrusted his small suitcase to a porter.

"Pity you can't come with me", he repeated, as they wandered up and down the platform; then, halting for a moment, "Of course it's none of my business, old boy. But you might do a jolly sight worse for yourself than marry the *conquistadora*. I gather she'd be quite willing."

"Did she tell you so herself?"

Geoffrey smiled, but did not answer. He took Miles's arm. They resumed their wandering. "A chap who hasn't got money nowadays", he went on, "might just as well be dead."

"But I've got a bit of money."

"Chicken food." Geoffrey's moon of a face creased in another smile. "I mean real money. What are you going to do when you've spent those few dollars you cleaned up in New York?"

"I haven't thought about that yet."

"Isn't it about time you did?"

"Yes. I suppose it is."

The train drew up to the platform before Geoffrey had time to say any more. But, once in his compartment, he let down the window, and leaned out of it, beaming, "Take my tip, and marry the girl". And, "Why shouldn't I?" thought Miles.

They shook hands. The stationmaster called, "*Partenza*". The moon of Geoffrey's face was eclipsed as the train slid out of view. And again Miles thought, "Why shouldn't I?" But the question answered itself while he walked back towards the hotel.

Men like Geoffrey and Ronnie Wallace were free. Marrying Halcyon, one would never be free. Even as her lover, one felt tied. And he hated being tied. Except for Halcyon, he might have gone to Berlin with Geoffrey, or taken a trip to Abyssinia.

He bought himself some cigarettes, and sat down at a café table on the sidewalk. The girl who served him proved talkative. She complimented him on his Italian. He was surprised to find himself appraising her dark hair, her luscious mouth, the cut of her figure; to find himself thinking, "After all, there are other women in the world".

Walking on, swordstick under arm, he came across the bridge to the edge of the sea, and rested again, on one of the benches there, thinking how flat life had gone all of a sudden, and wondering why.

XI

It was five o'clock before Miles came back to the hotel.

"*La casa Cook*", the hallporter told him, "has just telephoned. I put them through to the *signora*."

In her room he found Halcyon, who was writing out a cable, and looked up to say, "Everything is arranged. I have a wonderful idea. Let us spend tomorrow night in Monte Carlo. From there we can go to Paris".

Just before twilight a charabanc load of American tourists thronged the hotel. Watching them file on to the terrace for dinner, Miles thought, "Rome. Milan. Turin. Monte Carlo. Paris. They think that's travelling".

He slept alone that night, and badly. The tourists were just climbing aboard their vehicle when he and Halcyon started for the station next morning.

"We might have hired a car", she said. As though their railway fares weren't expensive enough!

A slow train took them to Genoa. They lunched at a hotel; and caught the rapide across the frontier.

"You will like Monte Carlo", said Halcyon; but Miles hated every moment they spent there—especially those hours in the casino, during which he wandered from roulette table to roulette table risking a few five-franc pieces, while Halcyon played *trente et quarante* with piles of plaques.

She won heavily; and ordered a bottle of champagne when they returned to their hotel. That night she again mentioned marriage. Next morning she insisted on buying him an elaborate gold cigarette case, which hung heavy in his hip pocket on their return to the casino.

Once more she won a lot of money. It seemed churlish not to let her pay their hotel bill. He could only revenge himself by filling her compartment with roses and lilies, faded by the time they reached Paris, where the manager of the Ritz greeted Halcyon as though she were a queen returned from exile; and where, within an hour of their arrival, she had made appointments with her dressmaker, her milliner, her shoemaker, and the like.

For three days she shopped frantically; and throughout those days there waxed in Miles Radcliffe, wandering lonely from café to café, a resentment which even the passion of their nights together—and never had he known her more passionate—could not kill.

The prime cause of this resentment eluded him. Trying to tell himself that he disliked extravagance, he was forced to admit, "Why shouldn't she do what she pleases with her own money?" and, evoking his objection to marriage, that she had not even mentioned the subject since their night in Monte Carlo.

"I still love her", he knew.

106

Yet all the time he knew, subconsciously if not consciously, that the situation was intolerable. And this knowledge strove harder and harder for self-expression, until that fourth and last evening in Paris, when she said, "Meelés, I am a little bored with the life of the boulevards. Besides, all my best gowns are packed. Let us drive out of town for dinner".

"If you like, *cara*."

"Then please order a car."

They left the Place Vendôme towards half past six. All the plane trees were in leaf and a spring sun shining. Halcyon gave the chauffeur some directions, and told him, "*Allez doucement. Nous ne sommes pas pressés*". It struck Miles that she seemed unusually weary. He said so, and she smiled, "I would not have it otherwise, my insatiable one"; and closed her eyes for a few moments as they circled the Place de la Concorde and crossed the bridge.

In those moments all his subconscious knowledge was in abeyance. There seemed to be no resentment in him, only a great tenderness, and a great wonder that any creature so utterly beautiful should be his. Once again she appeared to be completely submissive, conquered rather than conqueror. Pride rose in him as he laid a hand on hers.

At his touch her eyes reopened.

"It is a pity——" she began.

"What is a pity?"

"*Nada*. Nothing. I am very happy . . . You, too, *caro*?"

"*Si, cara*."

"And you must continue to be happy."

For a few seconds she fell silent. Then, being even more at home in Paris than in New York, she began to point out this building and that house, telling him a little of their histories. Soon they were on a long avenue of shops and factories.

"*No me gusta*", she said; and told the chauffeur to drive a little faster.

"Where are we going, Halcyon?"

"To a place you will like very much. It is not at all *de lujo*, but they give one very good food. Confess, Meelés. You do not care for the *vida de lujo*?"

"Not particularly."

"Say, rather, not at all. The life of luxury bores you. Do I speak the truth?"

"Yes. I suppose so."

A double line of cars blocked their way.

An *agent de ville* swung his white club and the chauffeur put on his brakes. A slight altercation followed.

"As for me", protested the chauffeur, "I *enfoue* myself of the man. And of his United States of Europe. Why should my patrons be inconvenienced just because he chooses to hold a meeting?"

The *agent* said, "Me—I *enfoue* myself of all politicians. But if you are not obedient, you will attrap a contravention".

As he signalled them on again, they heard shouts of, "*Vive Briand. Vive Stresemann*. Up the United States of Europe. Down with war". Their chauffeur turned round, and said, "The dirty Boche. And they cheer for him. Me, I fought at Verdun".

"In what regiment?" asked Miles.

"The artillery of field. With the seventy-fives. For three days and three nights we had no infantry in front of us. But the sale Boches did not pass."

Miles, anxious to practise the French he had not spoken for ten years, would have talked on; but Halcyon interrupted, "Chauffeur, if you do not keep your eyes on the road we shall have an accident; and I have already told you that I do not wish you to drive fast".

The man grinned, "Pardon, madam. As a married man, I understand perfectly"; and concentrated on his driving. Halcyon whispered in Guaraní, "How diverting. He thinks I am going to have a baby". And she added, "If I were, we should have to get married".

Then she fell silent again, while Miles thought how devilish awkward it would be if she were going to have a baby. But there his thoughts checked.

Soon they reached the tramway terminus at the end of the avenue. Another half kilometre, and they were off the pavé, rolling smoothly over tarmac. Here were many little villas, an occasional filling station, modest restaurants with quaint signs inviting one to eat one's fill for a few francs.

"But you do not like the life of the little bourgeois any more than you like the life of luxury", said Halcyon suddenly. "At heart you are the soldier. And yet, you are no patriot. Why is that, I wonder? To me it seems very peculiar. But then you are peculiar in so many ways, Meelés." And she smiled at him, thinking how young he really was, and how little he understood her. Did he really imagine—the poor stupid—that she could not read his mind?

"I know him so much better than he knows himself", she brooded. "And I love him better than he loves me. That is why I am so sad, of course. *Ay de mi*, I should have been born a man. Then I could have satisfied my body without engaging my heart."

Sadness grew at her heart while they were driven on, beyond the last straggle of villas, into open country; while she talked lightly of the clothes she had bought, of the journey before them. She was glad to be going home. It would be nice to see her mother again. The little matter of the arms could be arranged. Then they might either return to Europe, or visit Don Geoffrey in Trinidad.

Listening to her, interposing the few words requisite, Miles experienced no preoccupation. Her mere presence sufficed his momentary needs.

XII

The sun was still high behind the poplars when the car turned off the national road they had been following. A few more kilometres brought Miles and Halcyon to a village; and, beyond it, through woodlands, to a little restaurant on the banks of the Seine.

"We will eat in the open air", she said. "Help me into my cloak, *querido*."

A waiter led them through a long room, in which one or two other couples and a little family party were already dining, to a table under an orange awning. The proprietor bustled out to them, looked at Halcyon, twirled a stage Frenchman's moustache, and said, "It is a long time since one has seen you, madam. *Soyez la bienvenue*".

She ordered ecrévisses, chicken, a sweet omelette, and—on his advice—a bottle of Pouilly. Twilight fell, the fishermen on the opposite bank reeled in floats, sloped rods over shoulder and departed homeward, while they ate and drank.

When the waiter brought their coffee, he lit the electric table lamp.

"Switch that off again, please", said Halcyon, "it will only attract the insects"; and to Miles, "I will smoke tonight."

He handed her his new case, and flicked on a lighter she had given him in the early days of their love. She drew the smoke deep into her lungs. As she expelled it, her nostrils flared, and he heard her sigh, just once, before she began:

"I have something to say to you. It is very serious, and very difficult. But first I want to ask you a question. Do you love me enough to be quite honest with me?"

Night had now fallen over the river. But enough illumination filtered out through the lace curtains of the long dining room to show Miles her face. And, in that moment while he meditated his answer, her face seemed more beautiful to him than ever before. Because—for the first time—he seemed to be seeing, as it were, a light behind those eyes, still blue-black as the water of Lake Ypacarai, but no longer fathomless. And somehow or other this light made him feel a little ashamed.

"I hope I love you enough for that", he said at last; and she, slowly, putting down her cigarette:

"I, too. Because between a man such as you are and a woman such as I am there is no other way to . . . to the real tranquillity, which is not only a tranquillity of the body, but also of the soul."

She stopped there, and picked up her cigarette, and inhaled again, one quick pull after another, till the red flame of the paper might have been the flame of her own hair.

Then, abruptly, imperiously, almost as one man speaking to another, she said, "In marriage, there must be tranquillity of soul. If the good God gave us children—although, if He were going to do that, I fancy He would have done so already—I might find it there. But would you? I do not think so. I think you would chafe—not for other women maybe—but for freedom. Be honest, Meelés. *Palabra inglés*. Is not that so?"

Miles answered, after a long pause, "*Puede ser*. Possibly"; and once more Halcyon put down her cigarette, asking:

"Is that quite honest?"

Silence hung between them. At last, still ashamed, he said:

"No. Not quite. As a matter of fact, the whole idea of marriage is distasteful to me."

"*Porqué?*"

"I don't know why." He shrugged his shoulders. "It just is."

"Then let us renounce it. Once and for all, Meelés."

Her decision was a relief he could not conceal. His very breathing betrayed him. She said to herself, "*Pobrecito*. The poor little man. Always he has been frightened lest I should have a baby".

Aloud she went on, "But you see—do you not—how difficult everything will be for us in Asuncion? There is not only mother to be considered. There is the whole family. So perhaps——"

She paused there; and again silence hung between them. The light had gone from behind her eyes. Once more they seemed fathomless. Relief vanished. Sickeningly, Miles was conscious that disaster impended.

"So perhaps", she concluded, "it is best that we part."

Sheer surprise forced immediate argument. Why should they part? He still loved her.

"With your body", she interrupted. "But not with your soul. And one day the love of the body burns out. I have often told you so."

He said stupidly, "But that day has not yet come".

She answered without a second's hesitation, "How can you be sure? You speak only for yourself".

"You mean"—anger touched him—"that you are no longer in love with me?"

"No, Meelés. If I were no longer in love with you, I should be honest enough to say so."

"Then why do you suggest that we part?"

"*Quien sabé?* Who knows?" She in her turn shrugged her shoulders. "Maybe just because we are still in love with each other."

"I do not understand that, Halcyon."

"I was afraid you might not. So I will try to explain. Give me another cigarette, please. Light it for me. *Gracias, caro.*"

She took the cigarette, and blew a ring into the still air.

"Before you met me", she continued, "you had only bought your women. That suited you. Because, once you paid them, you had no more responsibility. But, in love, there is always a responsibility. And in our love that responsibility is mostly mine because . . . because I am older than you."

Denial rose to his lips. She silenced it with a gesture.

"I do not speak of years", she said. "Love such as ours is a sin. But it would be a greater sin if I kept you for my lover when you tired of me. And one day you will tire of me."

"Never!"

"Never is a long time, my friend. And supposing—for we must suppose this if we are to be quite honest with each other—that I were to tire of you; that, one night, lying in your arms, I were to say to myself, 'But he is no longer *querido de mi alma*, the beloved of my soul, he is only *querido de mi cuerpo*, the beloved of my body? That might happen. And even a worse thing."

"What thing?"

Halcyon hesitated a long time. Finally she said:

"You have perhaps forgotten. But once, long ago, you confessed to me that always, after you had been with other women, you experienced a revulsion. I, too, have known a similar feeling—though never with you. That might happen again. To either of us".

And after more time she continued, "We have loved each other so well, *querido*. So well—and so beautifully. If we part now, all our memories of each other will be happy ones. Do not blame me, do not be angry with me, because I am afraid to risk my memories".

Then, once again, he saw that strange light—which, though he did not

110

know it, was the true mother light—behind her blue-black eyes, as she concluded:

"It is only your vanity which makes you blame me. It is only your pride which makes you angry. Be honest with yourself, Meelés. Be quite honest".

And, "I'm trying to be", said Miles Radcliffe, after still more time.

For, secretly, subconsciously, ever since they had left Castello Gandolfo —and long before that perhaps—so many of these thoughts which she was now expressing had been his own.

XIII

Thunder drummed, lightning streaked the clouds, rain deluged the cobbles, as Miles and Halcyon were driven back in to Paris. All the way, they had spoken no word to each other. But his arm was still round her, and their hands were still clinging, when their car circled the Place de la Concorde. Because this—they had agreed—was to be their last, their very last, night together. And how could such misery be borne?

Once, during that night, she weakened, whispering, while her hands fondled, "*Quizas*, I shall not be able to bear life without you. If I send for you, promise that you will come to me".

And once, towards dawn, he weakened, snuggling to her and pleading, "Why must we part now? At least let me travel to Asuncion with you".

Nevertheless the mere fact that he could plead with her fretted him; and, leaving her, he put weakness away. She, not he, had decided that this must be the end of their loving. She, not he, must do the pleading if that decision were to be reversed. Maybe—surely—she would ask him to travel as far as Southampton with her? If so, he would not deny the boon.

But in Halcyon's mind—as she dressed herself—dwelt only the certainty, "He is a man for whom a mere woman will never be enough. Already he yearns for freedom. One day he will tire of me. Then he will hate me for having mastered him. Rather than that, I would endure any pain".

All morning, trivialities assuaged her pain. A hat, a diamanté belt, had not been delivered. She needed more scent. A new pair of shoes fastened too tightly over the instep. She must have some English money. And, insisting they must lunch in the crowded restaurant, she avoided any opportunity for the display of emotion.

Fatalism, too, forbade the display of more emotion. Part Spaniard and part Guaraní, she drew strength from the thought, "This was always decreed".

And towards the end, with all trivial tasks done, and her dressing case locked, and the luggage porter already wheeling away her steamer trunks, there came to her—this also by inheritance of blood—a sense of the fey.

"Courage", whispered her sense of the fey. "It is also decreed that this is not really the end. You will meet again—you and your loved one."

Whether the whisper foretold a meeting in this or in some after life, Halcyon did not know. Yet queerly it became the source of an even greater strength.

So that, at the very end—when, after that silent drive to the station, they

111

walked this platform arm in arm—when, arm in arm with him no longer, she gave him that one kiss, that one handclasp, and stepped aboard the train which was to separate them—she could still smile, could still say, "Not *adios*, Meelés. Only *hasta la vista*. Until we see each other again".

"But I shall never see her again", thought Miles Radcliffe, with the wheels already turning, and that long gloved hand already waving farewell to him from the railway-coach window.

For in him was no sense of the fey, only a fierce, almost irresistible urge to run, and run, and run, till he could catch up with that fast-disappearing railway coach, and tear the door open, and swing himself aboard.

BOOK SIX

I

FLUKE RADCLIFFE SNAPPED INTO HIS DICTAPHONE, "THAT'LL BE THE LOT";
replaced the mouthpiece on its hook; rang for his secretary Jean Higginbottom, and lit the second of his morning cigars.

"If ever a chap deserved a holiday, I do", he thought. "Damn it all, I
haven't had one since that b.f. Cuthbert Brendon blotted his copybook. And
he'd have blotted mine too if I'd given him half a chance."

The dour-faced Jean Higginbottom entered his new office; laid three more
letters on the elaborate desk to which he had treated himself at the expense of
his shareholders; and departed with the dictaphone cylinders. He glanced
at the letters; scribbled a note on each of them, and continued to think of
Brendon.

Served the fellow right, of course. A crook if ever there was one. Still,
gaol couldn't be much of a picnic. No cigars. And the privies must be
something horrible. Rising, Fluke went to his own—all white tiles and
chromium fitments, odorous with the same disinfectant Enid used for
Rosemary Lodge.

When he returned, he found Tom Clark, his new advertising manager,
waiting for him with the layouts for their autumn campaign.

"I think you'll find them fairly adequate, sir", said Clark; but Fluke
found them, "Too bloody highbrow. What's all this about Mercury? The
public's never heard of Mercury, except in a thermometer. And how many
of 'em even know what superheterodyne means? Take it from me, the
average listener-in doesn't give a damn why his set works. All he cares about
is how it works. Clear reception. That's the point you want to make.
Here's a new slogan I thought up last night."

He drew a scribbling block towards him; extracted a gold pencilcase from
a waistcoat pocket, and printed:

"TURN THE KNOB—AND IT DOES ITS JOB". To this he added
after some thought, "THAT IS ALL YOU NEED TO KNOW—WHEN
YOU'VE A RADCLIFFE RADIO".

"That's the stuff to give the troops", he concluded; and Tom Clark, once
of Balliol College, Oxford, picked up his layouts, musing gloomily, "This is
a nice sort of job for a chap who writes free verse for the New Politician in
his spare time."

Alone, Fluke thought of Brendon again. If Timothy hadn't happened
to warn one, "C.B. stocks are a bit wonky. They tell me he's got about all he
can carry", one might have agreed to Brendon's "investing" the reserve fund
of Radcliffe Radios Limited in Combined Cameras or the C.B. Finance
Corporation—and then one wouldn't half have been in the cart.

Instead, the judge had complimented one in his summing up: "Fortunately for the shareholders of another Brendon company, its vice chairman,
Mr. Radcliffe, was a man not only of acumen but of probity. He has told us
himself how he rejected, though under considerable pressure, the blandishments of the accused".

"Nice word, blandishment—might use it in an ad one of these days", ruminated Fluke; but the recollection of Brendon's gray face twitching as he stood to receive sentence made him feel a little shivery.

"There but for the grace of God——" he caught himself thinking.

On his desk stood the latest photograph of Enid and their four children. Still a little shivery, he regarded them. Enid, at thirty-eight, might have been a girl. That slimming course had certainly improved her figure. Soon, Simmy would be at Torrington. Philly looked like turning into a beauty. How tall Arty was—more like nine than seven. Gladdy, too, was going to be big.

And none of 'em would ever want for a thing!

II

A knock disturbed Fluke. He called, "Come". Derek Grayson entered, blinking through his hornrimmed spectacles. As usual he wore a sports coat and gray flannel trousers. Unusually he seemed depressed.

"I don't like the political situation", he said in answer to a question. "I wish to goodness you weren't going away."

The situation—thought Fluke—certainly was a bit tense. The Labour Cabinet had just split over a tenpercent cut in unemployment pay. According to the newspapers, the King was on his way back to London from Balmoral. But he only laughed, "Don't you worry your head about that, young feller-me-lad. Politics don't affect the radio business. The worse things are, the more people want to hear 'em. How about your scheme for making our own knobs? How much'll it cost?"

"I haven't been into the cost so far."

"You wouldn't", thought Fluke.

The trouble with all technicians was that they had no money sense. Give Derek his head—and they'd have a job to pay their preference dividends. But what a wizard of a designer. Their new all-mains model was going to be an absolute knockout. And Derek's articles in the technical press ("Not that I understand 'em", thought Fulke) meant a hell of a lot of prestige.

The telephone rang. Jean Higginbottom said, "The Automobile Association want to speak to you, Mr. Radcliffe". He boomed, "Yes, thanks. I've got everything now. Mind your chap meets me at Dover"; recradled the new hand microphone, and went on to Grayson: "Let's take a prowl round".

They left the private office, and passed through the new counting house, of which Fluke always told visitors, "Believe it or not, when I first started Radcliffe Radios, this used to be the whole blinking factory".

Crossing a courtyard, they climbed a ramp at which several lorries were being unloaded; pushed their way through a fireproof door; and lingered for a few minutes in the stockrooms, where Fluke flung a word to each of the supervisors.

In the main building, roofed with glass, nearly five hundred girls were fitting valves and transformers, loudspeakers and condensers, coils and knobs and wires and switches, into the pseudo-mahogany and pseudo-walnut cases which flowed in a slow continuous stream along the endless belts of the conveyors, all worked by electric power.

Here they found Alf—now graying in his middle fifties. Here, too, Fluke had a word for each supervisor; and occasionally for some particular worker, who would scarcely look up from her monotonous task of fixing a yellow wire to "point a" or a blue wire to "point b", as she answered, "I'm all right, thank you, Mr. Radcliffe", or "Thank you, Mr. Radcliffe, my Tom'll be at secondary school come Michaelmas".

And when they came to the tables on which the coils were wound, Fluke had a word for nearly every one of the winders, because these were the women he always referred to as, "My old brigade".

"Give him his due", decided Derek Grayson, "he may not know the difference between a short wave and a long, but he does know how to handle human beings."

Making their way back past the canteen and the recreation room, they fell to quarrelling about his latest scheme for an all-dry battery set—Fluke maintaining, as the whole trade were still maintaining, "It wouldn't pay. And how the hell would it work without an aerial?"

"You leave the aerial to me", said Derek. "We're using dry batteries for high tension, so why should we use wet accumulators for low?"

With more than a third of the houses in Great Britain still lacking electricity, Derek's idea seemed worth further experiment. Meanwhile, though, a glance at his father's watch told Fluke it was time for lunch, and a last talk with Rosaleen. A damn sound scheme of his—even if it did add a bit to the cost—to take Rosaleen abroad with them. Apart from looking after Simmy and Philly on the way down, her French would come in jolly useful.

He shouted into the house telephone, "I'm just off, Jean"; washed his hands; ran a comb through the sandy hair already receding from his broad forehead, and went for his car.

III

Twelve minutes of careful driving brought Fluke along the bypass, past the sign and down the side road to the Beehive. He parked his car, and stood for a moment, thinking what a fine job Dick Simmons had made of the new bedroom wing and the swimming pool.

Entering by the enlarged front door, and passing through the redecorated lounge, he heard chatter and the music of one of his own radios from the cocktail bar. A waitress in a primrose uniform smiled, "You're early today, Mr. Radcliffe". He boomed at her, "It's the early birds that catch the worms, Mollie. Tell 'em to keep me a nice lobster for lunch"; hung his soft hat on the usual peg, and barged into the slip of a room which Rosaleen used as her office.

She was answering the telephone. "I'm awfully sorry", he heard her say, "but we simply can't manage a thing this weekend."

Stephanie entered to interrupt over his shoulder, "Yes, we can. We've just had a cancellation".

Rosaleen said, "Hold on a minute, please"; and, later, "Very good, Captain Brown. We shall expect you and your wife by dinnertime on Friday".

"Captain Brown", mocked Stephanie, while Rosaleen made a note of the booking. "Of the Phantom Fusiliers. And his wedded wife, God bless her. Ring by Woolworths—returnable Monday morning. If we had to ask for marriage lines, this place would be a howling desert. Not that I care, as long as they pay their bills."

She went out. Rosaleen offered Fluke a chair. He sat down, and extracted a long envelope from the breast pocket of his pale gray flannel suit, beginning, "I got the A.A. to make you a duplicate copy of the route. Just as well to be on the safe side, don't you know. After all, either of the cars might have a breakdown. And Enid thinks half past eight tomorrow morning is cutting it rather too fine . . ."

IV

Fluke bustled off to his lunch. The old fusspot, thought Rosaleen. He couldn't make more of a to-do if he were taking a caravan through the Sahara. Then, just for a moment or so, her thoughts turned to Miles, from whom, ever since Christmas, when a picture postcard informed her that he was "Just leaving Guatemala", she had had no word.

Funny, how seldom one thought of Miles nowadays. These last two years seemed almost to have obliterated his image from one's mind. One had been too busy, and too happy in one's business, to have any man on one's mind, except perhaps Paul, for whom one couldn't help feeling rather sorry every fresh time he proposed.

Mollie brought in Rosaleen's lunch tray. She ate quickly and returned to her accounts.

At three o'clock Barbara Thaxted, who was to act cashier while she went on holiday, joined her from the restaurant. At half past four Stephanie looked in to say, "I'm just running over to Albanford. Keep an eye on things till I get back, dear". At five o'clock Eliza Cranbourne, who had taken on the job of housekeeper when they engaged their chef, telephoned, "Oh, Miss Adair, could you come along to the linen room? The laundry people are up to their old tricks again".

On her way upstairs, Rosaleen encountered one of their guests—a middle-aged man in tennis kit, with a hearty manner and a roving eye, who detained her, a little too closely, for nearly two minutes. How well she had grown to know that particular type!

Back in her office, she was informed by Jimmy, the barman, that he needed syphons, dark sherry, and at least six dozen of gin; telephoned the orders; typed a stiff letter to the laundry, and spent another hour instructing the not-over-bright Barbara how to balance the day book.

Usually she took an evening swim, but both her bathing suits were already packed; and anyway the pool, which she could see from her window, looked too crowded. Besides, Paul would be here to say goodbye any minute. Bother the man. Why couldn't he realise that nothing on earth would induce her to marry him—or, for the present at any rate, anyone else?

Paul proposed—for the sixth time!—while they strolled past the two hard tennis courts laid down that spring, and the new garage, towards the kitchen garden which supplied their chef with most of his fresh vegetables, despite her, "Please, don't start that all over again. It just doesn't get us anywhere", persisting, "But I can't help being fond of you", till she cut him short with a decisive, "You're not dying for love of me, my dear. You're not that sort. And even if you were, it wouldn't make any difference. You see, the older I get——"

"The more you like your independence", gloomed Paul.

Alone, with twilight falling and window after window beaming its kindly light on to the garden of which she knew every flower, on to the coloured umbrellas by the swimming pool and the many parked cars which told the tale of her success, Rosaleen fell to wondering if that were quite true.

"I'd rather have children——" she thought vaguely, while she and Stephanie took dinner together in the far corner of the restaurant after the guests had been served.

Two other tables were still occupied. At the nearer, a couple of obvious lovers held hands silently in the intervals between sipping coffee; at the farther, a party of four—the middle-aged man with the roving eye, another male of the same cut, and two buxom brunettes in their late thirties—made loud merriment over their liqueurs.

"Stephanie despises both lots", thought Rosaleen. "She doesn't really ike to see people happy."

Yet Stephanie had always done everything to make her happy. And once again, when they kissed, Rosaleen reproached herself, as so often in these last years, with ingratitude. No use blinking the fact, she simply couldn't care as much for Stephanie as Stephanie cared for her.

"I just like everybody a little, and nobody very much", she thought, head on cool pillow, tired limbs stretching luxuriously. "And I'm not sorry. Life's easier that way." But, just before she fell asleep, her imagination pictured a child's cot by her bed ; and, when she woke, it was from one of those motherhood dreams which had haunted all her adolescence, to the curious idea, "There's no reason to get married just because you want to have a baby".

The idea proved a trifle shocking. She jumped out of bed, drew her chintz curtains, and went to her bath.

At seven o'clock Mollie brought her a cup of tea, a boiled egg and some buttered toast. Thirty minutes afterwards she stood at the front door waiting for Ablett, Fluke's chauffeur. By then the prospect of a whole month's holiday was absorbing and exciting all her mind.

v

Fluke's big car looked like a pantechnicon. A curved luggage container had been clipped to its roof, two trunks and a suitcase strapped under a waterproof sheet on its grid. Inside was a miscellaneous collection of parcels. Ablett, in a new white dustcoat, with a linen cover to match on his blue cap, eyed Rosaleen's bags with displeasure, but cheered up a little when he had succeeded in stowing them away.

She climbed in beside him ; and they drove to Rosemary Lodge. There they found Fluke, watch in one hand, maps in the other, Enid, Simmy Philly, Fluke's sister-in-law Constance, to whom he had lent the Lodge for her holiday (on the condition that she looked after Gladdy and Arty, also present to see the safari start for Dover), Constance's three children, and his entire domestic staff.

Fluke, in pale gray plus-fours, tested the luggage straps of both cars with his own hand; ordered Rosaleen from the front seat to the rear; rearranged the parcels; mounted Simmy and Philly either side of her; handed Enid into his own two-seater; kissed Constance; boomed to Ablett, "All you have to do is to follow me", and took the wheel, declaiming, "Staff work, my dear. I flatter myself I haven't forgotten a single thing".

"Except our passports", smiled Enid, unzipping her handbag to produce them; and she added platitudinously, "Two heads are always better than one."

Exactly halfway to the coast, Fluke stopped; dismounted; waited for Ablett to draw up under the trees at the side of the road, and whispered through the window to Simmy, "Do you want to come for a little walk with me?"

Simmy looked at Rosaleen; flushed to the roots of his flaxen hair, and answered, "Yes, I would rather". Alone with her, Philly confided an identical need.

Driven on again, both children began to ask questions. How did you get a motorcar on board on a ship? Would the sea be rough? Did it hurt much being seasick? Mummy had taken some stuff that was supposed to stop it. Had Rosaleen taken anything? Coping with these and other questions, she caught herself thinking, "Four days of this—and I shall go crazy".

But perhaps one would be thinking differently if these two were one's own.

Simmy and Philly continued to be "slightly pestiferous", as she phrased it to herself, all the way to Dover; but on the Townsend wharf Enid took charge of them—and a man in Automobile Association uniform of Fluke, his new-lit cigar at the true Captain Kettle angle.

Meanwhile Rosaleen's mind showed her a dim picture of the last time she had crossed the Channel—in a boat so crowded that it seemed, to the little girl she was then, as though "it must simply sink with people". Queerly she remembered using those very words to her father; and his explanation that most of the people were "Belgian refugees".

That crossing—she further remembered—had been by night. But a loud boom from Fluke, "All aboard the lugger", dispelled the nineteen-fourteen memories; and she did not think of her father again until the mouth of Calais harbour opened, and they berthed at the quay.

She knew that quay; knew this market square through which—after a short delay for customs formalities—Ablett was now driving. "That statue is by Rodin", she heard herself telling the two children. "It's called The Captives. And those bells chime every quarter of an hour."

Bells chiming every quarter of an hour. And father still at the café. He'd be back soon. You would smell his breath when he bent over to kiss you goodnight.

Recollections of childhood vanished as they followed Fluke, who was hugging the right of the road at a nervous thirty, beyond the town. They had been first away from the ship; but nearly every one of the other cars

118

aboard passed them before they bumped over the cobbles of Montreuil; and it was nearly eight o'clock before they made Amiens.

There Enid—pleading a headache—soon took Philly to bed. But Fluke's war reminiscences kept Simmy and Rosaleen up for another hour. And next morning only Enid's reminder, "But how about the rooms we've booked all the way down, darling?" saved them from an impromptu tour of the battlefields.

That day Segrave Fluke, avoiding Paris, led the Plinley Green safari to Auxerre at an inspired thirty-five.

"Nothing to beat a continental motoring holiday", he foghorned over dinner. "I feel like a two-year-old. Tell the waiter to bring us another bottle of bubbly, Rosaleen"; and Enid realised it would be useless to plead a headache, as she might have known from the moment of their arrival when he said, "There are two beds in Rosaleen's room, so Philly may as well doss down with her".

"But I should hate it if he didn't want to", Fluke's wife consoled herself; and thought of Lucy for a moment.

What a fool Lucy was with her, "Oh, Timothy isn't a bit like that. He hardly ever worries me nowadays". Didn't she realise why?

VI

That night Rosaleen—finding sleep difficult—also thought of Timothy, and of a big blond he had once brought to a dinner dance at the Beehive, and of Stephanie's mocking comment while she made out their bill, "Why don't you charge him an extra pound for hush money?"

"Father—Fluke—Timothy", she speculated. "Three typical husbands. And if a girl does any better for herself than Fluke it's a miracle. Thank goodness I've got my own business." Yet, when she woke next morning, the sight of Philly still fast asleep in the other bed made her a little sad.

In a few more years she would be thirty. Ought you to have a baby much after thirty? Enid had been thirty-three when Gladdy was born. But then Gladdy hadn't been her first.

That morning the two children seemed more companionable. They "struck lucky", as Fluke put it, for lunch.

Towards mid-afternoon, accordingly, Philly, who had the family appetite, complained that she felt "a bit sick, Aunt Rosaleen". Fortunately Ablett found a shady place for the operation, and after half an hour's rest they were able to proceed.

But it took a long time, and any number of inquiries from any number of people who all gave them contrary directions, before they wormed their tortuous way through Lyons to their next hotel.

"Thought you'd had an accident", said a relieved Fluke, waiting for them on the sidewalk. "If this weren't such a b. awful town to find one's way about in, I'd have come back to look for you."

A good father, even though he must be a little trying as a husband. And you owed him a lot. If he hadn't taken you in when you were a refugee from Ireland, you might never have owned a share in the Beehive. All the same . ..

"All the same", decided Rosaleen, again sharing a room with Philly

119

"I'm glad I don't have to sleep with him." And from that she fell to wondering why no man had ever aroused in her, even imaginatively, that particular inclination.

"Am I really undersexed?" she asked herself, remembering a longago incident at the seaside. But, from the moment they started next morning, there was no more introversion in her mind.

Suddenly the business worries of which introversion had been the backwash fell away from her. Suddenly she began to enjoy herself. "This is Burgundy", she told the children. "Look. Those are vineyards. Soon the grapes will be ripe."

All that day—their longest on the road—the sun blazed from a cloudless sky. For lunch, they had a picnic. By tea time they were well down the Rhone Valley. The shades of Stanley and Livingstone hung abashed heads when Fluke touched Enid, who had drowsed away the last fifty kilometres, on the shoulder to announce, "We've done it. We'll be at Avignon in time for dinner".

"I used to know a song about Avignon", she murmured. "Isn't there a bridge or something?"

"Ancient palace of the Popes", quoted Fluke from the A.A. route they were following. "Oh, and a chap I met at the last Radio Manufacturers dinner told me to look out for mosquitos. His wife nearly got bitten to death there. This motoring doesn't half give one a thirst. What I need is a bottle of bubbly under my belt."

"As long as that's all you need—" thought Enid, longing for Westgate-on-Sea and hoping that they'd at least find some bridge players at Sainte Marie sur Mer.

At Avignon she slept, for the first time in her life, under a mosquito net, and woken inviolate was urged, "Up you get, darling. It's seven already, and we must see that ruddy palace before we push off".

They breakfasted in their room. As usual Fluke left her to pack the special case he had bought, "just for one night, old thing. Save an awful trouble on our way down". As usual he left a handkerchief under his pillow. Unusually, when she came into the hall, she found him arguing over their bill.

"Daylight robbery, that's what I call it", he grumbled. "And we're five minutes late already. Why hasn't that damn fellow Ablett brought the cars round yet? I'll pop over to the garage and give him a piece of my mind."

He went off in a huff, to return in a greater one, fuming, "He's changing a tyre. He says it went down in the night. If he'd get up in decent time, this sort of thing wouldn't happen".

Enid said, "If you go on like this, darling, you'll have apoplexy. I told you you ought to wear one of your open-neck shirts now we're practically in the tropics. Why don't we give the palace of the Popes a miss? It isn't as though they live there any more".

Fluke compromised. They'd just take a squint at the outside of the thing. But a merciless guide pounced on them as they drew up before that pile of uninspired masonry—so that it was nearly eleven o'clock before they escaped back to the cars; and well past two when they left Aix-en-Provence on what Fluke described as, "the last lap".

"I'm going to let the old bus rip now", he told Enid; and, putting his foot
120

as far down as he dared, actually achieved fifty-eight ("nearly a mile a minute, old thing") on one level stretch of empty road.

"Would you like me to keep him in sight, miss?" asked Ablett, turning to consult Rosaleen as his employer speeded up to this unparalleled velocity.

"No. Don't bother. We've plenty of time."

Ablett's face showed displeasure. They rolled on, passed by an occasional lorry, with the children somnolent and her own thoughts awander. This incessant motoring had grown rather tiresome. She would be glad to unpack and settle down. Bathing in the Mediterranean ought to be rather jolly. That walled town on the hillside looked attractive. Provence had been the land of the troubadours. One could imagine them, on foot or on horseback, making their way up to those walls through the sunscorched foothills . . .

"Excuse me, miss; but it looks as though that man wants us to stop."

Ablett's voice woke her from what must have been a drowse. Her eyes snapped open to show her the gray road curving upwards towards a long heap of stones, and three cypresses gauntly dark against red earth and the blue blaze of the sky.

Just beyond the heap of stones, the road narrowed and a big board announced, "Attention. Work in progress". There, one hand resting on a stick, the other lifted to halt them, stood a man in shorts and stockings, his chest naked except for a singlet and as brown as an Indian's.

Ablett, throwing over his shoulder, "Mr. Radcliffe's instructions were not to stop for anyone", hooted furiously. But the figure refused to give way; and, as their brakes went on, Rosaleen—half blinded by the sun and wondering whether she were really awake or still drowsing—heard a known voice begin in French, and continue in English, "Sorry to hold you up, chauffeur. But can you give me a lift as far as the next village?"

Letting down the window, she called, "Hallo, Miles!"

VII

Miles called back, as calmly as though they had met at Plinley Green station, "Hallo, Rosaleen. I've sprained an ankle".

Ablett reversed the car a few lengths to leave the road free. The four of them dismounted, Simmy saying, "It's Uncle Miles. And he's lost his shirt".

"Are you in pain?" asked Rosaleen as he hobbled up.

"Well, I'm not too comfortable. Simmy, run along to those trees. You'll find my rucksack there. Do you know what a rucksack is?"

"Definitely", said Simmy, using the word of the moment; and Miles, seating himself on the stones, took a crumpled packet of cigarettes from his back pocket.

"Do you happen to have a match on you?" he asked. Rosaleen handed him a booklet. He lit up, and quizzed the overloaded car, before continuing, "I thought I recognised Fluke in that closed two-seater. But the blighter must have thought I was a bandit. What are you supposed to be? The baggage van?"

"Something like that."

Simmy returned with the rucksack, and a battered hat, which Miles put

121

on, explaining vaguely, "I found I had a bit of time to spare before the ship sailed. So I thought I might as well get fit.

"Where are you all bound for?" he went on.

"Sainte Marie sur Mer."

"How far's that?"

"About sixty kilometres, sir", answered Ablett.

"Okay. That ought to do me as well as anywhere else. But you'll have to repack your traps."

"How about me and Philly sitting in front?" put in Simmy.

During the few minutes it took to rearrange the suitcases, Rosaleen gathered that Miles had spent the night at the walled town on the hillside, and hurt himself about an hour back just before he reached the national road.

"But mostly", he went on, "I've been sleeping in the open, because it's more fun. Curse this ankle of mine. I couldn't find a drop of water to bathe it anywhere. Do you mind if I take off my boot?"

He unlaced the boot. They were ready to start by then. Touching his bare arm as she helped him into the car, Rosaleen realised, pleasurably, how strong he was. But something about his expression puzzled her. This—surely?—was not the Miles to whom her last words had been, "Take care of yourself. Don't have any flying accidents".

The five years since that rainy Saturday evening when he drove her back to Fairholm had altered him completely. Better-looking than ever, he did not look . . . did not look . . .

"Happy", she decided, asking:

"And where are you off to this time?"

"I'm taking a bit of a holiday in Abyssinia. You remember Ronnie Wallace. Well, he's got a farm out there."

He offered her a black cigarette, which she threw out of the window after a few puffs, saying, "How can you smoke such things?"

"I'm not spoilt—like some people." His grin was the same. "Tell me about this place you're going to. Is it very *de lujo*?"

"What might that mean."

"*De luxe*", he translated.

"I don't know. Fluke chose it. I'm his guest."

"Fluke's making as much money as ever, I suppose."

"He deserves to. He works hard enough."

"So you said before."

He fell silent. The children turned round and began to chatter.

"Are we going to stop for tea?" asked Philly.

"No. But you can have some chocolate if you like, dear."

"Can I have some?" asked Miles; and a little later he said, "I don't think I'd better stay at your hotel. I haven't got much in the way of clothes for one thing. And for another it'll probably be too expensive."

"And for a third", snapped Rosaleen, surprised at her own ill temper, "you don't want to."

He eyed her curiously, smiling, "What on earth makes you say that?"

For no reason she could imagine, she snapped at him again:

"It's pretty obvious that you don't care for your family much. You hardly ever write—and you haven't been home in ages".

He burked the issue with a quiet, "Life's too short for quarrels. How's that pub of yours doing? Funny thing, I heard about it only the other day, from a chap who'd stayed there".

"I hope he approved."

"Rather. You and Stephanie must have worked jolly hard to get it going."

"We did."

Temper subsided. Once again—talking of her own affairs—she grew conscious of his good looks; and, presently, of a queer fascination he had begun to exercise over her. There was some mystery about this new Miles.

Still speculating about him while she talked about herself, she saw the signboard, "Sainte Marie sur Mer. 25 kilometres", and the arrow pointing right.

Ablett, never much good at finding his way, would have passed the turning. Simmy called his attention to it. How bright Simmy was. Just like his father. It must be awful to have stupid children. You couldn't really call Miles stupid. He was only . . . eccentric. At his age—over thirty—a man ought to settle down, ought to get married.

"You seem rather pensive all of a sudden", he broke in. "What are you thinking about? The boy friend?"

"Don't be so silly."

"Haven't you got one?"

"No. I have not."

The recrudescence of temper seemed to amuse him. He continued to chaff. She was getting quite a big girl now. Didn't Stephanie ever let her off the chain? How was darling Stephanie? Still anti-man? If so, Rosaleen ought to be careful. That sort of thing could be contagious.

"Oh, look", interrupted Simmy, turning round again, "there's the sea. And isn't it blue? Not a bit like it is at home."

In another kilometre the sea was at their very wheels. Soon they came to a little cove and a bathing beach. Beyond this beach, the road climbed a spine of land black from a recent forest fire. Spiralling down again, it brought them past little clumps of pine and occasional villas, and a sign that read, "The Inn of Mother Gaboriau—her beds, her wines, her bouillabaisse", to a long street, shops and restaurants on its one side, blue-painted cabins and yellow sand on its other.

Here crowds of people were bathing and some danced in shallow water to the music of a gramophone. "Margate on the Mediterranean", commented Miles.

"You'd better put on your boot", said Rosaleen sharply. "It's only about another mile to our hotel."

VIII

The hotel revealed itself, just beyond a level crossing, as a pinkwashed semicastellated edifice standing solitary in its own grounds. A short drive of white gravel led between hedges of pink and white oleander to the main entrance, either side of which were tables. At one of these, sipping champagne cocktails, sat Fluke and Enid.

"Well, I'll be damned", said Fluke, as Ablett put his brakes on. "You were right after all, old thing. That hobo who tried to stop us was Miles."

He rose, came to the car, and, hearing what had happened, declared he'd be further damned ("all ends up, old boy") if Miles should go to any other hotel. Clothes be damned, too. He'd already found out one needn't dress for dinner. What about a nice drink? The kids could have lemonade.

"And you'd better put yourself outside some beer before you unpack the bus, Ablett. Hi—concierge. See my chauffeur gets a bottle of beer, will you? And send the waiter along."

Philly whispered the customary demand. It was dinner time before Rosaleen met Miles again.

He had changed his shorts for a pair of knife-creased gray flannel trousers, his singlet for a sleeveless blue sweater. He wore a pair of canvas shoes with rope soles, and no socks. She noticed the professional bandage round his ankle, and asked, "Who put that on for you?"

"I did it myself, of course."

"And pressed your own trousers, I suppose?"

"No. I let the valet do that for me."

"How condescending of you."

Fluke, accompanied by Enid and the children, joined them before they could say more. They dined early on a glassed-in terrace which fronted the sea. Over their coffee Enid grumbled, "We seem to be the only English people here. I don't know what we're going to do with ourselves of an evening. I shall die if I don't get my game of bridge. And there must be moskies, because we've got curtains on ours beds."

"Dangerous animals—these French mosquitos", said Miles.

The sarcasm missed Enid, but hit Rosaleen. Just before they left their table, two or three couples—obviously English from the men's dinner jackets —drifted in.

"I shall put on evening dress tomorrow night", said Enid; and Miles whispered to Rosaleen, "Plinley Greenery for ever."

Despite herself, she smiled.

Much as this new Miles irritated her, he seemed so different—so pleasurably different—from the kind of man she was used to meeting at the Beehive. And the difference—a flash of intuition told her just before she climbed into bed that first evening—was that you always knew how the kind of men who came to the Beehive would react if . . . if you gave them the opportunity. As Stephanie had once put it, "They either bring their bit of stuff with them, or look for it on the premises".

But how Miles would react—granted similar circumstances—purely hypothetical, because you never had given any of the men who came to the Beehive even the opportunity for a flirtation—you hadn't the slightest idea.

She slept on that; but waking—glad of solitude after three nights of sharing a room with Philly—took herself to task for being over interested in the man. "He's nothing to me", she determined. Nevertheless, she was again aware of fascination when he joined them on the private bathing beach of the hotel.

Simmy and Philly, who swam like fishes, were still in the water. Enid was oiling her plump shoulders. Fluke—flat on his face in the warm sand— had covered himself with a towel after warning both of them, "Don't risk more than five minutes' sun the first day". Miles, still supporting himself on his stick, wore only the bandage round his ankle and a pair of white swimming shorts. His body might have been sunburnt gold.

He squatted down, native fashion, beside Rosaleen, asking:

"Been in yet?"

"No." She adjusted her bathing cap.

"I had a dip at dawn—and went back to bed again. Then I did a spot of telephoning, to see if I could get a bag sent over."

"Where from?"

"Toulon."

"How's the ankle?"

"Not too bad. Ready?"

"Yes."

She kicked off her shoes, and they made for the wheeled diving board.

"Ought you to dive?" she asked, as he put down his stick.

"I'll be all right if I take my time. You go first."

She poised herself and plunged. When she came up, she found him beside her. "Too deep", he said. "You didn't push off hard enough. When I'm better, I'll show you."

They crawled out to sea. Even though he had hurt his foot, she found it difficult to keep up with him, and was glad when he turned on his back.

She trod water, saying, "I never could float".

"It's easy enough. You've only got to arch your back. Try it."

She tried it, but failed. It seemed the old Miles who laughed at her, with whom she swam back to the shore, who sat by her while she dried herself. But it seemed a very new Miles who said, "I shouldn't sunbathe if I were you. A brown skin doesn't look at all well with your hair"; and who, when she retorted, "How do you know—from experience?" answered with the French quotation, "When a man discusses his experiences of women with women, he proves himself on the verge of senility".

The old Miles would no more have said that than he would have looked at one as though . . . as though he were mentally removing one's swimming suit.

"Hateful of him", she thought; then, queerly, "His figure's absolutely perfect. I wish mine were. I really am too thin."

Just before lunch she heard him at the telephone. He was speaking French, apparently to a woman. "No, my dear", he said. "I shan't be back till the ship sails. Yes. It is a great pity. But what would you? By hazard I have encountered my family."

Turning from the telephone, he seemed faintly selfconscious.

"How about a drink?" he asked.

"No, thanks."

"Okay. See you at table."

He went off. She restrained a violent impulse to follow him. Over their meal he devoted most of his conversation to the children.

"What do you want to be when you grow up, Simmy?"

"Oh, lots of things. I want to fly aeroplanes, and drive speedboats, and be a racing motorist."

"And how about you, Philly?"

"I want to be beautiful and have lovely clothes, like mummy."

"Is that all?"

"Well, of course, Uncle Miles, I shall want a nice husband."

"And plenty of babies?"

Philly brooded.

"Babies are rather messy", she said finally—and Fluke roared.

IX

Rosaleen—with a little mending and washing to do—passed the next two hours in her bedroom. Her chores finished, she wrote a letter to Stephanie. Afterwards she spent a little more time than usual before her mirror. Finally, having observed how many of the women wore trousers, she changed into the only pair she had brought.

"You're lucky to have such a flat bottom", said Enid, entering just as she was ready. "Fluke won't let me wear mine. He says I look like the fat boy of Peckham in them. What do you think of Miles? He doesn't alter much, does he?"

They made their way downstairs. By a table in the hall, on which a woman was displaying lace, shawls and a few swimming suits, Miles joined them. How stupid Enid was—thought Rosaleen—not to see the change in him. Why, he even carried himself differently. With a touch of arrogance? No—he was too selfcontained for that—aloofness.

Yet this aloofness—it seemed to her while they sat at tea in the open air—might be largely a pose.

Every now and again, too, watching him covertly, she was reassured of his unhappiness. And somehow or other this pleased her. Sooner or later she'd make him tell her why he was unhappy. It couldn't be anything to do with money. Because he'd just told Fluke, "The American slumps? No. They haven't done me any harm." So it must be something to do with a woman. Serve him right if it were. He'd always thought too much of himself. Look at the way he'd kissed her, that night he'd taken her out dancing. She'd been only a kid then. If he tried to kiss her nowadays . . .

"But you liked it", interrupted memory—and in that moment she realised, though only as a dim possibility, that she might be falling in love.

The possibility irritated her. Refusing to bathe again, she went for a solitary walk through the woods behind the hotel.

"Don't be ridiculous", she kept telling herself. "Being so interested doesn't mean a thing. Naturally you're interested in him. You've known him for ten years. You're one of the few people he ever writes to."

That night, however, she sat by her window for nearly an hour, thinking how beautiful this place was, and how peaceful, under a high moon, with the sea so quiet that one could barely hear the tiny waves plash on the shore. And after that, for the best part of another hour, she lay wakeful, wondering how she would feel if she were really in love with a man; till her imagination began to run away with her; and she had to shut off thought by switching the light on, and reading the only book she had brought with her, a rather dreary novel which soon sent her to sleep.

The clatter of trays woke her—but only to more introversion. She breakfasted in her room, and dawdled over a cigarette before she retrieved her swimming suit from the hooks outside the window, where it had hung, forgotten, since the previous midday.

"Careless", she thought. "Not a bit like me. I don't feel like myself at all this morning." And she grew aware of excitement as she made her way through the sandy path between the pine trunks to the beach.

Miles was not there. "He's gone into Sainte Marie to cash a cheque", Fluke told her. The trivial circumstance might have been a catastrophe. Never—it seemed to Rosaleen—had she felt so unutterably depressed.

Enid had scraped acquaintance with one of the English couples, who were just introducing two more of their own ilk. Rosaleen escaped to sea; and swam herself weary. It was past midday before Miles returned.

"You're not looking any too fit", he said over luncheon. "This climate can be rather trying till one's used to it. If I were you, I should take a good long siesta."

"What he really meant", thought Rosaleen, once more at her mirror, "is that I look a perfect hag."

She slept so heavily that the hands of the wristwatch Paul had given her were pointing to half past five before she woke, feeling rather guilty, because, being Fluke's guest, she couldn't do exactly as she liked.

It was too late for tea. She took a bath, hesitated at her wardrobe, finally plumping for her blue blouse and a short skirt of flowered silk. Further thought added a quaint necklace and a "costume" bracelet, both presents from Stephanie, before she went downstairs.

Fluke was entertaining his new acquaintances in the bar.

"So you took my advice", said Miles; and, looking her over, "That colour combination suits you. These champagne cocktails might be worse. Let me get you one." Fluke pressed her to a second; and boomed at Simmy and Philly in the adjoining ping-pong room, "Now then, you two, don't make such a row". Enid, perching bright-eyed on a chromium stool, smiled, "The poor darlings. It's not their fault. It's hereditary."

"One on the beak for his nibs", whispered Miles.

His eyes, also—it seemed to Rosaleen—were just a little too bright; and over dinner, with which they drank what Fluke insisted on calling "rosy wine", he proved unusually talkative. Taking advantage of this, she asked, "What were you doing with yourself in Guatemala?"

"Fishing."

"What for?" asked Simmy.

"Sharks."

He was lying, of course. He didn't want them to know what he'd been up to in Guatemala. He never wanted anyone to know what he'd been up to. Why must he always be so secretive? Why did he fascinate her so much? "He does", she knew. And in that moment she realised how easily she could fall in love with him if she let herself go.

But, of course, she wouldn't let herself go. Not like this. Not suddenly. Not without the slightest encouragement. And anyway, even if he did give her some encouragement, to fall in love with Miles—who loathed the very idea of family life—would be a catastrophe. Far better to marry Paul!

That last thought, and the images it conjured up, depressed her again. She was glad of Fluke's, "Hallo. What's this? Musicians?"

A man in white clothes with a red handkerchief round his head and a red

127

cummerbund round his waist, accompanied by a girl in Italian peasant costume with a guitar, appeared.

One or two people clapped. The man bowed. The girl played. He began to sing *Dolce Napoli*. The girl sang next—a song of which Rosaleen could not understand a single word.

"That wasn't Italian, was it?" she asked Miles.

He seemed not to hear. She repeated her question.

"Patois", he said.

"You understood it then?"

"Most of it."

"But I didn't know you even spoke Italian."

"There are lots of things about me you don't know."

He spoke almost angrily. She realised that she must have caught him off his guard. Depression vanished. Curiosity took its place.

A good deal of applause greeted the man's next song, *Santa Lucia*. When it subsided, the girl strummed a few bars; and Rosaleen, still curious, saw Miles start; saw a strange look in his elephant-gray eyes. He stared at the girl, almost as though he were hypnotised. Rosaleen saw his lips move in unison with hers, as she began to sing, "*La luna nuova, su su quel mare*".

That must mean the new moon on the sea—and the last lines, Rosaleen just understood, were something about a prow, and an altar, and stars, and love. To those lines, also, she saw Miles's lips moving in unison; and when the singer came round with the plate he gave her fifty francs. "*Grazie tanto, signore*", said the girl and passed on to another table.

"Throwing your money about a bit, aren't you?" foghorned Fluke. "Or are you trying to get off with her?"

"If I did, that big bozo would probably stick a knife into me."

"Oh, Uncle Miles, would he really?" chimed in Simmy.

"Rather."

"I say, has anyone ever tried to stick a knife into you?"

"Well, I've had one or two thrown at me."

"Do tell us about it."

"Perhaps I will some day."

Miles spoke lightly. His eyes had lost that strange look. To the others, he must seem completely normal.

"But he isn't", Rosaleen knew. "He's only on guard again."

And that night, just before she fell asleep, memory repeated his phrase, "There are lots of things about me you don't know".

What kind of things?

Sex things?

Confound sex. If she didn't keep a tight rein on herself, she'd be as bad as Paul, falling in love with someone who didn't give a damn for her.

Surely a girl didn't make that sort of an ass of herself at twenty-five?

x

"Not that sort of an ass of myself. Not at my age", thought Rosaleen, as she strolled down to the beach next morning. But, halfway along the sandy path between the pine trunks, she heard the swift pad of rope soles behind her and Miles calling, "Hallo there". Turning, she saw that he had discarded his stick.

"My ankle?" he said, answering her inquiry. "Oh, that's all right again. But I think I'll keep the bandage on till tomorrow, just *par precaution*. How did the bridge go?"

"I didn't play. What happened to you?"

"I took the bus into Sainte Marie. They've a little casino there."

"Did you gamble?"

"No. I just had a couple of drinks and came away again. Gambling rather bores me."

He stopped to light a cigarette. Today he wore a new sports coat over his bathing shorts. Obviously his bag had arrived. Curiosity—or could it be anxiety?—made her ask, "How long can you stay?"

"Oh, another two or three days, I expect. It depends on when my boat sails. She's held up at Marseilles for the moment. There's a strike on."

"It doesn't seem to worry you."

"Why should it? I'm not in any hurry."

They strolled on again; found Fluke and Enid lazing.

"Where are the kids?" asked Miles.

"They've gone off in a boat", said Enid vaguely. "Give me some more oil, Fluke dear? I'm browning up quite nicely except for my shoulder straps. If you don't wear a hat, Miles, you'll get sunstroke."

"Sunstroke? You don't know what real sun feels like."

Miles threw off his coat and squatted, lighting yet another of his interminable cigarettes.

"He oughtn't to smoke so much", thought Rosaleen. As though it mattered if he smoked himself sick!

Presently he asked, "How about that diving lesson I promised you?" and they went to the board.

"That's much better", he said, after she had taken three plunges. "Now for a good swim."

Ratiocinations, introversions, all the troublesome thoughts she had experienced since their meeting, disappeared while they swam side by side through the sunbright sea. Back on shore, peace lapped both her mind and her body. All that morning, all that afternoon and evening passed like a happy dream. Yet, because this happiness was so different from any she had ever experienced, Rosaleen could not help being both a little doubtful of it and a little afraid.

"This isn't real", whispered doubt. While fear whispered, "This can't last. Tomorrow you'll be yourself again". For, surely, her real self couldn't be so light of heart, so inconsequent, so . . . so feckless as to say, "I don't see why we shouldn't, Miles", when he suggested after dinner, "This place is like a morgue tonight. Let's pinch Fluke's car, and go for a flip".

XI

The English were already at their bridge, most of the French people at the casino. Only one old woman looked up from her book as Miles and

Rosaleen passed through the hall and out into the moonlight towards the garage, above which were the chauffeurs' rooms.

"Monsieur Ablett?" said the night watchman. "You mean the Englishman with the two cars. But yes. He is about to go repose himself." As he spoke, Ablett appeared on the outside stairway. Miles called up, "We're just going for a spin in the small car. Where's the ignition key?"

"In the lock, sir."

"How about petrol?"

"She's full up, sir. But Mr. Radcliffe's orders were nobody was to take her out except himself."

"He told me to tell you it would be all right, Ablett."

"Well, of course in that case, sir——"

The chauffeur went back to his quarters.

"You are a liar", said Rosaleen, as Miles pressed the starter button. "Supposing we were to have an accident. Fluke would be absolutely livid."

"All right, then. We won't have an accident."

After warming the motor, he let in first gear. Their headlights swept the oleanders. He turned east at the level crossing, and changed up, saying, "Not a bad bus, this. Do you remember the first time I ever drove you—in that Tin Lizzie?"

"Of course I do."

"You did look a funny little thing in your blanket. But you were jolly plucky."

It was the first compliment he had ever paid her.

"I didn't feel plucky", she said after a pause.

He drove a good kilometre without speaking. On their right, smooth silver under a full moon, lay the sea. On their left marched the dark regiment of pines.

"It's not bad here", began Miles.

"I think it's lovely."

"You didn't think it so lovely yesterday."

"How on earth do you know that?"

"Instinct, my dear."

"I don't believe you. I believe you were just guessing."

"But I guessed right, as you've already admitted." And he drove another kilometre in silence, while she thought, "Then he is a little interested in me after all".

Suddenly, her own instinct urged reprisal.

"You weren't quite yourself yesterday either", she said. "At any rate, not last night."

"What do you mean by that?"

"Oh, nothing, Miles." Instinct swept her on. "You didn't give yourself away, if that's what's worrying you. I'm sure no one else noticed it."

"Noticed what?"

"The effect that song had on you. Or was it the girl? Of course—it might have been the girl. Men do fall in love at first sight."

"It depends on what you mean by love." It seemed to Rosaleen that he had taken her up just a shade too quickly. "I don't believe in the as-long-as-ye-both-shall-live stuff myself,"

130

Silence seemed her best card. She played it.

"Do you?" he asked; and after another pause she answered, "I don't really know. I've never bothered about love. I've been too busy."

"But lots of men must have tried to make love to you?"

"Is that intended for a compliment?"

"Take it any way you like. I paid you a real compliment once. But, as far as I can recollect, you didn't particularly appreciate it."

The reference was obvious. She wanted to retort, "It isn't much of a compliment to kiss a girl when you've had too much to drink". But, once again, silence seemed her best card.

He lifted his right foot, and their steady speed slowed to a crawl. Why should she be feeling so excited? Was she so silly that the mere memory of a longago kiss could set her heart beating? And why—why on earth—were her toes curling in her shoes?

She thought stupidly, "I never really liked these shoes", and, not so stupidly, "Why didn't I say no when he asked me to come out with him?"

He was still driving very slowly. She began to feel a little afraid. She began to feel altogether afraid. This new Miles could be dangerous to her. But only if she lost her head. So she mustn't. She simply mustn't.

"Miles—oughtn't we to be going back?"

"We will presently. There's no room to turn the car here."

He answered her question as though it had been of no importance. He was treating her like a child. He always had treated her like a child. He didn't care a fig for her. Or for any woman. But he must have cared for some woman. Otherwise that song wouldn't have affected him so. And how about that telephone message she had overheard, "My dear . . . it's a great pity . . . but what would you"? Confound this curiosity about him. What did it matter to her if he'd cared for half a dozen women? It didn't matter a hoot. Nothing mattered—except keeping her head if he tried to kiss her again. But he wouldn't unless . . . unless she gave him an opening. Now how did she know that?

He was driving a little faster. Glancing at him, she saw his lips curl. Scornfully? Did he know her thoughts, then? What were his thoughts? He looked as though he had almost forgotten her.

The road, still running between sea and pines, widened. She heard herself say, "We could turn here"; heard him answer, "We could but we're not going to".

Fear touched her again, as his foot went down and the car swept to speed, its dipped headlamps illuminating kilometre stone after red-topped kilometre stone. Why was he driving so fast? Just to frighten her. But it wasn't their speed which frightened her. That only exhilarated her. It was this exhilaration—really—which made her so afraid because . . . because it seemed to be killing all thought, and all reason too.

She didn't want to think any more. She didn't want to reason any more. She just wanted to feel his hands on her, his lips on her, to lose herself in his kisses.

Afterwards? Never mind what happened afterwards. Why bother about that? Why bother about anything except . . . except the call of one's own womanhood?

Lost in emotions, she hardly realised that Miles was slowing. They were a little away from the sea now, trees on either side of them. The pines on their right opened. He braked; said, "It looks as though we ought to be able to turn here"; changed down and put the wheel over. Their tyres touched sand; ceased to roll. He shut off the engine, saying, "I could do with a cigarette".

"All right." He had spoken so calmly that her reason seemed to return. "If you really want one."

"What about you?"

"I'd rather not, thanks."

He fumbled in both jacket pockets; muttered, "Oh, dash, I've come away without any"; made to start the engine again—but took his hand from the starter button without pressing it. He had such nice hands, not flabby and clammy like Paul's. He was so much more handsome than Paul. So much more . . . virile. Reason vanished again. Instinct urged, "You've only to give him an opening". Fear had gone.

"It's a pity we didn't bring our bathing things", he said, still speaking very calmly. "This looks as though it ought to be a grand place for a swim."

"Yes. Doesn't it?"

"We might come here tomorrow."

"But it may not be as good as it looks. Shall we get out and see, Miles?"

He hesitated for an appreciable moment. She was aware of the hesitation, and of his eyes on her. He had such puzzling eyes. What lay behind them?

"We will if you like, Rosaleen."

"I think it would be rather nice."

XII

Rosaleen opened the nearside door and jumped out. Miles slid along the seat and joined her. Moonlight showed them a broad path between the pine trees. They set off side by side, drawing closer to each other as the path narrowed, sloping to the sea. The last few yards were rather steep. A rock nearly tripped her. As she half stumbled, he caught her by the elbow.

"Easy over the stones", he chaffed. But his voice had changed. His fingers were hot on her naked skin. She sensed emotion in him; and in herself a very turmoil of all the emotions.

They trod flat sand; but his fingers did not relax their grip. She saw vaguely that they were in the tiniest cove, sheltered from the road by the semicircle of pines through which they had come. Then he caught her by the other elbow and turned her towards him, so that she saw only his eyes.

His eyes seemed to be quizzing her. It was still impossible to know what lay behind them. She heard herself say, "Don't. You're hurting me"; heard him say, "Sorry"; felt his fingers relax.

His arms dropped to his sides. But they were still close to each other. She could see his nostrils flaring, ever so slightly, and a tiny vein throbbing at his right temple just under that patch of white hair which she had noticed

132

when they first met in Ireland. He'd been little more than a boy then; and she only a child. But now she was coming to full womanhood.

The apple of full womanhood was hers for the taking. She had only to hold out her hand.

And suddenly she was holding out both her hands—and he had gripped them, was pulling her towards him. Then an arm circled her shoulders, and she saw his eyes blaze. His mouth fastened on hers. She caught her breath, fought for breath, almost stifled by the fury of his first kiss.

But after that she gave him back kiss for kiss, the fingers of her free hand locked at his neck, pulling his head down, pulling his lips back to her lips every time they would have broken away. And, "Miles", she heard her own lips gasp between their kisses, "Oh, Miles. Oh, my darling. My darling".

Then, suddenly, she felt the strength go out of her, felt it ebbing from her knees as he lifted her, as he laid her full length on the warm sand.

He knelt over her, kissing her and fondling her, until her mouth, her breasts, her whole body might have been on fire. She could only whisper, "Be kind to me, Miles. Be gentle with me. I've—I've never been with anyone else".

"What ?"

His voice had changed again. It rasped between his teeth. And his eyes, too—those eyes up into which she lay looking—had changed. They still blazed, but with a different fire. He was angry with her. Why ? His hands were abandoning her. Why ? Didn't he want her any more—now that she was ready to give herself to him—now that she had so nearly given herself to him ?

"Are you telling me the truth ?" His voice still rasped. His eyes still blazed anger.

"Yes."

"You mean——"

"Just what I said."

"And you expected me——"

He rose from his knees. The fire went out of her body. Her lips were dry, her breasts ice. He stared down at her. She sat upright, staring back at him. He helped her to her feet. For a long time there were no more words in either of them.

"We'd better be getting along", he said presently ; and, after a little pause, "I thought you were only out for a bit of fun. I ought to have known better. Sorry".

Pride urged her to say, "I don't want your pity". Curiosity urged her to ask, "If that was all you were out for, why didn't you take your fun ?" But her lips were still too dry for speech ; and, under her frozen breasts, it seemed as though her very blood had ceased to run.

Hopelessly, submissively—all pride and all curiosity beaten out of her—she followed him up the sandy path, through the pine trees and back into the car.

"Rosaleen", he began there—and his voice seemed surprisingly tender, "we can't just leave things like this. I know what you're feeling. You're feeling that I've behaved rather badly."

"No, Miles." At last she found words. "It wasn't your fault."

"That's generous of you." He started the car and drove slowly on to the road. "But it isn't true. Let's be quite straight with each other."

"I'd—I'd rather not talk about it."

"But we must."

"Why?"

"Because we've known each other so long. Because we've always been such good friends."

"Friends!" she told herself bitterly; "I don't want his friendship": and, suddenly shamed again, "Not now. I've made too much of a fool of myself."

Aloud she said, "You're only trying to make things easy for me. You needn't. I shan't die of a broken heart just because you . . . you wouldn't do what I wanted".

He took her up instantly with a sharp, "Do you imagine I didn't want it too?"

At his words bitterness left her; and once again she experienced that turmoil of all the emotions, as she asked, "Then why wouldn't you?"

"It's a little difficult to explain." He had hesitated, but only for a moment or so. "I might have—if you'd been anybody else. But you see—I know this sounds rather silly—I've always felt a bit . . . a bit responsible for you, ever since I sent Fluke that telegram. And besides—well, it isn't as if I were in love with you."

He broke off. Glancing sideways at him, she realised—once again—that he must be unhappy. And, "Why couldn't I have made him happy", she caught herself thinking, "even if it wasn't for very long?"

Silence and their own meditations enfolded them. He drove on steadily under the setting moon. After a while he continued, "I'm afraid I didn't make myself very clear. And maybe that isn't the explanation. I don't want to set myself up as a Sir Galahad. But I guess I was pretty scared I mightn't be able to take care of you".

He broke off again. She said without thinking, "I don't quite understand".

"Don't you?"

"Yes." She pulled herself together. "Of course I do. I'm not as innocent as all that. It . . . it was pretty decent of you, Miles."

"Nonsense. I was only thinking of myself. If you'd had a baby, I should have had to marry you. And if there's one thing on earth I never want to do, it's to get married."

His voice had changed once more. This was the old Miles.

Why couldn't she be the old Rosaleen? Why had she wanted him so? Why hadn't she been scared of having a baby? Did she still want him?

"No", said her pride. "No. Not after the way he behaved."

And yet, had he behaved so badly? Where was he to blame? She'd thrown herself at his head like . . . like a love-crazed flapper.

"But you're not really in love with him", she thought. "It was just sex."

XIII

Sex.

Sex.

Sex.

All the way back to the hotel their very tyres seemed to be drumming the word at Rosaleen. Revulsion was on her.

"How he must despise me", she thought, not realising Miles was prey to an even deeper revulsion, at this hunger which only one woman—Halcyon, not seen for more than a year—had ever truly satisfied, but which could still leap on a man, insidiously, like a wild beast from a bough.

He did not speak again until they had garaged Fluke's car.

"I've been thinking", he said then. "How would it be if I faked up some excuse and went back to Toulon tomorrow?"

Once more, pride came to her help. She answered abruptly, "My dear man, you must decide that for yourself. As far as I'm concerned it's immaterial".

"Then I may as well stay till my ship sails. After all"—with a shrug of his shoulders—"there's no need for us to meet except at mealtimes."

Nevertheless his, "Good night, Rosaleen, my dear", struck another note of tenderness; and when, three days later, Fluke boomed, "Well, goodbye, old boy, don't forget to bring us back a couple of lionskins from Abyssinia", and Ablett drove him slowly away between the oleanders, she managed to draw a little comfort from a quotation remembered since her childhood:

"What is between us, we two know.
Shake hands and let the whole world go".

"Sentimental fool", she told herself. "He shook hands with Fluke, didn't he? He shook hands with Enid, didn't he?"

But he had held her hand a little longer than either Fluke's or Enid's. And somehow she knew that—had they been alone together—he might have kissed her again.

BOOK SEVEN

I

SENTIMENTALISING WAS NO USE. MOPING WAS NO USE. NEITHER WAS THERE the slightest use—meditated Rosaleen, with Miles gone from Sainte Marie—in selfreproach. The thing had happened. You couldn't alter it by harking back. You could only profit from the experience. By being on guard against similar ones.

Only—would there ever be a similar experience? Would any other man ever arouse that particular emotion? If so, it must be someone very different, some man who wanted a wife, a home, a family. The perfect marriage! Wasn't that too much to hope for? Look at Fluke and Enid. Look at Timothy and Lucy. Look at one's own parents. Look at all the other married couples one knew.

So why bother about marriage? Only because you wanted to have babies. And you couldn't possibly have babies without being married. It wasn't fair on them. Supposing, though—just supposing—that you had been going to have a baby by Miles?

What would you do in that case? Write and tell him? Blackmail him—it would be no better than blackmail—into marrying you? Probably. But how you'd hate yourself. So why not just be glad you weren't going to have a baby—and enjoy the rest of your holiday?

"That's what I will do", decided Rosaleen; and lived up to her decision —with only very occasional backslidings—all through that first fortnight of September nineteen hundred and thirty-one.

Her days were routine—the morning on the beach, the lazy lunch, the drowsy afternoon when one's head nodded over a book, another swim, cocktail time, dinner time, with bridge or a mild gamble in the little casino to follow.

She even indulged—just to prove her emotional immunity—in a very mild flirtation with a very mild young Englishman.

Then, with their suitcases packed for the return journey and only the overnight warning, "I feel awfully funny, Aunt Rosaleen. It's something to do with my head, I think", Simmy fell ill, his morning temperature a hundred and three.

The local doctor diagnosed, "A little nothing. A touch of our Mediterranean fever". But Fluke, panicking and fuming, "Blast. This'll throw all my staff work out. And he won't be back in time for beginning of term either", summoned a specialist from Marseilles.

"A little nothing at all", pronounced the specialist. "No food. A day or two more in bed—and, there you are, he will be quite fit to travel by auto."

It was while they were "travelling by auto"—on the afternoon the Plinley Green safari reached Lyons—that England went off the gold standard, and the pound crashed, and Enid asked, "Does this mean we shan't have enough francs to get home with, Fluke?"

But Leader Fluke only boomed, "Not on your life. I smelt this coming. I changed my whole letter of credit before we left Sainte Marie".

And he continued to preen himself on his foresight ("Shouldn't wonder if old man Snowden hadn't caught most of these blokes napping") while they watched his two cars, last of a full cargo, being manhandled aboard at Calais.

Whereafter the unkindly Channel, which has no respect for leaders, made even Fluke its sycophant, turning the white cliffs of Dover, as seen through the cabin porthole, to a most nauseous green.

II

Oh, but it was good—thought Rosaleen—to be at work again, to book reservations on the telephone, to hear the music of the radio and the slither of feet along the dance floor, to check up the cash every night and the bills every morning, to wrangle with the laundry, and bully the wine merchants, and argue about repairs with Dick Simmons, and gossip with Stephanie over a last cigarette before you dropped into bed . . . too tired to worry about anything except whether the plumber would keep his promise (only plumbers never did keep promises) and fix the hot-water tap in number nine, or whether that cheque you had taken from the young man in number twelve (such a nice young man and perhaps he really had been married to that nice young woman) would be met.

For what else was there to worry about? Politics? Not with this new national government in power. Economics? Not with "Your pound still worth a pound in England" and business so good at the Beehive. Bank failures in the United States? But here banks didn't fail. The Japanese attack on Manchuria? Let Paul shake his head over that, and say that the League ought to intervene.

Poor old Paul. He must always be shaking his head over something or other. Thank goodness he'd left off proposing to one. And thank goodness one had got over "that idiotic business" with Miles.

And yet—Rosaleen used to speculate in her rare times of leisure—would she ever quite forget those moments with Miles? Could she ever be like Stephanie, whom no man moved, who had no desire for children, whose only Christmas thought was, "We ought to take the best part of two hundred quid"?

No. She could never be a Stephanie. She could never be really happy without at least one baby of her very own.

She confessed this, one evening as they finished decorating the dance room with holly and mistletoe; but Stephanie only laughed, "It's easy enough, my dear. I'm sure there are plenty of men who would be only too willing to oblige you. I don't see why a woman should have to give up being a mother just because she doesn't want to be a wife".

And, that night, imagination rode Rosaleen, woken by the beat of heavy rain against her bedroom window, with its sharpest spurs.

Hundreds of women, thousands of them, had babies without being married. And she was making money. The Beehive would always make money. Besides, there were more legacies to come. Three of them. If you had enough money, you could do what you jolly well wanted to.

137

"So why shouldn't you do what you jolly well want to?" asked her imagination.

By next morning, however, such imaginings seemed altogether foolish. After all, she wasn't twenty-six yet. Sooner or later she would find some man she liked well enough to marry. Meanwhile, work!

III

Those holidays, Rosaleen and Stephanie had enough work for half a dozen women. No fancy-dress dance at the Albanford Assembly Rooms, no New Year's Eve party at Rosemary Lodge for them.

Twelve strokes of Big Ben on their own Radcliffe radio ("Model P.L. Superhet with the new magic-eye tuning") signalled the advent of nineteen hundred and thirty-two to their own guests—"All paying ones", as Stephanie remarked from the doorway of the dance room, "and all tight at their own expense".

But after that, with "Joey Giles and his Plinley Green Boys" playing *Auld Lang Syne*, even Stephanie waxed slightly sentimental, slipping her arm round Rosaleen's waist and asking, "Do you remember our first New Year in this place—how it snowed, and how nobody could come within a mile of us because the road wasn't made up?"

"Yes, I remember", answered Rosaleen. "And wasn't I in a panic our money would run out? You never were. You've always been marvellous. You do know how grateful I am, don't you, dear?"

For the first time in years Stephanie kissed her on the lips. Then, her cheeks flushing with sudden scarlet, she snapped, "Don't be such an ass. Gratitude indeed. As though you haven't had as much to do with it as I have". And very late that night, also for the first time in years, Stephanie Archer prayed to the God in whom her father had never quite taught her to believe, asking Him, incoherently, to make her as other women.

"Let me be pure in heart", prayed Stephanie.

She was the most normal of women. Nevertheless certain obscure thoughts continued to fret her; and after Twelfth Night, when Joey Giles's Boys again performed to the popping of champagne corks and a considerable profit, she visited Cambridge for a week, leaving Rosaleen to cope with the accountants.

"It looks like over two thousand net profit", Rosaleen told her on her return. "And we've written off everything we dare."

Fluke, who brought his codirectors to lunch next day, and was duly shown the trial balance sheet before he returned to the factory, bellowed, "Good for the family. Radcliffe Radios ought to pay twenty-five percent this year—and Archers must be fairly coining it, because the old man's gone and bought himself a car".

At the Beehive board meeting Paul proposed, "that we should now commence repaying our debentures". This was carried unanimously, but a more private proposal by Timothy refused.

"I'm quite sure Lucy doesn't understand you", said Rosaleen on the occasion of that private proposal. "If she did, she'd have divorced you

138

years ago. How about that synthetic blond you brought here in the summer? I'm sure she simply oozes sympathy."

Thus further assured of emotional immunity, she dismissed Barbara Thaxted, engaged a male bookkeeper, and—towards the middle of February—yielding to Eliza Cranbourne's persistence, changed their laundry.

Such things really mattered. The so-called sex life didn't. A successful businesswoman could do without a husband. She could even do without a baby.

So why—why on earth—should her heart miss a beat when Enid, who often brought her three younger children over to tea, said, "Just before we left the Lodge I had a telephone message. Who do you think it was from? Miles! He's back from Abyssinia. He's coming down tonight"?

One heartbeat. And then another. How silly she was being. She couldn't still be in love with the man. Dash it all, she never had been in love with the man, except . . . except for a few minutes. And he hadn't even been in love with her that long. He'd told her so. Horrid of him. He might at least have pretended.

Supposing she had pretended? She could have. Easily . . .

"Can we have lots of crumpets, please, Aunt Rosaleen?"

Philly and Arty and Gladdy were all speaking at once.

"Don't be so greedy", Enid reproved them.

Did Enid realise her own luck?

IV

It was the best part of six years—Miles Radcliffe remembered—since he last sauntered down these stairs and along this underground passage. But Plinley Green station hadn't even had a lick of new paint.

"And those blokes on the five-five", he thought, "might have been the very same."

It had been raining. Gray skies outlined the church spire. Tipping his porter, stepping into a taxi, he wondered, "Why have I come back?"

The main road beyond the railway arches had been widened. Here were fresh shops; there several more streets of "desirable villa residences". In Clareville Grove three new houses were under construction; and, as they drove in between the pillars of Rosemary Lodge, now topped with a brace of stone eagles, he saw that Fluke was building too.

"Billiard room, playroom for the kids, and a guest suite", shouted Fluke, meeting him in the oak-panelled hall. "Had to have 'em. What about my lionskins?"

"Rowland Ward's sending them down as soon as they're ready."

"Thanks awfully, old boy."

A manservant demanded Miles's keys and took his gear. Fluke led the way to the library; seated him in one of the saddlebags; poured whiskey, and began, "You're looking very fit. As usual. Wish I were. My digestion's gone to hell. Too much work and not enough exercise. Simmy's off to Torrington next term".

"How are the others?

"Fine."

"And Enid?"

"She's a bit fussed. Doesn't like having workmen about the place. But thank the lord there's nothing else the matter with her. And business is fairly sizzling. Have a cigar? We don't dine till eight. By the way, I hope you've brought dinner clothes." And his halfbrother talked on, while Miles listened, thinking, "Plinley Greenery—thy name is Fluke".

At seven-fifteen a gong rang, and he went up to the same little bedroom. The manservant had unpacked his gear. On his dressing table lay a small leather case, fastened with a press button. He opened the case, which he had found waiting for him in a registered parcel at his London club; closed it again.

Why should Halcyon send him her photograph? Why had she written "*Hasta la vista*" on it? Just when he was managing to forget, too. Hell!

He took a bath, dressed, and reluctantly kissed Philly, who had just finished supper in the nursery, on his way downstairs.

By the fire in the drawing room—its curtains already drawn—Enid sat listening to her radio.

"It's nice of you to put me up", said Miles.

"There's always room for one of the family. Help yourself to a drink."

Over dinner he experienced—for the first time he could remember—a touch of envy. Fluke, however much one might laugh at him, had always known what he wanted.

"And I haven't. Not for the last two years anyway", thought Miles.

While they were drinking coffee, the manservant announced, "Mr. Grayson's here, sir. I've shown him into your study"; and Fluke, booming, "Quite right, Parker. Sorry, old boy; but this is business", left him alone with Enid, who said, "Now tell me all about Abyssinia. Was it desperately uncomfortable?"

Entertaining her for an hour, showing her some photographs Ronnie had taken (including one of himself, sitting astride the first lion he had speared), Miles again felt conscious of a mild envy.

Come to think of it, there was something to be said for marriage. Since you couldn't do without women, why not have one of your own? But a woman of your own meant a home of your own, children of your own, the eight-thirty up every morning and the five-five down every evening.

"I could never stick that—especially the children", he decided. But could he stick many more years like these last? After all, he was rising thirty-three. Oughtn't a fellow to settle down at his age? Perhaps.

Up in his own room, he again opened the leather case.

The loveliness of this Halcyon. The happiness he had known with her. How much real happiness had he known since that moment when they parted at the Gare du Nord; since his sudden decision to fly to Berlin, to rejoin Geoffrey, during all those months he had spent, buying guns and running them to tinpot South American revolutionaries, with Geoffrey? And there had been no real happiness in Abyssinia either. Casual journeys, casual women, didn't really satisfy one.

Why—even Ronnie had his own woman, that French Eurasian with the downcast eyes.

"Pourquoi pas?" Miles remembered her saying. *"Il n'en saura rien. Moi, j'en ai besoin. Et toi aussi."*

Besoin! As though one were an animal. As though one would eat a friend's salt and sleep with his mistress!

The memory annoyed him. Snapping home the press button of the leather case which held Halcyon's photograph, he put it away in a drawer. *Hasta la vista*, forsooth. As if he wanted to see her again. Didn't he, though? Wasn't he still in love with her? Wouldn't he always be in love with her?

And that night he redreamed one of his earliest dreams of Halcyon, riding with her past blue-black waters into a dense green jungle, which he seemed to recognise . . . till a voice whispered, "I've never been with anyone else", and he woke to find a teatray at his elbow, and Parker drawing the chintz curtains.

V

"The master's compliments, sir", said Parker. "And would you care to go over the factory with him. If so, I'll order your breakfast in the dining room for a quarter past eight."

Miles ate in solitude. Before he had finished, Fluke entered, trumpeting, "Dunno how you can gorge yourself at this hour in the morning. It's all I can do to compete with half a grapefruit and a cup of China tea".

"Too many cigars?" grinned Miles. "Or too much brainwork?"

"Neither, old boy. Anno Domini. You wait till you're forty-two. My God, I nearly forgot. Those bloodstained decorators want to see me."

Fluke barged off. Miles poured himself a third cup of coffee and lit a cigarette. At nine o'clock precisely Ablett drove the big car to the front door. By then Fluke had a cigar between his teeth.

"This district's going ahead by leaps and bounds", he said, pointing out one mushroom patch of bungalows after the other, as they headed for the bypass. "In another ten years you won't know it." And on the bypass he gloated over several new factories.

"Progress, old boy. Progress. And a few years ago lots of people thought the old country was done."

"But isn't there a lot of unemployment?"

"Don't you worry. We'll cure that all right. I'm an optimist. Always have been. What I say is——"

Fluke continued to have his say till they entered his private office, where he buzzed for the dourfaced Miss Higginbottom, and told her, "This is my halfbrother, Miles. I want Mr. Grayson to show him over the factory. Take him along, will you? Are the travellers here?"

"Yes, Mr. Radcliffe. They're in Mr. Steele's office."

"Good. Tell 'em I'll be with 'em in two shakes of a duck's tail. See you later, old boy."

Thus dismissed, Miles followed Jean Higginbottom into a long room full of mysterious gadgets.

"But there's nothing really mysterious about radio, once you grasp the first principles, as they were laid down by Faraday and Maxwell", said Derek Grayson, peering at him through hornrimmed lenses.

"And who was Maxwell?"

"British mathematician. He proved the thing could be done—on paper —twenty years before Herz started to do it in the laboratory."

"But I always thought that Marconi invented wireless."

"A lot of chaps had their fingers in the pie before he was clever enough to start pulling the plums out. It's the same with most so-called inventions. One man, usually an Englishman, makes the original discovery. Then some foreign bloke, usually a Hun, does the technical spadework, because we're too damned lazy or too damned hidebound to bother about it. And after that some smart Alick with a flair for moneymaking turns up and scoops the pool."

Derek Grayson rode his hobbyhorse for a few minutes. They spent two whole hours in the factory.

"Pretty good show, eh?" boomed Fluke, when Grayson brought Miles back to his office. "This is Mr. Steele, our sales manager. We've just been having our quarterly travellers' conference."

"Glad to know you", said Steele, offering Miles a plump hand. "Mr. Radcliffe's just been telling me you're quite a dab at foreign languages."

"Let's leave that till after lunch, shall we?" interrupted Fluke. And Miles couldn't help speculating why he spoke a trifle more sharply than his habit. But his half brother's next words, "You'd better come along to the Beehive with us, Derek", drove the trivial speculation from Miles's mind.

Lunch at the Beehive meant a meeting with Rosaleen. "Bound to be a little awkward", he thought, when Fluke led him across the lounge of the hotel towards a glass sign which read, "The Honeycomb Cocktail Snuggery".

Rosaleen, however, did not appear till they were nearly through luncheon, and then all she said to him was, "Hallo! Enid told me you were back. Sorry I can't stay and talk to you, but Stephanie's up in London, and I've got to be here, there and everywhere".

She went to one of the other tables. Fluke produced a handful of cigars; called to their waitress, "We're quite ready for coffee, Mollie"; and continued, "Now go ahead, Steele; and before you start, I'll lay you ten to one in paper pounds he won't play".

"But it was your own scheme, Mr. Radcliffe", protested the sales manager; and turned sharp eyes on Miles.

Fluke's scheme, as elaborated with pomp and circumstantiality by the paunched and clean-shaven Steele, was simple enough. Radcliffe Radios Limited had "a certain number of continental agents" who might do better if "contacted regularly". But it was no good sending a home traveller out on that job. They needed a "man of the world", a "cosmopolitan", a chap who could take these agents "out and about a bit", talk to them in their own language, and . . .

"Help 'em to do a spot of bribery and corruption as and where necessary", interposed Fluke. "You know what foreigners are, old boy. Nothing for nothing's their motto."

"Floreat Torringtonia", grinned Miles, and quoted the school motto, "*Recte et Honeste.*"

"Uprightly and honestly", translated Fluke, also grinning. "Of course that would come out cheaper. But I don't see it bringing in much business. How would a job like that appeal to you?"

142

Somewhat to his halfbrother's surprise, but more to his own, Miles answered, "It sounds as though it might be rather fun. I'd like to think it over".

"Do", said Fluke, adding, "Of course you'd have to learn a bit about the business first. But that wouldn't take long. Call it a month at the outside. Then there's the question of how much we can afford to pay you. I'll talk that over with Mr. Steele this afternoon and let you know our ideas this evening."

VI

Fluke's ideas ("Five hundred a year salary, old boy, and any expenses within reason") seemed liberal enough. A full week, nevertheless, went by before Miles could be persuaded to "try it for three months and see how I get on". And, reconsidering the mental processes which had led him to this decision during the month of tuition which followed, they seemed more than a little obscure.

Financially, of course, he was in clover. The technical end of the business interested him. Travel had always been one of his passions. Try as he might, however, he could not see the job as a permanency, only as a stopgap. And a rather dangerous stopgap at that.

"Might find myself tempted to settle down if I make a success of it", he used to think. "And, hang it, I don't want to settle down. Not at my age. And not at Plinley Green anyway."

For therein—in "these intermittent attacks of Plinley Greenery", as Miles phrased it to himself—lay one's real danger, not quite so obscure, especially of a spring evening when one drifted over to the Beehive for a cocktail and a little chat with Rosaleen.

A jolly attractive young woman, Rosaleen. Took a lot of trouble about her appearance nowadays. No fool either. Look at the way she and Stephanie ran that business. A nice sense of humour she had too. And other senses. He might do worse—he might do a great deal worse—if he wanted to get married.

Dash it all, though, he didn't want to get married. That was the very last thing on earth he wanted. And yet, you couldn't do without women altogether. You got too hungry.

Confound this hunger. It'd get you into a mess before you were done.

"I'm flying to Berlin tomorrow", he told Rosaleen, one afternoon towards the end of April.

"But you'll be back?"

"Oh, yes. In about three weeks or a month."

"Fluke says he expects great things of you now you've picked up the business. He says you're absolutely cut out for a contact man."

"Fluke's always a bit of an optimist."

"So am I. I'm sure you're going to do splendidly—and that you'll end up by being made export manager."

From Berlin Miles flew to Milan, and from Milan to Paris.

A week later, Fluke's Catalan agent, meeting him at the Barcelona airport, lisped, "This is a great pleasure, *señor capitan*. Tomorrow is a national holiday. So I shall have the opportunity to show you our town. Tonight there is a party, given by *una amiga de mi amiga*, who trusts you will honour her house with your presence".

The girl friend of Señor Matric's girl friend welcomed Miles to her apartment with the conventional, *"Mi casa es á usted"*.

But there conventionality ended; and it was broad daylight, with all the flowerbooths blazing colour along the Ramblas, before he sauntered back to his hotel, remembering, dimly out of the boyhood when poetry had meant so much to him, "Passion ebbs and passion flows, But under every new caress The riven heart more keenly knows Its own inviolate faithfulness".

Confound this hunger again. And confound Maria Carmencita for having red hair.

VII

"It's your turn for a really good holiday. I don't need one at all this year", said Rosaleen; and Stephanie quizzed her before retorting, "So it appears."

The last dinner guests had left the long room; but Mollie was still laying the vacated tables for tomorrow's breakfast.

"Of course I know he doesn't like me", resumed Stephanie.

"Who doesn't like you?"

"I wish you'd leave off trying to play the innocent, Rosaleen."

"I wish you'd mind your own business."

"There's no need to lose your temper, just because you happen to be in love."

"But I'm not."

"Then why did you jump at the idea of letting him have a room?"

"I didn't jump at it."

"You gave him special terms."

"For a permanency."

"Permanency my foot! Do you really imagine that Miles will be content to work for Fluke all his life?"

"Fluke says he's done jolly well so far. They're offering him a two years' contract."

"Is he going to accept it?"

"Well—he hasn't quite made up his mind yet."

"But you've quite made up yours, haven't you?"

"About your taking a real good holiday this year", parried Rosaleen. "Rather. Why don't you try the Italian Riviera? Miles says it's simply marvellous."

"She's got Miles on the brain", thought Stephanie, but refrained from further teasing. Because after all she was only teasing—torturing?—herself.

They finished their coffee. Rosaleen went to her office. Stephanie sauntered through the last of the June sunlight towards the tennis courts, each occupied by a four. "The fool I am", continued her thoughts. "Rosaleen's bound to marry some day. So what the devil does it matter to me whom she marries?"

"Hallo there", said a voice; and, turning, she saw Miles. With him was

144

another man, tall and almost too handsome, golden of moustache and dark brown of eye, whom he introduced as, "Jim Bowlby. Jim and I have known each other longer than either of us care to remember. Could you manage him a room, do you think?"

"I shouldn't be surprised. You'd better ask Rosaleen. Rooms are her department."

"Right you are, I will."

The two men went off across the grass. Stephanie did not overhear Jim's, "A bit snooty".

But there was nothing snooty—decided Jim, the moment he set eyes on her—about Rosaleen Adair.

"Hasn't half come on since I last saw her", he ruminated, while Miles explained, "I ran into Jim on the aerodrome. I've been inquiring about a refresher course. He drove me back in his car. He's got to put up somewhere for the night, so I thought it might as well be here."

"Won't you join us for a drink?" asked Jim, after Rosaleen had shown him the room which adjoined Miles's.

"That sounds quite a good scheme. I'll be with you in twenty minutes."

She ran downstairs. They followed her at leisure; and sought the Snuggery. Jim seemed fairly prosperous. Over their whiskies and sodas, he confided:

"Among other things, I do a bit of car coping. That's what I was seeing Betterton about. And tomorrow I've got an insurance deal on. Then I sell second-hand guns. One way and another I manage to knock up about eight hundred a year. It's not so bad considering. By the way, you made rather a bloomer in asking after Mary. But I couldn't very well tell you so in front of Betterton. She and I had a divorce about two years ago".

He broke off. Miles said, "I'm sorry to hear that, old chap".

After a longish pause Jim went on, "It was all my fault. I made a perfect b.f. of myself. Thought I'd met my soul mate—and all that sort of rot. Mary behaved like an angel. But I wish to God she'd take me back. Perhaps she will one day"; and he broke off again, rising as Rosaleen entered the bar.

She sat down, and accepted a gin and tonic. Conversation turned to Ireland.

"A fat lot of good we did there", said Jim. "Dominic was quite right. De Valera's got his republic, *and* scrapped the oath of allegiance."

"But you did me a little good", smiled Rosaleen. "So we'll have the next round on the house. How long will you be staying, Captain Bowlby?"

"I must be off at crack of dawn, I'm afraid. Nice place you've got here. Miles is lucky to have such a good billet."

"Oh, we do our best to make him comfortable. Though some of his habits are rather peculiar."

"For instance?"

"Well"—laughed Rosaleen—"he will do his own washing and mending. And he insists on making his own coffee."

"Nobody in England knows how to make decent coffee", put in Miles. "And why shouldn't I do my own washing and mending if it amuses me?"

"It doesn't amuse him a bit, Captain Bowlby. It merely flatters his sense of . . . of selfsufficiency."

"Have it your own way, my dear", grinned Miles.

145

After a little more talk Rosaleen left the two men alone.

By now it was nightfall, and the Snuggery emptying.

"How long have you been staying here?" asked Jim.

"Only about a week. I'm working for my half brother."

"The devil you are. What as?"

"Oh, I'm a sort of glorified commercial traveller. I do the continent. It's rather fun in a way. But I don't think I'm going to stick to it."

"Why not? Doesn't he pay you enough?"

"The pay's all right."

Miles hesitated.

"If I carry on", he continued slowly, "I shan't make my head-quarters in England. Because then I'd have to pay tax on my American income."

"But where else can you live?"

"I rather thought of Paris. And another thing I've been thinking about is to get Fluke to stand me a plane. It'd come out much cheaper than railway fares. At least I imagine it would."

Secretly, however, Miles's imagination was still busy—as it had been busy ever since his first night at the Beehive—with the more important question, "What's scaring you?"

And, talking on with Jim—till the bar closed, till they had smoked their last cigarettes in the starlit garden, till they parted at the door of their bedrooms—he came slowly on the answer to that question. You could put it in two words, Plinley Greenery. Or you could put it in one word, coined to fit his own particular circumstance, "Rosaleenery".

Because, whatever Rosaleen had been out for last summer, you couldn't doubt what she was out for this. Otherwise why that joyous little outcry when she had been told about the proposal for a contract, "Oh, Miles, how wonderful. Now you'll really be able to settle down in England"?

Pretty plain, what that meant. And she'd been making it plainer every day since. Not crudely of course. There was nothing *crudo* about Rosaleen. But subtly, now with a look, now with a word, and always with the implied suggestion, "I know you better than most people do". Consider tonight's, "It flatters his sense of selfsufficiency", to Jim. Consider last night's, "Fluke sentimental? Not he. Miles is really the sentimental one", to Enid.

And who had given Fluke his cue for that suggestion, "Why don't you put up at the Beehive when you're at home, old boy? Save you fagging up and down from London every day"? Possibly Rosaleen. Though of course you couldn't be sure. Any more than you could be sure why you had fallen in with the suggestion, or whether you mightn't just as well swallow Plinley Greenery hook, line and sinker, safe job, marriage (after all, marriage didn't necessarily imply children,) and a villa-residence mortgaged to a building society included.

No, dash it all, you couldn't swallow that. Not with so much of the world left to see. The Far East, for instance. One day you really must hop a cargo boat to Hong Kong and call on Martin. Besides, supposing Halcyon turned up again?

"But she won't", he told himself; and so slept.

146

Jim's "crack of dawn" turned out to be nine o'clock. After they had breakfasted together, he drove Miles to the factory, where Jean Higginbottom said, "Oh, Mr. Radcliffe, Mr. Steele left a message that he'd like to see you as soon as you came in".

Steele, that morning, sounded rather gloomy about, "this continental business". They were up against too much competition.

"What I'd really like you to do", he went on, "is to take a hand in the home trade. And later on we might send you to Australia and South Africa."

At twelve o'clock Fluke boomed through the house telephone, "I'm feeding in town. You'd better come with me".

They lunched at the Savoy Grill, where Fluke seemed to know most people, including three alleged "practitioners in advertising", each transparently after his account. Afterwards they "toddled along to Portland Place".

The B.B.C. building, only just completed, struck Miles as one of the ugliest he had ever seen; and the gilded letters which greeted them as they entered the ill-lit reception hall made him laugh.

"Fee-fi-fo-fum, Reithus, Reithi, Reithe, Reithum", he recited on the way home. "Makes me feel as though I were in the Lower Fourth at Torrington again, doing Latin grammar with old Jellybags. The whole thing's typical. *Dios mio*, what a country!"

Fluke retorted rather crossly, "You're a regular bolshevik at heart, Miles. Why settle down in England if everything here annoys you so?"

"Who said I was going to?"

"But you'll have to if you sign that contract."

"Why? I could work the Continent just as well from Paris."

"But I thought——" began Fluke; and stopped, brooding, "Enid's wrong. He hasn't the slightest intention of marrying Rosaleen."

"Did Steele tell you his ideas?" he resumed.

"Yes."

"I rather agree with him. Besides—this is between you and me and the gatepost—I'm not too happy about Steele. He's just due for a new contract himself. And he's opening his mouth rather wide. I can get another sales manager, of course. But if you had a bit more training—say six months—I don't see why you shouldn't step into his shoes and eventually come on the board."

Some afternoons later—Fluke continuing persuasive—Miles signed and initialled three pages of near-English typescript which bound him, among other things, "to faithfully serve the company for a period of two (2) years from the twenty-fifth day of June nineteen hundred and thirty-two in the capacity of Continental sales-supervisor or in whatever similar capacity the company in its sole discretion shall appoint".

Dining at Rosemary Lodge that evening, he could have kicked himself for a fool.

"Why the devil did I do it?" he asked himself; and he was still asking himself the same question on that sunny afternoon, nearly a month afterwards, when he returned to the Beehive from what Fluke called "a run round the provinces, just to learn the ropes".

Compared with some of the places Miles had seen on his trip—especially one town in the distressed areas of which the traveller who drove him, eyeing the men in caps and mufflers at the grim door of the Labour Exchange, said, "I used to sell quite a lot of stuff here before they closed the pits, but now it isn't even worth stopping for"—Albanford, where he had alighted from the express, and Plinley Green, through which he had just been driven, seemed positive Utopias. Compared with all the hotels at which he had stayed his night or so, the Beehive, its shaved lawns, its flowers, its mellowing red brick walls and its gaily painted window frames all aglow in the hot July sunshine, seemed almost a home.

"Too much of a home?" he caught himself wondering, as he paid off the taxi.

Holland, the day porter, touching his cap, said, "Miss Rosaleen got your telegram. She's kept you the same room, Captain Radcliffe". And Miles's first sight of Rosaleen herself reminded him how often he had thought of her during these last three weeks.

She emerged from her office as he entered the lounge. Dash it, she really was attractive, almost beautiful; and so obviously pleased to have him back.

"How's the big businessman?" she asked, giving him a hand whose nails were now varnished.

"Pining for his tea."

"Would you like an egg to your tea, Miles?" Her hazel eyes gleamed humour.

"I wouldn't mind. They gave us a rotten lunch on the train. And can I have some watercress?"

"Watercress is an extra, sir", she mocked—and he noticed that her hair had been cut in a new fashion, revealing her ears.

"Pretty ears", he thought; and memory flashed him a very old picture of Rosaleen asleep, and of himself on a chair at her bedside, while dawn grew lighter and lighter beyond an unshuttered window, showing him the back of her head, the top coils of her golden brown pigtail, the curve of her left cheek. What kids they were in that picture. How heavily responsibility had weighed on him as he sat by that bed.

"Sentimental ass", he chided himself. "You weren't responsible for her then and you're certainly not responsible for her now."

His tea, served by Mollie in the garden, was delicious. This afternoon the Beehive seemed curiously empty, more like a country house than a hotel. He lit a black cigarette, and again fell pensive. Could this be the end of adventuring—the start of a different, a more equable, life?

Presently Rosaleen came across the lawn and sat down beside him.

"You'll be glad to know", she began, "that your *bête noire* went off for her holiday yesterday."

"Oh, come", he protested, "I don't find Stephanie as black as all that. Isn't the boot on the other leg?"

She thought that over, saying finally, "Perhaps you're right. I wish you two liked each other better. I owe a lot to Stephanie. Though of course if it hadn't been for you, she and I might never have met".

"More sentimentality", thought Miles; and changed the subject abruptly, talking about his trip, till she interrupted, "If you've got any decent cigarettes on you, I wouldn't mind one".

He slipped a hand to his hip pocket and took out a case she had never seen him use, an elaborate affair of chased gold with beautifully bevelled edges.

"Fluke's customers think the same way you do", he grinned. "So nowadays I carry stinkers for them."

"That's new, isn't it?"

"No. I've had it quite a while."

"May I look, Miles?"

"Do."

He slid the case open and handed it to her. Burning with sudden curiosity, she asked, "Who gave you this?"

"Why should you imagine anyone gave it to me?"

"Because I can't see you buying anything so expensive for yourself."

Miles grinned again, but refused to be drawn. He flicked on a lighter, also of gold and also unseen previously. "I bet some woman gave him both of them", Rosaleen said to herself. "Stephanie was quite right. I am in love with him. But I never knew it for certain till I saw him getting out of that taxi."

Aloud she said, "These are lovely cigarettes. Where did you get them?"

"At some shop in Newcastle. The fellow blends them himself. Or at least that's what he alleges on the label."

"Miles, why are you always so scornful? You never seem to believe anybody."

"Neither would you, if you were in the radio racket."

"Racket!"

"Radio's great cultural mission", scoffed Miles. "Why do your own thinking when the B.B.C. will do it for you?"

"You make me angry when you talk like that."

"You look rather nice when you're angry."

"How interesting."

"Isn't it?"

"No."

XI

"But of course it was interesting", thought Rosaleen, putting on a long frock for that night's dinner; and once again, after dinner, she sat with Miles in the garden, talking idly, thinking and thinking, "This year isn't like last. He's home now. Home for good. He's got a steady job, a two years' contract". And on the Saturday she broke a rule originally laid down by Stephanie, "You and I oughtn't to dance with the guests. People will only get wrong ideas about us". Such rubbish. When Miles danced so marvellously. Why shouldn't one have a bit of pleasure oneself, as long as the customers were properly looked after?

"But I don't think I ought to sit at your table", she said. "You have no idea what a place Plinley Green is for gossip."

"Then let's have half a bottle of fizz sent to your office."

"That would look well!"

"Perhaps you're right. It's a pity I haven't got my car yet."

"Miles! Don't!"

There was no need—she realised—to say more. He understood her meaning as well as she had understood his. That incident must never be repeated, never be referred to again.

"Sorry", he said after a pause; and she went back to her office, not altogether displeased with the way she had handled a situation which was bound to have arisen sooner or later if he were really . . . really interested in her. And of course he must be. His eyes, the pressure of his fingers while they were dancing, had told her that.

"I won't make a fool of myself this time", she decided. And by Sunday evening she felt quite sure that he must be more than a little interested in her, because that afternoon, when he came back from a round of golf with Fluke, they had fallen, somehow or other, into an argument about marriage, which ended with his admitting, "I'm not contending there isn't a lot to be said for it. Why, I might even commit matrimony myself one of these days".

Thrilling, to imagine oneself married to Miles. And all that week hope strengthened, because—for all his cynicism—he seemed so much happier, so much more contented than at Sainte Marie sur Mer.

By August bank holiday his little sports car had been delivered. She regarded the purchase as an omen. He would never have bought a car if he had the slightest intention of leaving England. Besides, he couldn't leave. He was under contract to Fluke.

The holiday rush of business over, he took her for an afternoon run and to tea at the aerodrome.

"Never been up?" he said. "I say, you are the oldfashioned girl. How about a flip round now?"

"With you?"

"Why not? Come along."

Climbing into the plane, she felt rather nervous. But once they took off she began to enjoy herself. He flew her for twenty minutes and made a perfect landing.

"We must do some more of that", he said, as they drove back to the Beehive. "It's a bit dull flying on an even keel. Next time I'll stunt with you."

"You'll do nothing of the sort."

"Oh, won't I?"

He grinned at her, a trifle masterfully. Yet the real mastery—she imagined —was her own. Last year, he had only wanted a bit of fun—and that only because she offered it. This year, he wanted companionship. Indirectly, he confessed as much next day, saying, "Dash it, why are you always so busy? Grayson's taking me up to town to see television demonstrated. I did think you'd be able to come with me."

So satisfactory, that Miles wanted her to be with him. But this year, she wasn't going to make herself cheap. She'd seen too many other girls do that since she'd been running the Beehive; and overheard too many men gossiping about them (Oh no, men never gossiped!) in the Snuggery. Besides, she didn't want . . . what she'd wanted last year, half as much as she wanted a child, two children, three children of her very own.

"And that's what I'm going to have", she told herself, taking tea at

150

Rosemary Lodge with Fluke and Enid, surrounded by Simmy, just home from his first term at Torrington, Gladdy, Philly and Arty, on the day before they all went off—by train this time—for Sainte Marie.

And the very next evening, it seemed as though dreams were to come true.

XII

That evening, with the Snuggery closed, and Milford, the night porter, only waiting for two more guests, who had gone out on a party, before he locked up, Miles sauntered into Rosaleen's office, and, touching her on the shoulder, said casually, "Hadn't you better call it a day, young woman? I'm just going for a stroll before I turn in. It'd do you all the good in the world to come with me".

She hesitated for a fraction of a second—his hand still on her shoulder—before agreeing, "All right. I will".

Once outside the hotel, both stood for a moment, revelling in the scene. It was a perfect English summer night, warm, dry, moonlit, the scent of roses in one's nostrils and, in Rosaleen's heart, certainty.

"My man", she thought. "My husband. The father of my children."

"Let's go down to the pool", said Miles.

He took her arm. They came along the herbaceous border, past the tennis courts, to the edge of the pool. For once he had no cigarette between his lips. Glancing sideways at him, she saw that they were drawn to a tight line under his narrow moustache. Then their eyes met and he smiled at her, "There's something to be said for England after all".

"You mean, you're happy here?"

"Aren't you, Rosaleen?"

"Mostly."

"What do you mean by that?"

"Well, one can't be happy all the time, Miles."

"No. Happiness isn't easy."

Still holding her arm, he fell silent, his eyes on the water. Presently his left hand closed on her right.

"You're rather a darling", he said, more to himself than to her. "And in one way you were quite right about my being more sentimental than Fluke."

He fell silent again; but his fingers tightened their grip.

"Why only in one way, Miles?"

"You wouldn't understand if I told you."

"All the same, tell me."

"I'd rather not. You'd only be shocked."

"Shocked." She couldn't help laughing. "Who's being oldfashioned now?"

He said gruffly, "Don't try to play the sophisticate. It doesn't suit you. You only know life from the outside".

"And you, of course"—she laughed again—"have really lived."

"Lived—and loved." He paused. "That sounds horribly sententious. But it happens to be true. So you may as well know it."

151

She said softly, "I knew last year. What does it matter?"

"Doesn't it matter to you?"

She hesitated once more—this time for many seconds. He released her hand and slid his arm away, facing her in the moonlight.

"Doesn't it?" he repeated. "Supposing I were still in love?"

"Are you?"

"Frankly, I don't know. It's so difficult to be honest with oneself. And"—after another pause—"it's a jolly sight more difficult to be honest with anyone of your sex."

Fear—or could it be delight?—struck her speechless. She could only watch him, puzzling herself about him, yet knowing, instinctively, that this was the moment for which she had waited so patiently, and so long.

"You see"—once again he spoke more to himself than to her—"girls don't really understand men. Not nice girls. The other sort are different. That's why one goes with them."

And after a third pause he went on, talking a little more quickly than his habit:

"For the last two years my life's been at a dead end. That's really why I signed up with Fluke. By the way, he wants me to be his sales manager and to join him on the board. So, as far as money goes I ought to be quite well off. Well enough to have a home of my own anyway".

"And a woman of your own, too."

For a moment the interruption struck him, too, speechless.

Then he said, once more speaking at his normal pace, "That's intelligent of you. And it's pretty near the truth. Though I shouldn't have put it so crudely myself. But I really am fond of you, Rosaleen—and if you'll be my wife I'll do my best to make you a good husband. Will you?"

And with that, his eyes kindling, he put out his hands to her, while she thought, "No. No. Never. Not on those terms. I shouldn't be your wife. I should only be your concubine". But already her hands were going out to his, and she was saying, "I'm fond of you, too. Only——"

"Only what, Rosaleen?"

His fingers had grown insistent. They were drawing her closer. Closer and closer. Slowly. Slowly and surely. Until, once again, she experienced desire, the whole hot, irresistible desire of her unslaked womanhood. Yet all the while thought tumbled over thought, and each thought shouting for expression, "You shan't beat me like this. You're going to know the truth too. I'm not in love with you. If I do marry you, it will only be because I want you for the father of my children".

And yet, if she did tell him the truth, if she didn't let him kiss her, now, now, with the flame kindling fiercer and fiercer in his hungry eyes, and those little pulses just beginning to beat, as she had seen them beating a year ago, at his temples, would he want her enough to marry her? Secretly, he was the sentimentalist. She must—she simply must—pretend.

"Only what, Rosaleen?" he repeated.

"Darling", she heard herself stammer, "don't—don't mind anything I say. I'm just being stupid. Stupid."

And stupidly—his arms round her, his mouth crushing hers, while thought still tumbled madly over thought, and every thought a deeper humiliation—she heard feet pounding down the flagstones that led to the pool, and a voice

152

calling, "Captain Radcliffe. Are you anywhere about? You're wanted urgently on the phone".

"This would happen at this moment", grinned Miles, releasing her as Milford ran up to them. But the night porter's next words, "It's a transatlantic call. They've been through to your club and the club put them on to us, Captain Radcliffe", wiped the grin from his lips.

"What the blazes——" Rosaleen heard him mutter. And at once he and Milford were running back to the hotel.

Automatically she ran after them; reached the main entrance; found Milford, who told her, "He's talking from your office". Still moving automatically, she ran on through the shadowy lounge.

Miles had left the office door ajar. She stopped; listened.

"Buenos Aires. Hallo, Buenos Aires", she heard him say; then, "Yes. That's right. This is Captain Miles Radcliffe speaking. Who wants me? Very well, put him on"; and after a moment's silence, "Hallo. Hallo. I'm here, Geoffrey."

And the next moment she heard, "Yes. I read something in our papers, but I didn't take it very seriously . . . As urgent as that, eh? . . . Brussels . . . Can't you send anyone else? . . . *She* wants me to . . . What did you say? With you. Yes. Yes. Of course I'd like to".

Soon his words grew incomprehensible; but Rosaleen recognised them for Spanish. He was talking to a woman.

"Althion", he said, "Althion"; and the very tone of his voice told her that this must be the woman with whom he had as good as confessed himself in love.

When he again spoke English it was curtly, crisply, "Okay, Geoffrey. I'll hop a plane. Be in Brussels by lunchtime tomorrow. Cable me the money and full instructions . . . You bet I'll bring 'em pronto, if I have to charter the *Mauretania*. Be seeing you in Asuncion . . ."

"So it's all gone phut", she realised. "Everything's gone phut!"

BOOK EIGHT

I

"IT'S A LONG, LONG WAY FROM THE CHACO TO PLINLEY GREEN", MUSED
Captain Miles Radcliffe, only Englishman to command a company of
Paraguay's crack regiment known as the Aca Veras, or Shining Heads.
"And this armistice doesn't mean the war's over. Not by a long chalk.
That Hun general and his Bolivianos are only playing for time."

He wriggled his bare toes, opened the jacket of his pyjamas, and, settling
himself still more comfortably on the rawhide bed under the mosquito net,
took another suck of maté through the silver tube of his gourd.

The temperature in this apology for a room—the best in this so-called
"fort", a collection of palmetto-roofed shacks they had captured ten days
ago—must be over a hundred. Outside—with the sun, vertical at midday
zenith, casting no shadows—it would be hot enough to fry an egg on a rock.

"But there aren't any rocks between here and Villa Montes", he thought.
"There's nothing but jungle. Must be three hundred miles of it. Still, we'll
get there one day. Or I don't know Colonel Estigarribia. Fancy, an army
like ours being commanded by a colonel who's only a little older than I am.
They might at least give him a spot of promotion after all he's done for
them. Dash it, we've never been outnumbered by less than three to one."

He took another suck of tea through the silver bombilla, and looked at
a photograph of Estigarribia, cut from an Asuncion newspaper, which
Tamoi, his bearer, reputed to be the oldest man in the army, had pinned to
the bullet-holed adobe of the outer wall.

A super-strong face, with that square chin. A super-intelligent face, with
that broad high forehead under its forest of upstanding black hair. Oh yes,
Estigarribia would lead them to Villa Montes all right. He'd sweep these
Bolivianos clean out of the Chaco. And then . . .

"Then I'll marry Halcyon", decided Miles.

He put the gourd away, rested his head on the hard pillow, closed his
eyes, and slept for a few minutes—only to be woken by the insistent pinging
of a mosquito, which he finally managed to slay. By then the toad—almost
as big as a rabbit, and nicknamed Hans Kundt after the German general
commanding the Bolivian army—had slithered from its pet corner to the
centre of the mud floor, where it now squatted, regarding him with stony
incurious eyes.

"Wouldn't half make Enid sit up if she woke and found you looking at
her, Hans", he thought ; and, so thinking, he remembered that tonight would
be the second New Year's Eve since he'd broken his contract with Fluke.

Fluke, still on holiday at Sainte Marie sur Mer, had written him a nice
stinker to Brussels : "If you were anyone else I'd damn well sue you for
damages".

Damages. What a joke !

Hans Kundt flopped closer, squatted again, blinked once and shot out
his tongue to engulf a fly. From the nearby hut came the regular raucousness
of snores ; from the jungle beyond the fort, the harsh squeals of vultures still

scavenging. So his chaps hadn't cleaned up those trenches yet. Tomorrow he must detail another burial party. And tomorrow it would be nineteen thirty-four.

He drowsed again; woke again to find the toad still staring at him. Come to think of it, he'd been a bit of a toad himself, chucking Rosaleen over like that , buzzing off to Belgium like that, telling her nothing except, "I'm sorry. But there's a war on and I've a job of real work to do".

Poor Rosaleen. She'd get over it, though. And those rifles, that ammunition had to be bought, had to be shipped. Even the Paraguayans couldn't go on fighting machine gunners with machetes for ever. And who else could Geoffrey have found to do the job ? Besides, he'd been straight enough with Rosaleen, told her there was another woman.

Thought diffused to a medley of pictures. Flashingly he saw himself packing his old valise, his battered guncase—the Sabina plane taking off from Croydon—the green of Haren aerodrome coming up at him—the little room where he sat studying Geoffrey's cabled instructions—the face of the bank manager who had said, "*Mais oui, mon capitaine*. We, too, have received a cable. There are five million belgas to your credit"—the grimy office in which he had haggled for arms with the two men named in Geoffrey's instructions.

An efficient bloke, Geoffrey. Knew the arms racket as well as he'd known the booze racket. But he'd missed one point—the draught of the ship. "Lucky I remembered she mustn't draw more than twenty feet", thought Miles Radcliffe, "otherwise we'd never have got her over Martin Garcia bar."

Then the vultures squealed again; and once more thought was a mere medley of pictures—the wharves of Antwerp—the single-funnelled *Etoile Belge*, chartered after nearly a fortnight of negotiation, with her hatches open —stevedores jabbering and her captain cursing and his cases swinging up from the quayside, dropping down into the hold.

"*Machines à coudre*. Sewing Machines. Stow away from boiler." Miles could still visualise the letters stencilled on those precious cases, as he lay sweating under his mosquito net in this Chaco *fortin* a thousand miles and more from the sea.

And now, in slow procession across the screenboard of his brain, swept the pictures of the sea—twilight down Channel and the night clouds driving —red dawn over Finisterre as she threshed into head winds—the Ushant light and a wave breaking inboard—presage of storm—and they met it off Lisbon—five knots, four knots, with the engines racing, shaking her plates as she pitched her screw free—pitched it and tossed it but rode the storm out —steaming south for the Grand Canary—steaming west with his precious cases—six knots, seven knots, eight knots, nine knots, into the calm of oily waters, into the wonder of tropic sunsets, greens and lilacs and mauves and purples, orange and scarlet and hot rose-madder, splashing the skies with incredible pigments, darkling the skies with incredible swiftness, till the whole black vault was one blaze of starshine, under which one steamed through seas of silver for the mouth of the Plate beyond Monte Video.

II

"But you don't give a damn for the sea, Hans Kundt, old boy. You've never even smelt it, and you're never likely to", thought Miles Radcliffe, wrenched from poetic reverie by the hypnotic eyes of the great toad.

Hans Kundt, as though for affirmative answer, engulfed another fly, flopped round and slithered off to his corner. The vultures, apparently satiate, had stopped their squealing. But the snores continued, keeping Miles awake.

He took the well-thumbed gourd from under his pillow, put the bombilla to his lips, and sucked another mouthful of maté. Imaginatively he was again aboard the *Etoile Belge*, standing on the bridge with her captain and the pilot, as dawn broke pearl-gray over Cerro hill and, one by one, the lights of Monte Video were extinguished.

"*Hay una lancha*", the pilot was muttering. "But it is not the launch of the *señor médico*. No. See, it is a speedboat." And in the bow of that speedboat, as she tore towards them, he recognised Geoffrey Thirkell.

The cleverest bloke, Geoffrey. You could always trust him to cut a corner.

"And we've got to cut 'em all, this trip", he had said, panting from his swarm up the ladder. "If we don't, we'll be too late. How about coal?"

"We can just make Rosario."

"Not good enough. Cheaper here. As a matter of fact, I've already fixed it."

And thanks to Geoffrey's "fixing" they were away across the Plate with full bunkers a good hour before dusk.

"How long shall we be held up at B.A. ?" Miles could still hear Geoffrey drawling. "Only long enough to pick up another pilot. Thanks to your pal the *conquistadora* we're free of the whole ruddy river. But don't ask me how that's been fixed, because I'm sugared if I know."

And it was then—Miles remembered—that he had first dared to ask, "When am I going to see her?" and Geoffrey's answer, "Quite soon enough for your peace of mind, old chap—and hers".

But he had not seen Halcyon for six long days and seven longer nights.

All those days and all those mortal nights the *Etoile Belge*, her screw half out of water, churned her slow way up the vast Parana, now a broad inland sea, its low banks of treeless scrub barely guessed on the aching horizon, now narrowed and bubbled to brown whirlpools by islands as big as an English shire. But those islands—Miles knew—could disappear, engulfed as easily as Hans Kundt could engulf a fly by the hungry river, between an up trip and a down.

Far beyond Rosario (and what memories of Halcyon in Rosario!) his ship had churned her way; past pink-washed villages, past ramshackle wharves where the peons piled the barges; past the clay banks on which the alligators basked in the steaming sunshine; past impenetrable green jungle walls, starred with red flowers and yellow, awrithe with serpents, abuzz and acrawl with insects; past San Lorenzo and Santa Fé and Diamante and the gleaming lights of City Parana, into wilder and yet wilder country—a land of red cliffs and humpbacked hills where the tacuara ferns at riverbank grew higher than the poplar trees in the garden at Rosemary Lodge, where giant birds flapped croaking from tree to tree, and giant butterflies, electric blue and copper scarlet and orange yellow, swarmed as one remembered the mayflies swarming on the river (only could you call that trickle a river?) that winds by Torrington—and if one shot an alligator the pirañas would disembowel him, drink the last drop of his blood, tear the last shred of flesh from inside his horny skin, almost before the noise of your shot finished echoing from sandspit to red sandspit across the muddied waters.

"Those cannibal fish give me the willies", Miles could remember Geoffrey drawling. "Last night I dreamt I fell overboard and that they were just getting their teeth into me."

But all those mortal nights on the slow way upstream to Corrientes Miles had dreamed only of Halcyon; and as they chugged away from Corrientes, by the red ruins of Fort Humaita—where, sixty years back, an Englishman's guns had held the water-pass for Lopez against the ironclads of the Brazilian Emperor's navy—into Paraguay, his hunger for her sharpened and sharpened, appetite unappeasable, smiting him sleepless, ache in his very loins.

This hunger, this physical ache for Halcyon! It was on one again—now—here—as one lay sweating under one's mosquito net—smiting one sleepless again—driving one crazy again, crazy with sheer longing to hold her in these arms, to fondle her with these hands, to kiss her with these lips, to kiss her and kiss her . . .

A perfect mating. A miraculous unity. Yet still more perfect, still more miraculous—or so it seemed to Miles Radcliffe—was that unity of mind and purpose which had been wrought between them during their first night in her mother's house . . .

III

Gradually—so gradually that only a man whose blood had been thinned by a whole year of fighting there could be conscious of it—the noonday heat of the Chaco began to abate. And, very gradually with that abating, there came to Miles Radcliffe a surcease from physical hunger. Yet still—though his eyes had closed again—memory forbade sleep.

In his memory those six long days, those seven mortal nights of his river journey from Monte Video, were over. At last the *Etoile Belge* had raised the city of Asuncion. There it lay, ghostly in the ultimate starlight, not a mile to starboard across the black glass of the lagoon.

In a few more minutes the stars would begin to fade, and false dawn turn the black of the glass to gray. Then true dawn would colour it to silver, and soon the Paraguayan sunrise would fleck the silver with gold.

"Is Halcyon there?" he remembered thinking. "Will she be on the quay to meet us?"

And now true dawn had already broken. Now, at long last, Asuncion was no longer a ghost city on the horizon of desires unaccomplished—but a real town.

How well one knew this little town—those cranes at water's edge, that cobbled street, the pastel shading of those flat roofs, dominated by the scaffolded cupola of the Oratorio, and the quadruple-pinnacled tower of that palace, its walls now peeling, which Dictator Lopez had built with the sweat and blood of an over-faithful people, who had fought almost to the last man at his bidding, while he lusted on a golden bed with his Irish paramour.

And today the grandsons and the great-grandsons of the men who had died for Lopez were fighting again, this time without guns, without rifles, without uniforms, most of them without even boots on their feet, in that dim green jungle on the other side of the lagoon. Yet already—if one could trust the gossip of the river—the bootless men had retaken the little forts of Pituanita and Corrales and Toledo and Boqueron. Already, armed with captured weapons, they were hacking their way on to Bolivia's advanced base at "Arce".

Could one trust the river gossip? Perhaps. Perhaps not. But did it matter which side was winning, or which side was losing, this war? Did anything matter to him, Miles Radcliffe, except Halcyon?

He recollected debating that question with himself—arguing with himself, "This isn't my war. I know the Chaco. I'm not going to fight in that stinking jungle"—as he stood for the last time on the bridge of the *Etoile Belge*, drawing closer and closer with every revolution of her screw to the wharves of Asuncion.

For still, peering his hardest, he could not perceive any but native women, with their cigars and their shawls and their baskets full of pineapples and oranges and that rock-hard bread which is called *chipa*, among the crowd along the quay.

"She's not there", he could remember himself muttering; and Geoffrey's, "I telegraphed her from Formosa. Those bally Argentinos must have held it up. Next time you charter a hooker, old chap, don't charter one without a wireless. The chances are that your *conquistadora's* either up country or in Concepcion. Never mind, you'll be seeing her one of these days."

One of these days! Or was he actually seeing her—could he really be seeing her—could that possibly be the Halcyon of New York and Paris and Milan, the Halcyon of the soft furs and the big hats and the shining shoes and the gossamer stockings, that figure in the drab green uniform, booted to the breeched knees, with a holster at its hip, running out and towards the ship from the customs sheds?

Impossible. And yet—and yet that figure might be Halcyon's. It had stopped. It had whipped off its sombrero. It was waving its sombrero. Yes. Yes. Halcyon. No head in all the world like hers.

They were almost alongside by then. Bow ropes and stern ropes had been heaved ashore. He could still see those ropes being coiled round the bollards, and the gangplank sliding down, and the crowd surging forward—could still remember the choke in his throat, the mist before his eyes and his heart thumping against his ribs, as the crowd parted to let her through and a sailor handed her aboard and he leaped down the bridge ladder.

"Meelés!" The very look in her eyes, the very tone of her voice, came back to him. "Meelés! You are in time. But only just. See, there are the lorries. At the airport the planes are waiting. Hurry. Hurry. Get me some rifles, some ammunition ashore. Not a moment must be lost. Not a single moment."

Then, turning from him and cupping her gloved hands round her lips, she had shouted in Guaraní to the waiting stevedores, "*Chébe. Chébe opacatuî*. To me. All of you. Unload me this ship. *Tîa ìuguî*. Sweat

158

your blood to unload her. How shall we attack Arce with only captured rifles and no cartridges?"

And all in a flash—as memory showed it to Miles Radcliffe—the covers were being stripped from the hatches, and the first crane load had swung ashore and men, himself among them, were piling ammunition box after ammunition box on to the first lorry. And almost before that first lorry-driver let in gear they were filling a second lorry, and yet a third, and yet a fourth lorry with cartridges and rifles. Nor might they rest, even for the full heat of noonday, with the planes already taken off from the mile-away airport and Halcyon still urging them, *"Tïaî uguî.* Sweat your blood out. Afterwards you shall eat your fill. Meanwhile you shall drink your *caña"*.

Not his war, this? Poppycock. As well say Halcyon wasn't his woman. And what a woman—this new, this transformed Halcyon in the soiled breeches and the dusty boots, with the big pistol at her belt and the sombrero cocked on her head and the cigarette between her lips, as she laced the *caña* which a shawled drinkseller had brought him with gin from her own hip flask, laughing, "Forgive me for dragging you half across the world only to make a peon of you, *amigo.* But your example is necessary. The attack is timed for dawn tomorrow. And with only two planes to carry the ammunition we dare not rest till sunset".

For not until the sun was setting had she driven him away from the water-front to her mother's house.

IV

That drive, too, memory brought back to Miles while he lay supine with closed eyes under the mosquito net—Halcyon's hand steady on the wheel as the car bumped over the cobbles of Libertad and Presidente Carnot and through a remembered plaza where the chivato trees shone orange and scarlet in the last of the sun; her hand lifted to sombrero brim as she acknowledged the salutes of those two wounded men in Plaza Independencia; her hand just resting on his arm as she slowed their speed through sudden twilight under the giant gum trees of Caballero Park.

Scraps of talk, too, he could remember. "Do not worry about your friend Don Geoffrey. He went to the hotel. He is very lazy. Yet he is also very tactful. We shall see him tomorrow morning. But tonight is ours. All ours, Meelés. At least—if you would still have it so."

If he would still have it so? *Dios !* If he would still have it so? *Madre de Dios*—as though he had ever wanted any other woman in all his life.

"But your mother, Halcyon?"

"She is not here. I sent her to Buenos Aires. The Bolivians may bomb the city. They have big planes. German ones. I have seen them myself. At Boqueron. At Corrales."

She'd been in the front line then. Fighting?

"Yes. For a little. Till the Colonel forbade it. There was another woman too. My cousin Mercédes. She killed three with a machete."

"And have you killed?"

"Not with a machete. Only with this pistol. There are notches on it. I will show you when we reach home."

"Quando llegamos á casa. When we reach home." How those words

159

had thrilled him—and that first kiss, snatched with twilight already fallen and the car halted for a moment under the dark tunnel of the trees.

"Impatient, Meelés?"

"*Si, querida*."

"Why? When we have the whole night for loving. Wait. Wait a little, *querido*."

Wait? *Dios. Madre de Dios*. Hadn't he waited for more than two years?

In his memory, she drove him on again, out of the park towards Barrio Cachinga, till the kindled swords of their headlights showed him a wide avenue bordered with carob trees, and there, at the end of the avenue, the double iron gates, the sloping parterres, the triple stairway and the eleven marble pillars of Casa Cardozo, flat-roofed above its seven Moorish arches, and that cool patio to which she had led him, whispering, "*Pichon mio*, the house is all yours".

"And you, also, Halcyon?"

"*Tonto*. Foolish one. Must I tell you that thrice over? Would you have me kiss you in front of my servants?"

For already—in the mirror of recollection—dark-eyed servants had come running to her handclaps and she was giving them orders: "We will dine out here, Pedro. Marietta, are my clothes laid out, is my bath ready? Tamoi—*sacramento*, why must you always be the last, Tamoi?—show the *señor capitan* to his room".

Miles could still see himself following Tamoi into that room, and hear the old man grumbling in Guaraní, "Once before I served a woman. But for that one, for the Irish woman of Dictator Lopez, I carried a rifle", and his own, "Nowadays, you are too old to carry a rifle", and Tamoi's "*Aãnỹ*. *Aãnỹ*. No. No. If you go to the Chaco, *capitã*, let me come with you. And together we will take *Amôtareỹmbeté*."

Amôtareỹmbeté. The word had defeated him. He could remember trying to puzzle it out, while he bathed and shaved and dressed himself in the silk clothes Tamoi brought; could even remember asking Halcyon what it meant and her answer, "The enemy's capital, of course. Have you forgotten one of the last phrases I ever taught you, *Apĩreỹ amôtareỹ, yepi yecotĩahá*? Never my enemy. Always my friend".

"*Yepi yecotĩahá. Siempre amigos*. Always friends."

The words, English and Spanish and Guaraní, sang themselves like a lullaby through the drowsy mind of Miles Radcliffe, lying there on his raw-hide bed in the heart of the Chaco; until, gradually, the mirror of recollection began to blur and he slept a while. Yet, even sleeping, some pictures of Halcyon haunted him; and, half awake again, it seemed to him that they sat once more drinking wine together at the cleared table in the moonlit patio of her mother's house.

"So you like these French fripperies I have put on for you", she was laughing. "Perhaps you would like me to varnish my nails again, and spend whole mornings at the hairdresser's. I confess I am a little disappointed in you, Meelés."

"*Porqué, querida?*"

"Because you always despised the *vida de lujo*. Because I imagined that you, being a soldier, would prefer me in my uniform."

And a little later she had said, "By tomorrow at dawn my men will have finished unloading the ship. What then? Wilt thou return to Europe in her?" and he, "Is that thy desire, Halcyon?" and she, "I will not name my desire. Decide for thyself. We Paraguayans are few. They of Bolivia are many. They have tanks, flame-throwers, aeroplanes, artillery, armies drilled by European officers. So perhaps if thou art careful, if thou art prudent——"

Careful! Prudent! With those eyes burning into his. *Carajo!* Did she think he was like Geoffrey, or like Fluke? Didn't she know that he had already decided, this morning, while he sweated on the quayside, that this was his war as much as her war if only she again became his woman?

And, "*Tonta*", he remembered himself laughing back at her. "My foolish one. There is no need for thee to name thy desire. It is the same as my own."

"Truly, Meelés?"

"Truly, Halcyon."

And after that there had been no need for any words save love words between them—and even of those, few, because, to each of them, as night waned over her mother's house, it seemed that they had reached the zenith of all human ecstasy, a union of their souls no less than of their bodies, consecrated for a common purpose to be achieved whatsoever the odds against them, till victory was won.

And from that night onwards—it came to Miles Radcliffe as his eyes opened to show him the bars of Chaco sunlight creeping slowly up the adobe wall—there had been no faltering from their common purpose, no doubt of ultimate victory, and, stranger still, no abatement of ecstasy even when they were separated, as they had been separated so often during this past year.

v

"It's a bit over a year", thought a more prosaic Miles, wide awake now and already parting the mosquito curtain to grope for his loose breeches and his soft leather riding boots. "Fourteen months to be accurate. And the best part of six weeks since I set eyes on her." Then, still more prosaically—because, although one never quite lost consciousness of this strange ecstasy, it was not the sort of mood in which a soldier on active service should over-indulge himself, "If she doesn't turn up pretty soon, I'll ask for a spot of leave and slip back to Concepcion".

In the meantime, though, what about the ration cart? Had it come in while he was asleep?

Pulling his boots over his breeches, he shouted for Tamoi. The old man, clean-shaven, hawklike of eye, leathery of face, and still black of long hair though he must be nearer eighty than seventy, came at his second call. The ration cart had not arrived.

"*Aánŷ, aánŷ*", grunted Tamoi. "We can starve for all they care in the commissariat. It was different when I fought under Lopez. Then we had full bellies."

"And what were they so full of—lead?"

Tamoi grinned at the jest; and Miles grinned back at him, thinking, "Old

161

sweats. They're the same in every army". Aloud he said, "Boil me some more maté".

"*Tá, capitã*. I will make the *caá guazu* at once."

Miles handed him the gourd, took off his pyjama jacket, washed in the tin bowl, and combed his hair at the mirror on the adobe wall. The cracked glass showed him that the white patch at his temple was a little larger than when he left England. Even to himself, his face looked leaner, older, more lined, and entirely colourless except for the red insect bites. And once upon a time he had imagined himself proof not only against mosquitos but against the tiny pulverins which made every night in the Chaco a prickling hell !

He dabbed some raw alcohol on the bites, donned his cotton singlet and lit a cigarette. Tamoi returned with the hot maté. The old man was chewing cola leaf, of which every Bolivian soldier carried a pouchful.

"The ration cart arrives", he grunted. "And about time too."

Pulling on his jacket and his only hat—made of linen and shaped like a pudding basin—Miles lounged out into the sunlight. Féliz, his top sergeant, saluted. He also announced, "Ration cart arrives".

"When ?"

"I judge it about half a league away. They should grease their axles better."

But, although Miles cupped a hand to his ear, he could hear no sound from the jungle which encircled the *fortin*.

"By which path does it come ?" he asked.

"Not by the right one. Roderigo must have lost his way. As usual."

Féliz spat his contempt. Half a dozen young men, stripped to the waist, joined them.

"*Caranchos*", said one, pointing to two vultures which had just flapped to the top of a distant tree. "That noisy cart has disturbed them."

It was not until three minutes later, however, that Miles could hear the creak of the axles. And once upon a time he had prided himself that his sense of hearing was almost as acute as a dog's !

The two skeletons of mules, and the crazy cart they drew, emerged from among the trees. The driver shouted "*Olé*", and slapped his flat-thonged *rebenque* on the mules' rumps as he crossed the clearing. More young men had come out of the huts. The cart halted, and they began to unload the rations : *chipa*, biscuits, sun-dried beef, bananas, pineapples, and manioc—a turnip-like vegetable against which even Miles's stomach had begun to revolt.

"Any letters, Roderigo ?" he asked the driver.

"None, *señor capitan*. Tomorrow perhaps."

"Any news ?"

"It is rumoured from Islâ Poi that the armistice will be prolonged for another fortnight."

"We have already heard that rumour."

"And doubtless the *señor capitan*, who knows so much, has also heard of the lady who arrived at Colonel Estigarribia's headquarters by aeroplane."

"*Cuando ?* When ?"

"It might have been yesterday afternoon."

The swarthy Roderigo wiped the sweat from his forehead with the back of his hand ; came as near to grinning as a gaucho may ; shrugged his shoulders, and swaggered off, swinging his *rebenque*, towards the palmetto roofed cook-house.

"Does everyone in this whole bally army know about me and Halcyon?" thought Miles; and he turned to Féliz, saying, "These animals will not do many more journeys".

"No. Poor beasts. The vampires have been at them."

Horse flies swarmed for the drying blood of the vampire bites on their backs, smaller flies clotted on their polls as the two apologies for mules bent their heads to suck brackish water from the two buckets. And the Bolivians had sent cavalry into the Chaco!

"*No es una guerra de caballero.* This is not a horsed gentleman's war", quoted Féliz.

"So why should I be enjoying it so much?" Miles asked himself; and, still sucking at the gourdful of warm maté, he wandered away towards the water hole, which had seemed dangerously low the last time he inspected it, think-ing:

"It isn't only because of Halcyon. Even without her, I'd rather be here than in Plinley Green".

But on that excitement gripped him. If Roderigo's hint were correct, if Estigarribia had lent Halcyon a good guide and decent horses, she might arrive tonight.

He came through the cluster of huts, by the smoke of the cookhouse, to the rough windlass under its screen of dried palm leaves. In this army one had to conduct such inspections without formality, especially if one happened to be a foreigner. Tigers in action, his men—once out of it—resented any but the mildest supervision. That much he had learned during his first week's soldiering with the Aca Veras from Alberto Roldan—killed nearly a year ago in the first big Bolivian attack on Nanawa.

A stout lad, Alberto. And since he'd taken over the company other stout lads had gone west, the last of them, Eusebio Piquart, less than a fort-night back, in the fight for this very water hole.

"It's about time they went me a couple more subalterns and some rein-forcements", he brooded, peering down into the well.

The water level seemed fairly satisfactory. He let down a bucket, cranked it up again, and eyed its scummy contents with distaste.

"Dunno why we're all not poisoned. Dunno how the dickens we've held 'em so long", he thought.

Then, once again, he remembered Alberto Roldan, and those four days, those four nights, in the trenches on the Nanawa-Gondra road.

VI

Miles emptied the bucket back into the well, overturned it and seated himself. Shadows were lengthening; but the summer sun still stood high above tree line, a ball of fire into whose eye one dared not look. Weird, that it couldn't give one sunstroke. A weird place altogether, this Chaco. From here the jungle might have been a green park. Yet—wander half a mile without guide or compass into that mirage of a park, and you might never hack your way out again.

163

Umpteen million acres of jungle, with only one navigable river, and only one track you could really call a road curving east and west from the high plateaux of the Andes along the swampy Pilcomayo.

No wonder General Kundt had flung everything he'd got into that first battle for Nanawa-Gondra. The only wonder was that his massed infantry hadn't broken through to the river; that one's own regiment and the Aca Me Quedo Yos and the Aca Carayas should have held the gap—held it for ninety-six mortal hours, under shellfire (when they didn't possess a single gun), under mortar fire (when they didn't possess one solitary mortar), under machine-gun fire (they could have done with a machine gun or two); held it and held it, letting 'em come on until one could see the whites of their eyes over the sights of the Bergmann, against wave after wave of assaulting infantry . . . held it and held it and held it, until, with one's own men (such as remained of them) down to their last cartridges, that wounded messenger had staggered along the trench and dropped to his knees gasping, "Colonel's orders. The Shining Heads will charge", and Alberto Roldan, waving his machete, went up and over, howling, "At 'em, the Aca Veras".

"Waterloo stuff", thought Miles, squatting on his bucket. "Doesn't seem true somehow or other."

Yet he himself had killed the killer of Alberto Roldan; slicing his head from his body with one cut of that heavy single-edged blade already scarlet to the cross-hilt. And how many more must he have killed on that twenty-fourth of January? How many since—with his machete, with his old Bergmann, with his two Colts, with the machine gun Féliz took single-handed?

For that battle had only been the beginning of this interminable jungle warfare—its end not yet in sight.

"No use kidding oneself", decided the soldier in Miles Radcliffe. "The Bolivianos aren't beaten. They'll come on again." And, rising, he walked back to the huts.

Some of his men were already feeding. He wished them good appetite, thinking how tough they were, and how gallant. Characteristically, no thought of his own toughness, his own gallantry, crossed his mind.

"Will the *capitã* eat now?" asked Tamoi when he reached his own quarter.

"No. I'll wait awhile."

"For *Yâra* Halcyon?"

"What do you know of *Yâra* Halcyon?"

"Nothing." Tamoi's black eyes were sly. "But something tells me she will be with us before the moon rises. See, I have set the *capitã*'s chair and table. Shall I now fetch him his *quatiá*?"

"*Tá.*"

The "book", as Tamoi called it, was a rough diary, which Miles wrote up every evening.

Taking it and seating himself on the canvas chair, he made the entry, "Twelfth day of armistice. Nothing doing"; and began to turn back the pages; musing idly, "If only I were a writer, I could make a real book out of this".

But even if he could write the thing, who would want to read it? To judge by the few newspapers one had seen during this past year, nobody in Europe and only a handful of folk in the United States took any interest in this war, one of the most bitter, one of the bloodiest, ever fought—against sheer aggression, against a big nation armed to the teeth, by a people whose regular army had numbered less than a thousand at the outbreak, and less than ten thousand in that first battle for the road to the river.

"We can all be killed for all they care", brooded Miles with a rare touch of bitterness. "But if some five-cent floozy of a cinema star divorces her husband she gets banner headlines. Because that does interest the Plinley Greens."

Quickly as it had come on him, bitterness began to pass over. Plinley Green, to the best of his recollection, hadn't been particularly interested, except from personal standpoints, in the Great War. It certainly hadn't worried its woolly head for the Troubles in Ireland. So why should it bother about what was happening in the Chaco? Would he—if it weren't for Halcyon?

Still turning back the pages of his diary, he considered that last question; as he had considered it so often since that night when they buried Alberto, watching Féliz scrawl, "*Muerto por la Libertad*" on the wooden cross.

"*Muerto por la Libertad*. He gave his life for freedom." But what was one risking one's own life for? A woman? Or a cause?

"Blowed if I know", he thought, looking up and westward over the tree tops into the fierce red eyeball of the declining sun. And as his gaze sheered away from the sun, barely two degrees above tree level but its light still blinding, he was haunted by more visions; by swift red visions of ambush and skirmish, of attack and counterattack, and of that second battle for the river, launched, as though to mock the veriest day of freedom, on the fourth of last July—launched with heavier guns (and still they had no guns), with bombing planes and tanks and flame-throwers (and still they had no tanks, no flame-throwers, and not one single fighter aeroplane), against the defenders of Nanawa-Gondra.

Touch and go, that second battle! Touch and go for five incredible months until the December morning—could it be less than three weeks ago? —when Estigarribia at last abandoned the defensive and flung every rifle, every bayonet and every machete forward against the Bolivians, hurling them back from Centeno-Gondra, smashing regiment after regiment of their conscript Cholos and Quechuas, who had no more stomach for this fight against free men.

"No wonder Herr General Kundt wants 'peace with honour'", thought Miles.

A drone—high and distant—recalled him sharply to the present. Jumping up, he ran into the hut and snatched for his fieldglasses. Inside another minute he had focused the plane—a Junkers—flying at about three thousand, straight for the *fortin*. Armistice or no armistice, one must have a crack at that chap if he came any closer . . .

But the plane was already banking; and, as the wings dwindled to a speck, the sun dipped below tree line.

Very soon, it would be night.

It had been night for a whole hour. Inside this hut, with the cheesecloth drawn across door and window and the oil lamp burning on the table, it was so hot that you nearly stifled. But, if you went out, the mosquitos and the pulverins would get you. You couldn't be quite safe from them, even here.

And those weren't the only horrors of this Chaco night—loud with the shriek of insects, the belling of giant toads, the bark of alligators and the snarls of the jaguars.

"Your move", said Féliz, playing king's knight to king's bishop seven; and Miles lit another cigarette while he studied the board.

He advanced a castle. Féliz took it with a pawn—and put his queen in jeopardy. Miles closed the trap.

"*Coños*", swore Féliz. "Your game. And tonight I imagined myself beating you easily."

"Why?"

"Because you have not yet eaten", answered the top sergeant, and came as near to grinning as Roderigo had done.

Miles poured some more of the amber *caña* into their cups, reset the pieces, and turned the board. Tamoi poked his head through the cheesecloth over the door and announced, "The moon rises".

Féliz grunted, "Then we shall not have time for another game. Besides, I ought to visit my sentries—though why it should be necessary to post sentries during an armistice only the *capitan* knows".

"Must I tell you again"—they had been disputing this point since the nineteenth of December—"of the famous Christmas truce in the Great European war, and how it was ended by a German officer shooting one of our men in the back?"

"But we are not fighting against Germans. The Bolivian officers are men of honour."

"And gallant fighters. Only—their army is not commanded by a Bolivian."

"Well, you are in command here", said the top sergeant; and drained his *caña*, and put on his pudding-basin hat, and saluted and went out.

"I will now lay the table for dinner", said Tamoi, entering; and presently, having anointed his face and hands with oil of citronella, Miles followed Féliz into the night.

The belling of the toads, loudest at sunset, was beginning to die away. Only one alligator barked, intermittently, from the nearby creek. But the perpetual buzz of mosquitos might have been that of a saw; and just beyond the smoke of the fire, piled high with logs of *palo santo* wood, round which a bunch of his men squatted to play *truco*, a card game he had never been able to learn, it was as though Miles pushed his way through a flame-lit meshwork of angry wings and angrier bodies. While beyond that meshwork, visible only as black sprays in the beam of his flashlight, the pulverins swarmed for his disfigured face.

"I swear they like this citronella", he thought, slapping cheeks and lips and forehead with vain hands.

A few more strides brought him to the one place in the clearing which, for some reason he had never been able to discover, was moderately free of insects. There, switching off his flashlight, he halted; and stood for a while, impressed—despite the mounting excitement caused by Tamoi's certainty that Halcyon was really on her way to him—with the savage beauty of the jungle, newly lit by a crescent moon.

For months now, this appreciation of beauty had been growing on him —and with it a sense of how little one mere man, himself, counted in this vast continent of which Paraguay was the tiniest republic—where men had been fighting and dying since the beginning of recorded time.

"Same all over the world", went on his thoughts. "Nothing but wars. Seems silly." Yet war was the only trade which he, Miles Radcliffe, really knew.

A rustle at his feet disturbed thought. Instantly the rustle was a vicious hiss; and the rattlesnake had struck for the leg of his boot. He jerked the pistol from his belt with one hand, switching on his flashlight with the other. But the snake whipped away before he could fire; and in its wake scuttled a brace of centipedes.

A nice health resort, the Chaco. Without his boots he'd have been for it. Funny, that the rattler should have struck without provocation. They didn't usually. And centipedes rarely hunted in couples. What were they hunting? By jingo, a tarantula. There he was—goggle-eyed and as big as a soup tureen on his ten hairy legs. This ought to be a fight worth watching.

The enormous spider, however, scared by the light, scuttled off into the undergrowth just as the centipedes reared up to tackle him—and almost simultaneously Miles heard the jingle of harness and the sentry's challenge, "Halt. Who comes here?"

Running, he heard the answer. Where the jungle path debouched into the clearing, he saw Halcyon, riding astride, her legs long in the stirrups, her face veiled. The guide rode with her. Behind them, dragging a handcart, walked three Lengua Indians. She reined back her pony, and greeted him, without removing her veil, "*Féliz año nuevo*, a happy New Year to you, Meelés"; and leaned forward from the sheepskin saddle to give him a gauntleted hand.

He kissed the back of her gauntlet.

"*Buenas noticias*", she went on. "The armistice is prolonged and I have permission to stay with you."

"Here?"

"*Porqué no?* I have been in the front line before."

"I am afraid you will not find it very comfortable."

"Comfortable or not", laughed Halcyon, "here I stay."

She pressed her pony on. He walked beside her. When they came into the firelight the cardplayers rose. Them also she greeted, "*Féliz año nuevo*", and to Tamoi, who was waiting for them at the door of the hut, she said, "*Roĭ mbae ñĕmbômbucaha*".

"Fertile year, *Yâra* Halcyon?" grumbled Tamoi. "Say rather, *roĭ caruai reheguâra*, year of starvation."

"You will speak differently, my old one, when you have unpacked that cart."

Miles held back the cheesecloth, and she passed into the hut.

"*Que lujo*", she smiled, lifting her veil; and, spying Hans Kundt in his corner by the washbasin, "So you already have a sleeping companion. Now there will be two of us. Will the animal be jealous if you kiss me,

167

Meelés?" And this was the woman—he remembered as he took her in his arms—for whom the best suites at the Ritz in Paris or the Saint Regis in New York had hardly been luxurious enough.

She pulled off her gauntlets; and again memory haunted him. These long hands—once so white, so soft, rose or scarlet of nail as the fancy took her—were now hard and brown, scarred and workmanlike, like his own. And her face, also—despite the veil—insect bites had disfigured.

Seeming to follow his thoughts, she asked, "Would you rather have me as I used to be, Meelés?"

"Thou knowest I would not", he answered; and, because this was the truth for both of them, they did not kiss again, being content to sit and talk while Tamoi and the Lenguas unpacked the cart.

"This armistice", said Halcyon, "does not mean peace. Last week I was in Monte Video. The politicians of the Argentine and Brazil and Chili and Peru talk and talk. But they get nowhere. Now the League of Nations wishes to interfere. They are sending a commission to investigate. *Que barbaridad*. The Chaco has been ours legally for more than forty years. I would rather die than see us surrender a square metre of it. You, too, I hope."

Her eyes glowed. In that moment she was all Paraguay—a little nation with a single mind, a single purpose.

"The grandest little nation in the world", thought Miles Radcliffe. "And she's the grandest woman. But would I rather die than give up a few hundred, or even a few thousand, square miles of this rotten jungle? Not likely. Why —if she were a Bolivian, the chances are I'd be fighting just as hard for the other side."

And since that seemed the final answer to the question he had been asking himself ever since the night he and Feliz buried Alberto Roldan, he could only lay a hand on her arm, smiling, "We do not talk of death in the Aca Veras, Halcyon—only of *mala suerte*".

"*Mala suerte*", she repeated. "Bad luck. Yes, that is better. And it won't happen to either of us."

But a little later, she said, her eyes glowing again, "Promise me one thing, Meelés: That if the bad luck should be mine, thou wilt go on fighting".

And:

"If that were to happen", answered Miles Radcliffe, "what else should I have left to live for?"

Because that, surely, must be the ultimate truth.

VIII

All through this year of jungle warfare—it came to Miles as he watched Halcyon busy with a pocket comb at the cracked mirror—his mind had been groping after that ultimate truth. Now, finally, he could see it plain.

For the very first time in his life, he might count himself truly happy. Cause or woman—surely they were both one—he had at last found something worth fighting for, and, if necessary, worth dying for. Could any man ask more of life, or death, than this?

"No man worth a pinch of snuff", he decided; and moved towards her.

168

She looked at him over her shoulder, laughing, "Leave me alone. I am busy. Go and see what that old fool Tamoi is doing".

But Tamoi entered while she still spoke.

The old man carried two enormous baskets. He laid them on the floor and went out again.

"Bring the box", Halcyon called after him in Guaraní.

"What box?"

"The striped one. With the glass eye."

Her jacket was already off. She rolled up her shirtsleeves and knelt to one of the baskets.

"*Lujo*", she laughed, unpacking and handing up its contents to Miles. "Two bottles of veritable champagne. A ham. A tin of caviar. The caviar may have melted. But if so we will drink it like soup. And afterwards, music from Europe."

"*Como?* Music from Europe?"

"*Si, si.* Out of the box with the glass eye. A regular *milagro*. Wait till you see it."

Then Tamoi carried in the first portable radio Miles had ever seen—and just for a second he thought of Fluke, booming across the dinner table at Rosemary Lodge, "Derek's still working on that all-dry battery set". But with the caviar opened and the ham cut and the wine uncorked and Halcyon seated opposite to him, Fluke's England seemed a million leagues away.

"*Salud y pesetas*", he toasted her.

"*Salud*", she smiled back at him. "As for the *pesetas*, I do not imagine I shall have any left by the time we have finished with the Bolivians."

"*Tonta.*"

"Perhaps I was foolish. Last week I gave President Ayala my jewelry and my last hundred thousand American dollars. Of all my fortune, nothing remains except a few hectares of quebracho forest. Art thou angry with me, Meelés?"

"Why should I be angry?"

"Am I not your affianced?" She drained her glass. "When this war is over, would you marry a woman without a dowry?"

"You know I would marry you tomorrow, if only you were willing, *querida*."

But Halcyon could only answer, as she had answered more than once before, "To what purpose. Since it seems that the good God is not willing that I should have a child by you". And after her second glass of lukewarm champagne she said, this thing also having been said before, "For two lovers without children marriage is only a social convenience. While this war lasts we do not need that convenience. So let us go on living *en amistad* till the day of victory". And after yet a third glass she was in his arms, laughing:

"No. No, my friend. Curb yourself. Since we have waited so long, we can wait a little longer. I would not sleep this New Year in, even with you beside me. Moreover it is not alone for you and me that I have brought wine. Listen".

Listening, Miles heard his men singing round the campfire.

"Let us join them", said Halcyon.

So they joined them; and his men too toasted her, in the harsh red wine of their country, in orange juice and *caña*, with the fireflies dancing and the

169

firelight leaping and the radio playing, now from Europe, now from North America, and now from their own city of Asuncion, as Halcyon turned the controls.

"*Mârâneỹ, Yâra*", they toasted her. And, as midnight sounded from their own city, Féliz produced his prize possession, a regulation army cap which had belonged to his great-grandfather, and put it on Halcyon's head, crying, "*Viva Paraguay. Muere Bolivia*".

The regulation cap of the old Paraguayan army—that very symbol of liberty the pikemen and the musketeers of France wore, as they marched singing Rouget de Lisle's new song out of Marseilles—was still perched on Halcyon's red curls when she and Miles returned to the hut.

Inspecting herself in the cracked mirror, she laughed, "I have only to take off my boots and *bombachas* to be a real *sans culottes*, eh, *pichon mio*?" And Miles laughed back at her, "If you can do that, after mixing *caña* and champagne, *querida*, you are indeed *la conquistadora*".

"Do you dare to imply that I am not completely sober?"

"*Si, cara*—I would even go so far as to say that we are neither of us quite sober."

"If that is really the case", said Halcyon, eyeing the great toad, and speaking with vinous deliberation, "perhaps I had better ask Hans Kundt to maid me."

She subsided on to his only chair and readjusted the cap of liberty.

"That animal", grinned Miles, "would be of no more use to you as a maid than his namesake has been to the Bolivians as a general."

"Then what must I do? Come to bed with my boots on? Surely that would be—how do you say in English—rather shocking?"

"Very shocking indeed. Therefore it must be prevented. At all costs. Even if I have to go on my knees to you."

He knelt as he spoke. She stretched out a leg. Once again, as he tugged at toe and heel, the only Englishman who commanded a company of the Shining Heads caught himself thinking what a long way it was from Plinley Green to this outpost in the Chaco. And a while after that, still holding her close to him on the rawhide *catre* under the thick mosquito net, Miles Radcliffe caught himself thinking many thoughts which he might not utter, even to this woman he loved more than life itself.

For although both their souls and their bodies were long since consecrate for a common purpose to be achieved, whatsoever the odds against them, until victory should be accomplished, they could never—it came to him in that moment of final revelation—be truly one.

"Even if you and she were to die together", said the voice of that final revelation, "you could not be truly one." And when he woke, long before the dawn, it was to the fear that nags in secret at all who seek for happiness in earthly love.

"Not for ever", whispered the fear that lies at the heart of all earthly love. "Not even for very long. So pray that you be the first to go, Miles Radcliffe." And when, still only half awake, he asked, "How can I pray to a God I've never believed to be real?" fear answered, "At least, you know that I am real".

So Miles, not daring to stir lest he should wake his woman, prayed to his fear, making a god of it. And this false god comforted him, more than a

170

little, during the days of alternate storm and sunshine which followed, with the half selfish thought, "She's safe enough. I'll send her back the moment there's a hint of trouble".

But Halcyon, during those days and nights, needed no comfort except her lover's. Because, already, her secret soul had passed into that realm of the fey which was hers—as it could never be Miles's—by inheritance of blood.

"All this", she used to think, "must have been ordained long ago."

And on their last night together, with the armistice just concluding, she said, strangely submissive, "Thou art quite right. We are both soldiers and must obey our orders. I will start back for Islâ Poi before sunrise".

It still lacked a full hour and a half to sunrise when Tamoi burst in on them, shouting:

"*Capitã, Capitã,* we are attacked!"

IX

A burst of fire from his forward machine-gun post seemed to confirm Tamoi's words. Within ten seconds Miles was pulling on boots and breeches, grabbing for jacket and belt. As always in an emergency, his mind worked coldly. The machine gun had stopped. Probability—a false alarm.

He told Halcyon to get dressed, and to lie on the floor if she heard any more firing. Then, slinging the Bergmann over his shoulder, he went outside.

A lamp had been lit in the main hut. Féliz was already rousing the men. Miles called to him, "*Que hay?*"

Féliz called back, "*No sé*. But it is unlike Pepé to lose his head and shoot at shadows".

"*De acuerdo.* I agree. Man the trenches."

"*A las trincheras*", shouted Féliz; and Miles turned to find Tamoi at his side.

"Shall I order the *Yâra's* horse to be saddled?" asked Tamoi.

"Not yet. Stay with her. See that she does not leave the hut till I return."

"It were better that she and the guide should go now, I think."

"Do not argue. Do as you are told."

Tamoi's rope-soled *alpargatas* shuffled away. Miles stood for a moment longer, accustoming his eyes to the darkness—pitch beyond the glow of the lamp. Then he shouted to Féliz again, and clicked on his flashlight.

Rain had fallen while he slept. The main path across the clearing squelched under his bootsoles. He reached the withered palm tree, split by lightning, which marked the way to the machine-gun post; stood again, listening.

This was the dead hour before dawn when even the insects seemed to be resting. Hallo—another shot.

The shot, a single one, came from his left-flank listening post. As it ceased echoing, the sentry fired twice more—and Miles heard a troop of startled *karayá* monkeys yell blue murder. The fearsome yelling receded, as they swung away from him through the branches.

He went on, his mind still working coldly and logically. The enemy must have sent out a few scouts. They wouldn't attack before dawn. They'd

171

never had enough woodcraft for night work. If any attack developed, it could only come from the west. Islâ Poi lay east. He'd send Halcyon off as soon as he knew what the position was. Confound these *caraguatá* plants. He ought to have insisted on their being cut down.

Skirting the *caraguatás*, which his men would never destroy because their roots contain water, he reached three huge inverted bottles of those queer trees known as *palos borrachos*. Now he was within a thousand yards of the machine-gun post—and need only follow the white arrows till he came to the ditched tank. Good fun he and Féliz had had stalking that tank, till its stifled crew stopped for a breather. War was fun. And to think that all this past year he might have been selling radios in Birmingham or Manchester. But the thought that he might also have been married to Rosaleen did not cross Miles's mind, concentrated again as he followed the white arrows painted on the trees.

The tank, put completely out of action by the grenade which Féliz had lobbed into the opening manhole, was already half swallowed by the jungle. Lianas tied its rusting tracks like ropes. Turning his flashlight on it, he saw scores and scores of white ants, the last fragments of wood and cushion in their mandibles, crawling up out of the manhole, across which a positive cascade of purple orchids drooped from an overhanging branch.

Curiously he remembered other orchids, at Halcyon's shoulder, as they stood to watch the magic of the twilight falling over New York. How right she'd been—even then in New York—about the Bolivians. They'd planned this war years ago. Any man ought to have seen it coming. But only one clever woman did.

"She is clever", he thought. Still—nobody was clever enough to dodge a stray bullet. So the sooner he got forward to his post, the sooner he found out what Pepé had fired at and got back to her, the better. Inside sixty minutes it would be light.

A shallow communication trench led from the tank to the post. Halfway along this trench Miles gave the owl-hoot which he and Jim had used in Ireland. One of Pepé's men hooted in reply, and parted the branches which camouflaged the emplacement, saying:

"We heard them on the move. Pepé thought that we hit one of them. He has gone to find out. *Maté, capitan*?"

"*Gracias.*"

Squatting by the machine gun, Miles put the offered bombilla to his lips. "How long has Pepé been gone?" he asked.

"He went at once. He should be back by now. Yes, here he comes."

Once again his men's ears were too keen for Miles, who could not hear Pepé's movements, snakelike through the short grass, until he was within a few feet of them and crawling for the low semicircular parapet.

"*Uno*", reported Pepé, squatting down and wiping his machete with a piece of rag. "It was kinder to kill him. This, from the feel of it, is a new kind of rifle."

He handed over the captured rifle. Fingering the stock and bolt, Miles recognised it for a short Lee-Enfield. And many of the prisoners taken at Centeno-Gondra had been wearing British khaki with plain buttons.

"*Inglés?*" asked Pepé.

"*Si.*"

172

An uncomfortable silence, broken only by the suck of the gourd, now passing from hand to hand, followed. After a while Pepé said, "It will soon be light. The man we hit was not the only one. If they attack this post at dawn, the *capitan* may find it difficult to return to the *fortin*".

"That is possible", answered Miles. "But it is no use my returning until I know more. And besides, you may need a little help, Pepé."

Another silence, somehow friendlier, followed. Soon, kneeling to peer over the mud parapet, Miles could see distant treetops, feathers of sepia against the indigo of false dawn. But between the post and the treetops lay a three-foot carpet of impenetrable mist.

Squatting again, he drew from his side pocket a rough map he had made, and inspected it, just to confirm memory, with his flashlight.

Once the mist lifted, this camouflaged post should be able to enfilade any frontal assault on his forward trenches. But if that one burst had given its position away, the enemy might attack the post first.

He peered over again. The carpet of mist was undulating, thinning to a faint breeze which he knew for the forerunner of dawn. Momentarily he remembered Halcyon. She could have been away by now. Pity. He might have made a mistake there. Still, she'd be all right as long as she kept under cover. The Bolivians couldn't be in any great strength. Whatever happened, he could hold the fort till the reserve company came up—as they would at the first sound of heavy firing.

"Hist!" interrupted Pepé. "I hear something."

Once more Miles heard nothing. But the machine gunner, obedient to Pepé's signal, was already traversing.

"Hold it", commanded Miles. "What did you hear, Pepé?"

"The clink of a breechblock."

A gun banged. A light shell whizzed before the words were out of his mouth. Six more shells sizzled high over the emplacement and burst in the jungle behind. Almost simultaneously they heard sporadic rifleshots from their own trenches—the nearest one less than five hundred yards to their left.

"Did you see the flash of that gun?" asked Miles.

"Yes. Why must we hold our fire, *capitan*?"

Miles explained. Pepé grinned approval.

"But the moment we see anything, we may shoot?"

"No."

The next burst of shellfire, however, proved too much for the machine gunner, who loosed off a belt at the flash.

"Headstrong blighters", thought Miles. "If that chap spotted our flash we'll be for it."

He repeated his orders. The machine gunner apologised. His loader handed him another belt. Telling Pepé and the five riflemen to keep well under cover, Miles took another squint over the parapet. The mist had almost disappeared. To his front he could already distinguish separate tree trunks. The range to the nearest of those tree trunks—memory informed him—was a thousand and fifty yards, but for more than half that distance the ground was dead.

He looked to his left, over a clear field of fire, towards the trenches Féliz was manning. Their orders, received overnight, had been specific. In the event of the enemy attacking, the *fortin* must be held to the last man.

173

"If the Bolivianos really mean business", he thought, "the sooner our reserve company comes up the better."

Then the gun banged, shells whizzed again, and he ducked automatically. The gunner, however, had not spotted them. What the deuce did he think he was shooting at? Apparently, the clearing. He seemed to be lengthening his range. Must be firing by guesswork. Not likely to hit anything. Too many trees in the way. Pity about Halcyon, though. And, just for the split of a second, Miles caught himself panicking, lest a chance shot should hit his own hut.

In that split second he decided the gun must be put out of action. Question —how?

He put his head up again, looked to his right and succeeded in spotting the exact position of the gun. A minute later he was telling Pepé what he intended to do.

"Let me come with you", begged Pepé, his dark eyes shining.

"No. You must stay here in case they attack the trenches."

"You do not think they will attack us then, *capitan*?"

"Not until you start firing."

"*Pecado*. What a pity", grumbled Pepé, who was not yet eighteen.

X

Miles slung his automatic rifle; crawled back to the communication trench; crawled out of it, and ran in a semicircle, stooping from tree trunk to tree trunk for the best part of half a mile.

"V.C. stuff", he thought, as he dropped breathless to ground among more *caraguatás*. "Damn silly of me. Dunno why I'm doing it. Fun, though."

For that momentary panic about Halcyon had disappeared in the old, cold, pleasurable excitement of battle—and his nostrils flared a little, as he worked his way forward on knees and elbows, guiding himself by the intermittent pom-pom-pomming of the gun.

He edged still farther away from the gun, so as to be sure of coming at it from a flank. In about five minutes, each pom was a pain at his eardrums, and he judged himself almost close enough. Now, peering cautiously round the trunk of a *palo borracho*, he could actually see the thin funnel-ended muzzle. But the gun crew was still hidden from him—as he from the gun crew—by another of the bottle-shaped palms.

He drew back and waited for the gun to fire one more burst; rose, ran and dropped to ground behind that other *palo borracho* with the last flash still leaping red from the muzzle.

"Got 'em cold", he thought, but deafness and sheer lack of breath and gouts of sweat in his eyes forced him to wait a full minute longer.

Then, almost in one simultaneous movement, he was on his feet, round the trunk, sighting and holding back the trigger of the Bergmann.

Still shooting, he saw the gunlayer topple sideways from his seat and three others crash forward on their faces as his bullets cut the legs from under them at less than fifty yards. The rest ran—but not far. Miles dashed for the gun, from under which, just before he reached it, there rose—to his

174

complete amazement—a figure with both hands above its head, crying "*Camarada*".

There was no mistaking that guttural accent.

"*Deutscher?*" snapped Miles, pointing his rifle at the man's belly.

"*Ja.*" The face was sullen. "*Ich bin deutscher Kanonier.*"

"Then you know how to put this gun out of action."

"*Das ist einfach, aber——*"

"It is equally simple", grinned Miles, "to let you have some lead in the stomach. So get to work and be quick about it."

His sullen face greening with terror, the German fiddled with the breech of the gun; detached an oblong piece of metal which appeared to be the firing mechanism, and handed it over.

"Now off with you!" snapped Miles.

The man fled for his life; stumbled; picked himself up, and plunged on again, making for what appeared to be an opening in the jungle. As he vanished, invisible rifles cracked; and Miles, also, took to his heels. Bullets pinged uncomfortably close until he reached the sheltering trunk of the second palm. But after that it was easy enough to keep out of sight.

He made the *caraguatás*, skirted them, and halted for a breather.

"Sun's just coming up", he thought. "Doesn't look as though they meant having a real crack at us."

Didn't it, though? Those must be Féliz's riflemen. Firing rapid too. And that was Pepé's machine gun chattering.

Miles covered the eight hundred yards to the communication trench in less than three minutes. The next ten were too hot for thought.

"*Coños de mi padre*", swore Pepé, wiping his forehead at the end of those ten minutes. "But we've stopped 'em."

"Temporarily", said Miles.

The whole field of fire between them and the left-hand trench, which had also stopped shooting, was littered with brown shapes, some motionless, others writhing. Of their own eight, two riflemen lay dead; and one of the machine-gun crew so badly wounded that Miles fed him a tablet of morphia, telling him to hold it under his tongue.

The lull lasted just long enough for the gun to cool. But the next attack, instead of being directed against the trenches, was launched straight at the post from the dead ground to their front.

"*Treinta metros*", ordered Miles, as the line of heads appeared above the dry grass—and because that order was historic, dating from the first battle of Nanawa-Gondra when the Aca Veras had been almost down to their last cartridge, the machine gunner obeyed it, holding his fire until the heads and bodies were within fifty paces.

"You won't get much farther", thought Miles, squinting at a Bolivian officer over the sights of his Bergmann.

Then—awfully as in some nightmare—he heard Tamoi—only, how could it be Tamoi?—grunting behind him, "*Ỹmé, ỹmé. Angabeỹ*", and Halcyon's —only, how could it be Halcyon's?—"Run back to the camp, old man, if you are so afraid of a little danger".

He turned his head for the fraction of a second, and had a quick glimpse of Halcyon, stooping to snatch up a dead man's rifle, rising, putting the rifle to her shoulder.

175

She was kneeling beside him. For the first and only time in his life he swore.

"God damn your eyes, woman. Why the bloody hell can't you obey orders?"

She swore back in Spanish, "*Me cago en tus ordenes*". He saw the flame spurt from her rifle; wrenched his eyes to his front; saw the enemy all round and the Bolivian officer almost on top of him; heard the first belt clack madly through the machine gun; saw clean down the muzzle of the Bolivian officer's pistol; saw the flash leap from that muzzle; felt the Bergmann kick as he held back the trigger.

But even while he took the first pressure on that trigger, he had been conscious of a bullet thudding into flesh, of Halcyon staggering backwards, of the rifle dropped from her hands . . .

And after that all Miles can ever recollect is the fall of the scarlet curtain through which a man sees faces, and only faces, when he goes berserk.

He does not even remember his bare hands squeezing the life out of that Bolivian officer, who had shot Halcyon not knowing her for a woman—only her poor head, pillowed on his knee after he leaped back into the gun emplacement, and her poor bloodless lips asking, "Have we beaten them off, Meelés?"

"*Si, querida.*"

"Good! Oh, good!" The long lashes fluttered on her graying cheeks. "The other company will be here within an hour. They have been delayed. They sent a messenger. But I was afraid he might not find you. That is why I came myself. Do not be angry. Just kiss me."

As he bent and kissed her, gently on the forehead, her blue-black eyes opened their widest and the long lashes ceased to flutter.

"*Mala suerte*", she whispered. "But thou wilt go on fighting? Thou wilt keep thy promise?"

"*Si.*"

"*Palabra inglés, querido?*"

"*Palabra inglés, querida.*"

Her lips smiled. But no more words came through them—only a little sigh.

He put his arms round her; held her living body for its last moments on earth.

XI

A priest of Halcyon's own church read the burial service over that rough coffin which Miles Radcliffe had insisted on making with his own hands. And, after his men had fired a last volley over the plain wooden cross on which he himself had cut "*Muerta por la Libertad*", that same priest tried to comfort him.

But for Miles there was no comfort in any priestly words—only in that "word of an Englishman" pledged when his loved one lay dying. And even this only seemed a comfort because—keeping his pledge faithfully—he, too, might encounter death.

Time and again, during those desperate months when the Paraguayans,

176

still outnumbered by three to one, swept forward from Nanawa, he courted death, not over-rashly, because he was too good a soldier, but with a coldly calculated daring that made his name a byword for courage even among the men of the Aca Veras.

First into the enemy trenches before their base fortress of Ballivian, it was his company that hung on there, day after incredible day, night after incredible night, repulsing counterattack after counterattack until, of all those who had gone over the top with them, only he and Féliz, Tamoi and Pepé, and one wounded machine-gunner were left to hold the tiny gap, through which, at long last, the men of the Aca Carayas and a remnant of the Aca Me Quedo Yos stormed with drawn machetes howling, "*Viva Paraguay. Muere Bolivia*".

By then General Kundt, ruthless and stupid with all the ruthlessness and the stupidity of the least far-sighted race on earth, had been disgraced for squandering more than sixty thousand lives. But Bolivia could still afford to squander lives—and all that July, all that August and September and October of nineteen hundred and thirty-four, while Estigarribia's lines swept forward in the north, while Picuiba spouted blood, and Irendegua spouted blood, and the corpses piled up round the well of Carandaytay, and men died like flies in the reeking mud at Cañada Strongest, the great fortress on the Pilcomayo still resisted, until—even to Miles Radcliffe—it seemed that there could be no final victory such as Halcyon had dreamed of in this interminable war.

For already, by that October, he was utterly weary of war, with only his pledged word holding him, and even his desire for death abated because he had courted it overmuch.

Yet the word he had given to his own especial dead might not be broken ; and once again, on that November day when the great fortress fell in smoke and flame, he was among the first who fought their way forward through the stink of the fires and the exploding ammunition dumps. And out of that day also he came scatheless, thinking, as he dropped to sleep with Tamoi beside him, "Surely this will be the end".

Yet still this war came to no end. For the Bolivians still held Villa Montes. And now at long last the League of Nations showed its hand, granting arms to Bolivia and forbidding them to Paraguay, lest a poor nation should win too complete a victory over a rich.

But, because Paraguay was rich in the things of the spirit, the half starved boys of the Aca Veras and the Aca Carayas and the Aca Me Quedo Yos and all those other regiments whose flag was the red, white and blue, and whose symbol was the cap of liberty, only laughed, or cursed, according to their natures, as they chewed their sun-dried *charqui* and sipped their maté to the lashing thunder of the December rains.

"*Politicos* or no *politicos*", laughed Féliz on the night they heard that news, "Estigarribia will have at them again ; and we will beat them completely."

Miles Radcliffe, however, was among those who cursed, "*Me cago en la Sociedad de Naciones*" ; and next day at dawn he remembered, for the first time in years, Dominic Mahoney's "But the shame of ut, the black shame, will be England's", and Jim Bowlby's answer, "By Christ, you're damn right about that".

177

For his own *politicos* must have voted for the resolution forbidding arms to Paraguay, and how could he, an Englishman, hold up his head if his own country helped to rob this heroic little people of victory? Whereafter, very curiously, there resurged in him the desire for death.

So that, once again, when the orders came for them to move forward against Villa Montes, he began to court death, no longer with the cold calculated daring which befits a soldier, but hotly, madly, over-rashly, with a greater passion than he had ever courted Halcyon.

Yet still, all through that February, and that March, and that April and that May, death's wings only singed the hair of the crazy fighter whom the veterans of the Aca Veras recall, even nowadays, as "The mad Englishman. *El loco inglés*".

XII

El loco inglés woke to partial sanity one June morning in nineteen hundred and thirty-five, having slept—for the first time in eighteen months of almost continuous action—on a real bed. Rising, he went to an open window; and rested his elbows on the sill.

Directly below him lay a cobbled street. Peering down, he saw an old woman, dressed all in black, carrying two buckets, which she filled at a little fountain in the opposite wall.

Looking over the broad top of the pink-washed wall, he saw a patio, green with palm trees, beyond whose feathery tops stretched flat roofs of gray tile, these too broken here and there by little patches of greenery. Beyond the roofs a cluster of foothills reddened to the rising sun. Farther still—miraculously—appeared higher ranges.

"Not the Andes?" he asked himself. Then recollection flooded back, answering, "But they are. We've won. The war finished yesterday. This is Villa Montes. And I'm still alive."

Féliz, too, was alive. And Tamoi. He'd have to do something for old Tamoi. But what could he do for himself? He himself wasn't really alive —only living.

Somehow or other, though, he'd have to go on living. Where? In Paraguay? No. He could never be happy again in Paraguay. In England? No. He'd never been really happy in England.

What was happiness anyway? Just a dream. But at least he, Miles Radcliffe, had had his dream; found something—someone—worth fighting for, and if necessary worth dying for.

The real ecstasy of love, the real ecstasy of battle. He'd known them both. But now they were over.

In that moment he swore to himself:

"Come what may, I'll never marry. And I'll never fight in another war".

BOOK NINE

I

"PHWAT DID OI TELL YOU THAT DAY SEVENTEEN YEARS AGO WHEN OI CAME near to bating the loights out of Jim Bowlby? And now you've heard the end of ut, Moiles. The British Navy's been kicked out of Oireland for kapes."

Dominic Mahoney—red as ever, his huge chest bulging open the soft shirt he wore with his tuxedo—switched off the news and poured himself another two fingers of Scotch.

"That guy Chamberlain must be nuts to give up those bases", he went on. "But I guess everyone's nuts in Europe. 'Tis glad Oi am to be an American citizen."

He tossed off his drink, and went on: "Folk ought to be coming aboard pretty soon. Guess Oi'll have a look round. Help yourself to another highball".

"Thanks. I will."

Dominic swivelled his chair; rose, and left the cabin. By the decanter tray on his desk stood a calendar whose exposed leaf read, "Tuesday April 26. 1938". Through the uncurtained porthole Miles could just see the high lights on Telegraph Hill.

"Funny set-up, this gambling ship", he thought. "Not outside the three-mile limit. Dunno how it's wangled. Graft, I suppose."

He poured himself a little whiskey; almost drowned it with soda, and added three cubes of ice. The inner door of the cabin opened, revealing Dominic's blond Lou, surprisingly like his memory of Dominic's blond Edla, in a backless evening dress with a white ermine coatee on her over-braceleted arm.

Lou said, "Hallo"; dropped her coatee on to the sofa; mixed a highball in the third glass, and took the swivel chair.

"Did that hotel fix you up all right?" she asked.

"Yes. And I'm very grateful to you."

"It's a good little joint."

She took a pack of cigarettes from her elaborate bag. Miles flicked on his lighter.

"And how do you like San Francisco?" she continued.

"I've hardly got acquainted with it yet."

"You will", smiled Lou; and eyed him, thinking, "Handsome. And how? Calls himself a globetrotter. But Dom says he used to be in the liquor racket. Wonder what his racket is nowadays."

Smiling back at her, "I expect so", Miles wondered—as he had been wondering ever since early yesterday morning, when the cargo boat on which he had taken cheap passage from Honolulu docked at the waterfront—why he should have come to California.

"Might just as well have gone to Australia", he thought. "Doesn't matter where I go nowadays." And the smile vanished.

"Guess he's pretty tough", Lou told herself. "Guess I could fall for him, though. Hell, I oughtn't to have to run around with a man of Dom's age, and me not twenty-two yet."

Aloud she asked, "You going to play tonight?"

"No. I'm not much of a gambler."

Lou smiled again, but only with her mouth; took a drag at her cigarette, a sip of her highball.

"I went to the movies this afternoon", she went on. "Daphne Stoddart's just swell in her new picture. She and Mackay are in town. They're stopping over at the Mark Hopkins."

"And who might they be?"

"Gee, where've you been hiding all these years—Alcatraz with Al Capone?"

"I've managed to keep out of jail so far. But I'm not a picturegoer. So please enlighten me."

Thus pressed, Lou explained that Daphne was one of the three Stoddart sisters, all stars, and Andrew Mackay, her husband, "one of the best directors ever".

"Scotsman?" asked Miles.

"Yeah. From Little Rock, Arkansas. Guess his folks must have been Scotch, though. He's not her first husband, of course."

"Why of course?"

"My! Don't you even know she was married to George Upjohn before he hitched up with Arabella Arnold? I thought everybody knew that."

"Well, I'm afraid I didn't. Sorry, Miss Lou."

"Oh, can the Miss. It don't suit me. Hasn't since I was eighteen."

"Okay, Lou."

Dominic's blond continued to talk Hollywood. Miles Radcliffe's mind wandered. Why had he come to the States? Why should he have run into Dominic almost the moment he stepped ashore? Queer, how one was always running into chaps one knew. Take that last meeting with Ronnie Wallace in Aden. Poor old Ronnie. The Eyeties hadn't done him much good when they pinched Abyssinia . . .

"Dom—he don't care for the pictures much either", said Lou. "He says they're too sentimental for his taste. Me, I guess I am sentimental."

Her ice-blue eyes appeared to soften. They appraised Miles with slightly too much interest. He was glad to see Dominic in the doorway, to follow him on deck.

II

The fog had cleared. To port blazed the great hump of San Francisco City. Lower and to starboard shone the twin diadems of Berkeley and Oakland. Between, loop after great loop of light, and every loop doubled by the dark mirror of the waters, the giant bridge spanned and spangled the Bay, across which crawled the bediamonded beetles of the ferries.

"Gee, but it's swell", breathed Lou, slipping an arm through Dominic's. "And it'll be sweller still next year when they have the Exposition. They're working late tonight."

"They work late most nights", said Dominic, pointing to a coronal of arc lamps not quite midway of the Bay bridge. "Guess they've got to, or it won't be ready."

From under those distant lamps on Yerba Buena Island, Miles could just hear the thump of a piledriver, an occasional whistle, the puff-puff-puff of donkey engines.

"Where'll I be next year?" he was asking himself; when Lou called Dominic's attention to the speedboat just circling for their ladder, at the foot of which stood a sailor with a hook.

The lordly manner which Dominic assumed to welcome his first boatload of "guests", with all of whom he shook hands and most of whom he addressed by their christian names, amused Miles. Two more speedboats arrived before he made his way down to the saloon.

Both the faro game and the roulette game—Dominic had been at some pains to assure him—were "absolutely on the level". But the roulette wheel had two zeros ; and, little though gambling interested him, he knew enough about faro to realise that the dealer is at no disadvantage.

Play was for ready money, which included many silver dollars ; and the opening stakes moderate enough. The players, some thirty in all, could be roughly classified under two heads—young men and women obviously out to enjoy themselves, middle-aged men and women obviously out for profit.

Soon bored with watching, Miles moved away from the tables and perched himself at the bar, where a Japanese houseboy was dispensing free drinks and a plethora of solid refreshment. After a while Lou joined him.

"We're getting out tomorrow", she said.

"Why?"

"I wouldn't know that."

Her eyes went blank. He realised that he had made a social mistake. She ordered herself a club sandwich. A steward ran down the companionway and whispered to Dominic, who was standing by the roulette table. The pair of them disappeared. From outboard came the phut-phut of a speedboat's engine at quarter throttle. "Spot of trouble?" speculated Miles. But a few moments later Dominic was ushering another party—six of them, all in evening dress—down the companionway, and Lou had clutched him by the arm.

"Look who's here", she said. "Daphne Stoddart and Andrew Mackay."

Questioned in a whisper, she indicated the shortest of the three women and the tallest of the three men.

Both halted midway between the two gaming tables. The woman's face —familiar, now that one saw it in the flesh, from newspaper photographs and an occasional poster—was almost too coldly cleancut for beauty. Only the eyes, very long of lash and smokily blue under the plucked demilunes of the eyebrows, betrayed character. Her hair—Miles noticed—was pale gold, soft, silky and apparently not synthetic. She carried herself perfectly, with what seemed the faintest touch either of arrogance or selfconsciousness.

The star's husband, nearly as tall and almost as broad of shoulder as Dominic, looked all the athlete, until one observed the heavy cane on which he supported himself. His face also seemed queerly familiar. But not from any photograph. Somewhere or other one had actually encountered this man with the big nose, with those clean-shaven, slightly overjowled cheeks, with those humorous hazel eyes and that high forehead. Only—the face had been years younger, no gray at those prominent temples, no creases in those cheeks.

"Where the blazes——?" Miles asked himself, but memory remained elusive until Mackay, having seated his wife at the roulette table, approached the bar with Dominic. And even then one couldn't be quite sure.

The pair took stools at the other end of the counter. Mackay hung his leather-handled cane on the rail.

"Thanks, I'll have a Bourbon", he said. Lou rose and sidled over. Dominic introduced her. She came as near to curtseying as an American girl may, affording Miles more amusement. Then, abruptly, his eyes met his man's and it seemed to him that the recognition must be mutual.

He saw Mackay turn to Dominic and whisper a question or two. Dominic called along the counter, "Moiles, I'd like you to meet a friend of mine".

Miles joined them. Andrew Mackay offered a powerful hand, saying, "I've no memory for names. But didn't I once give you a shoulder holster?"

"You did. And I've still got it."

"I've a kind of idea, too, that I gave it you for saving my life."

They were still grasping hands, but Mackay's words made Miles feel rather uncomfortable. He was aware of Lou's eyes goggling hero worship. Releasing his fingers, he protested, "I didn't do anything of the sort".

"Oh, no." Mackay laughed. "You just rode away and left one greenhorn of a Yankee sergeant wounded in a shell hole with the Heinies potting at him from three points of the compass. You never rolled that machine-gun post flat and covered the retreat of a detachment that was only supposed to be under instruction. And it wasn't you who jumped out of your tank and carried me across the open to that dugout."

"I didn't carry you by myself."

"Sure you didn't. You only carried me the last few yards, when the other chap I had an arm round couldn't make the grade."

"The other chap being dead", Andrew Mackay explained to Lou and Dominic; and would have elaborated the tale further, if Miles's discomfort had been less obvious—and his carefully pressed blue suit less bare of nap.

"Down on his luck", thought Andrew Mackay, not realising that it was the best part of two years since Miles's last appearance in the big store on Regent Street to which he had been originally taken by Jim Bowlby. "Wouldn't be running around with the Mahoney crowd otherwise. Have to do something for him if he'll let me." And he began to fish for information, asking, "How long have you been here and how long do you intend to stay?"

"Stalling", decided Andrew Mackay when Miles answered, "I haven't made up my mind. I only arrived yesterday. It was a bit of luck running into Dominic."

"I'd like you to meet my wife when she's a little less busy. Pardon me for a moment", went on Daphne Stoddart's husband; and, taking his cane from the bar rail, hobbled to where she was sitting.

"He's one of the biggest salaried men in Hollywood", confided Lou.

Dominic went towards the faro table, at which a slight dispute had arisen. This settled, he relieved the payer-out—a wizened little chap who might have been half Chinese—at the roulette wheel. Lou slipped from her bar stool and stood behind his chair.

182

"All limits doubled", he announced. "Five hundred dollars on the even chances. Numbers in proportion."

"I'll go the limit on red", said Daphne Stoddart, handing five notes from her pile to the croupier, who promptly threw one of the zeros.

Alone, Miles remembered Halcyon gambling at Monte Carlo. What a long time ago that seemed. Silly to let oneself think of her. She'd been dead four years. And love had died with her. Casual women again. Casual journeys again. Life without any real purpose. Quite amusing, though. As long as one didn't take it too seriously. At least, one was one's own master. Footloose.

He asked the boy for another highball, and lit a Havana cigarette. Presently, twisting his head, he saw Daphne Stoddart rise from the table. She and her husband conferred a while. They came over—and he was introduced.

At close quarters the star developed more charm, her whole face dimpling to the smile which accompanied her handclasp and her, "I'm glad to meet you, Captain Radcliffe. Andrew's spoken about you so often, though he never could remember your name".

Miles asked her if she'd won.

"I broke even", she answered. "I'm not crazy about gambling anyway. But we were taking dinner with Joe Kerstlen and he insisted on bringing us here."

Mackay, glancing at his wristwatch, said, "Joe won't quit till all hours. We might call it a day after you've had your orange juice".

"But will there be a boat?"

"Sure there will. I told that fellow to hang around till we wanted him."

He ordered two orange juices from the houseboy, and, turning to Miles, continued, "I'm due to make a speech at the Commonwealth Club tomorrow. We've an evening date too, and we're flying to New York on Thursday. So I can't invite you to take a meal with us. But if you're not doing anything around five o'clock, do come along to the Mark Hopkins".

"Yes, please do", echoed Daphne.

"I'd love to", said Miles.

They chatted for a few minutes. He accompanied them to the deck; shook hands once more, and watched them descend the ladder. Both waved to him from the speedboat. Waving back, he thought, "I might just as well have gone ashore with them".

But it was not until three and a half hours later that a sleepy night porter let him into the modest hotel recommended by Lou.

III

The bells on the clanging trolley cars woke Miles before eight. Simultaneously the telephone shrilled; and Dominic was saying, "Sorry, me boy, but Oi guess Lou and Oi can't make lunch. We're getting out of town roight away. Be seeing you some place or other, I expect".

Hardly waiting for his answer, he hung up. Miles drew the curtains and looked out of the narrow window, which gave on to a blank wall of yellow brick.

"Shan't stay in this joint longer than I can help", he decided. "Can't even see whether the sun's shining."

He shaved, stripped, soaped, showered and dressed himself in the usual twenty minutes; let himself down in the automatic elevator; had his shoes shined, and sauntered out through a lobby which seemed overprovided with spittoons. Two blocks brought him into Market Street. Outside the doors of a cafeteria hung its price list, which he consulted before going in.

A chatty waitress in the cleanest linen brought him his order of coffee, ham and eggs, and hot waffles.

"You're British, I bet", she said. "Come to the Coast on business?"

"No. I'm just looking round."

"Well, see you find what you're looking for."

She pattered off to another table. Miles ate with his usual appetite, wondering what sort of trouble Dominic had struck (for obviously he had struck trouble) and what to do with himself till five o'clock. He ought to do some shopping. He needed socks, shirts, underwear and at least one new suit. That could wait, though. He'd inspect the town first.

Strolling through the incipient sunshine of a windless day, stopping here and there to price clothes in a store window, he soon made Union Square. Along the rails by the palm trees buses were parked. Billboards round a ticket office advertised sightseeing tours. A little scornful of himself—hadn't he always despised tourists?—Miles decided to take one of the trips.

"Leaving in ten minutes", he was told; and secured a goodish seat, next to a very fat man with a wart on his nose, who proved even more informative than the guide with the megaphone at the rear end of the car.

"You being British", said the warty one, as they sped away from the tangled churchyard of Mission Dolores, "should know who was the first Britisher to land in California. But I betcher don't. It was your Sir Francis Drake. Prayer Book Cross, he landed at. And they called it that because he held the first Church of England service there. You'd be Church of England, I suppose? I was brought up Christadelphian. No drinking, no smoking, and no theatregoing. Did my dad wallop the pants off me when he caught me with my first pack of cigarettes?"

Personal reminiscences continued to the intermittent salvos of information through the guide's megaphone all the up and down way to Golden Gate Park. There they stopped for a while; and Miles contrived to escape into the aquarium.

But at their next stop, the Cliff House, he was not so fortunate, being treated to a hot dog, and a lecture on sealions, several of which were basking in hot sunshine on the nearby rocks.

"The real name for those rocks", he was further told, "is Punta Lobos— *lobo*, 'case you don't know it, being the Spanish for seal. And, talking of Spaniards, an uncle of my wife's was one of Teddy Roosevelt's boys in Cuba. What do you think of this Roosevelt? Me—I'm all for him."

"I'm afraid I don't know anything about American politics", said Miles; and needed no more speech until they returned by Presidio Barracks to the city, where the warty one wrung his hand enthusiastically and disappeared into a drugstore. "Being in need of a gargle", decided the lecturer.

Miles entered another drugstore and fed lavishly for sixty cents. It seemed strange to be in an American city after more than a year spent in the Far East and the South Sea Islands. But somehow or other—though he had never cared overmuch for cities—this one rather appealed to him. If he could only find more comfortable quarters he might stay for a while. He might even stay permanently, if he could find some kind of a job.

IV

Surprised at this last thought—surely one didn't want to settle down with one's income still intact and so much of the world left unseen?—Miles took another stroll, managed to buy himself some Brazilian cigarettes, priced more clothes, had his hair cut and inquired his way to the Mark Hopkins.

"Walk there, suh?" said the coloured boy, pocketing his dime. "On the hottest day we done had this spring? No, suh. You hop on dat dar trolley."

The indicated trolley car decanted Miles at the top of Nob Hill—the last gradient of which he judged to be about one in three—at ten minutes to five precisely. The lobby clerk, turning from the phone, said, "Mister Mackay isn't home, Captain Radcliffe. But he'll be back shortly. Mrs. Mackay says will you please come right up".

A bellhop who seemed overlarge for hopping escorted Miles to a bronze-gated elevator which seemed too small for the size of the hotel, and out of it to the door of an apartment in whose hall waited a maid with a rather too obvious French accent. The maid, having relieved him of his shabby hat, ushered him in to a sitting room, which appeared to resent having been turned into a flower store and dwarfed its sole occupant, who lay tiny and at ease on a colossal sofa.

"Andy won't be long", said Daphne Stoddart, stretching up a hand. "Have you had tea yet?"

"Well, as a matter of fact, I haven't."

"Then let's."

She gave an order for three China teas to the maid. Miles took a chair beside the sofa. The telephone rang. Daphne put the ivory microphone to one ear and said, "Hallo, Joe . . . You can't make it before half nine? That'll be all right . . . Sure . . . Andy says not more than three weeks".

The conversation continued. Miles took another glance round the be-flowered room. Once upon a time he himself had lived in American luxury. "How long ago?" he wondered. "The best part of nine years."

His glance came back to the little woman with the lovely hands and the page bob of pale gold hair. Memory shot him a picture of Halcyon, of their suite at the Saint Regis in New York, of her brother-in-law bending to kiss her long fingers.

"Well, so long, Joe", said Daphne, and recradled the phone.

She made conversation, asking him how he had spent his day. He told her of his trip, and she smiled at him, "That's the kind of thing I'd like to do. But of course I can't".

"Why ever not?"

"Because folk would be sure to recognise me."

"And supposing they did?"

His naïveté seemed to amuse her. She explained that she would be pestered by autograph hunters, by people anxious to shake her hand, to tell her how much they liked her pictures.

"Don't you like them?" she asked.

"Frankly, I've never seen one. I don't believe I've been to the flicks half a dozen times in my life."

Never having been in England, the word "flicks" was new to her. She meditated a moment before saying, "You're rather a unique person, Captain Radcliffe. Don't you go to the theatre either?"

"Not if I can help it. I'd rather read a book any day."

"Do you read much?"

"I have latterly", said Miles—and stopped.

"What kind of books—novels?"

"No. I'm afraid I haven't much use for fiction."

A waiter knocked, wheeled in a table. The maid followed and poured out their tea. As she asked Miles, "Sugar, m'sieu?" Andrew Mackay entered, came over, grasped him by the hand, and bent to kiss his wife on the forehead. Discarding his cane, he took the end of the sofa. The maid filled the third cup.

"Joe's just been on the phone", said Daphne. "He's put dinner off half an hour. And he wanted to know how soon we'll be back. I told him three weeks."

"Was he satisfied?"

"Is he ever?" The star displayed all her dimples. "I don't know why you renewed your contract with him, Andy."

"There are worse guys in the industry than Joe."

The maid had left them. Andrew Mackay drained his tea at a gulp, put down his cup, and offered Miles a cigar. His wife said, "Captain Radcliffe's just been confessing that he never goes to the pictures or to a theatre if he can possibly help it."

"How's that?" asked Mackay.

"Well, the few pictures I've been to just didn't happen to amuse me. One of them was a war picture. And you never saw such tosh. They had what looked like a twelve-inch gun bang in the open, and you could have danced a quadrille in the alleged trenches."

"Not guilty", laughed Mackay.

He turned the conversation. What had Miles been doing with himself all this time?

"Oh, lots of things. After the war I served in Ireland. That's where I first met Mahoney. By the way, he rang me up this morning. We were going to have lunch together. But he couldn't manage it."

"I'm not very surprised to hear that."

Mackay did not elaborate. The phone rang again. He scooped it up, listened, and said, "She's resting right now, I'm afraid".

"Who was it?" asked Daphne.

"Some newspaper girl or other. New to the game, I guess. Isn't it about time you did go and rest, honey?"

"Yes, I suppose it is."

She rose, and Miles with her. As they shook hands, he was sharply aware of her attraction, its essence simplicity and a poise which he now

186

recognised to be neither arrogant nor selfconscious, but merely natural—like her hair.

"I wish you could have dined with us", she said. "Andy would have liked that real well."

V

After the door, which revealed a glimpse of bedroom, closed behind Mackay's wife, Miles remained standing for a moment, fascinated by the view through the three long windows.

The sun was just setting; but the Bay still shone smooth as glass. From this height one could see clean across it to the northern mainland. While he watched, the lights of both bridges were flashed on, and the shore lights, and the lights of a Sausalito ferry boat. Somehow he was reminded of a sunset he had watched with Mary and Martin Halliburton from the Peak in Hong Kong. When he mentioned this, Andrew Mackay, still conscious of that shabby suit, said :

"You seem to be quite a traveller. Where else have you been?"

"Oh, most places."

"I haven't been around as much as I'd like to. Though I know the States better than most Americans. Right after the war I got into the tourist game. On the publicity side. That's how I started in making pictures—to advertise steamer lines and railroads."

He broke off, thinking, "This chap's as tight as an oyster. He's always going places. But how does he manage it? Steamer trips cost money".

"Ever been in Rio?" he resumed.

"Once or twice. But never for more than a day."

"Buenos Aires?"

"Yes. I know the Argentine fairly well. I once tried to farm there. A chap who hadn't much experience took me into partnership because I could speak Spanish and knew something about handling labour."

"How did it work out?"

"Fine." Miles grinned. "We happened to hit the green gold boom and cleaned up a hundred per cent profit before we'd cleared half our acreage."

"The green gold boom?" queried Mackay. "What's green gold anyway?"

"Yerba maté. You call it maté tea. It's drunk all over South America. I don't know what we'd have done without it in the Chaco."

"Hell's bells", broke in Andrew Mackay, whose hazel eyes had glinted understanding at the first mention of the word yerba, "were you in the Chaco war?"

"Oh, I saw a bit of it."

Miles, anxious—as always when under such examinations—not to be too communicative, failed to notice the other's excitement. But the next questions, "Which side did you fight for? Paraguay. That's grand. Which regiment were you in? The Aca Veras. That means Shining Heads in Guaraní, doesn't it?" took him entirely by surprise.

Automatically he corrected Mackay's pronunciation "Guarany" to the correct "Guaranee".

"How did you come to know about the Aca Veras?" he asked.

For answer, Mackay stretched out a hand to the telephone table, picked

187

up a book—at which, Miles remembered, his wife had been glancing when the maid brought him in to her—and handed it over.

Miles looked at the title page. "Land of To-morrow", he read. "A Story of South America. By R. W. Thompson." Facing the title page was a photograph captioned, "Above the Hidden City".

"I know where that was taken from", he said, recognising, in the background, the twin peaks of Illimani and Illampu; and once again memory shot him an old picture—of a train halting at Alto after the long mountain climb from La Paz.

"Did you ever run into this guy Thompson?" interrupted Mackay.

"No."

"We've been trying to contact him for the last three months. But it's no go apparently. He's gone off on some other trip."

Mackay stopped talking—but not thinking. Miles flipped through the book. Presently he came on two photographs, one of Estigarribia, with a couple of staff officers whom he also recognised, the other of the light railway from Casado up which he had first travelled to the front.

"This looks rather interesting", he commented.

"I'll loan it you if you like. We've another copy in the studio." And Mackay, continuing silent, continued to think his hardest.

"Kill two birds with one stone", he said to himself finally, and aloud, "If I could find Thompson, I'd pay him five thousand dollars and his fare to Hollywood and back. How'd you like to collect the dough instead of him?"

That time surprise struck Miles completely speechless. "Chap must be off his nut", he decided. But already the other was explaining:

"It's like this, you see. Some while ago Joe bought a story about the Chaco war. The story's punk; and the author's died on us. Not that she'd be any good if she were alive. When we came to check up, we found that she'd never been closer to Paraguay or Bolivia than Indianapolis. But Joe still wants the story done, and Daphne's crazy to play the heroine. She's a golden-haired Bolivian girl in love with a Paraguayan officer".

"The devil she is", grinned Miles, finding his voice; and Mackay grinned back at him:

"We'll have to cross that strain, I guess. Give her an American father and educate her at Vassar. But that's not the snag. The snag is, and I've told Joe so—as a matter of fact I've told him I won't do the story unless I can get over it—that I'd just hate to have my name on the kind of war picture you were talking about just now. And I'm bound to—I'm bound to make one damfool break after the other—if I can't find someone to put me wise about the actual scrapping. Do you get me?"

"Yes. I get you", said Miles, speaking rather more slowly than his habit. "But five thousand dollars seems an awful lot of money to pay for a little information."

"Aw, shucks", retorted Andrew Mackay, momentarily reverting to the doughboy. "Forget the money. The question is: Are you on?"

VI

It was past seven before Miles, with Reginald Thompson's book under his arm and another of Mackay's cigars between his teeth, emerged from the

Mark Hopkins. A night wind had risen; tore at his hat brim as he trod warily down the steep sidewalk. Of all the queer things which had happened to him in his thirty-odd years, this seemed the queerest. He simply couldn't make head or tail of it. "Money for jam", he kept thinking. "And the chap actually offered to advance me five hundred dollars to bind the contract. Seemed quite upset when I refused 'em too. Am I bats or is friend Andrew?"

For they had come to christian names before they were through.

Still puzzling, he reached the foot of the hill; refound Kearney and Market Streets, and chanced on a restaurant which struck him as "rather *de lujo*". But with that letter signed "Andrew Mackay, For Kerstlen Pictures Inc" tucked away in his billfold, money seemed to have lost a good deal of its value. He pushed his way through a revolving door; was ushered to a table; ordered "a sea-food cocktail", a tenderloin steak with sweet potatoes, and, on the advice of his waiter, whom he discovered to be an Italian, a half bottle of Californian wine.

Queer or not, the Hollywood happening was true. Andrew had even insisted—despite his protest, "I may as well warn you I broke the only other contract I ever made"—on his signing a duplicate of the letter. Before the end of May he must be at the Kerstlen Studios. Meanwhile . . .

"Dunno quite what I'll do", he brooded. "Might buy a used car here— Andrew said I'd need one—and toddle round a bit. I'd like to have a look at the redwood country. Read something about that. When I was quite a kid. In a novel, wasn't it?"

The name of the novel eluded him until he had finished the last rare morsel of that succulent steak; and only on his way back to his hotel did he recollect the name of its author, Jack London. Once in bed, however, *Land of Tomorrow* soon wiped out that dim boyish recollection of *The Valley of the Moon*.

Reginald Thompson's book runs to four hundred and fifty pages. Miles read and revelled in every one of them—the magic of words conjuring back to the magic of his imagination known cities and known people, the very rivers, the very jungle odours, the very trees, the very fireflies, the very humming birds, the very sunsets of the Paraguay he had loved so well.

Yet all the while his imagination revelled, he was aware of pain. Because Paraguay could never be the land of his tomorrow. Because Paraguay was the land of his yesterday beneath whose fertile soil, and that wooden cross on which he had carved, "*Muerta por la Libertad*", lay buried the last cold ecstasy of battle, the last hot ecstasy of love.

He finished the book and put it away. But no sleep came to him when he switched off the light.

Hours ago the trolley bells had ceased their clanging. For at least an hour he had not heard the vague drone of the elevator. But every now and again the wind that sweeps in from the Pacific through the Golden Gate still buffeted at his open window; and still pain haunted him, ghostly in the dawn.

Painfully he remembered that other dawn, in Villa Montes; that other window from whose casement he had watched the foothills of the Andes redden to the sunrise, and the two oaths he had sworn, and thinking, "Isn't it about time I got back my sanity?" Painfully, still sleepless, he relived his return to Asuncion, a city of poverty, of streets muddy and grass-grown, along whose sidewalks went the wounded and the women in black.

Halcyon's mother had worn black on that afternoon when he sat with her, in the remembered patio, telling her of the provision he wished to make for Tamoi. "But I", Halcyon's mother had said, "will provide for Tamoi. Because you, *señor*, have already done enough for us." And of her daughter she would only say, "Do not reproach yourself. It was written that she should die. And since she died so gloriously we must not doubt that all her sins have been forgiven".

The faith of true patriots. The faith of true Romans, as his father had been wont to call them. But neither of these faiths was his. He could only escape from this house, from this city, from this land which was overfull of remembrance. And he had escaped next day.

Up the Parana his trail led him—with only his thoughts or some chance-met acquaintance for company—beyond those mighty Cataracts of Iguazu which make Niagara seem like a millstream, into a country of no maps, where globetrotters may not venture and whoso wanders more than a day's journey from the river bank is apt to die, not too swiftly, of thirst.

Twice while he groped his way through that country Miles nearly died of thirst, and once of a fever for which a naked Indian woman with breasts that hung almost to her knees drenched him and drenched him, he too naked under a heap of blankets alive with lice, while the medicine men clicked fishbones against fishbones.

And after this medicine he began to yearn for the company of his own kind.

"You must have had the lord's own luck", said the first of his own kind, a long lean Devonian with a red beard already graying encountered on the upper reaches of the Madeira. "I've been hunting birds, butterflies and orchids all up and down this country ever since the Boer War. But I wouldn't make that trip alone for the best dairy farm in the valley of the Otter. What on earth did you do it for?"

"Oh, just fun", Miles recollected himself prevaricating, and the Devonian's, "Where are you trying to get to now? Down the Amazon to Para, eh? Well that's easy enough as long as you've got the money." And, dismissing his canoe men one week later, he had made Para in a little over five.

"And wasn't I glad to get there?" he remembered. "Wasn't I glad to be on a real ship again, to smell the sea instead of those rotten mangrove swamps?"

For the first boat out from Para—again by the lord's own luck—was to call at Port of Spain, and there he ought to find the one man of his own kind to whom he might speak of Halcyon.

But even to Geoffrey Miles only spoke of Halcyon once—late that first night, as they lay side by side on long chairs, with moonlight silvering the palm trees and the cicadas shrilling, and the scarlet blossoms of the hibiscus round which the hawk moths fluttered so still that they might have been cast from metal.

"Never look back", Geoffrey had said.

Yet here he was, looking back on the trip he and Geoffrey had made round Europe, where George the Fifth was already dead and the Germans already occupying the Rhineland and Spain seething for civil war.

Still undecided, that war. You had seen a little of it. And in the east, too, at Shanghai and at Nanking, you had seen battles. But only as a spectator, not caring which side won. Let the Huns have their Rhineland. Let them have—hadn't they just taken it?—Austria. Let fascists or socialists —a plague on both their houses—boss Spain, and the Japs do what they liked to China. Your own soldiering days were over.

"And your love days?" Miles asked himself.

But from that question thought shied, reared like a stallion, plunging and fighting against the taut bit of his selfcontrol.

VII

After a while, Miles managed to curb thought, to repress the one memory which perturbed him as no other memory of all the years since he had lost Halcyon. And after that he drowsed for a little, only to be woken, once again, by the shrilling of the telephone bell.

"Andrew here", said the voice at the other end of the wire. "Say, listen. After you left last evening Daphne and I had quite a talk. How would you like to get acquainted with Hollywood rightaway? If you would, why not make our home yours? I can easily call my secretary on long distance. She'll fix everything at the house; and I'll tell her to have Nikko Longmore, he's the scenarist you'll probably be working with, show you around till we get back. You'll like Nikko real well."

"I'm sure I will, only"—still scarcely half awake, Miles felt singularly stupid—"is it really necessary?"

"Necessary? Why, no. We just thought you'd be happier that way."

"It's awfully decent of you—but—well, as a matter of fact I rather thought of using my three weeks to take a trip to the redwood country."

It had struck Miles that the name Nikko Longmore sounded familiar. But already Andrew was saying, "That's all right by me if it's all right by you", and "So long, Miles. Don't forget your deadline".

A good bloke. And even more hospitable than most Americans.

"Can't imagine Fluke doing a thing like that", thought Miles.

But the mere thought of Fluke—how one had laughed when he boomed across their brandy glasses, "Believe it or not, old boy, I'm in the running for a knighthood"—seemed as though it might conjure up, in those pictures which were still occasionally apt to haunt one's imagination, that most perturbing of all memories.

It was a long time now, six months at least, no, more than that—why, he could actually remember the date, the tenth of September last year, and the room in Hong Kong, so different from this one, though much the same fog filtered through its wide windows—since he had spent so sleepless a night.

VIII

The fog cleared while Miles breakfasted at the nearby cafeteria.

"I suppose you couldn't tell me where to buy a good used car for about a hundred and fifty dollars?" he asked the same waitress who had served his ham and eggs on the previous morning.

"Couldn't I?" she smiled. "Why, my boy friend's in the used car

191

business. And he'll treat you right, too. You go around and see him. His place is only a few blocks away, just off Kearney Street."

Accordingly, by next morning's breakfast, Miles was in possession of a second-hand Chevrolet, and, by lunch time, of the necessary plates and papers. That afternoon he bought himself a suit of ready-to-wear clothes, socks, shirts, underwear, a Rand McNally road map—and a cheap reprint of Jack London's *Valley of the Moon*, through which he glanced while he was dining and which he compared with the road map on his return to the hotel.

BOOK TEN

I

THE GIRL IRENE SAID, "THANKS A LOT. NO. I GUESS I'D BETTER HIKE FROM here. It's only about a mile anyway—and seeing me in a machine with you might give my folk ideas".

She picked up her light grip and walked off, humming, "It was swell while it lasted". Miles watched her till she disappeared where the field track met the woods.

It had been a queer little affair—begun at that filling station way back between Red Bluff and Redding, whose attendant had said in his slow drawl, "You wouldn't believe, sir, the way some folk in this country treat an automobile. Take a look at that young woman sitting on that there bench. She's ridden all the way from Los Angeles without checking up on her oil level. And now she's mad at me for telling her her old jitney's only fit for the Japs. And they only pay scrap metal prices. As I've also been telling her. Comes from Medford, Oregon. I reckon she'll have to hitchhike now".

So what could you do, being bound that way in so far as you were bound any way, yourself—except offer Irene a lift as far as Medford? But they'd turned off highway ninety-nine once they were through Redding. And then the storm came on. And then they found the autocamp. And then . . . then the thing just happened.

"Pity", thought Miles.

He climbed back into the Chevrolet, and drove on for Rogue River, meaning to unroll his old valise there and camp like "Saxon" and her "Billy" in Jack London's book—whose descriptions, allowing for the time lag of more than a quarter of a century, had proved amazingly accurate ever since he drove out over the Bay Bridge and headed for Sacramento. Another spring storm, however, made him change his mind.

Next day, having slept in a poorish autocamp, he swung south and west away from Grant's Pass for the sea. Time was getting short. Another week, and he must be in Hollywood—a grim place if you could trust Irene, who'd spent her last dollar trying to get screen work there and not possessed "more'n enough money to buy gasolene and peanuts" when her car packed up.

"Poor kid", he caught himself thinking, just before he fell asleep in Crescent City. But within another forty-eight hours he had as good as forgotten her. And two nights later, camping lonely where azalea buds were just bursting to bloom among the giant burls at the foot of a redwood tree which must have been bigger than the oldest oak in Torrington playing fields a thousand years before the first Icelander sailed his longship to this America, he re-experienced, just for a moment, the perturbation which had haunted him twice before, once in Hong Kong and once in San Francisco.

Telling himself, sharply, "You fool. You utter idiot. You'd know all right if anything like that had happened", he scourged perturbation away.

193

Next night, trespassing into the Game Refuge, Miles camped again. And all next day, south from Ukiah, he followed the trail which an author dead these many years had blazed for him, gladdened by the spring sunshine, by every lush valley, by every purling stream, by every farm where the fruit trees blossomed and every range whereup the madroños or the manzanitas marched for the horizon—gladdened, and, above all, grateful, as never in all these years since Halcyon's death had he been able to feel truly grateful, for the mere gift of life.

His last night north of San Francisco he spent in what must originally have been one of those "three little hotels in Glen Ellen, right next door", to whose proprietor "Saxon" had sold her vegetables. But nowadays the hotel was no longer little. Nor could he identify, though he spent several hours pottering round Caliente and Boyes Hot Springs and El Verano, the precise whereabouts of "Madroño Ranch".

So towards noon he drove back to Petaluma and south along the concrete of highway a-hundred-and-one till he made Marin County, and the tunnel, and crossed Golden Gate Bridge.

A fleet of American warships was steaming to anchor up the Bay. He watched them from his driving seat, while he consumed the hardboiled eggs, the sandwiches, the fruit and the can of beer he had bought in Sausalito, imagining that he recognised a cruiser in whose wardroom he had been entertained by an officer of Marines during his stay at Pearl Harbour.

A stout fellow, that officer of Marines. But maybe just a shade too certain that the Japs would never take on America. Martin Halliburton thought differently. A bit of a panicker, Martin. He'd been right so far, though. The Japs had done exactly as he predicted when one met him—nine years ago that must be—in New York.

"And things in Europe don't look any too rosy either", brooded Miles Radcliffe. But the little mood of pessimism soon passed.

He tossed the remnants of his meal to the gulls ; consulted the town plan in Rand McNally, and soon found himself at the flyover between Skyline Boulevard and the coast highway. By nightfall he was in Monterey ; and at twilight next day he made the long green seafront of Santa Barbara, and a hotel from whose prices he fled back to the town.

There he found a room and a bath for two dollars, a garage whose mechanic promised to have his car washed by "seven o'clock tomorrow morning, you can rely on our service, sir", a Spanish-looking restaurant, and a Los Angeles and district telephone directory, in which he discovered that "Longmore N." lived on a street called Petunia in a place called Beverly Hills.

"No. I wasn't at all surprised when you phoned", said Nicholas Longmore. "You see, I'd already had a letter about you from Andrew, and he mentioned that you'd been in the Tank Corps. Did you have any difficulty in locating me ?"

"Not the slightest. I came in on Ventura and turned off by the golf course into Beverly Glen Boulevard."

"You always were pretty good at mapreading. D'you remember my nicknaming you Little Peter the Pathfinder?"

"No. I'd forgotten that."

They were still standing under the pergola which led up to the little house in whose shady front garden his one-time major had been sitting when Miles drove up.

The house, of red tiles and green plaster, was imitation Provençal. Longmore, in his knife-creased white trousers, his silk shirt and his brass-buttoned double-breasted coat of blue flannel, might have been dressed for Cannes.

Miles followed him through a narrow darkish hall into a low room which looked out on to flowerbeds where a gardener was watering zinnias.

Almost as tall as Jim Bowlby—with the same air of the beau sabreur and what remained of his hair equally golden, but blue-eyed and, nowadays, clean-shaven—Longmore, who must be at least forty-eight, carried himself like a young athlete. On one wall of the room Miles noticed a rack of foils.

"Do much of that?" he asked.

"Fencing? Yes. I'm rather keen on it. I play a good deal of lawn tennis, too. That's one comfort about this place. One can get any God's own amount of exercise. What games do you play?"

"Oh, most of 'em. But I'm not particularly keen. How long have you been in Hollywood?"

"Since the Flood. Or before the talkies. Nineteen twenty-six to be accurate. This section was only waste land then. But I had a hunch about it. And I got in on the ground floor. Land's the only thing if you want to make real money. I could quit pictures now if I wanted to. But I don't quite know what I'd do with myself if I went home."

Longmore shook a cocktail. Drinking, Miles recollected a farmhouse kitchen on the Western Front and a conversation which had ended, "What am I going to do when it's all over, Peter the Pathfinder? Be an author if I can".

"Did you ever write that novel?" he asked.

"I did." His ex-major's tone was almost apologetic. "And sold the film rights. And came out here on a three-months' assignment. And here I've stuck, doctoring scenarios with one hand and buying up town lots with the other, for twelve years. Call me a well-to-do beachcomber and you won't be far wrong".

Longmore fell silent, his blue eyes a trifle sombre. Then he changed the subject, asking the usual, "What have you been doing with yourself all this time?"

"Oh, lots of things", answered, also as usual, Miles.

Talk turned to Andrew Mackay.

"You saved his life, I gather."

"So he alleges. I wonder if that's why he's overpaying me."

"Overpaying you! My dear chap, there's no such word in Hollywood's vocabulary. Another cocktail?"

"No, thanks."

"Then"—Longmore glanced at his gold wristwatch—"how about a spot of lunch?"

"All right. I'll find somewhere to doss down afterwards."

"Don't worry. That's all been taken care of. Andrew told me to get in touch with his secretary the moment you rolled up. You're expected at his house round about seven. He and Daph won't be back till Wednesday or Thurdsay. But Pat's there."

"Who's she?"

"Daph's youngest sister. Now I'll go and get the car out."

"We could go in mine."

"We could—if we were my gardener." And Longmore, laughing, led the way to his garage, where they climbed into an open Cadillac, painted red and black with white leather upholstery.

"You seem to do yourself pretty well", thought Miles.

<h2 style="text-align:center">IV</h2>

Nikko Longmore drove slowly along Petunia Street, between empty sidewalks and hedgeless front gardens and low houses of varying architecture —none of which, he explained, had been built more than five years. Magnolias were in bloom. Here and there jacaranda trees flowered, parma-violet in the midday sunshine. Nostalgically Miles remembered taller jacarandas, a whole avenue of them, and Halcyon murmuring, "*Que lindo*". Where could that have been? Buenos Aires? Rosario? Asuncion? Curious—how easily one forgot.

"This was mostly waste land, too, when I arrived", said Longmore, as they swung right along Wilshire Boulevard. "We'll feed at the Victor Hugo. Afterwards I'm taking you to see some friends of mine in Pasadena. Or rather Altadena. They're a bit snobby, but they've got a peach of a swimming pool—and a daughter, also rather a peach, with whom I'm in what the French call rather a delicate situation."

And over lunch, for which he chose a lonely table, Longmore confided:

"The damnedest unluckiest wound. I'd have given every penny I've ever made, any time these last twenty years, for a nice wife and a couple of brats".

They made palmy Pasadena towards three o'clock; and there, once again, Miles was nostalgically reminded of South America. These trees— oranges and lemons, cork and rubber, pepper and banana and eucalyptus— seemed as familiar as these Spanish houses. But, once away from the city, they came through what might have been European parkland, beyond which rose a range of mountains.

"The Sierra Madre", said Longmore. "Quite good shooting there. Bears, they say. Do you care for that sort of thing?"

"Oh, I've done a bit of it in my time."

"Queer bloke", thought Miles's ex-major. "Doesn't give much away."

He drew in at elaborate iron gates hung between pillars of masonry; shifted gear and circled up a white gravel drive. The house stood high on a long walled terrace blazing with flowers. The precise style of its architecture defeated Miles. There was something of the Mission about those yellow

196

walls and the grilles at those upper windows and the lines of that curling roof. But the ground floor windows were french, and that bell tower Italian renaissance, and this loggia pure modernity.

Out from the loggia, at sight of the Cadillac, ran a girl.

V

The girl, dark and very sleek, with an almost perfect figure, said, "Hallo there, Nikko. The others are all down at the pool". Introduced as "Caroline van Ness", she gave Miles a hard little hand and the conventional greeting. They strolled through the loggia, through a lofty hall, whose curtains were of dark red Venetian cotton velvet, through a drawing room hung with Lelys, its furniture beautifully blent of Chippendale, Hepplewhite and Chinese lacquer, on to smooth turf and down a flagged path at the end of which two Judas trees flaunted in rubeate glory against the hot Californian sky.

Steps led to a blue pool, more than a hundred feet long, bordered in green marble, gay with a Japanese pavilion and varicoloured umbrellas. There were people in the water, people in the pavilion, people under nearly all the umbrellas. On a diving board high enough even for Miles, poised the figure of a gray-haired man.

The man dived. Caroline van Ness said, "Father's crazy. He'll break his neck one of these days. Come along and meet mother, Captain Radcliffe".

Mrs. van Ness, prominent of nose and sharp of feature, wore a lace frock, had hoisted a lace parasol, and appeared to possess a sense of humour.

"I'm like the old lady who lived in a shoe", she began. "I've so many children I don't know what to do."

She pointed out half a dozen of them, and called one, a tall youth with crinkly golden hair, over.

"Caroline's taken Major Longmore to inspect the water lilies", she said. "That girl never had any manners. This is Captain Radcliffe, Tom. Please look after him"; then, "We don't usually have such a crowd of a Sunday. But this is a homecoming party. Mr. van Ness and I have only just returned from Europe. We met a Sir Philip Radcliffe while we were in London. Is he a relation?"

"I've a halfbrother of that name. He makes radios."

"Now let me think. I believe Sir Philip did tell us he was interested in radio. Yes. I'm sure he did."

So Fluke had got his knighthood. And Enid was "m'lady". What a scream!

The ensuing hours proved pleasant, though a little trying, because Tom van Ness took his duties as a host so seriously, introducing Miles to more people than he had been accustomed to meeting in a month.

"I feel rather dazed", he confessed when, Longmore having at last retrieved him from the pavilion, they climbed back into the Cadillac. "I don't know how many houses I haven't been asked to visit."

"From which one gathers", observed Longmore, "that you did not mention you had anything to do with the movies", adding, "I played that card for all it was worth with Caroline. And what do you think her answer was 'My dear Nikko, I'm not in the least classconscious.' Hades. What am to do with that girl? The next thing I know she'll be proposing to me."

"Well, you can always refuse her", grinned Miles. But the grin left hi lips as he remembered . . . that one incident of these last years which h wanted to forget.

VI

Twilight fell, and was night, before Longmore's Cadillac purred back t Petunia Street. Soon Miles's Chevrolet was following it to the gates o Bel Air and through them up a curving road.

The short drive which led to the Mackay home was steep and heavil overhung with shrubbery. What one could see of the house looked faintl Burgundian. A butler, obviously English, emerged from a turreted porch.

"Will you be staying for dinner, sir?" he asked Longmore.

"No. I only came to show Captain Radcliffe the way. How's the worl with you, Jenkins?"

"I'm sorry to tell you that my wife's poorly again, sir."

"I say, that's bad luck."

Longmore drove off. Jenkins, having removed Miles's valise and case from the Chevrolet, informed him that the chauffeur would take it to th garage, and led him into a heterogeneously furnished room, with a dee sofa, many bookcases, and snuff-coloured curtains. A woman who reminde him a little of Stephanie rose from the desk at which she had been writing and said, "How do you do, Captain Radcliffe? I'm Ruth Alderson, Mr Mackay's private secretary. I have an airmail letter for you".

The letter, on paper embossed, " Kerstlen Pictures, Inc. New York Offices", read, "*My dear Miles. This is just to greet you if we don't happen home before you arrive, and to say how glad we are to have you stay with us. Your agreement provides for an advance of* $1000. *The cashier's department at the Studios has been instructed to pay it over to you rightaway. My wife joins me in good wishes*".

"Is this usual?" Miles asked himself. "Or does Andrew imagine I'n broke?"

Jenkins showed him to an octagonal bedroom, panelled in green silk with French furniture; and began to unpack his suitcases.

"Will your big luggage be coming on by train, sir?" he asked.

"I'm afraid that's all I've got."

"You'll find clothes terribly expensive here, sir."

"Meaning I'll have to buy some, eh?"

"Well, you certainly need a new dinner jacket, sir."

The man laid out his blue suit and went to draw his bath.

Tubbing himself, Miles continued to speculate about Andrew's letter Did he owe his job with Kerstlen Pictures to the fact that he had save Andrew from being taken prisoner? Rotten, if he did.

Downstairs, in a lounge hall which, like the bedroom and bathroom seemed overluxurious, he found Ruth Alderson smoking a cigarette throug a long holder and fiddling with the controls of a radio. She switched of and said, "I've just been listening-in to some news from Europe. How d
198

you feel about the position? My opinion is that Hitler means to have Czechoslovakia".

"I'm afraid I don't know much about it. You see, I haven't been in Europe since nineteen thirty-six."

"But you read the newspapers?"

"Oh, occasionally."

A hidden elevator whirred. A door clicked open. From behind the staircase came a girl in gray trousers and a scarlet turtle-neck jumper, who held out an exquisite hand, saying, "How do you do? I'm Patricia Stoddart. I'm so sorry I wasn't here to welcome you. Ring for dinner, will you, Ruth? I'm simply starving".

Patricia had the same pale gold hair, the same smoky blue eyes, and was just about the same height as Daphne.

"But she's about three times more alive", decided Miles.

The three of them dined at a long oak refectory table illuminated with wax candles in silver sticks. Jenkins served them with cold soup, a roast done to the turn, avocado pear salad, and a trifle. Ruth ate in silence. Patricia pattered all the time. Her lips, which curled fascinatingly at the corners, were infinitely mobile, but rather too inquisitive.

She insisted on being told Miles's age ("I'm twenty-five next birthday"), whether he were married ("I've been married three times to Daph's twice, but I've never been lucky with it"), how much he knew about pictures ("Nothing at all, Captain Radcliffe? How refreshing") and what he really thought about the abdication of Edward Windsor.

On learning, "I was in England when it happened", she asked, "Whose side were you on?" and seemed very surprised when he answered, "I'm afraid I didn't really bother about it".

"Why not?"

Miles's, "Oh, I was just leaving for the East about that time", struck Ruth Alderson as rather unconvincing.

"He'll take an awful lot of knowing", she thought, and, with Patricia still at her very brightest, "I've seen Pat in this mood before. If she asks him to take her dancing, I shan't feel at all happy about it."

Meanwhile Pat was saying, "I don't have to work tomorrow. So how would it be if I showed you around?"

Miles answered:

"That butler of yours seems to think I ought to spend most of the day at a tailor's. He didn't seem too impressed with my evening clothes. And I'm supposed to call in at the studios".

Pat smiled:

"I know a perfectly swell tailor. And I'll go along with you to the studio".

"More trouble", thought Ruth.

VII

Andrew Mackay said, "Sure, it's hokum, Nikko. But I reckon we can get away with it. As far as I can see there's nothing more to be done with his script except pep up the dialogue. Joe will have it that Sol Rosenblum is the best man for the montage. I'd rather have had De Saumarez. He

199

did a fine job on 'Way Up the Amazon'. But you know what Joe is. You and Miles must get together with Sol as soon as you can. And look here, Johnny, Miles feels that sketch of the fort still makes it look a bit too solid. That's so, isn't it, Miles?"

"Well, yes. They were only shacks, you see. At least most of them."

"More like this", said John Anderson, the young scenic artist who sat next to Miles at the round table; and, picking a sketch from the folder at the foot of his chair, he transformed it with a few quick strokes of the pencil.

"And I'll have to have the well a whole lot farther away from the 'dobe hut", went on Mackay. "If it's too close, that scene where Daphne draws water under fire won't mean a thing."

The conference continued. His part now a mere listener's, Miles let his mind drift. Already it was more than six weeks since his arrival in Hollywood—five since he had moved into his own apartment—and four since his last meeting with Pat, who ought to be back from location by tomorrow evening. What had the girl meant with her, "Then we might go places"? Easy enough to guess.

"Nuisance", he decided. "Don't want to be worried with that sort of thing."

For his job, entirely consultative, had never proved too onerous to prevent him from playing lawn tennis at the Athletic Club, or swimming from the sands at Santa Monica, or exploring a countryside which—once one escaped from the "dreary quadrilateral", as Nikko phrased it, bounded by Culver City and the Santa Fé depot at Los Angeles—had proved wide enough.

"Well, I think that settles everything. So we might break off now."

Andrew's voice recalled Miles to the present. He rose with the others and followed Nikko Longmore—immaculate in beige gabardine and brown and white shoes—past the chromium-plated office where an immaculate lady receptionist was just telling an equally immaculate film agent, "I'm rea sorry, Mr. Schuylenberg, but Mr. Mackay won't be able to see anyone til tomorrow", to their own room.

"Let's contact Rosenblum", said Longmore, sitting down at his desk and scooping up the telephone.

Miles, in white flannel trousers and a sports coat of pale gray Englis worsted, ordered at what then seemed astronomical prices from Pat's "swel tailor", lounged to the window, which was wire-netted against flies.

Below ran a concrete path. Through the thin netting he could see the south wall of number one studio, high as an aircraft hangar's. Between th path and the wall lay a little flagged garden, freak of Joe Kerstlen's fancy and his especial pride. Miles remembered Pat showing him that garden. If h had guessed right, would she be such a nuisance? Confound one's imagina tion. Confound this hunger. Didn't a man ever get over it? Even Long more wished he had a wife. "And children", thought Miles.

Once more reminded of the one incident he wanted to forget, he wa glad of Longmore's "Rosenblum wants us to lunch with him".

They washed and left the room. A long corridor led through a swingin wire screen into sunshine. Longmore put on smoked glasses and a Panam hat, grumbling, "It's as hot as hell today".

"You don't know what heat is", grinned Miles.

They passed through a doorway into a cool passage. Longmore pocketed his glasses and hung his hat on a peg. They entered the commissary, where Sol Rosenblum had already taken a table and was busy whispering into a telephone. Longmore introduced Miles. They chose and fetched their own dishes.

"*Ja*", said Rosenblum over coffee. "De script I see him. Already I make a simple liddle plan."

But, once they reached his room, the expert's plan for the montage—three sequences each composed of more than a hundred flashes—proved so complex, and his knowledge both of English and the Chaco war so rudimentary, that Miles soon broke into German, of which—fortunately—Longmore possessed a smattering.

Rosenblum, making occasional notes, listened carefully; and pricked up his pointed ears when Miles mentioned General Kundt and the mass assaults at Nanawa-Gondra.

"*So*", he said. "*Das ist gut.* I can there a little anti-nazi propaganda make."

VIII

On their way back to their own room, Longmore said to Miles, "That poor devil had a big job with Ufa. They kept him in a concentration camp for God knows how long. Do you think there's going to be another war?"

"I was in Germany about two years ago. To have a look at the Olympic Games. They seemed friendly enough."

"So they did before the last one. I'm a bit worried."

"I can't say it worries me."

On his desk Miles found a characteristic note from Ruth Alderson: "A.M. wants to see you. Ring me". Rung, she said, "He's free now, Captain Radcliffe. You can come right over".

Andrew Mackay sat alone in his businesslike room, its shades drawn against the sun.

"Joe's been at me", he began. "Someone's been telling him that the Bolivian troops wore old German army helmets. I've forgotten what they're called."

"*Pickelhauben.*"

"Yes. That's right. Is it true?"

"Not to my knowledge. What's the point?"

Andrew hesitated, playing with a paper knife.

"Politics", he said after a longish pause. "The more we can make the Bolivian army—after all, they were the aggressors—look like the German army, the better Joe'll be pleased."

"And so will Rosenblum, I imagine."

Miles gave a précis of his talk with the montage expert.

"There's too much anti-nazi propaganda coming out of Hollywood", frowned Andrew. "The public doesn't go to the pictures to be preached at. And our public's international."

He elaborated the theme, closing with a quiet, "What goes on in Europe is none of America's business".

H—WWE

"Or of mine?" wondered Miles.

The mental question proved just a mite disquieting. A chap on the radio last night had sounded pretty pessimistic about Czechoslovakia. Probably, though, the whole trouble'd blow over. Troubles usually did. And anyway —no more wars for him. That book had been closed at Villa Montes. And closed for keeps.

Andrew talked a little longer—about the title of the film, still undecided after half a hundred suggestions—and dismissed him. The empty hat peg in their own room proved that Longmore had decided to call it a day. Miles took his own hat; collected his shabby Chevrolet from the parking place, and drove out through the iron gates which a guard with an automatic at hip unlocked for him, past the filling station into Venice Boulevard.

The usual breeze was blowing. As usual, he stopped at the golf club, for which Andrew had given him a card, and treated himself to a drink.

IX

Twilight fell—silly, there being no summer time!—just as Miles reached the food store on Wilshire Boulevard whose Chinese owner, having prospered and multiplied, now rented him four rooms on the upper floor, originally constructed for his own occupation.

"Velly fine chellies", said Tio Khie Hong, found on the sidewalk. "I send you some up. News from China velly bad tonight. War with Japan last long time. Maybe fifty years."

Miles thanked him, unlocked his private side door, pulled some letters from the mailbox and went upstairs.

He had been lucky to find this place; luckier still to find a landlord like Tio, one of whose manifold relatives kept it clean.

A second staircase led straight up from the store. At the top of this was another door, with a snap lock of which Tio kept the only key. A hand rattled the knocker on this door. Opening it, Miles looked down on the sleek head of Tio's eldest, a boy about ten, who proffered a large box of black cherries, beginning gravely, "Be pleased to accept gift from honourable father", only to chuckle, "Say, captain, wouldn't I be swell in a Charlie Chan picture?"

Alone again, Miles put the cherries in the icebox; and sat down at the kitchenette table to open his mail.

This envelope with an English stamp and the superscription "Radcliffe Radios Limited" must obviously contain Fluke's answer to his congratulations on the knighthood.

"Took his time about it", thought Miles, and slit the flap.

Mrs. Van Ness's information had been accurate, Fluke beginning, "*Thanks for writing to me, old boy. Yes. It's quite true. I was made a K.B.E. in the last Honours List. I suppose you don't realise that none of us have had a line from you since you left for the East. Still, better late than never*".

Scraps of family news followed. Enid was as fit as a fiddle. Simmy had been at Cambridge for the last year; Philly would come out next. Arty had been operated on for appendicitis. The letter ended, "*Fancy your having a job in Hollywood. Wonders will never cease. Don't be surprised if her ladyship and I roll up there one of these days. There's some talk of our making a trip to America".*

"Funny", brooded Miles. "Not a word about Rosaleen."

The next envelope, forwarded from his New York bank, bore the Hong Kong postmark; and, reading Martin Halliburton's letter, Miles forgot all about Fluke's.

Martin and his Mary must have gone crazy. They were volunteering, he to fight and she to nurse, for China. *"I know what you'll think"*, wrote Martin. *"But the way we see it is that if the Japs aren't stopped it'll be our turn next, and after that America's. Tell your Yankee friends so with my compliments."*

"That would be popular", thought Miles.

Two more envelopes contained advertising matter, and the last his bank statement, which he checked before taking his bath. Afterwards he opened a tin of soup, heated it on the electric stove, cooked himself a dish of ham and eggs, and set to on the cherries, eating more than half the box.

"Turning into a regular old bachelor", he brooded, inspecting the shelves in his sitting room and taking down one of his latest purchases, a secondhand copy of Goethe's *Faust*, printed in Holland. Presently he was reading one of his favourite passages :

> *"Sie kämpfen sich, so heisst's, für Freiheitsrechte,*
> *Genau besehen sind's Knechte gegen Knechte".*

Rather pleased with a paraphrase pencilled in the margin, " 'Fight for your freedom!' Thus each leader raves. The truth? That slaves are murdering other slaves", he was just reassuring himself that nothing on earth would ever induce him to be a soldier again, when the telephone rang, the operator said, "Captain Miles Radcliffe? You're wanted on long-distance", and he heard Patricia Stoddart's, "Hallo there, Miles. I'm starting back first thing tomorrow. If you haven't got a date we might go places Sunday".

Instinct prompted prevarication. Almost immediately, however, he had invited her to take lunch with him, and was promising to call her at Andrew's.

"Weak of me", he thought ; and the thought nagged at him until—thirty-six hours later—he heard Jenkins's, "Miss Patricia, sir? One moment—and I'll put you through."

"Let's lunch somewhere we can talk", she said that time. "And I'll tell you what we might do afterwards. Andrew's been given two seats he can't use for the final of the Jitterbug Contest."

"What on earth's that ?"

"Haven't you ever heard of jitterbugging? I just love it. Where will we dine ?"

She decided on the latest craze in restaurants. As he hung up—he had been telephoning from the studio—Miles saw Longmore eyeing him curiously.

"Hitching one's wagon to a star", pronounced his ex-major, "is apt to come a bit expensive. I'd watch my step if I were you. She's just about due for another husband."

"Don't be such an ass."

"All right. You wait and see. Where are you feeding tonight?"

"Murphy's."

"Mind if I join you?"

"Rather not."

"Good."

Longmore, Carlo Neroni, his Italian fencing professor, and Pierre Benoist, an ex-champion French epéist, arrived late to find Miles already tackling the large proprietor's largest steak and an enormous stein of beer.

"Strengthening yourself for Sunday's ordeal?" chaffed Nikko Longmore, and was amused to see Miles flush.

Dinner over, the Frenchman and the Italian slid into a dispute about the conquest of Abyssinia. Successful in knocking up their verbal swords, Nikko fell to wondering whether he wouldn't, after all, take out his papers as an American citizen; and looked up to see Caroline van Ness just entering the restaurant.

Caroline had a young man with her. She came straight towards him. He rose and met the pair just before they reached the table. She held out a hard little hand, saying, "You know Julius, I think, Nikko. He and I have just made up our minds to get married".

"Congratulations", said Miles, when his ex-major sat down again—and it was Longmore's turn to flush.

The Italian commented, "*Bella donnina*"; and the Frenchman, "*Ravissantes, les petites Americaines*".

About such conquests, they were in complete accord.

X

Tio Khie Hong did not open his store Sundays. Neither did his female relative come to clean.

Miles woke at his usual seven, cooked breakfast, which he took at a nearby drugstore on working days, washed up, aired and made his divan bed, and decided it was about time he cleaned his guns.

"Might sell them", he thought, oiling the Bergmann. "All except the shotgun anyway. Always a bore smuggling them through the customs." But something akin to sentiment forbade. How many years of his life had he spent using these weapons? What fun they'd been. Even that last year in the Chaco, looking back on it, didn't seem too bad.

Just as he relocked the guncase the telephone rang, and Jenkins said, "One moment, sir. Miss Patricia wishes to speak to you".

Pat's voice sounded gay—and faintly provocative. She'd be expecting him around twelve for a cocktail. Would he mind if her sister Helen took lunch with them? He'd like Helen. Only he mustn't like her too much.

Miles changed his old gray trousers and singlet for a suit of Foochow silk bought in Canton just before the Japs began bombing it; took a little more trouble than usual over the set of his tie and the brushing of his hair, still jetblack except for the white patch at his right temple; went downstairs, and let himself out by his private door.

The day promised to be unusually hot. ("In more ways than one?" he speculated with a touch of cynicism.) He opened all the windows of the Chevrolet, which he never garaged; drove past the vacant lots along the side turning and back across the boulevards until he made the gates of Bel Air.

Several other cars were parked along Andrew's drive. Their glitter made his own conveyance look rather dilapidated. In the turreted porch he encountered Daphne and a diminutive man with an overlarge head and very bright eyes whom he knew for Joe Kerstlen. Daphne introduced them. Joe said, "Pleased to know you, Captain Radcliffe", and stepped straight into a chauffeur-driven limousine.

"Go right in", smiled Daphne. "I'll be along presently."

She wandered off round the house. Miles wandered in.

The hall was fairly crowded. He shook hands with Andrew, and found Pat by the cocktail table with Helen. They were so alike that they might have been twins—distinguished only by their mouths (Helen's, he thought, looked a trifle sulky), an inch in height (there Pat had the advantage) and their style of hairdressing, tight gold curls for Helen and a page bob for Pat.

Both women wore white, and each of them was drinking a tomato juice. Helen said, "I do hope you don't mind my tagging along for luncheon". Pat twinkled, "What do you expect him to say? That he just hates it?" and laid a possessive hand on his arm as she continued, "Fix yourself a drink, Miles". Ruth Alderson joined them. Once more Miles was struck by her resemblance to Stephanie.

"How's our phenomenon?" asked Ruth, explaining to Helen, "We call him that because he's the only man in Hollywood who admits he doesn't know a single thing about pictures. And he never goes to one if he can possibly help it."

"I met a man like that once", said Helen; and she added, rather surprisingly, "He told me he preferred his emotions first hand."

Andrew hobbled over and mixed in the conversation. After a while Pat asked, "Have you bought yourself a new car yet, Miles?"; and, learning that he still drove the Chevrolet, went on, "I'm not going to ride in that flivver".

She stepped to the house telephone; called into it, "Oh, Jake. Is that you? I want the Packard rightaway please". And five minutes later Miles was wringing her new chauffeur warmly by the hand.

Jake Folinshaw explained that he had come out to California for his health. Sadie was fine. She'd gotten her a job in a downtown department store. They had a swell little apartment. Miles must come and take supper with them sometime. Would Miss Patricia be wanting him again?

Pat, already at the wheel, seemed to hesitate before she said, "No. I guess you can have the rest of the day off, Jake". Miles climbed in beside Helen. Jake closed the door. As she drove off, Pat asked, "How did you two come to know one another so well?"

Afraid of her curiosity, Miles answered:

"We used to be in a business together once. But that was a long time ago. The last time I met him he was driving a taxi in New York".

The answer seemed to satisfy Pat; but he caught Helen eyeing him sideways. "She's got the most brains of the three", he decided. "She's a bit suspicious too. She's wondering what my background is."

It was not, however, until halfway through their lunch in a pseudo-Hawaiian restaurant that Helen Stoddart interrupted his reminiscences of the real Hawaii with a quiet, "You seem to have been most everywhere. He's a regular soldier of fortune, isn't he, Pat? Why don't you write your memoirs, Captain Radcliffe? I bet they'd be thrilling. And you might make a lot of money".

Off his guard for a moment, Miles answered, "I'm afraid I'm not as keen on money as most people".

"Does that mean you've enough to live on without working?"

"Yes. As long as I live carefully."

"Who the hell wants to live carefully? I'm sure I don't", laughed Pat.

XI

Towards half past two Helen said, "Well, I'm off to Hollywood Park to play the races", and called for a taxi. Once she and Miles were alone, Pat seemed to relax.

"The trouble with Helen", she confided, "is that she's rather high hat. She'd get more parts if she were to open up a bit. She's easier to look at than either me or Daph. She's got a nicer voice, too."

"I dispute that."

"Well, Daph's easier to look at than I am anyway."

"I dispute that too."

Miles's compliments seemed to please. A waiter brought the bill, which came to twelve dollars. It struck him that dinner would cost at least double. He remembered Longmore's, "Hitching one's wagon to a star is apt to come a bit expensive". Pat said, "This is a nice place. I've never been here before. We must come again".

She went to powder. He tipped the waiter a dollar fifty, and gave the man who brought the Packard to the door a quarter. "You drive", ordered Pat. "I'm feeling lazy and I want another cigarette."

After the Chevrolet it was a joy to handle this big engine. He said so, and she laughed, "They're cheap enough—only about two thousand—you ought to buy yourself one. Don't go so fast, or we'll have a speed cop after us".

He obeyed her. Their way took them some eight miles downtown along Sunset Boulevard into the business section of Los Angeles.

"I'd almost as soon ride in a trolley car as that flivver of yours", said Pat, when they halted at a traffic light.

"Have you ever been in a trolley car?" grinned Miles.

"Sure. I used to ride to school in one. Dad kept a five and ten cent cigar store. Now Daph and I and Helen keep him in imported Havanas. What did your dad do for his living?"

"He was a clergyman", said Miles, shifting gear as the lights changed.

"Is he still alive?"

"No. He became an army chaplain and was killed in the Great War."

"Turn left at the next block. Is your mother still alive?"

"She may be."

"How do you mean—may be? Don't you know?"

"I haven't the slightest idea." Confound this girl's curiosity. "She ran away while I was still a baby."

Pat gave him another direction, and meditated.

"Don't you even remember what she looked like?"

"No."

"Say, that's tough."

Queerly her comment annoyed him. What right had this "playactress", as his father would have called her, three times in the divorce court herself, to make reflections on his mother? His mind switched back across the years. He was sitting in Fluke's study, thinking, "Mother must be a little like I am. I expect that's why she ran away from the vicarage".

Patricia Stoddart's, "That's the stadium. I wonder where we'd better park", recalled him sharply to the present. "National Jitterbug Contest", he read on an enormous poster, and could just hear a band playing the fastest swing music, as he declutched and shut off that sweet engine.

Pat pulled on the shady hat which had been lying across her knees and took a pair of sunglassses from her handbag. He helped her out. Along the gravel path between slips of green lawn, she took his arm. Her hands really were exquisite. She wouldn't be so curious if she hadn't taken a fancy to him. Why be annoyed?

An attendant inspected the ticket she produced, and directed them along a cool concrete passage. "I had Ruth Alderson change our seats", she explained. "You don't get any fun unless you sit with the real fans."

Steps led upwards, and back into the full glare of the afternoon sunlight. The next attendant said, "Unless I'm vurry much mistaken, you're Miss Patricia Stoddart. You ought to be with the judges, Miss Stoddart. Wait right here till I get you a cushion".

He fetched two cushions and shepherded them to their seats. The music had just stopped, but a hundred couples were still standing on the raised platform in the centre of the grass oval, on which other couples sat or strolled.

"Thank you", smiled Pat to the boy and girl who had squeezed closer to make more room for them.

"You're welcome", said the boy.

Loudspeakers trumpeted a torrent of words. Handclapping broke out all round the stadium. Pat signalled to a uniformed popcorn seller and bought two bags from his tray.

The boy put his arm along the back of the seat. The girl leaned against it. "When in Rome", thought Miles. He put his arm along the seat, and Pat leaned against it. The band began to play. The couples on the platform began to jitterbug, slowly at first, then faster and faster, madly and more madly, to the swing music. Little shivers ran through Pat's body. Her feet tittuped to the music. He could feel the muscles of her right shoulder tensing and flexing against his hand.

Gradually, to commands he could not follow, the platform emptied. Now only a dozen couples were left. Now only six—five—three—one of them coloured—one of the men in sailor's rig. The coloured man swung his partner clear off her feet, tossed her and caught her.

"Oh, good", said Pat.

The music stopped. Her body ceased to shiver. She sat forward and began munching popcorn.

"How do you like it?" she asked.

"I'd like it better if I knew what it was all about."

207

"Well, you see", began Pat, "it's a national contest. And today's the final."

"Are they amateurs or professionals?"

"Amateurs. They come from all over the country."

The loudspeakers blared again. He gathered that the judgments were supposed to be by popular applause. Subsequently he lost interest in the performances—but not in Pat, who insisted on staying till the prizes were distributed by a smaller light in her own firmament.

By then she had eaten three bags of popcorn, drunk several coca-colas and made friends with the boy and girl next to them, shaking hands with both, and dimpling happily when the boy said, "It sure has been swell for us knowing you, Miss Stoddart. We plan to be in the final ourselves next year".

"Nice kids", she said, taking Miles's arm again as they left the stadium. "I have enjoyed myself. Let's run around a little."

"Right you are."

It was just past five o'clock. Well before six they were driving north along the beaches under a cooling sun for Santa Monica. With Pat unusually silent, Miles fell to thinking of Halcyon.

"What are you feeling so sentimental about?" she asked.

Her intuition surprised him.

"I'm not aware of feeling sentimental", he prevaricated.

"But everybody feels that way sometime or other. I know I do. Have you ever been married?"

"No. I've escaped that so far."

"Aren't you cynical?"

She fell silent again, telling herself, "I wish he weren't so handsome. He's the handsomest man I've ever met. I thought so the first time I ever saw him".

After another mile she said, "Let's stop".

He braked on a bare stretch of road. To their left stretched sand, and the blue Pacific just ruffled by the evening breeze. On their right a line of oil derricks climbed the inland dunes. She took a pack of cigarettes from her handbag. He flicked on his lighter for her, and lit one of his own.

"Haven't you ever met anyone you wanted to marry?" she probed.

Miles hesitated. Truth—or would it be only half the truth?—seemed the easiest answer.

"Yes, once", he said.

"Then why didn't you?"

"She died."

"You poor man."

Pat laid a hand on his arm. Automatically his fingers touched hers.

They sat silent again, taking occasional puffs at their cigarettes. He was aware of the hunger. A car rolled by them, and several more cars, before she next spoke, saying a little triumphantly, "Then I was right. You were feeling sentimental. But never mind. You'll find somebody one of these days. How long are you planning to stay in Hollywood?"

"Only till Andrew's finished his film. My contract'll be up then."

"But you could get another. I guess I could fix something for you. Let's go. I wonder if I'll dine with you after all. Would you mind very much if I didn't?"

She released her hand from his. The apparent alteration of demeanour puzzled him.

"What's made you change your mind?" he asked.

"Well"—she hesitated again—"one reason is that I've got to be on the set early tomorrow."

"And the other?"

Pat smiled—her lips crinkling adorably at the corners.

"If you're the man I imagine, you should know that without my telling you. It doesn't mean that I like you less than I did anyway."

Their farewell in the turreted porch came dangerously near kiss point.

"I'm not a monk", thought Miles.

XII

Pat's letter reached Miles two days later.

She'd been thinking about him a lot. As soon as she'd gotten through with her picture ("We're on the last scenes right now") they must have that dinner they'd missed. It'd be just too bad if he didn't stop on in Hollywood. Even though he didn't care for pictures he ought to see *Men Only Love Once*, Did he really think that was true? Meanwhile she remained his affectionately.

He framed his reply carefully, promising to see *Men Only Love Once*. which was playing at a nearby theatre; and went the following night. The picture told of an overfaithful widower, falling—to a few wisecracks and a lot of celluloid—for the blandishments of a lady who had also been married before.

Four nights afterwards, by which time they were almost ready to begin shooting their own picture, Andrew invited Miles to a party at the very restaurant where Pat had suggested they should dine, and seated them together. During the meal she devoted most of her conversation to her other table neighbour, Joe Kerstlen. But during their first dance—and she was all of a dancer—she said, "I wish this party were just you and I. Don't you, Miles?" And during their second dance, a rhumba, she abandoned herself to him so completely that there was no need for words.

Bringing her back to the table, he felt just a little afraid. It would be easy enough—imagination showed him—to lose his head with this young woman. He'd had one experience of that since Halcyon was killed. And one experience was quite enough.

Pat did not dance with him again, and the party broke up shortly after midnight. The old hunger kept him wakeful. At his age a man just couldn't live like a monk. And, dash it all, she wasn't a girl. She'd had three husbands already. She'd known just what she was up to when they were doing that rhumba.

Her next move was a telephone call which woke him towards one o'clock in the morning. She couldn't sleep. Did he ever get that way? The other night she'd forgotten to ask him whether he'd been to see *Men Only Love Once*. He had. Well, what did he think about it? Wasn't it just too human? And after a good ten minutes of one-sided conversation, she said, "Oh, Miles, I felt so lonely I just had to call you. Don't you ever feel lonely, living a by yourself?"

She waited for his answer. After a longish pause he admitted, "Sometimes". After another pause Pat sighed into the microphone, "I guess I'll have to hang up now", and did so, leaving him slightly troubled.

XIII

Miles's troubles—he decided over next morning's breakfast at the drugstore—were, first, that he couldn't escape from Hollywood till his contract expired; secondly, that he couldn't be frank (one didn't say to a woman like Patricia Stoddart, "I'm not in love with you"); and thirdly, more complicatedly, that he didn't really want to escape either from her or from Hollywood.

For once in these last three years—maybe for once in his lifetime—he had lost the desire to wander. This place, this climate, this easy job and this cosmopolitan atmosphere suited him down to the ground.

Wasn't he, moreover, just a little in love with Pat?

Driving the eight miles to Culver City, his imagination grew perturbingly active, showing him her hands, her figure, the way her lips crinkled at the corners; and that evening he took supper with Jake Folinshaw, whose Sadie, turned a little shrewish by the passing years, said, "I don't like for Jake to be a chauffeur. Americans oughtn't to be servants. And I don't like that movie woman he's working for either".

"Jealous—that's what she is", grinned Jake.

"Of you? Say, that's real funny."

She went to cook their tenderloins. Later, while she washed up, Jake, his keen blue eyes quizzing Miles through the smoke of his ten-cent cigar, said, "Now if Sadie was married to you, she might be jealous. I drove that jane and Daphne home from that party they took you to. Real mad she was when Daphne razzed her about her insisting you be invited. The way some dames talk, you'd think they reckoned their chauffeurs hadn't gotten any ears".

Sadie's return stopped her husband's gossip, but not Miles's imagination. Towards ten o'clock, having invited them to a return dinner, he took his leave, still thinking of Pat.

The July night was hotter than usual and the moon at her full. His way took him along Petunia Street. All the lights in Nikko Longmore's house were burning. He stopped; went in, and found himself one of a party who were nearly all English. Longmore introduced him to a movie journalist newly arrived from London.

"How long are you staying?" asked Miles.

"That rather depends on Hitler. Personally I don't feel he's quite ready to march yet."

A girl, also just out from England, chimed in, "Don't listen to him, Captain Radcliffe. He's got Hitler on the brain. The Germans don't want to fight us again any more than we want to fight them".

"Well, let me tell you this", said one of the few Americans present, Hank Bronford, a middle-aged author whom Miles had met at the studio. "If there's a scrap, don't reckon on our helping you out again."

"No politics, Hank", interrupted their host; and the subject dropped—

to be resumed for a few minutes next morning before he and Miles began work.

"How do you feel about this Sudeten business?" asked Longmore.

"I really haven't thought about it."

"Would you go home if there were another war?"

"Not likely."

All the same, his ex-major's question worried Miles, though only at intervals, until another letter drove it clean out of his mind.

"Why aren't you ever at home?" Pat wrote that time. "I called you last evening. And the evening before." News followed. She was through working, but couldn't make up her mind where to go for a vacation. Maybe she'd stay on in Hollywood. For a while anyway.

A postscript read, "But I shan't stop on here, though Andrew and Daph want me to. I think I'll take an apartment".

They were already shooting Sol Rosenblum's montage. Miles had to be on the set by eight. That evening, while he was still in his bath, the phone bell rang. Naked and dripping, he heard Pat's:

"Hallo, darling. Why haven't you answered my letter? Where do you think I am? Right around the corner from you at the Beverly Wilshire. Would you like to give me dinner at the Brown Derby—and maybe we could come back here for a drink afterwards?"

And when he hesitated, she went on, "Of course, if you'd planned to dine with anyone else, you've only to say so".

So what was a chap to do?

XIV

As Miles entered the Brown Derby, he remembered that it was "helps' night out". All the semicircular couch seats and all the straight sofas in the outer room were already occupied. He passed through it, greeted by a few acquaintances, to find the inner room almost as full.

Next to the only corner table vacant sat a party of six, among them the English movie journalist he had met at Nikko Longmore's, who said, "I believe I know your brother. Isn't he chairman of Radcliffe Radios?"

"Yes."

"Won't you join us?"

"Thanks, but I'm waiting for a lady."

Miles sat down and inspected the menu. What the deuce was this fellow's name? Torrance. No. Todhunter.

"Hallo there", interrupted Pat.

Hatless, gloveless, and dressed with extreme but, as he could not help realising, the most expensive simplicity, she looked her very best—and, in that soft light, the merest girl. She wore no flowers, and only one piece of jewelry—a necklace of small sapphires whose colour matched her eyes. "Good evening, Mr. Todhunter", she smiled.

The journalist rose, shook hands, and introduced the rest of his party.

"Don't forget I'm interviewing you the day after tomorrow", he reminded her.

"I'm not likely to do that."

211

She demanded a cigarette, a cocktail, and beer to follow, but refused to say what she would eat, telling Miles to choose.

He suggested cold soup, one of the entrées, and—doubtfully—a jam omelette. She accepted all three suggestions. When Todhunter called for his check and shepherded his party from the restaurant, she whispered:

"Thank goodness they've gone, darling. Now we can really talk. Listen. I've got quite an idea for you. At least it's not mine really. It's half Andrew's. Why shouldn't you join an agency?"

"What kind of an agency?"

"Well, you see"—crumbling a tiny piece of bread between her lovely fingers—"Daph and I and Helen make all our contracts through the Californian Play Company. But we're rather thinking it'd be a good thing to have a change. And if we do, if you could go to Phil Schuylenberg and tell him that you could bring us over, why, he'd take you on his payroll at the drop of the hat."

"But how would your sisters feel about it?" asked Miles, playing for time, while he wondered (not that there seemed much need to wonder) what lay behind that second "darling" and this peculiar offer.

"They've got to pay agent's commission anyway. And Phil Schuylenberg's a topnotcher. He handles . . ."

She named half a dozen biggish stars; and dropped the scheme as suddenly as she had broached it, smiling, "But don't let's worry about business any more tonight. Finish your drink, and we'll go along to my apartment".

So—once again—what was a chap to do?

XV

Miles paid his moderate bill. In the outer room Pat stopped at one of the tables, saying, "Oh, Phil, I'd like you to know Captain Radcliffe. He's done a swell job for Andrew on that South American story".

"Won't you two sit down and have a drink with us?" asked Schuylenberg. Pat, however, excused herself; and Miles followed her out.

A sea mist had blown up. Sparse traffic hurried along the wide roadway. She took his arm while they waited for the lights; but relinquished it once they were across the boulevard. A few paces brought them to the Beverly Wilshire and through doors of glass and metal, opened by a porter who said, "Good evening, Miss Stoddart", into the high marble lobby, its centre table massed with flowers.

"A package just came for you, Miss Stoddart", said the clerk who handed over her key. "I sent it right up."

They entered the elevator and were decanted at the fifth floor. Along the corridor Pat took Miles's arm again, saying, "Wasn't it lucky our running into Phil?"

A bright hall led into a large sitting room, lit only by rose-shaded bracket lights. On a side table lay a long package.

"More flowers", said Pat. "How lovely. Undo them for me. There's a darling."

Untying ribbon, lifting lilies from cellophane, he thought, "I might have sent her some. But tomorrow'll do".

The card tied to the lilies read, "With love from Ruth Alderson".

"How perfectly sweet of her", went on Pat. "Let's put them in water rightaway. I know I saw another vase somewhere or other. Oh, yes. A blue one. It's in the kitchen. Go and fill it for me, there's a darling."

Three darlings altogether! One must watch one's step . . .

A fullsize kitchen and pantry—complete with all utensils—opened out of a dining room. Miles found the vase and filled it at the pantry sink. As Pat arranged the flowers he was conscious of her full attraction, and hunger ousted sense. They'd been nearly at kiss point once before. Presently they'd be there again. Pity he wasn't more in love with her. Still—he could always pretend . . .

They made conversation.

"Why, I could cook dinner for a dozen people on this range", said Miles.

"You're not trying to tell me you can cook?"

"Can't I just? It's one of my best accomplishments."

She picked up the vase. He said, "Allow me"; and took it from her. As he did so, their hands met. Would it be pretence if he made love to her? Again the old hunger ousted sense.

They made more conversation.

"For a bachelor", she smiled, "you seem singularly domesticated. What other housework can you do?"

"Wash. Iron. Mend clothes. Darn stockings."

"My! Where did you learn all that?"

"Believe it or not, Pat, I'm selftaught."

"You must be terribly clever, Miles."

Back in the sitting room, she told him to put the vase on an occasional table behind the brocaded settee.

"Do you know what I'd like? Just one glass of wine", she continued, and, picking up the telephone, asked for room service.

A waiter appeared with the wine list. Pat gave the order. As she did so, Miles remembered how long it was since he had drunk champagne—and the lukewarm taste of those two bottles Tamoi had uncorked for him and Halcyon on a New Year's Eve in the Chaco. *Dios*, if one could only put back the clock of the years!

"Miles, I believe you're feeling sentimental again."

Her voice broke the memory. Confound the woman, she was altogether too cute. Like Rosaleen. Why on earth should he be recollecting Rosaleen, who hadn't even troubled to answer his last letter? It was years since that . . . that night at Sainte Marie sur Mer.

"Confess", chaffed Pat.

"My dear"—he spoke slowly—"I may be lots of things, but I'm not a sentimentalist."

"No?" Mirth danced in her blue eyes.

"No."

"Very well. I'm wrong. Tell me what you really are."

She moved to the settee; patted it for invitation. He seated himself warily; but couldn't help recollecting the French proverb, "*Il faut prendre son plaisir où on le trouve*".

"Maybe you're a romanticist", she went on, eyeing him. "Helen declares

213

that's what I am. When I was a little girl I used to write poetry. Do you like poetry?"

"I do rather."

"How British you are. The British always qualify everything they say. I wonder why."

"Oh, it's just one of our national characteristics."

The waiter knocked; entered; opened the half bottle of champagne, and twirled it in the ice bucket.

"We'll let it be for a while", said Pat. "Good night, Albrecht."

"Okay, Miss Stoddart. Good night, Miss Stoddart."

The man went out.

"May I smoke?" asked Miles.

"Surely. If you want to."

"Won't you have one?"

"No, thanks."

He lit up. It seemed silly to feel afraid. He might not be much in love with her. But she was fair game.

"I think we'll have our wine now", she said after a short silence.

He stubbed out his cigarette; rose; filled the two glasses; handed her one of them.

"*Salud y*——" he began, still standing; and stopped dead.

Salud y pesetas. How often he had drunk that toast with Halcyon! *Dios*, why couldn't one be faithful to one's memories?

"Well, here's luck", said Pat.

She sipped and put her glass on the table. He sat down again. She edged closer, regarding him thoughtfully, her eyes now darker than the sapphires at her neck. Presently she laid a hand on his knee.

His eyes, too, began to darken. Memories faded. He became aware of the hunger—ready to pounce—pouncing. His hand covered hers. He heard himself say, "I wonder about how much you like me".

"That's what I'm wondering too."

Her hand felt cool. She appeared altogether cool, completely mistress of a situation just a little—imagination seemed to be telling him—beyond experience.

He raised her hand; turned it over, and put his lips to the palm. She said "Oh, no, please". He slipped an arm round her shoulders. She let it lie there. When he drew her to him, she resisted. Her resistance only increased his hunger.

"Look here——" he began.

"Where?" She sought refuge in laughter.

He took both her hands. They didn't feel quite so cool now. Her eyelashes were fluttering. He dropped her hands, put both arms round her, caught her to him. Her eyes closed; but her lips opened as his mouth fastened on hers. In another moment she was drinking his kisses as though they had been wine.

"My sweet", she gasped between their kisses. "My sweetest."

Then, suddenly, he felt her body stiffen and her mouth eluding his. Her eyes opened. He saw them, dark with passion, with a hunger that matched his own.

For a long second neither spoke. He could hear the thudding of her heartbeats.

214

"Quit play-acting", he heard himself say; and once more his mouth fastened on hers, once more she drank his kisses . . . until, once again, her mouth eluded him, and her body stiffened, and she said, her lips trembling:

"I'm not play-acting, as you call it. I'm crazy about you. I've been that way ever since we met. Only—only we mustn't, darling. Not till we're married. You do see that, don't you? You wouldn't have me behave like . . . like a tramp, would you, my own honey?"

Her own honey?

Hell!

XVI

"I thought I knew something about women", brooded Miles Radcliffe standing—more than an hour later—at the open window of his own sitting room. And on that, just for the split of a second, he remembered another woman, telling him, "Don't worry. I wouldn't marry you if you went on your bended knees to me. Run away and enjoy yourself—you always have run away and enjoyed yourself . . ."

Meanwhile, though, what of Pat, with her, "We could be married tomorrow. I wouldn't want a big wedding. I wouldn't want any publicity. If Phil Schuylenberg takes you on his payroll, you'll have quite a little money. And I've got plenty. I'm not extravagant. I'm not like Helen. I don't play the races"; with her, "You say it wouldn't work. How do we know unless we try?"

Gosh, how weak he'd been. But he mustn't be weak any more. He must be faithful to his memories, to that oath he had sworn at Villa Montes. Shrugging his shoulders, he moved from the window to his desk.

It took him a whole hour to compose that letter. The last sentences read: "I'm not in love with you enough to marry you. That's the truth. I'm sorry. Forgive me".

"But of course", he knew, "she won't."

He closed and addressed the envelope; went downstairs, and posted it in the nearby mailbox.

Afterwards he returned to his window. The night had cleared. The big studio on the mile-away hill must be working late. He could see a blaze of lights there. A queer place, this Hollywood. What had Longmore once called it? "The world's largest illusion factory."

But how much of the world was truth, and how much illusion? Did you ever find out?

215

BOOK ELEVEN

I

SOL ROSENBLUM SWITCHED OFF THE RADIO AND MUTTERED, IN THE SAME language it had been squeaking at them for the last half hour, "What have I told you all long? *Der Mensch ist verrückt.* He is completely mad. *Das heisst Krieg*".

"It certainly looks like war", admitted Miles.

"*Aber warum?*" asked Grete Rosenblum. "But why?"

In contrast to her father's, the girl's hair was the true German blond. But her blue eyes betrayed an equal panic.

"More coffee, *Herr Hauptmann*?" she asked.

"Please."

Her hand shook as she lifted the heavy pot. Miles took it from her and filled all three cups.

"Don't worry", he said. "It may all blow over."

Would it, though, with Hitler howling for the immediate surrender of the Sudetenland, with Chamberlain back these four days from Cologne, with Daladier, the French Prime Minister, and General Gamelin in London, with trenches being dug there, and gasmasks being served out, and the school-children to be evacuated, and the Fleet mobilising? And if it didn't blow over, what about that other oath he had sworn in Villa Montes? Wouldn't he have to go home?

Rosenblum was off the handle again. Words poured through his square teeth. His pointed ears kept twitching and twitching. Perspiration beaded his pale face. "Your dear Aunt Alice, your dear Uncle Herbert", he groaned at his daughter. "They will never escape now. And just when it was all arranged, just when they had as good as obtained their permits."

"*Liebes Väterchen*", coaxed Grete, "calm thyself."

Rosenblum, however, raved on, while Miles thought, "I could start tomorrow. The picture's practically finished".

Weakness again. Hadn't he sworn never to fight in another war?

Presently his host recovered selfcontrol.

"You must excuse", he said. "I become too excited. At least I have my dear daughter safe and sound."

"*Und drei Liften Möbel*", smiled Grete, glancing from the heavily framed pictures to the enormous carved sideboard, which took up a whole wall of the cluttered room.

The word *lift* for a vanload of furniture was not new to Miles. Many of these better-off exiles brought their household goods—so utterly unsuited to American living conditions—with them.

"Three?" he cut in.

"*Ja.* Three. It cost colossal money. But Mr. Kerstlen was so good. He has promised, too, that he will give me a screen test. But first, of course, I must learn to speak English."

"And it is Mr. Kerstlen's wish", interposed Rosenblum, "that my little scene where the Bolivian soldiers are being taught the *Parade Schritt*—how do you call it, the goose step—should not be cut. I told Mr. Mackay so on Saturday, Captain Radcliffe. But he said he must have your opinion. Will you help me, please? And will you also say to Mr. Mackay that I hope to be well enough to come to the studio myself on Wednesday?"

They talked technicalities—Andrew wanted other flashes cut—for a little longer. Then the girl escorted Miles to the automatic elevator.

"Do you think there is any hope of peace?" she asked as they shook hands.

He tried to reassure her; but felt that he had failed.

II

Outside, the sunshine was hot and the Californian sky cloudless. A good part of the world, this. Pity that Fluke couldn't see it. He didn't seem to think there was much hope of peace either. Otherwise he wouldn't have telegraphed from New York that he and Enid were catching the *Queen Mary* back to England. A bit of a panicker? Perhaps.

"Shan't hurry my stumps—whatever happens", determined Miles.

He started up his old Chevrolet and headed for Venice Boulevard. As he braked at a traffic light, another car drew alongside and he was hailed by Jake:

"Hallo there. I got in day before yesterday. We sure had a swell trip. Was you ever to Colorado Springs?"

The bell rang. The lights changed. Jake shot ahead. So Pat was back from her vacation. Would one be meeting her again? Only by accident. Naturally she hadn't answered one's last letter. "Mad at me", thought Miles.

Latish at the studio, he wandered on to the set and over the cables to where Andrew, hunched in a canvas chair, had been supervising the final retakes.

"Is that about the last one?" Andrew was asking.

"All but nineteen and twenty-two."

"Okay. Let's get on."

The actors appeared. The board clapped. The interminable—and, to Miles, interminably boring—procedure continued for another hour. Finally Andrew expressed himself satisfied; the Kliegel lights were switched off; the script girl rose from her hard seat, and the camera men and the microphone men wheeled back their machines.

"Four days ahead of schedule", said Andrew. "Good enough. Do you want to see me about anything, Miles?"

"I do rather."

"Well, let's go along to my room."

He hauled himself upright on his stick. They made their way through the bizarre medley of scenery into open air.

"Anything new from Europe?" asked Andrew. "I only had time to look at the headlines before I left the house this morning."

"Yes. Hitler's just made a speech. I heard some of it over Rosenblum's radio. He's foaming at the mouth a bit; swears that if he doesn't get what he wants by the first of October, he'll blinking well take it."

"The double-crossing louse."

Andrew stumped on round the low wall of the flagged garden. They came to the back door of his offices and into his room.

217

There were various memos on his desk. He riffled through them, depressed one key of his dictograph and called, "Get me Mr. Kerstlen, please".

A voice called back, "Mr. Kerstlen's secretary's just been on the wire again, Mr. Mackay. He's in conference right now, but he'll be free around six o'clock".

"Okay. Send in tea for two, please."

"Certainly, Mr. Mackay."

Andrew switched off the dictograph. Miles gave him Rosenblum's message.

"I'm not having that goose-step stuff in if I can help it", he said. "Sol can go boil himself. But I can't tell Joe that. You'll have to help me there."

"How?"

"You'll see. Joe's having the montage run through for him again. Probably this evening. He's in a rare state, I don't mind telling you."

"What about?"

"This war, of course."

"Well, it isn't a war yet."

Andrew—thinking, "You can't rattle the British"—smiled. A girl brought a teatray.

"It's a long time since you were last up to the house", he said, putting down his cup and lighting a cigar. "By the way, Pat's back."

"So I've just heard."

"And you don't get anything out of them without a can-opener either", continued Andrew's thoughts.

Miles felt slightly uncomfortable; obviously Andrew was probing. But the dictograph buzzed before he could probe deeper—and, for the next fifteen minutes, having said, "Hang around till Joe rings, will you, Miles?" he was on the phone.

"Dog's life, however much he's paid for it", thought the listener. "Still, he seems to enjoy it. There's one thing about the States. People don't grumble like they do at home."

Andrew's next call was from Daphne. Would he be back in time for dinner? "I'll make it if I can, sweetheart. But don't wait for me." Then one of his secretaries brought in a trayful of letters; and, while he signed them, the dictograph buzzed once more.

"Put him on", called Andrew; and into the phone, "I happen to have Captain Radcliffe with me now, Mr. Kerstlen. I'd very much like for him to come along too."

He recradled the instrument, signed the last of his letters, and took his stick from the chairback, telling his secretary, "If anyone wants me I'll be in number four projection room". There, after waiting for ten minutes, they were joined by Joe Kerstlen and two minor executives. "Let's get on with it", said Joe.

The little man with the big baldish head, the tiny feet and the bespectacled black eyes, seated himself by the desk in the front row of fauteuils and switched off the reading lamp. Andrew lowered himself into the next fauteuil, and called over his shoulder to the operator in the box behind them, "Run it slow, please".

The room darkened. The projector began to click. Watching the flow of pictures on the little screen, Miles's mind took him back across the years.

218

"Clever", he thought. "It does give one an idea of the fighting. That tank looks just like the one Féliz and I scuppered. Though it's only a model." But several shots—as he had already told Rosenblum—were travesties of the truth.

On Andrew's order the operator rewound his spool and ran it again. When the lights came on, Joe barked, "What's wrong with that anyway?"

"Lots, in my opinion, Mr. Kerstlen", answered Andrew. "To begin with it's anti-Bolivian. And to go on with it's anti-German. We're telling a love story, not making a propaganda picture."

He developed his argument. Bolivia and Paraguay were at peace nowadays. Why stir up bad blood in South America? And there were too many anti-nazi films being made. Why drag in the goose step? Why show a German ship unloading arms for the Bolivians? The British had sold them rifles too. And guns. And uniforms. Captain Radcliffe wanted a good many of these shots cut. And he was their expert. Why hire expert advice, if one didn't mean to follow it?

"I didn't hire him", fumed Joe. "You did. And what in hell do we care about Germany? They don't buy our pictures. For all we know they're starting up a second great war right now. As like as not they'll bomb Prague tonight."

"But the Bolivians never bombed Asuncion or any other town in Paraguay", interrupted Miles. "And Mr. Rosenblum shows them doing it."

Andrew gave him a glance of approval. One of the minor executives said, "Then I certainly think that ought to come out, Mr. Kerstlen", and the other, "If there is a war in Europe, won't we have to take the Neutrality Act into consideration?"

Andrew raised further objections. Joe Kerstlen continued to fume. Finally he thumped the desk with one hand; gesticulated with the other; broke out, "We'll talk this over tomorrow morning, but I warn you I'm not going to be browbeaten"; rose to his full five foot four, and stalked from the projection room. His two executives followed—one of them turning to wink reassuringly from the door.

"I need a drink after that", declared Andrew. "Come along back to my room. You did fine, Miles. Joe won't give us any more trouble."

"It didn't sound like it."

"You don't know him as well as I do. Once Joe says he won't be browbeaten, it means he's licked."

The sun had gone down while they argued. Night fell as Andrew produced a bottle and glasses.

"Here's to peace!" He tossed down three fingers of neat Bourbon.

"At any price?" asked Miles.

Andrew hesitated.

"You aren't a cripple", he said after a long pause. "You didn't spend the best part of two years in hospital, wondering if you'd ever be on your feet again—and how the heck you'd earn your living even if the surgeons weren't feeding you a lot of boloney. I guess I'm scared—not for myself, I won't be there—but for all the other millions of poor devils who may have to go through what you and I went through, and not come out of it so lucky. And it won't be only men next time. It'll be women and children too. Look at what's going on in Spain. Look at what's going on in China. I don't want that to happen in England. Or Germany."

"Neither do I. I'm not potty", grinned Miles.

But, as he drove homeward, he experienced—for the first time in many years—a faint stirring of patriotism. What was he, a trained soldier who had seen more active service than most, doing here in Hollywood with England on the verge of war?

III

That night of Monday, September the twenty-sixth, nineteen hundred and thirty-eight, Miles cooked his own dinner, and sat down to a travel book by Peter Fleming. But the printed page could not hold him; and after a short while he began to play his portable radio, bought more than a month ago when things first looked serious.

Tuning in to the German news service, he heard a rehash of the Führer's speech; then more tales of Czech "atrocities", almost obviously bunk. A local station gave him scraps of European news. Chamberlain believed peace by negotiation still possible. The French were manning the Maginot Line. Italy remained calm—Hungary and Poland resolute in their claims for territorial revision. The London Stock Exchange continued to mark down prices, and the *Queen Elizabeth* would be launched tomorrow. All this by courtesy of The Red Devil Soap Corporation—"and don't forget, you housewives, that Red Devil is the very devil for dirt".

He switched off and walked to the window. A nice mess things seemed to be in.

A ring at the side-door bell sent him downstairs. There he found Nikko Longmore, who said:

"We saw your lights on. Can we come up, or wouldn't it be popular?"

"No female impediment tonight, if that's what you're hinting at", grinned Miles.

"We", disentangling themselves from the Cadillac, emerged as Lionel Barry, an English playwright with whom Miles had a passing acquaintance, and three unknown young women, also English—and no more sober than the time, now getting on for midnight, warranted.

Miles led the five into his sitting room, and went to the kitchenette for more drinks. One of the young women, dark-eyed, Eton-cropped, and casually introduced as "This is Eleanor Rowley. She's by way of being a novelist", followed him and perched herself on the table.

"We've been to the bloodiest party", she began. "I hate Hollywood and I simply loathe Americans."

"Then why come here?"

"Why does anyone? Except to make money. Isn't that why you're here?"

"No. I rather like it."

"And Americans?"

"Yes. And Americans."

"Well, they make me sick."

Eleanor Rowley lit a cigarette, and watched him prod ice from the tray. "Are you a pansy?" she asked, as he dropped the cubes into a bucket.

"Not so that you'd notice it."

"Well, that's one comfort."

220

"Do you need comfort?"

"No. At least I don't think so. If you're not a pansy, why do you have flowers in your kitchen?"

"I happen to like flowers."

"You don't like me much, I gather?"

"Perhaps you're nicer when you haven't had quite so much to drink."

She sniffed, slid from the table and threw her cigarette on to the linoleum. Miles picked it up and stubbed it out in an ashtray.

"What happened at the party you allege to have been so sanguinary?" he asked. "Did someone turn you down?"

"No. They turned me up. The wrong way. It was that beast Hank Bronford. I can stand a lot. But I'm damned if I'm going to stand him, or any other American, saying we're afraid to fight."

"So you and Hank got on to politics, eh?"

"Yes. And I told him where he got off."

Miles arranged the glasses, the shaker, the bottles and the ice bucket on a tray, and carried them—Eleanor Rowley again following—into the sitting room.

From the moment he fixed their drinks, talk turned on the recent spat.

"You behaved like an idiot, Eleanor", said Longmore.

"I rather admired her for it", countered one of the other young women.

Lionel Barry drawled, "Manners none and habits beastly. Hank was paying for dinner, and he's as much entitled to his opinions as we are. I don't see what all the fuss is about. Hitler stated quite clearly that he didn't want a war and that he has no more territorial claims in Europe. So why don't we give him the Sudetenland and have done with it?"

The third young woman, whose red fringe almost touched her pale eyebrows, said, "I suppose you'd give him his colonies back too. And you're supposed to be a socialist".

"Communist", corrected the playwright.

The Rowley girl cut in, "Don't make me laugh, Lionel. I can't take it. Will you go home if there's a war?"

"No. I shall stay here and do propaganda."

"You would."

"Shut up, Eleanor." The red-headed one helped herself to more gin. "You've already caused as much trouble as the Treaty of Versailles."

They all fell to discussing that treaty, rehashing every argument for and against it which Miles had heard, over and over, during this last month.

Their talk bored him, and his thoughts drifted. It was not until nearly an hour later, however—and by then they had finished his bottles and eaten his last cracker—that he found himself alone.

IV

Miles tidied the sitting room and carried the dirty glasses to the sink. These so-called intellectuals—he thought—were always rather futile. They talked and talked—and got nowhere. If Lionel Barry and those three young women were fair samples of England, he preferred America. Men like Andrew Mackay and Jake Folinshaw, even a woman like Patricia Stoddart, at least knew what they wanted. They didn't fox themselves with nebulous generalities. Why shouldn't Hank Bronford be anti-British? One had been a bit that way oneself in the Chaco. And one hadn't appreciated the idea of an English prime minister flying hat-in-hand to curry favour with the Huns either.

"Never pays to treat that race like gentlemen", thought Miles. "All they understand is a good sock on the jaw."

He slept on that; but woke more philosophical. Probably the thing would be settled. So much the better if it were.

Just as he was off to breakfast at the nearby drugstore, his telephone rang.

"This is Eleanor Rowley", said the throaty voice at the other end of the wire. "I behaved like a rotter last night. Sorry. My agent's bringing me over to the Kerstlen Studios this morning. Will you be there?"

"Probably."

"Then I may look you up and grovel a little more."

She hung up. The newspaper he read with his ham and eggs told him nothing. Arrived at the studio, he could discover nothing to do. At half past eleven she came in, accompanied by Nat Owers, who handled the literary side of the Schuylenberg agency.

"Are you very busy, Captain Radcliffe?" asked Owers. "If not, may I leave Miss Rowley in your charge for a while?"

He explained that he had an appointment with the head of the story department and left them alone.

"I don't often get so tight", she began; and Miles, telling her to forget it, found her not unattractive, though rather too dark for his taste and rather too prone to ape the man. She wore no hat, sat with her legs crossed, and smoked incessantly.

"Nat Owers is trying to get me an assignment", she said in answer to a question. "But he doesn't look like bringing it off. And anyway I'm not sure I want one."

"Sour grapes?" grinned Miles.

Nikko Longmore, already working on another scenario, lounged in; said, "Hallo, Eleanor. What the deuce are you doing here?"; picked some papers from his desk, and lounged out again.

"I wonder if you'd do something for me", she went on.

"Anything in reason."

"I want to see a gambling ship. Nikko won't take me. Neither will Lionel. And they say I oughtn't to go alone."

"What do you want to do that for?"

"Copy, for one thing. Could we make it"—her unmanicured fingers extracted a Smythson diary from her bag and flipped through its thin blue pages—"Saturday night?"

She explained that the particular ship she wanted to see was called the *Happy Chance*; gave him her telephone number; extorted his promise to dine with her ("You'll have to provide the car and find out how we get on board, so that's only fair"), and was re-collected by her agent. Miles rang Ruth Alderson, who said, "No. Mr. Mackay's busy right up till seven o'clock. I'm sure he won't be needing you". Deciding he might as well take the rest of the day off, he drove to the flying field, one of his latest haunts.

"I'm trying out a new bombing crate as soon as I've had a bite to eat",

222

said his friend Billy Williams, the test pilot. "You can come along if you like."

They flew towards the Mexican border. For a few minutes the Texan let Miles handle the controls.

"If this war starts up", he drawled when they made their landing, "I reckon I'll volunteer for the British Air Force. My folk came from England. What'll you join up in? Tanks again, I suppose?"

From the flying field Miles drove to the salle, which he had also taken to frequenting, for a sabre lesson.

"Nice. Corsica. Tunis", exploded Carlo Neroni. "The Duce is right. We must have them, even if we have to fight the *maledetti francesi*. But I should not care to see us go to war with England."

"I bet you wouldn't", thought Miles.

Pierre Benoist, the French epéist, came in while he dressed.

"*Neroni est fou*", he said. "*Et nous aussi*. If France and Italy do not combine, the Boche will dominate the whole of Europe. Me, I fear the worst. Me, I am most gloomy."

And late on that Tuesday night—after a solitary dinner at a German restaurant he had discovered, most of whose customers seemed to have suddenly become the most fanatical Nazis—even Miles felt a little gloomy. Because, dash it all—oath or no oath—he'd have to go home if this thing didn't blow over. That much, at least, had been made quite clear by Billy Williams. You couldn't let Americans volunteer to fight for your country and stay put yourself.

He turned on the radio. "President Roosevelt", he heard, "is addressing a last appeal to the rulers of Europe. In a few hours the British House of Commons will be holding what may well be its most epoch-making session. A second world war looms on the horizon. The destiny of civilisation hangs in the balance. It is rumoured in Washington . . . A report from Tokyo states . . . Berlin announces . . . Doctor Benes, the President of Czechoslovakia, declares . . ."

But what did it all boil down to? That he, Miles Radcliffe, who had sworn never to fight in another war, might be forced into this one. Forced into it! That was the real trouble. Practically conscripted. What by? Other people's opinions? His own conscience? The mere fact of nationality?

The questions puzzled him. Switching off the swing time which followed the news, he thought, "Nonsense! I needn't go. I shall be thirty-nine next birthday. Billy Williams is ten years younger. Confound it all, nobody can make me go. I've had enough fighting to last my lifetime". And, waking, he thought, "I've never done anything I didn't want to".

This might have proved illuminative. But by then he was in no mood for illumination—only for news.

V

The news came, astoundingly, just after Miles reached the studio, on that sunny morning of Thursday, September the twenty-eighth, nineteen hundred and thirty-eight.

At one moment Longmore was saying, "Well, it's all u.p. I heard most of Chamberlain's speech on my wireless while I was having breakfast. God

223

knows why he ever went to Cologne. It hasn't done a damn bit of good as far as I can make out". At the next moment Sol Rosenblum had rushed in on them, babbling, "I come to see you about de montage, Captain Radcliffe. Mr. Mackay he will not budge. But dot can vait. You heard vot happens. No. *Mein Gott*, it is de miracle. To de House of Commons, just as Herr Chamberlain finish his speech, der com a telegram. Tomorrow he to München fly. Dere he and de French Prime Minister meet Hitler and Mussolini".

"Where's that rumoured from ?" asked Longmore. "Wall Street ?"

"No. No. It iss not a rumour, I tell you. It iss official." And within another minute Miles was saying down the telephone, "Right you are, Andrew. I'll have that done. Yes. Mr. Rosenblum's just told us. You can confirm it. Thanks. Oh, rather. I think it's fine too".

But did he think it fine ? Didn't this mean . . . just what Lloyd George's letter to de Valera had meant seventeen years ago in Ireland ? Old memories —of Jim Bowlby's face, and Dominic's, and the scowling face of Ronnie Wallace—haunted him as he recradled the phone.

Sol Rosenblum stayed long enough to make his final point, "You and Mr. Mackay must haf your way about de little shots, Captain Radcliffe. But it iss a pity. A great pity". Alone, Miles and his ex-major looked at each other without speaking for quite a while.

"What do you make of it ?" asked Longmore finally. "Presumably it'll mean peace."

"For how long ?" Miles shrugged his shoulders. "As far as I can see, it's just a bit of face-saving."

"Our face or France's ?"

"Both, I imagine."

"Hitler'll get his own way, of course. It makes one wonder what the hell we fought for last time."

"I seem to remember something about making the world safe for democracy", scoffed Miles.

Cynicism was on him. Queerly, even with suspense over—only a fool could imagine there would be a war now—he experienced no relief at the solution of his personal problem. The fact that he was still free to do as he pleased gave him no pleasure. Rather the reverse.

He lunched in the commissary. Nobody except himself—as far as he could gather from scraps of conversation—seemed certain of peace.

A little after five o'clock Andrew, stumping past his room, looked in at the open door, and called, "Hallo there. I'm going off for an hour. Ride up to the golf club with me".

"I'm all for Chamberlain", said Andrew over their highballs. "He's put his pride in his pocket to save Europe—and maybe us too."

Just before they parted, he handed Miles a card which read, "Major Dominic Mahoney takes pleasure in inviting you to spend a profitable evening aboard the good ship *Happy Chance*. Ten minutes by speedboat from Long Beach", remarking, "I never gamble and Daphne doesn't want to go".

Arrived home, Miles called Eleanor Rowley, and again cooked his own dinner. Afterwards he took a long walk through the deserted streets. His mind seemed altogether confused. This—since the last thing he wanted was to soldier again—seemed quite absurd.

His morning paper carried banner headlines, "Chamberlain Flies To Munich". By four o'clock, Coast time, the news of a midnight agreement was all over the studio. Dining with Longmore at the Brown Derby, Miles overheard nothing but approval. Nevertheless, just before he fell asleep, he remembered Halcyon raging as she repeated the words of a Paraguayan delegate to one of the many conferences held while they were fighting in the Chaco, "Peace is worth more than a place in history".

"The coward", he could remember her raging. "What is peace without honour?"

Strange that her face, the very tone of her voice, should have come back so vividly. Why could he never quite forget her? Never! Even while he held other women in his arms?

VI

That night, strange dreams troubled Miles Radcliffe. He woke listless. And the mood lasted all day.

He could hardly bother to read the evening papers, column after column describing Chamberlain's return to London, his drive from Heston aerodrome to Buckingham Palace, the frantic enthusiasm of the crowds, his smile as he stood at the window of Number Ten Downing Street to declaim, "My good friends. Peace with honour. Peace in our time".

Peace or war, national honour or national dishonour—what the deuce did it matter to him? Let the *politicos* get on with their politics. He told Eleanor Rowley so, dining with her on the Saturday at Perino's.

Her comment, "I don't believe you're as unpatriotic as you pretend", annoyed him. He quoted his favourite couplet from Goethe.

"Translate", she ordered. "I don't speak a word of German."

"And you set yourself up to be an educated woman!"

"There's no need to be rude", she snapped. And of course there wasn't, though he had taken such a disfancy to her. A really irritating young woman. Rather the same type as Ruth Alderson and Stephanie. Good-looking, though. And no fool.

As he drove her to Long Beach—following a scene over who should pay for dinner, which nearly led to an open quarrel—she broke off a sentence to say, "I'm still wondering why you made such a fuss about taking a meal from me. Are you by any chance that legendary character, the hundred-per-cent predominant male? If so, you oughtn't to be living in America——the land of the hundred-per-cent predominant female".

"Then you don't like your males dominant?" grinned Miles.

They were at the jetty by then. She jumped out. A speedboat man approached. Miles asked him, "How much'll you charge to take us out to the *Happy Chance*?"

"Trip's free, if you've an invite. If you haven't, nothing doing."

Miles produced the card. The man flashed a torch at it; and led them down stone steps to the boat.

"Seem to have seen you somewhere", he said, as he took the wheel and started up his engine.

"Try Trinidad, Lefty."

"Gosh! You've got some memory, captain. Tell you who I saw around the other day. Ferrety Jake. He's altered more'n you."

"You haven't changed much. Meet Miss Rowley."

"Pleased to meet any friend of the captain's, miss."

"How do you do?"

Eleanor did not offer to shake hands. Obviously she was a little unsure of herself; and this amused Miles.

"Lefty and I", he went on, "used to be shipmates."

"I didn't know you'd been a sailor."

The two ex-members of Geoffrey Thirkell's rumrunning gang made poker faces at each other. Lefty put the boat to speed.

Soon, they reached the ladder of the *Happy Chance* and were hooked in. "Be seeing you", called Lefty, as they climbed aboard.

Dominic was on deck. "Moiles, for the love of Jasus", he said. So was Lou. Miles introduced a bewildered Eleanor.

Dominic told Lou to take them to his cabin for a "bottle of the bhoy". Lou, on her best behaviour, only made one break, "This is a sweller ship than we had up to Frisco, Miles. Maybe you and Miss Rowley would care for to see one of our bridal suites".

"Later on perhaps", grinned Miles.

Lou offered them more champagne. Eleanor refused, asking, "Can we be shown the gambling rooms?" and, alone with Miles after Lou had escorted them down the companionway into the saloon, "Is this a bawdy house as well as a gambling hell?"

"Worse than that. The gambling is only a blind. Dominic's one of our leading white-slave dealers. I didn't want to tell you before, but I'm his Hollywood agent. By tomorrow you'll be on the road to Buenos Aires."

"Don't I have to be doped first?"

"We prefer beating them up. It comes less expensive."

"You'd like to do that to me, wouldn't you?" asked Eleanor, her dark eyes twinkling with sudden fun. Off his guard for a moment, Miles answered, "It might do you good".

There were three gaming tables, all crowded. She moved away, and stood watching one of the roulette wheels. Presently she changed a bill and leaned over to place her chips. As Miles joined her, the croupier called "Thirteen". He saw that she must have won; saw her plastering thirteen and the adjacent numbers. She turned her head, whispering, "Go away, blast you. Or you'll spoil my luck".

"All right. Keep your wool on. I'll be at the bar."

At the bar, he thought how much he disliked girls who used bad language; and heard the croupier call, "Seventeen".

Then thirteen repeated; and a few minutes later Eleanor, stuffing hundred-dollar notes into her handbag with fingers that still trembled, took the adjoining stool.

"I gather you've been fortunate", said Miles.

"Fortunate. Christ! I put up the last ten dollars I had in the world, and they weren't mine, either, they were Lionel Barry's. Barman, give me a double brandy. Neat."

The glass clinked against her teeth. But a second double steadied her. "Let's go", she said. "I've had quite enough excitement for one night."

226

A different speedboat took Miles and Eleanor ashore. In the car she told him the rest of her story. To his mind it paralleled Irene's. A letter from Nat Owers, suggesting that he might be able to secure her an assignment, had tempted her to spend all her savings on "a trip to this lousy Hollywood". But Nat Owers was "a skunk and a stool pigeon". He'd let her down.

"So now you'll go home?"

"Not bloody likely. I've got a novel to finish first."

"How long will that take you?"

"God knows. I haven't started it yet. Nobody could work where I'm living. By the way, why do you hate my guts?"

"I don't." At least, she had guts—paying for his dinner with her last twenty-dollar bill and putting up the rest on a double-zero roulette wheel.

"Oh, yes, you do."

He dropped her at a cheap apartment house where radios and gramophone still blared at the passing trolleys.

"You're probably telling yourself you owe me a meal", she said then. "Well, I'm not proud. How about"—once more flipping through her blue diary—"Tuesday?"

"All right."

As he drove his five miles home, Miles found himself liking her better. Tuesday disclosed an entirely different Eleanor, her hands manicured, her hair washed, and her manner almost submissive.

"I've been having one of my crazy fits", she explained. "Too much worry about money. Too much hooch. And not enough to eat. Now I'm going on the wagon till I've finished my book."

He took her to his favourite Murphy's. They ate planked steaks. She drank ice water and talked about the debate which was still going on in the House of Commons.

"Are you liking Americans any better?" he asked.

"All except Hank Bronford. I slapped his face last night."

"What for?"

"He said that Chamberlain had sold the Czechs down the river."

"What did he do when you slapped him?"

"Slapped me back first—and apologised afterwards."

"It all sounds rather childish. How about some more coffee?"

"Thanks."

She took a cigarette from her case. Flicking on his lighter, he thought, "Hank Bronford's not so far wrong".

But what did it matter to him if the Sudeten frontier went the same way as Austria and the Rhineland? Chamberlain's optimism—fatuous though it seemed—might be justified. And so far both the oaths he himself had sworn were unbroken.

On the way home to her cheap apartment house, Eleanor said, "I'm off the day after tomorrow. But I don't quite know where. Do I improve on acquaintance? If I send you my address, will you write to me?"

"I'm afraid I'm not much of a writer, and I don't expect to be here more than three weeks longer myself."

All the same, he kissed her good night.

BOOK TWELVE

I

ONE HAD ENJOYED THESE LAST THREE WEEKS. EXCEPT FOR "THE WAR THAT didn't happen", as Longmore called it, one had enjoyed one's whole time in Hollywood.

"But the going's a bit too soft for my taste", thought Miles.

Still making casual conversation with two dinner neighbours, Ruth Alderson and Helen, he glanced up and down the long candle-lit table at which Andrew and his Daphne were entertaining a dozen people, among them Joe Kerstlen and Pat. So far, he had only said how-do-you-do to Pat. Better if he could avoid her for the rest of the evening.

"Coffee, sir?" asked Jenkins, very much the ducal butler with his three hired waiters.

"Thanks."

Ruth Alderson fitted another cigarette into her long holder and said, "I think it's too bad of you not to stay for the première". Helen chipped in, "My dear, he's a soldier of fortune. They never stay anywhere—even when the loveliest ladies implore them". He countered quickly, "Did you?"

She razzed back, "You don't mean to say you've forgotten?" and turned to the leading man in the picture, entitled after prolonged argument *The Girl in the Chaco*, who was seated on her other side. Ruth talked across the table to Phil Schuylenberg. Miles remembered a packet he had left in the cloakroom. He must get Andrew alone presently. A good bloke!

Joe Kerstlen thumped the table and insisted on making a speech. He wished to propose "the very good health of our dear friends Daphne and Andrew, and success to their latest masterpiece, *The Girl in the Chaco*—a surefire winner or I don't know the first thing about pictures". Andrew replied; and the party left the table.

All the other ground-floor rooms had been cleared of furniture. Already a small orchestra was tuning up, and cars arriving with other guests. Miles, a little selfconscious about his dinner jacket because nearly all the men were wearing tails, asked Helen for the first dance. "Why didn't you ask Pat?" she mocked. "Are you scared?"

"I'm much more scared of you."

"Why?"

"Because you're so intelligent."

"What a pretty compliment. I wish you weren't leaving us."

"So do I—in one way", Miles couldn't help thinking; and just for a while, dancing with her, a regret outside experience—always before, he'd been glad when the time came to wander on—touched him. You couldn't go on wandering all your life. You'd have to settle down sooner or later. This place was as good as any, better than most—nice climate, plenty of exercise, good money to be made if you knew how to go about it. He'd have been on easy street, for a year or more anyway, if . . . if he'd taken that job with Schuylenberg. But that would have meant marrying Pat.

228

Towards eleven o'clock, deciding he'd played the coward long enough, he went up to her. She said, "Hallo, stranger". He asked her to dance.

"You've got a nerve", smiled Pat. "But I don't see why we shouldn't. Daph says you're going away tomorrow."

"Yes. I am."

They danced without further speech. When the music stopped, she held out her hand, saying under her breath, "Maybe it wouldn't have lasted. But I can't help wishing we'd tried".

Watching her next partner slip his arm round her waist, watching one of those exquisite hands yield itself, Miles experienced another touch of regret.

He went to the cloakroom; fetched and unwrapped his packet; wandered into the dining room, now equipped with a buffet. There he found Andrew drinking a glass of champagne.

"Enjoying yourself, Miles?"

"Rather. Have you got a minute to spare?"

"Surely."

"Could we go into your workroom?"

"Why not?"

A narrow passage led to the workroom, bare of furniture except for a desk, two chairs, a dictaphone and a table covered with books. On the walls hung the collection of Indian and other pipes which was Andrew's one hobby.

"Sit down", he said, still leaning on his cane.

"I shan't keep you a moment", said Miles. "Only I didn't want to give you this in public."

He produced one of the few possessions he really prized, a gourd with a chased silver mouthpiece, saying: "Souvenir of the Chaco".

Against the dark mahogany of the gourd glittered a round plaque, also of silver, on which he had had engraved, "Andrew Mackay from Miles Radcliffe. Beverly Hills. November, 1938".

"Thanks a lot". Andrew put on his spectacles to read the inscription. "I'll treasure this."

He spoke in his usual voice, but Miles sensed that he was deeply moved.

"I'm real sorry you're not staying", he went on. "So's Daph. A time ago we rather thought—well, that you mightn't be leaving us."

He stopped there; and laid the gourd on the desk.

"I'm sorry to be going, too", replied Miles; and, fumbling for his words, he continued, "You've been awfully good to me. I know what was in your mind when you first offered me the job."

Andrew flushed. He, too, fumbled for his words.

"I don't quite get you."

"And I didn't quite get you—at the Mark Hopkins. If I had——"

"You'd have turned the job down, eh?"

"Probably."

"Well, I'm glad you didn't. I don't know what I'd have done without you."

"Honestly, Andrew?"

"Honest Injun! Here's my hand on it. And good luck to you."

"Good luck to both of you", said Miles.

They returned to the buffet. At once, newcomers surrounded Andrew Miles decided to go; looked for Daphne; found her, and said goodbye.

Miles drove back to Wilshire Boulevard, through a rare pelt of rain, feeling singularly sentimental. This apartment—it appeared to him as he went up his private stairway—really had been a home. Now he was off again, first to San Francisco; then wherever fancy and some chance ship might carry him. Should he look up Eleanor on the way?

He took her letter from his desk and re-read it. One sentence baffled him. "The real reason why I'd like to see you again is to convince myself that I haven't been misled by a most extraordinary likeness." Now what the dickens did she mean by that?

Still undecided, Miles tore the address heading from her letter and put it in his billfold. All his goodbyes were now said. He'd had his last fencing lesson from Neroni, his last flight with Billy Williams, his last drink with Nikko Longmore, his last game of lawn tennis at the Athletic Club, his last round of golf, his last meal with Jake and Sadie. Tomorrow the florist would send his flowers.

"*Strich darunter*. Draw a line under it", as Sol Rosenblum said after their final wrangle over his montage. The Hollywood chapter was closed.

He shrugged his shoulders, smoked a last cigarette, and went to bed. When he woke, it was still raining. He cooked his breakfast and finished his packing. What a lot of gear he'd accumulated. Far too much for a wanderer. Did he really want to go awandering again? How easily you got used to a bathroom of your own, books of your own, a car of your own, plenty to eat and a soft bed to sleep in every night.

Soft! Operative word. You'd have to harden yourself up again. How about shipping to Australia as a deckhand? That'd learn you! Pensive, he strapped his old valise a couple of holes tighter; and went down by the inner stairway to the store.

Tio Khie Hong sat in his little office.

"You go now?" he asked. "Wantchee boy bling down baggage?"

"No. I'll do that myself, thanks. I only came to bring you my keys."

Tio accepted the keys, opened a drawer and took out a tiny box of red lacquer.

"Please accept little plesent", he said. "Bling luck in battlee."

Opening the box, Miles saw a sliver of jade incised with an ideograph and eyeleted to a very thin silver chain.

"Wear lound neck", explained Tio. "Put on now, please. You soldier. One day, perhaps, fight for Free China."

Chain and jade slipped easily under Miles's loose collar. The idea that he might ever fight for China seemed rather grotesque.

Tio's eldest had already left for school. Upstairs Miles found the mysterious relative, who must have let herself in by the private door, peering here, there and everywhere to make certain all his belongings were packed. He gave her five dollars; and, despite her protests, carried his own luggage down to the car. Six pieces—nine counting the tennis racket, the golf clubs and the radio. Lucky that the old Chevrolet had a luggage grid.

As he drove off, he thought—rather queerly—of a very different car, also overfull of gear, and himself saying, "But you'll have to repack your traps a bit", and Simmy's, "How about me and Philly sitting in front?"

But from that, memory switched to Patricia. Why on earth had he omitted her name from his list of people who ought to have flowers?

Pulling up at a florist's, he remedied the omission with red roses. Now the Hollywood chapter really was closed.

III

Inside another half hour, Miles had left the world's largest illusion factory behind him. Rain ceased. Switching off his screenwiper, he was vaguely harassed by another memory—of a drive through snow when a wiper had refused to function. "Ended with my kissing her", he thought. "Wonder why she never answered my letter . . ."

What a nuisance such memories could be!

Ten miles on towards Santa Barbara, the steering wheel, dragging suddenly sideways, nearly landed him in an accident. Dismounting, he found his right front tyre flat. All his tyres were nearly down to the cotton. But it hadn't seemed worth his while to buy new.

He took off his coat, jacked up the Chevrolet; and, changing the wheel, wondered at this new aversion to getting his hands dirty.

Soft? Why he was turning into a regular sissy. That's what too much money did for you. Nice—all the same—to feel that he still had quite a wad of Joe Kerstlen's dollars in the bank.

New habits were hard to break. Miles lunched at the best restaurant he could find in Santa Barbara; and treated himself to a couple of new Goodyears, telling the garage man to put them on. Strolling idly, a good cigar between his teeth, his eye was caught by a jacket in a bookshop window. Green letters above an impressionistic picture read, *Youth Asks. By Eleanor Rowley*.

He walked in; and, buying the book, thought how extravagant he had become. This carelessness with money would have to stop.

More rain fell as he drove slowly north by the known highway out of Santa Barbara. Stopping for coffee in San Luis Obispo, he decided to take the coast road. Dusk saw him beyond Harmony. It was colder here, with a great wind sweeping in from an angry sea.

Chance guided him to a modest hotel, already heated for winter. After dinner—there were only three other guests, all men and all taciturn—he retired to his bedroom and read through *Youth Asks* in less than two hours. The style of the book irritated him. He found the story inconclusive and the characters unreal. They talked too much and did too little. None of them seemed to know what they wanted. But—did he know that himself?

Sunshine woke him. White clouds scudded across blue skies while he sat at breakfast. Overnight he had almost made up his mind to ignore Eleanor's invitation and push straight on for San Francisco, rejoining highway a-hundred-and-one at Salinas. The sooner he stored all this surplus gear and left off living like a sissy the better. But his beloved redwoods made him change his plan.

He came on a great seaward canyon of them within an hour; and loitered afoot till well past midday. The tourist season was over, the big hotel shut. He lunched frugally in a log cabin. The woman who served him, answering

231

casual inquiry, said, "The Horse and Hound Inn? Why, no, sir. I never heard tell of it. There's a Highland Inn over Carmel way. Maybe that's the one you're thinking of".

"Well, never mind. It's not important", said Miles, smoking another of his three-for-a-dollar cigars.

He drove away from the redwoods. Once again only chance was his guide. Beyond Point Sur he braked at the foot of a hill and dismounted to examine his luggage grid, which had developed an irritating rattle. There he saw the weatherbeaten sign, "Three miles to the Horse and Hound".

Even then he hesitated. Dash it all, Eleanor Rowley was nothing to him. But the sky was no longer blue, and he'd wasted so much time already, and anyway . . . anyway one might take a look.

IV

Shifting gear for another hill, with the first drops of a big storm splattering his windscreen, Miles saw a second sign. Soon he came to an open gateway and a narrow road twisting through a wood.

"Looks a bit gloomy", he thought. Simultaneously, however, he had stepped on the brake pedal and was turning his wheel.

Thunder pealed, a streak of lightning lit the wood, trees creaked, and he heard the bark of a big dog as he drove into a red gravel clearing. Through the sudden onlash of the downpour he perceived a straggle of low wooden buildings, clustered round a larger one, also single-storeyed, which stood a little higher than its fellows on an outcrop of gray rock.

Steep steps and a rough wooden handrail led up the rock to a log porch. More dogs barked furiously, as he dismounted, slammed the car door and ran for shelter.

The house door opened before he reached the sopped coconut matting of the veranda. The boy in the cotton clothes, obviously a Filipino, said, "Missee come soon. Me make tea. Excuse please", and disappeared.

"Funny sort of place. Funny sort of welcome", thought Miles, entering straight into a low room over thirty feet long.

He moved to an open fireplace in which a huge fire of wood crackled, and glanced about. Those windows looked as though they gave on to the sea. The blanket on that far wall might be Mexican. Nice antler trophies. Two of these rugs were deerskins—one an African lion. That radio must have cost a lot of money. The vase full of green branches on the piano could be genuine Ming. Comfortable chairs, by jove. Who might "Missee" be? Not Eleanor. She couldn't be expecting him. To judge by the amount of shelving, all crammed to capacity, whoever owned this place must have a perfect passion for books.

Miles was just stooping to examine the low shelves either side of the red brick fireplace, when dog's claws pattered over hardwood, a switch clicked, lights glowed in the wooden chandeliers, and a woman's voice said, "I'm sorry to have kept you. I've just been out to feed my labradors. Down, Ravager. Manners!"

The black dog, which was nosing Miles with suspicion, couched on the tawny lionskin.

232

"What can I do for you?" asked the woman; and, looking her over, Miles saw that she was tall, almost his own height, very smooth of complexion and still jetblack of close-cropped curly hair, though apparently in her fifties. A tweed riding coat covered her fine bust; on her long legs she wore jodhpur breeches. Her brown boots were caked with red gravel. The colour of her eyes—neither quite gray nor quite black—struck him as rather remarkable. So did her mouth, almost the true Cupid's bow, with perfect teeth and lips that might have been a girl's.

"I could give you a bite to eat", she went on. "But if you're looking for a room, I'm afraid I can't manage it. We closed down for the winter yesterday."

"Miss Rowley isn't here any more then?"

The woman—she might be English with that accent—approached a pace, and stood speechless for the best part of a minute. He was aware of a tense scrutiny.

At last she said, with the tiniest catch in her voice, "If you came to see Miss Rowley, you must be Miles . . . Miles Radcliffe. She left a letter for you. That's how I know who you are".

Then she grinned, and the grin might have been his very own, as she continued, "The last thing your father ever said to me was, 'Sooner or later, Marguerite, your sin will find you out'. And now it has. Don't you know who I am?"

"*Madre de Dios*", thought Miles.

For the best part of another minute he, too, stood speechless.

Then he grinned, and his grin might have been her very own, as he asked, with the tiniest catch in his voice, "Even if the hotel is closed, couldn't you manage to find me a room?"

"If you want to stay."

"Of course I want to stay . . . mother."

"Need you call me that?"

He approached a pace. Hailstones thudded like bullets on the roof. Like gunfire, thunder roared and lightning flashed beyond the seaward windows. The dog growled.

"Quiet, you", ordered the woman, in a deep voice which resembled his own except for a slight huskiness.

Instinctively he put out his hands; drew her to him, and kissed her—a little gingerly—on one cheek.

A sudden shyness was on both of them. After a little pause she said, "That wasn't really necessary. I never did anything for you".

"You gave me life."

"For what it's worth."

"Mine's been a pretty good one so far. Hasn't yours?"

"Well"—she paused again—"it doesn't owe me much."

Thunder pealed, lightning flashed once more.

"I'll go and get you that girl's letter", said the woman who was his mother. "Then we'll have tea."

They took tea by the fire.

"What did the Rowley girl have to say?" she asked.

"Nothing of any importance."

"Do you want to see her again? She hasn't gone very far."

233

"She can go to Timbuctoo for all I care."

"You don't sound exactly grateful."

"And you?"

Miles laughed. His shyness was going over. Instinctively again, h
touched one of her hands. They were the same shape and of the same
strength as his own.

"I don't know yet", she laughed back. "Would you like to stay till
find out?"

"I'm not at all sure"—shyness might be going over, but you had to pick
your words—"that I don't want to stay permanently."

Her eyes might have been a man's.

"You don't look", she said slowly, "as though you were cut out to be a
mother's darling. You'll find existence rather dull here."

Existence dull? With this woman who intrigued him more than any he
could remember meeting. What had she meant with her, "Life doesn't owe
me much"? Sentiment or no sentiment—mother's darling, indeed!—dash
it all, he was just not going to let himself feel sentimental—he'd stay until
he found out.

V

You weren't going to find out much, in fact you'd be lucky if you found
out anything—Miles discovered that first evening—by asking direct questions.
This woman—still a little difficult to think of her as your mother!—had all
your own reticence. Keep talk impersonal—and you could not wish for a
more charming, a more erudite, companion. Display curiosity—and you
might as well have been fencing left-handed against Neroni. You just
couldn't penetrate that adroit defence.

"I haven't been in Europe for five years", was one of the few scraps of
information he managed to elicit before dinner.

But if the frock in which she reappeared, though a little unfashionable,
weren't a Paris model, he'd never seen the Rue de la Paix; and the scent she
used—elusive as her personality—might have been Halcyon's. Why should
she remind him of Halcyon? They weren't in the least alike . . .

The storm abated, the wind began to die down, while they were dining.
After the houseboy, to whom she gave her orders in his own tongue, had
served their coffee, they spent an hour browsing among her books. The name
on the bookplates was "Marguerite Murillo". The volumes were in many
languages. She admitted readily enough that she knew French, Italian,
German, Spanish, Portuguese, and "quite a little Russian".

That, however, concluded the evening's revelation; and, when he would
have kissed her good night, she drew back, saying with a touch of cynicism
that seemed rather familiar, "Don't you feel we ought to know each other a
little better before we become too ostentatiously affectionate?"

"*Comme vous voulez, madame*", chaffed Miles.

His little room was bare but quite comfortable. Waves beating on rock
sang him to sleep.

Another Filipino woke him with tea, and asked what time he would like
breakfast.

"What time does madam have hers?"

234

"Missee breakfast in bedroom."

"Right. I'll have mine in half an hour. Ham and eggs if you can manage it."

His mother, dressed in the same tweed coat and jodhpurs, entered the big living room while he was drinking his second cup of excellent coffee. She carried a shotgun under her arm. Ravager fawned on him, as she began, "I'm going round the estate in a few minutes if you care to come with me".

"Okay. What's the gun for, mother?"

"I spotted a few grouse yesterday evening. Please don't go on calling me that. It makes me feel about a hundred."

"But I must call you something."

"Then why not"—with a shrug of her fine shoulders—"Marguerite?"

Following her down the rock steps on to the red gravel, Miles was shown round the outbuildings, most of them two-roomed cottages.

"I kept open last winter", she said. "But it didn't pay."

"How long have you had this place?"

"Oh, a fair time."

They entered a biggish garage. Next to his own car stood a station wagon, and a low open machine which he recognised for a racing Isotta.

"Do you drive that, Marguerite?"

"I haven't lately."

No change out of her so far! But, when they came to the range of kennels, she opened up a little, volunteering, "I've had quite a good year with my puppies, though I only breed them for a hobby. I used to breed horses too. Now I've only got a couple of youngsters out at grass".

"You've a lot of ground, I gather."

"No. Only about five hundred acres. Most of it's on the other side of the road."

Ravager and another dog she had loosed at heel, they took a path through the wood, crossed the road and cut diagonally up a rough field. Two horses came to her call. She gentled them. They loped away.

"The grouse were feeding there", she said, pointing to a haystack in the next field and slipping cartridges into the breech of her gun.

That morning they flushed no grouse. But, just as they turned downhill from her boundary fence after two hours of hardish going, Ravager put up a brace of sage hen, which she bagged with a right and left. Her dogs retrieved the birds, both shot through the head. Miles said, "Good work, Marguerite".

"Your father taught me how to use a gun——" she began; and stopped, biting her lips.

He had an early vision of that "sporting parson", his father, in Norfolk jacket and knickerbockers; remembered him in hunting kit too.

"You know he was killed in the Great War, of course?"

"Oh, yes. I heard that."

Nothing more enlightened his curiosity until the evening. Then, her eyes on the rockbound sea, already gray in the twilight beyond the windows of the big living room, she asked, "Does my name convey anything to you?"

"Only that you must have remarried."

She parried with silence and riposted with questions.

"Have you ever been married?"

"No."

"Any particular reason?"

"No."

"Are you . . . allergic to children?"

He realised she was bringing the fight to him and gave ground warily.

"That's a conceivable explanation."

"It would be a very natural one. You're wrong about my having re
married. Once was quite enough."

The implied reflection on his father irritated him.

"Then"—he turned away from the window and lit the last of his blac
cigarettes—"how did you come to be called Marchesi?"

"I may tell you one of these days. But you'll have to open up a bi
yourself first. All I know about you is that you've been working in Holly
wood—and I only got that from Eleanor Rowley. You're not an actor, ar
you?"

"Actor? Me? Good lord, no."

A telephone bell rang for the first time since his arrival. She went of
to answer it and was away for several minutes.

"I have to go to San Francisco tomorrow", she said on her return. "The
chances are that I shan't be back for a week. What would you like to do
about it?"

"Shall I drive you there?"

"No. I'm going by train."

"Can I stay till you come back?"

"If you want to. You may be rather bored."

"If I am, I'll run over and look up Eleanor."

"Somehow I don't imagine"—had her eyes twinkled at him?—"that she'd
amuse you for very long."

VI

The rest of that evening duplicated their first one. Plenty of talk about
Marguerite's books; but nothing in the least illuminative about herself.
Miles did not attempt to kiss her good night; and she went off in the station
wagon, driven by Juan, her number-one houseboy, while he was still at
breakfast with Ravager, who showed pleasure when he uncased his own shotgun.

That morning he killed a brace of grouse. The afternoon he spent writing
long letters to Geoffrey Thirkell and Martin Halliburton, shorter ones to
Ronnie Wallace, care of a bank in Aden, and Jim Bowlby, care of Cox's,
London. On an impulse he wrote to Fluke, but changed his mind about
telling Fluke that he had met his mother. A final impulse made him scribble
on a picture postcard of the Inn to Rosaleen, "Staying here for a bit. Hope
you still flourish".

After supper he found an inscription in one of Marguerite's books.
"*Voce d'oro. Cuore di diamante*", read the masculine handwriting. "*Ma
spero sempre. Milano. Agosto, 1902.*"

Voice of gold. Heart of a diamond. So she'd been a singer. Queer,
with that husk in her voice.

All next day storm lashed the woods and raging seas blinded the windows. He searched the books for more clues but discovered nothing. At nine o'clock the phone rang and Juan summoned him with the single word "Missee" to her office.

"How are you getting on?" she asked.

"Fine, thanks."

"Good. You might just keep an eye on the horses for me. By the way, I forgot to tell you about the deer. There are a few blacktails in the canyon. If an old man with a long beard asks you for your permit, just say you're"— she hesitated a perceptible second—"you're a friend of mine."

Miles also hesitated a second before he laughed, "Okay, mother".

Without hesitation she gurgled back at him, "Good night, sonny boy. And don't forget to say your prayers".

Pleased, he hung up; read Bret Harte—a new discovery—for a couple of hours, and went to bed.

After breakfast he uncased a smallbore rifle which had taken his fancy when he was last in London; asked the number-two houseboy to cut him a few sandwiches, and set off for the canyon, on the lip of which—about a hundred yards beyond the boundary fence—he encountered the old man with the beard.

At nightfall he returned with his deer, which he had gralloched himself— and a very little more information. "Missee" had been living in "these parts" for about five years. 'Fore that, the Inn had belonged to another Britisher. "But he went and died. Reckon he must have left it to her in his will." The canyon formed part of a big ranch owned by "one of them San Francisco millionaires". He was a friend of Missee's too. "Older nor me", confided graybeard. "His father struck it rich in forty-nine. Mine useter work for him."

That night the phone rang again. It was a little disappointing to recognise the voice at his ear for Eleanor's. He experienced a little difficulty in prevaricating. "Yes. It turns out that she and I are related", some awkwardness in admitting, under pressure, "As a matter of fact she's my mother".

"What a story!" said Eleanor. "Do come over and tell me all about it. You can drive here in a couple of hours easily. But don't come till next week because I simply must get on with my novel."

"Thank the lord for that", thought Miles.

VII

Three more days—two of storm and one of fog—passed in pleasant solitude. On the fourth morning the sun broke through. Miles caught and saddled one of the young horses, rode south by a bridle path along the cliffs. No countryside could have been wider, wilder, or more suited to his mood. Hollywood seemed ten thousand miles away, Plinley Green a million.

Some of his sensations on that ride—though his inexperience failed to recognise them—were those of the average man who comes, after long wandering, home; others were akin to, and yet utterly different from, his best feelings for Halcyon. Of one thing only did he feel quite certain. He must find out very much more about Marguerite.

237

The unclipped chestnut, restive at first, flagged on the way home. He slid from the English saddle, did the last three miles on foot, turned the animal loose again, and walked back, carrying the harness, to the Inn.

"Missee come," Juan told him. "Me fetch."

VIII

Telling Juan, "I'll come with you", Miles was conscious of a vague excitement; and this excitement grew keener while they waited, after a fifteen-mile drive during which they only passed a few log cabins, at the wayside depot.

Questioned, a lone porter informed him, "On time? Sure the train'll be on time. Twenty-two and a half minutes after schedule. Never known for her to vary. 'Cept on Thanksgiving an' the Fourth of July".

Juan, cold in his cotton clothes, went back to the station wagon. A few passengers appeared. Walking back and forth alongside the rails (there was no platform) Miles wondered what Marguerite could have been doing in San Francisco. Had she a lover there? Ridiculous. She must be fifty-seven or eight. But she didn't look it. Dressed for dinner, she might have been forty. A really beautiful woman. A thoroughly intriguing woman. Queer, that she'd never remarried. Queer, that she'd hinted herself allergic to children. They must have a lot of characteristics in common. Take her talent for languages . . .

The distant engine-bell broke the threads of introspection. Watching the smokestack puff up the grade, he remembered another train rolling away from him while a long gloved hand waved from one of its many coaches. There *was* something . . . something of Halcyon in Marguerite.

The bell ceased to clang. Brakes grinched on steel. Doors opened. Two darkies jumped to ground with their steps. He saw her before she saw him; thought, "That's a nice tailormade you're wearing"; called, "Hallo there".

Her elephant-gray eyes glowed as they met his. Her nostrils flared a little, as she called back, "Hallo yourself. How nice of you to come and fetch me".

A darkie hauled out her cases; handed her down. Before Miles quite knew what he was doing, he had kissed her.

She stiffened, mocking, "There's no need to be so demonstrative. Especially in public. I feel positively embarrassed".

"If I have made a gaffe, my dear Marguerite"—Miles grinned as he broke into French—"I can only offer you my most sincere apologies."

She answered him in the same language, "The greatest of all gaffes is to be premature. Please do not presume on the accident that we happen to be mother and son".

Her smile—he imagined—might have been Halcyon's own. It lingered on her lips the whole evening. Just before they went to their bedrooms she interrupted a bookish conversation with, "We have been complete strangers to each other for the best part of forty years. You seem to think we can bridge that gap by mere sentimentality. Tell me something. Have you ever been truly"—she fumbled for the right words—"*en rapport* with a woman?"

Miles flushed.

"Once," he answered after a considerable pause.

"You really loved her?"

He nodded.

"How did it end?"

"She was killed."

"Poor you." One of her fine hands touched him ever so lightly on the forearm. "And yet you've been fortunate. More fortunate than I."

Resentment that he should have been the first to impart a real confidence made Miles say:

"But you left father for another man".

"Not entirely." Her hand was still on his arm, her gaze quite steady. "I had other reasons. You, for instance."

"Me?"

"Yes. I'd always loathed the idea of having children."

"Then why did you marry him?"

"Primarily for escape, as I see it now. Lots of girls did in those days."

She broke off and rose from the sofa on which they had been sitting.

"Here endeth the first lesson", she smiled; then, "Please tell me the name of the woman you were so much in love with".

"Her name"—he, too, had risen—"was Halcyon."

"Spanish?"

"No. Paraguayan."

"Was she very beautiful?"

"I still think so."

"I thought the same about . . . about the man for whom I left your father. I have thought the same about . . . about one other man. But . . . but I have never been truly *en rapport* with anybody, man or woman. Maybe that's why I'm finding this . . . this situation so difficult."

"I'm not finding it too easy either."

"Shall we go on trying to . . . to bridge the gap?"

"I'd like to."

"So would I."

IX

Gradually, sometimes helping, sometimes hindering each other—the very similarity of their characters their main difficulty—those two bridged the gap of the years between them. But November was December, New Year over, skies clear and osiers greening by the stream at the foot of Antelope Canyon, before they came to confidences. And still there were spiritual waters to cross.

Always, when they were in company, they felt a little awkward. As one slow-spoken neighbour confided to his companion when they drove away after a business call, "I reckon those two might be strangers". As Eleanor Rowley, who visited them once or twice before she returned to London, put it to a shipboard acquaintance, "They behaved more like a man and a woman who didn't want you to guess that they were in love with each other than a mother and a son".

239

For in so many ways—and, at long last, in all spiritual ways—they were the lovers that a mother and son may be when both have suffered overmuch. But only Marguerite saw this coming to pass; transcendentally, by the light of an imagination which had always shrunk from the responsibilities of motherhood, even as it had shrunk from that supreme selfgiving which alone sublimates love.

And only Marguerite knew how jealous she might have been if Eleanor's casual, "How about coming back to England with me, Miles?" had evoked any but the casual answer, "Thank you, I'm quite happy where I am".

Happy. Even with Halcyon—it appeared to Miles—he had never known greater happiness. Yet this happiness, he being a man, was essentially empirical. They were such companions. They were so alike. You could tell her almost anything.

His imagination only painted present pictures—one of himself, as he had never yet dared realise himself, and the other of a personality which seemed, always allowing for the difference in their sex and generations, the very counterpart of his own.

"I've never been afraid of anything—except money and having children", she said once; and at another time, "I couldn't bear the idea of staying put till I was over fifty."

Meanwhile, blent with and complementary to the picture of her personality, there developed the circumstantial story of her life.

By the second week of March, with the poppies just ready to bloom, and Marguerite still in two minds about reopening the hotel, because "it'll leave us no time for our rides or our talks of an evening", that story was as good as complete.

X

Marguerite's story unfolded itself in all its completeness one afternoon as Miles lay drowsy in a long chair on the veranda after the hardest ride they had yet taken the young horses, stabled now and greedy for their corn.

He saw her as a girl genius, barely eighteen, crazy to escape from narrow-minded parents, from a multiplicity of brothers and sisters, from that very atmosphere of "Plinley Greenery" which he himself had always abhorred.

"We were poor too. Starvation poor. The only amusement we ever had was music. I used to sing a bit. In the choir, mostly. My one ambition was to train for the operatic stage. But whenever I suggested that, father told me nice girls didn't become actresses. So what could I do except marry the first man who proposed, especially when he promised me a horse to ride—I'd always loved horses—and fifty pounds a year pin money?"

"What on earth's pin money, Marguerite?" he remembered himself asking, and her, "They call it a dress allowance nowadays. I'm . . . I'm afraid I wasn't very good value".

"Don't say things like that."

"Don't be so sentimental. I can't jump out of my skin, even to please you, Miles. My marriage was a disaster."

A double disaster! ("My mother hadn't told me anything. And he

240

. . he always thought it rather shameful.") Lying here on this veranda
—Ravager beside him—Miles could sympathise with both of them, but
mostly with her.

She'd been so young, little more than a child. And she'd never wanted
a baby.

"She dreaded the idea as much as I must always have dreaded it", he
thought; and the visions which his mind had been making blurred.

His visions of the young Marguerite, he had found, often blurred. It was the
same way with his visions of the men of whom she spoke—his father, and
that boy, "he really was only a boy, terribly handsome, but so gentle, so unlike Simeon", with whom she ran away to Italy, and that other, who had
written, "*Voce d'oro. Cuore di diamante*", but whose hopes had never been
realised, although it was he who paid for her singing lessons.

"I paid him back", Miles could hear her saying. "I've never been be-
holden to any of my lovers. Don't look so shocked. You've never been
able to live like a monk, you tell me. So why expect me to have lived like a
nun?"

Ravager's tail thumped the matting. His tongue licked Miles's hands.
More visions blurred, dissolved, faded one into the other, much as Sol
Rosenblum's montage flashes.

"It's funny," he thought. "I've never really been able to confide in anyone before. There were reservations, even with Halcyon."

Yet there was still one reservation, even from Marguerite.

His eyes closed, but visions of her still pressed on him—faster now, always
faster, as the Scala at Milan, and the Costanzi in Rome, the opera houses of
Paris and Berlin and Vienna and New York and St. Petersburg ("But not
Covent Garden. Somehow or other I could never bring myself to take an
engagement at Covent Garden") rang with applause for the latest soprano,
Marguerite Murillo.

"And then, then Italy came into the war . . . I felt I ought to do something about it. Silly of me. Everybody told me so. But I've always done
what I wanted."

And so had he!

The next vision showed a hospital on the Italian front, and Marguerite,
dressed as a nurse, in the fever wards. And a little way on in the story a
doctor, not knowing who she was, said, "The typhoid might have left you
deaf in both ears, *signora*. As it is you are very lucky. There should be no
other consequences except this little weakness, this little huskiness, this little
roughness of the vocal chords".

"So that was that", she had told him. "I consulted other doctors, of
course. I must have been to every throat specialist on the Continent—and
here in America. But none of them could do anything. As a singer I was
finished. When I knew for certain, I went a little mad."

How mad, these other visions proved.

All across the world she had gone, seeking sanity (even as he himself had
sought sanity after the Chaco), but finding it nowhere, finding no solace for
the gift she had lost.

"You're looking shocked again, Miles. Why? You're no plaster
image of a man. And I'm no plaster image of a woman. We're human
beings, both of us. The first day we met, I told you that life didn't owe me

anything. Once my voice went, I was an artist *manquée*. If I'd frustrated myself I could never have won tranquillity."

For in the end, thanks to the Englishman who had left her this place ("He was dying when we met. I nursed him for four years. Not for money. I'd my own money. From the first day I began to earn it, I've always been careful of money"), she had won to tranquillity, with her dogs, with her sport, with her hotel work ("Not very valuable work, but it kept me busy"), with music ("It's funny you should have so little feeling for music"), and with her books.

Dash it all, he'd left her browsing among her books. Confound it all, she might have let him drowse a bit longer—she needn't have turned on the radio yet awhile.

But inside another second Miles was off his chair, into the house, and listening to a broadcast which described the occupation of Prague by German troops.

They heard the broadcast through. When it finished, she said, "That's the end of Czechoslovakia. So much for appeasement! I don't suppose you'll be with me much longer".

"What nonsense." His voice rose a betraying semitone. "Even if this means another war, I shan't volunteer."

"Because of your oath?" Her eyes, so like his own, quizzed him.

"No. Because of you."

"So"—her body flinched, but not her spirit—"he'll be a good little boy and stay home with mother."

"Don't be such an ass, Marguerite."

"Aren't we both being rather asinine?"

But that night, for the first time since she had left her husband's house, the woman whose legal name was still Marguerite Radcliffe begged the god of her unbelief, "If You really exist, let me keep him just a little longer".

And that night Miles, also, prayed.

This present happiness—both realised—could not endure.

XI

Both knew that happiness could not endure. But, even to their private selves, they would scarcely admit the knowledge.

"*Vogue la galère*", thought Marguerite. And Miles, "There's always the chance of a miracle". Meanwhile, eager for distraction, she decided to reopen the Inn.

"You can help me," she said.

"How?"

"Oh, all sorts of ways. You might do some of the book-keeping. We have to fetch most of our provisions. People like their cars put away and brought round for them."

"Do I touch my cap when they tip me?"

"Don't worry. Very few of them will. You look too superior. Now run away while I talk to Juan. We shall need more help. And I always advertise our opening. It's a pity you're not as clever at that sort of thing as Fluke seems to have been." For he had talked a lot about the Beehive and a little about Rosaleen.

Business, at first, was confined to a few passing motorists, who rarely stayed for more than a couple of nights, and whose conversation, when it turned on Europe, did not encourage Miles's belief in a miracle.

Memel had already been surrendered. Great Britain was negotiating a pact with Poland. At Easter, Mussolini pinched Albania. On the twenty-sixth of April, England introduced conscription. Just as the radio finished telling them that news, the postman brought a belated answer to the letter Miles had written Geoffrey Thirkell.

"*I only got yours last week*", wrote Geoffrey from Paris. "*I've been running about a bit, picking up a few dishonest pennies and a whole lot of information. Tried to pass it on to the French, but they only made raspberry noises at me. They'll be for it all right, and so shall we, unless Chamberlain does another Munich. The balloon'll go up this summer, I imagine. I shall make tracks for Trinidad before the end of July.*"

When he showed Marguerite that letter, she laughed, "Raspberry noises. How like the French. It would never surprise me if they ratted on us".

"Or Mussolini might rat on Hitler."

"Italy will dash to the rescue of the winner", she quoted; and let the subject drop.

That May they were always letting the subject of war drop. It touched them too closely. And by June business improved, giving them little time to talk international politics, of which she seemed to know a great deal. Only late of an evening would they have an hour of solitude—each hour the more precious because, secretly, neither could help thinking, "For how long?"

They could sentimentalise a little now.

"I wish I'd known you sooner, Marguerite."

"I feel the same sometimes. But perhaps we weren't ready for each other."

"There's something in that. I mightn't have liked you so much when you were—er—on the rampage."

"Rampager yourself, Miles. But you'll break loose again. I rather thought I saw signs of it last week. An attractive young woman! She mentioned that she might be coming back . . . without her husband."

"She mentioned the same thing to me."

"How forward of her. Did you furnish the necessary encouragement?"

"Of course I didn't."

"Puritan!"

"*Et toi?*"

"*Touchée.* I admit my own reformation."

Conversationally they were as intimate as—even more intimate than— that. Yet one last confidence Miles continued to withhold.

She was so sensible. She would only laugh at his dread of a contingency that could hardly have happened without his knowledge.

No. That just couldn't have happened. So *why* worry about it? And why worry about this war that still might not happen—though Jim Bowlby's letter seemed as certain as Geoffrey Thirkell's?

The King and Queen would hardly be visiting Canada and America if things were as serious as Jim made out with his, "*Anybody but a blind man ought to be able to see what's coming. I'm putting my name down for the R.A.F. reserve. They take men up to fifty-five".*

(And that was the man who had said to you, a lifetime ago in Ireland, "I'm going to send my decorations back. The King's welcome to them, and, as for the blasted Country, it's not worth fighting for"! So how could you "stay home with mother" if the Huns really marched?)

Still—Jim didn't really know anything. Neither did Geoffrey. Neither did Martin, who wrote from a place called Chungking, *"This show and the Spanish one are only the start of global war".* Or Ronnie Wallace, back in British Somaliland, and apparently certain, *"One day the Eyeties'll have a crack at Egypt".*

But then neither did Fluke, whose letter arrived by the same mail as Ronnie's, and ended, *"Hope all this war talk isn't panicking you. It's just bilge in my opinion".*

"What do you think?" Miles asked Marguerite, after she had read both letters.

"My dear, what's the use of thinking?"

For, once again, *"Vogue la galère".* Nothing in her life ever had lasted. So why should this?

"Even if there isn't a war", she used to think, with June gone, and the Fourth of July over, and every one of her cottages full; "even if Miles stays on here in California, we shan't always be as happy as we are now."

She was as much in love as that; but in love—at long last—spiritually. This consolation, her best one, she hugged, as some tortured nun might hug a crucifix, to her wounded heart.

"Simeon was right", she knew. "My sin has found me out. These breasts should have suckled his little lips. These hands should have guided his tiny feet. This mind should have helped to open his mind."

Yet always clear in her own mind remained that other consolation. When the time came for them to part, her suffering would be the keener. Because, whatever wrong she had done him, her son—at least—was not one of those miserable halfmen who pass through life tied, as it were by invisible navel cords, to the maternal womb.

XII

Parting was not yet. But it seemed very close to Marguerite on that August evening when—all their chores done and all their guests gone to their cottages—they took the Isotta, which Miles had tinkered into some sort of order, and he drove her, under a full moon that dimmed the starlight south towards Point Sur and the redwood canyons for a midnight bathe.

He thought as he drove. How he had grown to love, how well he knew, this wild corner of California. How often he had swum in Abalone Creek, and ridden that trail through the chaparral to One Nugget Valley, so well named because that was all, just one nugget, the goldrushers ever found.

Here, the sea. North and south, the two rivers. Inland, the high sierra. This winter, he said suddenly, they might go skiing in the high sierra;

and she smiled at him, "Why, yes. That's quite an idea. It's one of the few sports you've never tried your hand at"; and fell silent, musing, "But you won't be here this winter. Or any winter".

"A penny for your thoughts, Marguerite."

"You know them." She could not even manage a grin. "Yours are the same. We're not a pair of lovers. There's no need for you to play pretty with me. These Moscow conferences are England's last bid for peace. But they won't come to anything, and when they fail——"

She broke off, biting her lips.

"Don't be so gloomy."

"How right you are. Let's enjoy ourselves while we still can."

But she fell silent again, only breaking that tense silence to tell him of a dirt road that led to the sea through pines.

These pines—though he had never taken this road before—seemed curiously familiar to Miles. So did the path down which they went after they had parked the car and changed into their swimming suits. The last few yards of its slope were steep and narrow. A rock nearly tripped Marguerite. She half stumbled, and he caught her by the elbow, chaffing, "Easy over the stones".

It was then that he knew why this whole scene, tiny cove sheltered by a semicircle of trees, flat sand, sea aglitter in the moonlight, should look so familiar; and later memories fretted him while they swam.

"So stupid", he thought, crawling his fastest through the ice-cold water. "Don't see why I shouldn't tell her, though. She knows pretty well everything else about me." And, back in the car, drinking the hot coffee laced with rum her forethought had provided, he gave her the one confidence hitherto withheld.

As he had suspected, the tale—told a little haltingly—only made her laugh.

"Don't talk as though you were a Don Juan", she said. "A woman of that age should be able to take care of herself. Why this exaggerated sense of personal responsibility?"

"I've—I've always felt a little that way for her."

"Then it's high time you got over your fatherhood complex."

"Fatherhood complex? Me! You know I've always loathed the idea of being a father."

"Precisely. That's one reason why you're letting your imagination run away with you. My dear idiot, don't you realise that it is only imagination? You'd have heard soon enough."

"You really think so?"

"I don't think. I'm certain. And now"—laying a hand on his arm—"now that you've rid your bosom of all this perilous stuff, won't you take pity on an old lady who's probably caught her death of cold bathing at midnight, and let us go home?"

She staged a sneeze. He reached back for her tweed cloak and insisted on draping it round her shoulders.

"You haven't really caught cold, Marguerite?"

"No." She could have kissed him for his anxiety. "Of course I haven't."

"You're sure? How about a mustard bath when I get you home?"

"You're not getting me home. Hand over that wheel. And I'll show you how a racing car ought to be driven."

They changed places. Once on the highway, she put her foot down, till he protested, "Steady the Buffs. You're doing well over eighty".

Pressing the brake pedal, she laughed, "The first time I ever handled this machine, they clocked me in at a hundred-and-twenty for the measured mile".

XIII

It was nearly two o'clock in the morning before those two put the Isotta away in the garage. As usual, they walked arm in arm across the gravel and up the steps to the main building. As usual, they kissed each other good night. "What a woman", thought Miles. "What a pal. What a companion." For he had never been so happy—no, not even with Halcyon.

Yet morning found him curiously depressed; and every now and again, throughout the week that followed, this curious depression would leap on him—much as he could remember an older hunger leaping—like a beast from a bough.

No happiness in his life—he would feel in such moments—had ever lasted. So why should this one? It would go over. It was going over. Daily. With every leaf you tore off this calendar. Almost hourly. Every time Marguerite switched on this radio. Curse the radio. Why had it ever been invented? Bad news travelled fast enough anyway. You had to listen, though. Because of those broadcasts from Moscow. You knew, Marguerite knew, the whole world knew, how much hung on those Anglo-Russian conferences in Moscow. If they failed . . .

And they had failed; Stalin and Hitler were to sign a pact!

Full confirmation of the Russo-German agreement—the first news had only been a flash—seemed almost a relief. By chance, the big living room, where they had first set eyes on each other more than ten months ago, was empty.

"So that's that", said Marguerite, switching off the tale of paeans from Berlin, of "excitement" in Paris, of "readiness" in Poland, of "complete calm" in London; and she walked to the seaward windows; stood there for a while, mastering herself, before she went on, as calmly as though she were suggesting a trip to Nugget Valley: "You'd better start for New York tomorrow. You may have a job getting a berth otherwise".

"But this"—momentarily his calm equalled hers—"doesn't necessarily mean war."

She turned to him, took a step towards him, asking, "Doesn't it?"

"Even if you're right" (and of course she was) "there's no need for me to go."

"Isn't there?"

"No." (But you'd fought all this out with yourself last September in Hollywood!) "At least not immediately."

Silence held them for a while—the width of the lionskin apart.

Then Marguerite's chin lifted, and Miles had the impression that she was squaring her shoulders, as she said, "If you are going—and of course you must —I would rather you went immediately".

246

"Why?"

"Because it will be easier for both of us."

"I can't see that."

"Can't you?"

Her nostrils flared a little. One of her feet moved, was drawn back. He saw her cheeks flush, her hands clenching, the pupils of her eyes dilate in the elephant-gray irises.

"If you love me", she began, and it was the first time that word had ever passed between them, "do as I ask."

"Today . . . mother?"

"If you love me, son."

She checked speech, upper teeth biting lower lip till a speck of blood reddened there.

He tried to say, "Of course I love you, mother". He tried to move, to take her in his arms. But no more words came to either of them, only the mutual thought, "So this is how it feels—this is what people mean when they talk about being heartbroken".

For neither of them had ever experienced that feeling until now.

BOOK THIRTEEN

I

"I CAN QUITE UNDERSTAND YOUR NOT WANTING TO; BUT THAT'S THE LAW, I'M afraid, Captain Radcliffe."

"But my money's been in America for donkeys' years."

"As far as I know—but I shall have to make certain—your securities can remain there for the present, provided you register them with the Treasury. But you cannot keep a dollar balance at your New York bank."

"Do you think that the Treasury will take over my securities?"

"I should say they're bound to. But when they do they'll pay you for them in sterling."

Miles—still without a war job, though it was more than a week since his return to England—said, "I see". The same manager with whom he had opened his first banking account, when he received his original commission in the Tank Corps, handed him two forms and explained how they should be filled in.

"You've come back to join up, of course?" he went on.

"Yes. If they'll have me. What do I do for money while my dollars are being transferred?"

"Don't worry about that, Captain Radcliffe. You can draw on us for anything in reason."

They discussed details. The manager rang for a clerk, who returned with more forms and a cheque book. A few minutes later Miles found himself in Pall Mall.

II

By now there was nothing strange about this wartime London. Miles no longer looked up at the balloons. It seemed quite natural—though still rather futile in the light of his experiences during the air raids on Nanking and Canton—that doorways should be lightly sandbagged and windows disfigured by crisscrosses of flimsy paper. Equally natural—though equally futile—appeared the fact that nearly every civilian carried a gasmask either in a cardboard box or a fancy container.

"I suppose I ought to get hold of one and carry it, just for the look of the thing", he thought.

By the railings outside the bank stood a newsman whose placard read, "Polish Line Straightened".

Miles bought a paper, tucked his swordstick under his arm, skimmed through the communiqués, and eyed the placard again, thinking, "Bunk. They're being smashed to smithereens". Simultaneously a hand slapped him on the shoulder, a known voice said, "Miles, by jingo"; and, turning, he faced Jim Bowlby, resplendent in blue.

Jim wore a round cap cocked rakishly over his right eye. The left breast of his jacket displayed his wings, the puce-red ribbon with the little bronze Victoria Cross, the white and transverse violet of the D.F.C., the paler red of

248

the Légion d'Honneur, the 1914 star, the Allied and the Victory ribbons. On his lapels shone the two brass VRs of the R.A.F. reserve. His buttons glittered. The rings on his sleeves proclaimed him a squadron leader. Gloves, cap, shoes and uniform were obviously brand new.

"Who do you think you are? Boom Trenchard?" grinned Miles, mock-saluting. "Won't you take me for a ride in your aeroplane, sir?"

"We call 'em aircraft nowadays", corrected Jim. "Come along into the bank. I'm just going to cash a cheque. Then I'll buy you a spot of lunch."

He took Miles by the arm; and time rolled back for each of them when they stood at the counter where Miles had once drawn fifty pounds.

Jim passed his cheque through the grille. This time, as not last, the cashier only said, "How will you have it, squadron leader?"

"Oh, pounds'll do."

Jim slipped five notes into a sealskin case as obviously new as the rest of his outfit; and, once more, they left the bank.

"Where are you stationed?" asked Miles.

"The Air Ministry. Why on earth didn't you let me know you were home?"

Miles hedged. He'd been rather busy.

"Looking for a job, I suppose. Well, I can fix you up with one in two shakes of a duck's tail."

"A flying job?"

"At your age, old chap? Hardly. Let me see, don't you speak quite a lot of foreign languages? Intelligence ought to suit you."

"I came home to fight, Jim. Not to sit on my tail."

Miles stopped to light a black cigarette, of which he had found a supply in Soho. Jim preferred one of his own gaspers. They cut through St. James's Square and up into Jermyn Street. Another news placard read, "Poles Fighting Back".

Miles asked, "Do you know how things really are?"

"Lousy", whispered Jim.

They entered a restaurant which was new to Miles. The cloakroom attendant refused Jim's service gasmask.

"We're not allowed to take them, sir."

"What bloody nonsense!"

Jim carried his respirator to a long bar and dropped it on the floor by his stool.

"My usual martini", he ordered. "Same for you, Miles?"

"I'd rather have whiskey, thanks."

The uniform made Jim look years younger than when Miles had last seen him in the autumn of nineteen thirty-six. He looked healthier too—almost the beau sabreur of their days in Ireland, except for the bald patch at the back of his golden head.

They talked this war with their drinks, the "Troubles" with their meal.

"My Mary's married again", volunteered Jim. "She's going to have a second kid. Not the best time for it—and he's in the navy. So Martin Halliburton and his Mary are helping the Chinks, eh? Good for them. We were a tough bunch in the old crowd, weren't we? Gosh", leaping to his feet, "if that isn't Ronnie. Looks as if he's alone too. I'll go and haul him over."

Ronnie Wallace—in plain clothes like Miles—accepted the invitation. His eyes still reminded Miles of a snake's, but his hair had gone iron gray and he never smiled once while he ate.

"Aye, I'm hame. But I'll no be hame long", was all he would volunteer. "You mark my words. This is only the beginning of things. There'll be doings in Abeessinia before we're very much older."

"How do you make that out?" asked Jim. "We're only fighting the Boche——"

"Up to the noo, Jim. But I dinna trust the French."

Glancing at his wristwatch, Ronnie excused himself.

"Queer bird", remarked Jim, lighting another gasper. "I don't trust the French either. How about a glass of port?"

"No, thanks."

The hero of Miles's boyhood continued to give his ideas on the war until the cloakroom attendant handed them their hats.

"Come along back to the Ministry with me", he said then. "And I'll see about fixing you up with a job."

"Oh well, it can't do any harm", thought Miles.

A taxi took them round Trafalgar Square and down Whitehall into the car-crowded cul-de-sac of King Charles Street. Dismounting—and letting Miles pay the fare—Jim saluted a superior and was saluted by the porter in the gold-braided top hat.

"You'll need a pass, old chap", he said.

They went up a few stairs and turned to their right. A messenger seated at a desk wrote Miles's name on a pink slip. They returned along the corridor and climbed another flight of stone stairs.

"Wait here", ordered Jim.

Opening a door, he left Miles to kick his heels on a long gloomy landing. In about ten minutes he reappeared, saying, "It's all right. You can come in".

The outer room held three other officers, all busy writing. Jim led through it into a smaller room, which was carpeted; and presented Miles to a biggish man who sat at a cluttered desk.

"This is Captain Radcliffe, sir. He's come back from America to join up."

"Splendid fellow." The air commodore rose, offered a freckled hand and pushed over a cigarette box. "What were you in last time? Tanks, eh. But you've taken your ticket since. That's all to the good, of course. Still —Bowlby tells me you're thirty-nine. A bit long in the tooth, what! You've been to the War Office, I gather?"

"More than once, sir."

"Have you put your name down for the Officers' Emergency Reserve?"

"No, sir."

"Why not?"

Miles explained. If he put his name down for the army reserve he might be kept hanging about for months.

"I thought we might fit him in with us, sir", interposed Jim.

"Can't be done, I'm afraid, Bowlby. I took on another body this morning and that fills up our establishment. If I were you I should run him along to Monty."

But "Monty's" establishment, also, was full; and half an hour later Miles was on his way to see "a bloke called Crashaw. Room four hundred and twenty, Adastral House", to whom Jim had telephoned before handing him back his pink pass.

III

Crashaw, a harassed civil servant, took Miles's name and the address of his club; offered him another cigarette, and a form. The Air Ministry's procedure—explained Crashaw—was the same as the War Office's. You'd be sent for when you were needed, with no guarantee how you'd be employed.

"Well, I'll think it over", hedged Miles.

He slipped the form into his notecase, walked out along Kingsway, and found a teashop.

Why the blazes had he been in such a hurry to come home? This coffee was foul; the information imparted by his bank manager dashed irritating. His American securities had always been his sheet anchor. Now he'd have to pay British income tax. Your money or your life? The country didn't seem to want his life, but they grabbed his money pronto.

Once again, as so constantly since his arrival in London, he fell to wondering, "Why did I come home at all?"

The high September sun still silvered the barrage balloons when Miles left the teashop and took a bus back to the modest club of which he had remained an overseas member. Walking the last few hundred yards from Marble Arch, he was again struck by the number of houses which were curtainless and empty of furniture.

The whole metropolis, compared with his few recollections of it, seemed empty. How scared people were of raids. How amusing it had been to watch 'em scuttle, and the traffic all stopped, the first and only time the sirens sounded. How furious that warden had been with him because he wouldn't take cover. And only a false alarm after all.

There was no bar in the club, and nobody in the lounge. Miles walked up to his own room (no elevator, if your please!), undressed, slipped on a dressing gown, went to the public bath (only one tub for each floor, if you please!), and wondered what to do with himself for the rest of the evening while he changed his clothes.

He'd dine out. This club gave him the pip. London gave him the pip. Not being able to choose his own job gave him the pip. He'd better ring up Fluke tomorrow. Why hadn't he rung Fluke up before?

"Dunno", he told himself. But of course he did know. The old dread was still there, however certain Marguerite might be that nothing could have happened. Oh lord, how he missed Marguerite.

IV

Miles broke open another packet of cigarettes, filled the gold case Halcyon had given him, pricked and squeezed another capsule of petrol into his lighter, and was just leaving the club when he encountered a dark man in khaki, who said, "Aren't you Miles Radcliffe? I'm Timothy Archer. You know, Enid's brother".

Timothy, very dapper with his Military Cross and the three stars of a captaincy, insisted on standing a drink.

"I joined this pothouse a couple of years ago", he explained. "Comes in jolly handy now I'm at the War House"; and in answer to a question about his wife, "Oh rather. Lucy's fine. So are my kids. Peter's a territorial Archie gunner. Pamela's trying to joins the Waafs. You know Fluke's Simmy is in the Air Force?"

"No. I—er—haven't been down to Plinley Green yet."

"Really? Why ever not?"

Miles burked the question, prevaricating, "I've only been home a day or so". Timothy rattled on. He'd been lucky to get his three stars. Most chaps had to rejoin as second loots. The Stock Exchange was n.b.g. since this adjectival war. He'd seen it coming, started pulling strings last March. Wouldn't be at the War House very long. Wangle himself out to France pretty soon. Couldn't stay for another snifter. Had a date. Must go and change.

Watching him stride away, Miles thought, "That's torn it. Now I'll have to get on to Fluke, otherwise he'll be offended". But tomorrow would be soon enough for that.

The lounge began to fill. He ordered another whiskey; drank it, and left the club. A few minutes took him into Hyde Park. Orators were orating. He listened to one of them from the fringe of a little crowd. "If this were Germany", he thought, "that bloke would find himself in a concentration camp."

A queer place, England. He'd never felt really at home here. Least of all, this last week.

Strolling on, he observed four anti-aircraft guns, some wooden hutments, and a sentry talking to a girl. Beyond these, a balloon was just being hauled down. Dull jobs. Wouldn't suit him. But did he really want any soldiering job? What about his oath?

"Might as well have stayed on at the Inn", he brooded. And, again, his thoughts turned to Marguerite. How much he missed her comradeship. As much as he had once missed Halcyon's? More!

Three soldiers in battledress passed him. But they didn't carry themselves like soldiers. They slouched.

He stopped to examine some trenches and a dugout. One good storm —and they'd be waterlogged. Fifty yards more brought him across a roadway to flowerbeds. Better kept than the trenches! Significant, that.

Still more significant seemed a scrap of conversation between two loitering youths. "So they haven't pinched you for the Forces yet, 'Erb?" "Not much. I'm reserved, I am." "Me, too. Lucky for us, ain't it?"

And he, at his age, had paid his own passage to volunteer.

The clock at Hyde Park Corner showed Miles it was time for dinner. As he turned left down Piccadilly, a beggar with a silver badge in the buttonhole of his greasy jacket whined, "Spare a copper for an ex-service man, sir". Miles fumbled in trouser pockets, found a sixpenny piece, and walked on again, thinking, "Probably a fake".

Outside a club which he did not know for the Cavalry, he boarded a bus and was driven to Piccadilly Circus, its traffic sparse and its Eros sand-bagged.

All the theatres in Shaftesbury Avenue were open. At one of them he saw the tail end of a queue. Turning out of the avenue into Soho, he replenished his stock of black cigarettes.

"The mobilisation twice in twenty-five years!" grumbled the Frenchman who owned the shop. "It is an exaggeration. Where is the money to come from? That is what I ask myself, *monsieur*."

On the pavement, one Italian was chattering to another, "This war is not our affair".

"Is it mine either?" thought Miles.

He came to the door of a restaurant, inspected the priced menu in the brass frame, entered, was shown to a corner table, and ordered the set dinner. Dimly illuminated and nearly empty, this place, too, gave him the pip.

But the food and the baby flask of Chianti might have been worse, and the coffee was almost drinkable. As he asked the waiter to bring him another cup, a party of six—two middle-aged civilians, a young man in naval uniform, and three girls, one of whom wore khaki—came in. The girl in khaki stopped at his table and held out a hand. It was a second or so before he recognised her for Eleanor Rowley.

"When did you get over?" she asked.

"Oh, I've been in London about a week. What do you think you're masquerading as? A vivandière?"

Eyes twinkling, she retorted, "Oh, I've still got a few kisses to spare"; and explained that she was "M.T.C."

"What's that when it's at home?"

"Mechanised Transport Corps. We drive cars and that sort of thing. How did you leave your mother?"

Her question seemed to carry a double meaning. He was glad when —after a little more conversation—she rejoined her companions. Sporting of Eleanor to join up, though. And, had it not been for her, he would never have known Marguerite!

Sentimentalising again—would one never have done with sentimentalising?—he stopped at her table on his way out of the restaurant. She gave him her telephone number.

"Ring me up if ever you're wanting a vivandière", she smiled. "I expect you'll be in uniform next time I see you and simply plastered with medal ribbons."

Uniforms and ribbons. As though they mattered to him!

What did matter to him? England?

But England was only Plinley Green.

His oath never to fight in another war? But that oath was already as good as broken.

Marguerite, then? But Marguerite hadn't *sent* him home. He'd have come anyway. He'd decided that a year ago in Hollywood.

Walking back to his club through a London strangely beautified by the moonlight, he remembered Billy Williams drawling, "If this war starts up, I reckon I'll volunteer for the British Air Force".

And once again patriotism brushed him—but only with light wings . .

253

Miles woke before dawn; and, although he slept again, it was fitfully, his mind haunted by dreams of Marguerite.

Sleeping, he heard her voice once more, kissed her goodbye once more, surprised that they could speak, could kiss, so calmly, with no outward show of the emotions which had been tearing at them all these last hours.

"I'll come back as soon as this show's over", he said in his dream; and she, "You're sure you haven't forgotten anything?" and he, "Not a thing. Look after the rest of my gear for me. And take care of yourself . . . mother."

"You take care of yourself . . . son. And don't forget to send me a cable as soon as you're safe in England."

Safe! As though war had actually been declared. As though either of them were in danger. What nonsense they were both talking. Did people always talk nonsense when their hearts were breaking? This heartbreak. God, how it hurt. Even in a dream. Was he only dreaming? Weren't these words real?

"Well, au revoir, mother."

"Au revoir, son. Don't drive too fast. You've plenty of time to catch the plane from San Francisco."

And now, in his dream, he heard car wheels thrumming, "Happiness. Found and lost. Lost forever. Why? Turn back. Turn back before it's too late".

"Only a dream", he knew, his eyes opening.

But soon his eyes closed again, and the dream-wheels were thrumming once more.

And now a great plane took air; and all California, all his beloved California, slid swift under this giant wing-tip.

Until, suddenly, twilight darkled beyond the wing-tip, and stars shone, and the sun again. And all this while engines were drumming, "Happiness. Lost. Unless you turn back at Chicago".

But already, in his dream, he was away from Chicago, flying for New York, and away from New York, past the Statue of Liberty—only, what had become of his own liberty?—in a speeding ship.

Always before you had been able to escape on a ship. But from this ship with the darkened decklights there was no escape. You were in prison—chained—with Marguerite beckoning and beckoning—while the voice of an old man threatened you, "Evil things. Evil things. Evil things".

As though there could be any greater evil than this being a prisoner, than this loss of Marguerite, than this knowledge that you would never see her again, never talk with her again, never kiss her again . . .

But on that, Miles woke; on that, sweating and shivering, he jumped from bed, ran to the window, and drew the blackout curtains; flung the window wide.

It was barely sunrise. Cool air, breathed deep into his lungs, forced back reality. The terror to which he had woken lifted.

So it had been only a dream after all!

He put on a dressing gown; shaved; looked at his watch; and saw that he had a good hour to spare before the valet brought his tea.

"Might as well fill in those forms", he thought, and, having found his American bank accounts and the list of his securities, sat down to write.

The forms were simple enough; but he checked the figures he had written twice before he signed them.

So that was that. And now why not sign one of these other forms—either the War Office's or the Air Ministry's? Just as well to clinch things. Then you'd be free of all responsibility. It wouldn't be your fault if they gave you a cushy job instead of a fighting one.

Dash it all, why wouldn't they take him back in the Tanks? Only because, "I'm afraid you're rather too old for us, Radcliffe". And what had that air commodore called him? "A bit long in the tooth."

Still undecided about signing either form, Miles inspected himself in the mirror over his washbasin. If he lied about his age, they'd have him by the short hairs the moment they looked up his papers. But supposing he rejoined as a Tommy? They wouldn't have any papers then. He'd lied a year on to his age in nineteen sixteen. Why not lie a few years off it in nineteen thirty-nine?

He played with the idea for a while; and put the forms away in his suitcase. There lay the octagonal red lacquer box Tio Khie Hong had given him on the day he left Hollywood. Fingering the sliver of jade, which he still wore round his neck, he remembered the Buddha Martin Halliburton had worn in Ireland and what Tio had said about fighting for Free China.

Martin, rising sixty, was fighting for China. But England, apparently, didn't think a trained soldier rising forty fit for a commission. And if he brought his own weapons, he was lucky not to have them confiscated. The fuss that customs official had made when one opened one's guncase. The fuss the police had made about renewing one's firearms certificate. What did they expect a fighting man to bring home—a teddy bear and a baby's comforter?

Thank the lord—that dream hadn't half upset one—here came tea.

VI

No breakfasts—Miles had discovered his first morning at the club—were served before half past eight. Down earlier than usual, he spent ten minutes in the street, twenty reading the papers. Another week—it seemed—would put paid to Poland. Where would the Hun go for honey then?

The soldier in him considered this question while he ate his eggs and bacon. A drive through Holland and Belgium—and the Maginot Line, from what he had seen of it three years ago, could be turned. But that wouldn't happen before next spring. So why rush off and enlist as a Tommy? Plenty of time for that.

Deciding thus, he looked up to see Timothy Archer, pale of face with black circles under his eyes, taking the next table.

"I feel like death", confessed Timothy.

"You look it", grinned Miles, suddenly reminded that he must ring up Fluke before Timothy passed on the news of his homecoming. "What time did you get in?"

"Just in time to shave and change."

255

Timothy gave his order; opened his paper, and only nodded as Miles left the room.

Neither of the telephone boxes in the hall was occupied. Miles lit his seventh cigarette that morning; looked up the Rosemary Lodge number in the book; and asked the woman on the switchboard to get it for him.

A voice that seemed vaguely familiar answered his, "Can I speak to Sir Philip, please?" with a forthright, "No. I'm afraid you can't, he's just gone off to the factory".

"Is Lady Radcliffe there?"

"Not at the moment. I say, aren't you Uncle Miles?"

"Yes."

"Well, I'm Philly."

"The deuce you are. And how's the world with you, Philly?"

"Lousy. I've had to put off my wedding."

"I didn't know you were engaged. Congratulations. Why have you had to put off the wedding?"

"Because they sent Bill to France yesterday. He's in the same fighter squadron as Simmy. How long have you been home?"

"Not long."

"When are we going to see you?"

"I was wondering whether I could come down for the weekend."

Philly, remembered as a bouncing girl of eighteen with sandy hair, boomed Flukily:

"You can't unless you sleep on the billiard table. Mother's gone all patriotic. We've got ten evacuees in the house. And they don't half smell either. Gladdy and I have had to double up in one room. And Arty doesn't go back to Cambridge till the end of the month. Blast. Those infernal slum children are after the apples again. Could you ring up at lunchtime? Mother's sure to be in by then".

She hung up without waiting for his answer.

Feeling rather old—Arty, remembered in his cradle, must be over eighteen—Miles paid for his call; and meditated yet another visit to the War Office.

"But what's the use?" he thought. "They'll only tell me to sign on the dotted line."

Lighting yet another cigarette, he determined to take the day off.

A ten-mile hike—twenty would be better—might help him to come to a decision about joining the ranks.

Back in his room, he changed his town clothes for a pair of gray flannels, heavy brogued shoes and a sports jacket. Before leaving it, he gave a last glance at the two photographs—one of Halcyon in her uniform, the other of Marguerite dressed as Carmen—on the little table by his bed.

They weren't really alike, those two. And your thoughts of them weren't alike either. You loved them both. But after a separate fashion. And you'd always keep that first oath sworn at Villa Montes . . . You'd never marry . . . If you got through this show alive, you'd go back to California . . .

Dimly aware of the confusion in his mind, Miles slammed the door on his photographs, ran downstairs, and out, hatless, swordstick under arm, into the London sunshine.

Three minutes' walk brought him to a tube station. At the booking office, he heard himself say, "Please give me a return ticket to Plinley Green".

VII

"Habit", Miles told himself, as the collector clipped his ticket and he stepped on to the escalator. But his mind was still confused.

The first train in was marked, "Albanford. All stations". Automatically he stepped on board.

The long carriage emptied at Paddington, and ran from underground to overground just before Baron's Court.

Memories had him while they rolled on, stopping and starting every three minutes. He was coming back from Ireland to The Firs. He was coming back from South America to Rosemary Lodge. He was coming back to Rosemary Lodge from Abyssinia. He was coming back from the Midlands to the Beehive. He was travelling down from London to the Beehive. Only for a week, though, before he went East.

Nonsense. It was the best part of three years since he'd gone East. And he wouldn't go near the Beehive—he wouldn't go within miles of it—today!

His mind began to clear. He decided to alight at Thatch Lane; to buy himself some grub, to take the public footpath over Thatch Down golfcourse and hike through Motley Wood.

The girl in the station kiosk sold him a big bar of chocolate, a packet of biscuits, and an orange which bulged his pocket. A railed walk led to a stile, which he vaulted. The golfcourse was deserted; the footpath across it forked. He climbed a big bunker by one of the greens to make sure of his bearings. That spire on the hill was Harrow School. Fork right—and you should see the wood when you topped the next rise in the fairway.

Hallo, planes!

He sighted the planes. Single-engined fighters. Those Spitfires one was always reading about. Nine of 'em. Keeping nice formation too. Queer, to think of Fluke's Simmy flying an eight-gun fighter. You remembered him and Philly in their pram, and Rosaleen wheeling them. "Miles", she was saying, "what a lovely surprise. We didn't expect you down till much later."

No use her expecting him today!

The Spitfires dwindled to specks. Miles quickened his pace; breasted the rise, and saw Motley Wood—oak and elm still in full leaf, no hint of brown or gold telling of autumn—at the foot of a long slope.

Swordstick at the trail, he doubled for half a mile; found his breath a little short; wondered if he were smoking too much—and stopped to light yet another cigarette.

Motley Wood, like the golfcourse, seemed entirely deserted. He flung away his cigarette; stamped the butt out, and hiked haphazard.

Oh, but it was good to be among trees again. For the first time since leaving America, he began to feel a little happy. Dash it all, why not enlist and have done with it? No responsibilities, when you were in the ranks. And yet, you might still have one responsibility. Oughtn't you to make sure of that before you joined up?

257

Thought grew vague. Presently he came on a grassy ride and broke into a double again, uphill till he reached the far edge of the wood.

Once upon a time this had been the loveliest view in the whole neighbourhood—open country nearly all the way to Albanford Abbey. But today there were too many houses, too many railway lines, too many factories, too much . . . "Plinley Greenery", thought Miles.

The old distaste on him, he turned away from the view, and squatted down by an oak bole to eat his lunch.

Hunger satisfied, he took the orange from his pocket; sliced off the top with his penknife, and sucked out the juice. He heard a rabbit scuttle through undergrowth. A thrush flew down, pecked at the biscuit crumbs he had thrown away. Why did men live in the Plinley Greens? Why must there be wars? Why must he fight in this one? He'd killed enough men in his time. He might be killed himself this time. Then he'd never see Marguerite again.

Idly, he began to play with the handle of his swordstick; fingered the catch; slid the blade from its triangular scabbard. There was a tiny spot of rust on the foible of the blade. He rubbed off the rust with a dock leaf; rose, and tried a few lunges. Once upon a time he'd thought what fun duels must be. Queer, that there should be no more fun in such fantasies. And there wouldn't be any fun for him in this war either. He wouldn't be fighting because he wanted to. Those days were over. *Cué.*

The Guaraní word brought back Halcyon. Halcyon brought back Marguerite. Thoughtful, he resheathed his sword-blade; and looked at the view again.

That factory—once white, now camouflaged—was Radcliffe Radios. Marguerite's intuition might have been wrong. If . . . if anything had happened, Fluke would be sure to know.

In another second he was on his way, by the remembered shortcuts, down the vale.

VIII

In a sunk lane between high hedgerows, Miles's memory faltered—and his resolution wavered. He was being silly, letting his imagination run away with him. After a while, however, he went on again, till he found the pond.

Skirting this pond, he came to the gateway of Oplady Farm; and past cowsheds to a narrow road. Two miles of fair heel and toe round several sharp corners—at one of which he was nearly run down by a carelessly driven car—brought him to the bypass. Since he'd come so far, why not go the whole way and make sure?

The factory gates stood open. In the asphalted courtyard he saw a big car, engine already ticking over, Ablett at the wheel. Down the steps from the office came Fluke, followed by Derek Grayson. Miles called, "Hallo there".

"Hallo yourself", foghorned Fluke.

In the second before they shook hands Miles perceived that his halfbrother—still with a red carnation at his lapel and a cigar case bulging his handkerchief pocket—had put on still more girth. A gold watchchain looped his waistcoat. A pearl gleamed in his silk necktie. Under his arm he carried a huge wallet of brown leather with a brass lock.

Derek Grayson also shook hands, and said, "Welcome, stranger".

"Philly rang up to say you were home", went on Fluke. "Why the hell didn't you let me know you were coming? Not that it would have made any difference. I'm being run off my feet. Government work. No money in it. This bloody hundred-per-cent excess profits tax! Still—Radcliffe Radios are doing their bit. Sorry I can't stay and talk to you. Got to make a dash for it. Minister of Supply just phoned. Another conference. Drive us off our nuts with their blasted conferences. Where are you staying? Your club. Good. I'll call you there. Tomorrow or the day after. Come along, Derek. No rest for the wicked."

So saying, he wrenched the car door open; pitched his wallet inside; practically pitched Grayson after it; jumped in; slammed the door; sirened, "Let her rip, Ablett. We've only forty minutes"; and went off at knots.

"Nice brotherly welcome", thought Miles.

The car was through the gates by then. A watchman relocked them; and approached, saying, "You can't go in unless you've a pass. Who might you be wanting to see, sir?"

"I've seen him, thanks. How does one get out?"

"By the side gate, sir. I'll show you."

Back on the bypass—singularly bare of traffic—Miles stood for a long moment, his mind once more confused.

Fluke must be making some secret war gadget. If there were any other secret, Fluke and Enid must both know it. Should he go along and see Enid? Or should he . . .

Dash it, the thing had been worrying him for the best part of three years. Why not put his mind at rest before he joined up? Not necessary? All right. Spin a coin. Heads he would. Tails he wouldn't.

He took a penny from his pocket; tossed, and caught it.

The penny came down heads.

IX

Memories blacked-out thought, as Miles, walking his fastest, crossed the tarmac of the bypass and turned left along the footpath. Head up, sword-stick swinging, he came past the roundabout to the sign which read "This Way to the New Beehive". Once in the side road, he stopped for yet another cigarette.

As he flicked on his lighter, memory seemed to be repeating:

"It's a pity you smoke so much. But then you always did . . . That was why I fainted . . . Yes—in Ireland . . . What kids we were—— . . . Oh no. I'm quite grown up nowadays . . . It's four years since—since you went away . . . Sore at you for breaking our engagement? My dear, that's ancient history . . . And we were only engaged for about five minutes . . . When are you off East? Not for another week . . . You must be awfully bored at your club. Fluke can't put you up? Then how would you like your old room for your last week? You'd love it. Flatterer! But even a businesswoman likes being flattered".

A businesswoman! So how could one have imagined . . . how could one possibly have imagined . . . how on earth could one still be imagining . . .

"But I'm not", Miles swore to himself. "It's only that I want to make quite sure."

His cigarette had gone out. He tossed it over the hedge and walked quickly on. Another few yards—and he would see the Beehive. Yes. There it was—its window frames still white, its red brick walls only just a little mellower, the virginia creeper only just a little higher, than his memories.

He came closer, entered the grounds. This lawn was still smooth as a billiard table. But last time no dahlias glowed in that border. It had been too late in the year for dahlias. What year? Nineteen thirty-six, of course. The only time he'd been home since . . . since Halcyon was killed. And again, for the split of a second, memories blacked-out thought.

Except for a waitress reading a magazine, the chairs, still painted pale yellow, at the tables under the orange umbrellas were empty. Miles crossed the lawn, and the girl rose. She wore the familiar linen uniform; but her face was a stranger's.

"Is Miss Adair anywhere about?" he asked—queerly glad that she should not know who he was.

"No, sir. Miss Adair went home after lunch and she won't be back till dinnertime."

"Doesn't she live here any more, then?"

"Oh no, sir. She lives at Old Cottage."

Old Cottage. Another memory. You went past the tennis courts, through the kitchen garden . . .

"Would you like some tea, sir?"

"No, thanks."

"Perhaps you'd care to see Miss Archer, sir? I'm expecting her back in about half an hour. She's only gone to an A.R.P. meeting."

"Thank you. But I won't wait for Miss Archer."

The girl stared after Miles, thinking, "He's a gentleman all right; but there's something funny about him", as he went to wash his hands.

x

As always, the front door of the Beehive stood ajar. The same blue vases in the lounge held golden rod and Michaelmas daisies. But another strange face eyed Miles from the office window. And surely that grandfather clock —its hands now pointing to three-thirty—had stood on an upper landing, just outside Rosaleen's bedroom. One remembered it ticking, as one tip-toed back to one's own . . .

In the cloakroom he found the same green soap, the same notice, "Visitors are requested to empty the lavatory basins after use, and to put their towels in the basket provided for that purpose".

Smoothing his hair at the mirror, he experienced a last scruple. If he went to the cottage, Rosaleen might imagine . . .

Such nonsense! She'd been quite sensible about the thing. They'd parted good friends. She'd always known where a letter would find him.

Best get this job over without dwelling on it. Silly job really. He'd have heard soon enough, if . . .

Resolute again, he made his way past the locked door of the Snuggery, and round the tennis courts into the kitchen garden. A gardener was lifting potatoes. Yet another new face. They must have changed the entire staff.

Once more, memories blacked-out thought. Vividly against the screen-board of recollection he saw Castle Kilranan blazing—Geoffrey's room in barracks—a shabby Rosaleen wheeling Simmy and Philly in their peram-bulator—snow on the windscreen of Fluke's car as he drove her back from Dominic's party—and that other drive, through the Mediterranean moon-light beyond Sainte Marie sur Mer.

Vividly he relived those moments by the swimming pool when he had asked her to marry him. "Darling", repeated the microphone of recol-lection, "don't mind anything I say. I'm just being stupid."

Stupid! Who was being stupid now? *Cué* to all that! What had she herself called it? Ancient history. He hadn't been really in love with her when he asked her to marry him. A word from Halcyon—and he had left her.

But when he came back to her? No! He'd never really loved Rosaleen. Not even for that one crazy week, his last in England before he sailed East. And she? She'd treated the whole incident so lightly. She'd let him go without a single tear. She hadn't been afraid. So why should he be?

For now, suddenly, as Miles opened the postern gate in the far wall of the kitchen garden, a fear beyond any in experience clutched at his very entrails; so that he could hardly close the postern for the trembling of his hands.

He tried to fight fear, telling himself, over and over, "She wouldn't have kept it to herself. No girl would. She was only a girl. Even that time". But the fight made his knees tremble, so that it was with difficulty he reached the bend in this lane along which they had wandered arm in arm on a Decem-ber evening the best part of three years ago.

"One of these days", repeated the microphone of recollection, "I mean to buy Old Cottage."

And there stood the cottage, rebuilt, repainted, gay with all the flowers of early autumn, its chimney smoking, its mullioned windows agleam in the September sun.

<h1 style="text-align:center">XI</h1>

Fear had gone over. His limbs no longer trembled. But a strange awe—also beyond experience—was on Miles.

A low white gate led into the front garden of the cottage. He pushed the gate open, and made his way over grass-edged flagstones between rose trees to an oak door.

A bell chain hung by the door. He pulled, and the bell jangled. He pulled twice, three times. But the door remained shut; and after what seemed a long while, gingerly, almost as though he had been a trespasser, he turned the handle and went in.

Only the scent of roses, the tick of a clock, and one last recollection greeted him. "I shall make these two groundfloor rooms into one", Rosaleen had said. "Over there, I shall have a french window so that I can walk straight out into the orchard."

The french window was open. Through it, in another moment, came Rosaleen herself.

He saw that she had been running; saw that she was out of breath and her cheeks flushed.

Then she stopped dead; and her cheeks whitened, and she put one hand to her heart.

"You!" she said; and stood there, eyeing him—never had he seen those hazel eyes so hard, or those full lips so resolute—without another word.

She stood thus for what seemed an eternity. At last her hand came away from her heart and she said—never had he known her voice so cold—"I felt it might be you. That was why I ran so fast. I knew this war would bring you back. You've always loved war. It's fun to you. Everything's fun to you. I was. But that's . . . ancient history. You . . . served your purpose. Or rather mine. So now will you please go, before they——"

"They!"

"——run after me." She brushed the interruption aside. "I told them not to. But they're not very obedient yet. They're such mites. Both of them."

"Both of them!"

"They're mine." Again she disdained the interruption. "Utterly and entirely mine. The only things in the world I ever wanted. I told you you'd served your purpose. Now go. Before they see you."

But already, glancing beyond her, Miles saw those two little, brightly clad scraps of humanity, running hand in hand out of the copse on the far side of the orchard. One of the scraps stumbled. The other stopped to pick it up.

His eyes betrayed him. Rosaleen turned; called over her shoulder, "Stay where you are, children. Mummy won't be very long"; and turned back to him.

For the third time she said, "Go!"

Anger flicked him with its first lash. He stood his ground.

"Why should I? I'm their father."

"Even if you are"—her, too, anger was flicking—"you've no proof."

For long moments silence held them rigid.

At last Miles said, thinking how stupid it sounded, "What are they? Boys or girls?"

"Girls."

"Why didn't you write and tell me?"

"Why should I?"

The children had run back into the copse. Once more silence held Miles and Rosaleen rigid—till anger flicked him with its second lash.

"You ought to have written", he said; and took a step towards her.

"You mean"—she did not recoil—"I ought to have blackmailed you into marrying me?"

"Don't be idiotic, Rosaleen."

"I'm not being idiotic. I've thought it all out. I thought it all out before . . . before I pretended I was in love with you. That's what I did it

262

for. That's the only thing I did it for. But you've no proof. Even if you had, you couldn't force me to marry you."

And for the third time silence held them—in a rigidity that might have been death's.

Then, once again, Rosaleen said, "Go!"

"Supposing I refuse?"

"You can't. This is my house. They're my children."

"And mine."

"No."

But her eyes flinched; and in that moment Miles knew, irretrievably, that he must break both the oaths he had sworn at Villa Montes.

The knowledge maddened him.

"If they're not mine"—his eyes were hot—"whose are they?"

"Paul's." She had not hesitated.

"Another lie."

"At any rate, he wanted me to marry him. And that's more than you ever did. All you ever wanted of me——"

"Don't, Rosaleen."

"Don't what? Tell you the truth for once?" Her hand was at her heart again. "That I hate you. That I've hated you ever since you threw me over and ran off to South America. But at least I got what I wanted from you when you come back again."

"Then you admit——"

"That you're their father. Yes. For what it's worth."

"It's worth their . . . birthright."

"Who cares about legitimacy nowadays?"

"They will"—another voice interrupted—"when they grow up."

And that voice, Stephanie's, continued to Rosaleen: "I thought it must be Miles when I was told that a man had been inquiring for you. I came at once. I couldn't help overhearing what he just said. As you know, I've never liked him. And I don't suppose I ever shall. But he's right, my dear. And we're wrong. Both of us. It's been my fault even more than yours. I should have insisted on your letting him know. Then he'd have come home and married you before they were born."

"But I don't want to marry him."

"We can't always do what we want in this world, my dear. And quite possibly we shan't be able to in the next world either", said Stephanie, and strode away through the apple trees, to where the other two children were still playing in the copse.

XII

"My grandchildren!" thinks Marguerite Radcliffe, watching those "other two" at play with a litter of labrador puppies on the veranda of the Horse and Hound Inn. "It's funny how one comes to happiness."

And much the same thought comforts Rosaleen Radcliffe every time she breaks off from her office work (and goodness knows how much office work running a place like the Beehive means in this year nineteen forty-two) to begin a letter, "Dearest Jocelyn and dearest Carole".

263

It was a terrible wrench to part with your children, of course. But you had to give Miles right when he insisted on their being sent to California.

"For obviously", thinks a more prosaic Rosaleen, "you can't always do what you want in this world."

And after that, before she goes on with her letter, she is apt to consider Miles for a while, neither over-sentimentally nor over-romantically, neither hating him (not that she ever really hated him) nor loving him overmuch (not that she hasn't grown to love him more than a little), but just commonsensibly, as a grown-up wife should consider a grown-up husband.

"The poor darling", she'll think, "he isn't finding this war any fun, though he always writes so cheerfully. But perhaps it's just as well he shouldn't. He was always a bit childish about his soldiering . . ."

And, "More than a bit childish", thinks Sergeant-Major Miles Radcliffe, with the khamsin wind blowing all the dust of Egypt into his eyes.

But, even with that dust blowing, the eyes of his mind are clear.

He can see himself, nowadays, both for the boy he was; and the man he is—one little man among millions fighting, and loathing every moment of the fight, just to ensure the elemental decencies; and for the man he may be if death spares him—just one little man among millions of those "Plinley Greeners" whom his boyhood so despised.

"For obviously", thinks a more prosaic Miles, "if the men and women of today—if people like Rosaleen and myself—only did what we wanted to, it wouldn't be fair on the children, on the men and women of tomorrow."

And in this thought, maybe that peace which passeth all understanding, Sergeant-Major Miles Radcliffe finds more spiritual happiness than he ever found with Halcyon.

Or even with Marguerite!

THE END